Lecture Notes in Computer Science 7731

Commenced Publication in 1973
Founding and Former Series Editors:
Gerhard Goos, Juris Hartmanis, and Jan van Leeuwen

Editorial Board

T0223496

Roberto Di Pietro   Javier Herranz
Ernesto Damiani   Radu State (Eds.)

Data Privacy Management and Autonomous Spontaneous Security

7th International Workshop, DPM 2012, and
5th International Workshop, SETOP 2012
Pisa, Italy, September 13-14, 2012
Revised Selected Papers

 Springer

Volume Editors

Roberto Di Pietro
Università degli Studi Roma Tre
Largo San Leonardo Murialdo, 1
00146 Rome, Italy
E-mail: dipietro@mat.uniroma3.it

Javier Herranz
Universitat Politècnica de Catalunya
c. Jordi Girona 1-3
08034 Barcelona, Spain
E-mail: jherranz@ma4.upc.edu

Ernesto Damiani
Università degli Studi di Milano
Via Bramante, 65
26013 Milan, Italy
E-mail: ernesto.damiani@unimi.it

Radu State
University of Luxembourg
rue Alphonse Weicker, 4
2721 Luxembourg, Luxembourg
E-mail: radu.state@uni.lu

ISSN 0302-9743   e-ISSN 1611-3349
ISBN 978-3-642-35889-0   e-ISBN 978-3-642-35890-6
DOI 10.1007/978-3-642-35890-6
Springer Heidelberg Dordrecht London New York

Library of Congress Control Number: 2021954547

CR Subject Classification (1998): K.6.5, E.3, K.4.4, C.2.0-6, C.5.3, H.3.4-5

LNCS Sublibrary: SL 4 – Security and Cryptology

Typesetting: Camera-ready by author, data conversion by Scientific Publishing Services, Chennai, India

Printed on acid-free paper

Springer is part of Springer Science+Business Media (www.springer.com)

Foreword from the DPM 2012 Program Chairs

The current volume constitutes the revised proceedings of the 7th Data Privacy Management International Workshop (DPM 2012), which includes revised versions of the papers presented at the workshop. The aim of DPM is to promote and stimulate the international collaboration and research exchange on novel data privacy topics. This 7th edition of the workshop was co-located with the ESORICS 2012 symposium in Pisa (Italy). Previous issue for the DPM workshop were held in 2011 in Leuven (Belgium), 2010 in Athens (Greece), 2009 in Saint Malo (France), 2007 in Istanbul (Turkey), 2006 in Atlanta (USA), and 2005 in Tokyo (Japan).

The program of this year's workshop consisted of the presentation of the 13 accepted full papers (out of 31 submitted papers), and three keynote lecutures. The accepted papers deal with topics such as location privacy, case studies in citizens' privacy, authentication with anonymity, privacy in distributed systems, privacy policies, or automated privacy enforcement. Each paper was reviewed by at least three reviewers.

We would like to acknowledge and thank all the support received from the Program Committee members, external reviewers, and the Organizing Committee of ESORICS 2012, the General Chair of DPM 2012, Javier López, and the General Chair of ESORICS 2012, Fabio Martinelli. We would like to warmly thank Joaquin Garcia-Alfaro for all his support and for the great task he did as the Publicity Chair of DPM 2012. We want to thank Institut TELECOM for providing the USB devices with the proceedings of DPM 2012 that were distributed during the workshop.

Last, but definitely not least, we would like to thank all the authors who submitted papers, all the attendees, and the three prestigious keynote speakers who accepted our invitation to give a talk for all the attendants of DPM and SETOP 2012. Virgil Gligor, who gave a talk entitled "On the Foundations of Trust in Networks of Humans and Computers;" Chris Mitchell, who gave the talk "Re-using Existing Security Infrastructures;" and Pierangela Samarati, who gave a talk on "Supporting User Privacy Preferences in Digital Interactions."

Roberto Di Pietro
Javier Herranz

Foreword from the SETOP 2012 Program Chairs

Today's global challenges in security are largely due to sudden paradigm shifts. Traditional ICT systems are being replaced by a complex global infrastructure, where continuous, dynamic adaptation and reconfiguration challenge most classic assumptions of security-by-design. The Research Track of the International Workshop on Autonomous and Spontaneous Security (SETOP) Workshop, co-located with the 17th annual European Conference in Computer Security (ESORICS 2012), aimed to bring together the research community tackling this challenge.

Each paper was reviewed by at least three independent reviewers from the international Program Committee, undergoing a thorough and rigorous review process. Among the many submissions we received, the Program Committee selected ten papers for presentation in the workshop Research Track. We believe that these papers provide a unique view of ongoing security research work in a number of emerging environments that are becoming part of the global ICT infrastructure, from content-centric to mobile and wireless networks. Also, some of them cover the key role of run-time enforcement in process and service security. The workshop keynotes, held in collaboration with the parallel DPM Workshop, tackled these multifaceted challenges and solutions from various perspectives.

Putting together a successful workshop is always a team effort; therefore, some acknowledgments are necessary. We would like to thank the key co-organizers of this workshop, starting from our General Chair Frédéric Cuppens and the colleagues who chaired the Industrial Track, Louis Granboulan and Olivier Heen. Our heartfelt thanks also go to all the authors who submitted to SETOP. The research work presented in this workshop represents a step further toward securing the global ICT infrastructure.

Ernesto Damiani
Radu State

7th International Workshop
on Data Privacy Management – DPM 2012

Program Committee Chairs

Roberto Di Pietro   Roma Tre University of Rome, Italy
Javier Herranz   Universitat Politècnica de Catalunya, Spain

Workshop General Chair

Javier López   Universidad de Málaga, Spain

Workshop Publicity Chair

Joaquin Garcia-Alfaro   TELECOM Bretagne, France

Program Committee

Carlos Aguilar Melchor   XLIM Research Institute, France
Mohd Anwar   University of Pittsburgh, USA
Ero Balsa   K.U. Leuven, Belgium
Erik-Oliver Blass   Northeastern Univeristy, USA
Emiliano De Cristoforo   PARC, Palo Alto Research Center, USA
Vanesa Daza   Universitat Pompeu Fabra, Spain
Josep Domingo Ferrer   Rovira i Virgili University, Spain
David Evans   University of Cambridge / University of Derby, UK
Jordi Forné   Universitat Politècnica de Catalunya, Spain
Sebastien Gambs   Université de Rennes 1, France
Flavio Garcia   Radboud University Nijmegen, The Netherlands
Joaquin Garcia-Alfaro   TELECOM Bretagne, France
Wei Jiang   Missouri University of Science and Technology, USA
Guillermo Navarro   Autonomous University of Barcelona, Spain
Jordi Nin   Universitat Politècnica de Catalunya, Spain
Melek Önen   EURECOM, France
Andreas Pashalidis   K.U. Leuven, Belgium
Abdullatif Shikfa   Alcatel Lucent Bell Labs, USA
Claudio Soriente   ETH Zurich, Switzerland

Alessandro Sorniotti	IBM Zurich, Switzerland
Vicenç Torra	IIIA-CSIC, Spain
Carmela Troncoso	K.U. Leuven, Belgium
Yasuyuki Tsukada	NTT Communication Science Lab, Japan
Alexandre Viejo	Rovira i Virgili University, Spain
Lena Wiese	Stiftung Universität Hildesheim, Germany

Organizing Committee

Joaquin Garcia-Alfaro	TELECOM Bretagne, France
Guillermo Navarro-Arribas	Autonomous University of Barcelona, Spain

External Referees

Berker Agir	K.U. Leuven, Belgium
Damià Castellà	Rovira i Virgili University, Spain
Azadeh Faridi	Universitat Pompeu Fabra, Spain
Oriol Farràs	Rovira i Virgili University, Spain
Kunihiko Fujita	NTT Communication Science Lab, Japan
Philippe Gaborit	XLIM Research Institute, France
Michael Herrmann	K.U. Leuven, Belgium
Merel Koning	Radboud University Nijmegen, The Netherlands
Prakash Kumar	Missouri University of Science and Technology, USA
Anil Kurmus	IBM Zurich, Switzerland
Javier Parra-Arnau	Universitat Politècnica de Catalunya, Spain
Constantinos Patsakis	Rovira i Virgili University, Spain
David Rebollo-Monedero	Universitat Politècnica de Catalunya, Spain
Bharath-Kumar Samanthula	Missouri University of Science and Technology, USA
Jan Stanek	IBM Zurich, Switzerland
Fabian Van Den Broek	Radboud University Nijmegen, The Netherlands
Jose Luis Vivas	Rovira i Virgili University, Spain
Jorge Villar	Universitat Politècnica de Catalunya, Spain

5th SETOP International Workshop on Autonomous and Spontaneous Security – SETOP 2012

Program Committee Chairs

Research Track

Ernesto Damiani	University of Milan, Italy
Radu State	University of Luxembourg, Luxembourg

Industrial Track

Louis Granboulan	EADS, France
Olivier Heen	Technicolor, France

Workshop General Chair

Frederic Cuppens	TELECOM Bretagne, France

Program Committee

Gildas Avoine	Catholic University of Louvain, Belgium
Massimo Banzi	Telecom Italia, Italy
Michel Barbeau	Carleton University, Canada
Michele Bezzi	SAP Research, France
Carlo Blundo	University of Salerno, Italy
Joan Borrell-Viader	UAB, Spain
Lionel Brunie	INSA-Lyon, France
Mike Burmester	Florida State University, USA
Jordi Castellà-Roca	Rovira i Virgili University, Spain
Ana Cavalli	TELECOM Sud Paris, France
Iliano Cervesato	Carnegie Mellon University, USA
Stelvio Cimato	Università degli Studi di Milano, Italy
Mauro Conti	Università di Padova, Italy
Isabelle Chrisment	LORIA-INRIA, France
Frédéric Cuppens	TELECOM Bretagne, France
Nora Cuppens-Boulahia	TELECOM Bretagne, France
Vanesa Daza	Pompeu Fabra University, Spain
Sabrina De Capitani di Vimercati	Università degli Studi di Milano UNIMI, Italy
Josep Domingo-Ferrer	Rovira i Virgili University, Spain

Steering Committee

Table of Contents

Data Privacy Management

Autonomous and Spontaneous Security

Fair Anonymous Authentication
for Location Based Services

Panayiotis Kotzanikolaou[1], Emmanouil Magkos[2],
Nikolaos Petrakos[1], Christos Douligeris[1], and Vassilis Chrissikopoulos[2]

[1] University of Piraeus, Department of Informatics,
80 Karaoli & Dimitriou, 18534 Piraeus, Greece
{pkotzani,npetrako,cdoulig}@unipi.gr
[2] Ionian University, Department of Informatics,
Plateia Tsirigoti 7, 49100, Kerkyra, Greece
{emagos,vchris}@ionio.gr

Abstract. We propose an efficient anonymous authentication scheme
that provides untraceability and unlinkability of mobile devices, while
accessing Location-Based Services. Following other recent approaches
for mobile anonymity, in our scheme the network operator acts as an
anonymous credential issuer for its users. However, our scheme supports
credential non-transferability, without requiring embedded hardware security features. In addition it supports *fairness* characteristics. On one
hand, it reduces the trust assumptions for the issuer by supporting *non-
frameability*: the issuer, even in collaboration with the LBS provider,
cannot simulate a transaction that opens back to an honest user. On the
other hand, it supports *anonymity revocation* for illegally used credentials. Our scheme uses standard primitives such as zero-knowledge proofs,
MACs and challenge/responses. We provide formal security proofs based
on the intractability of the Divisible Diffie-Hellman assumption.

Keywords: Anonymity, fairness, non-frameability, non-transferability.

1 Introduction

Ongoing research seeks for efficient and *fair* solutions that correctly balance
access control and privacy requirements in anonymous authentication [6,9,3].
A basic goal from the point of view of a user, is authenticating to a service,
without revealing the user identity (*user untraceability*) and without allowing
the linkage of different accesses (*transaction unlinkability*). Another requirement
for the user is *non-frameability*, *i.e.*, it should not be possible for anyone, even a
collaboration of entities, to successfully simulate an anonymous access that opens
back to an innocent user. From the point of view of the service provider, a goal
is preventing users from transferring or sharing their credentials with others
(*non-transferability*), from using a one-show credential more than once (*non-
reusability*), but also establishing accountability when users behave dishonestly.
In such cases it may be required to trace a transaction (*anonymity revocation*)
and/or revoke all the anonymous credentials of a user (*credential revocation*).

R. Di Pietro et al. (Eds.): DPM 2012 and SETOP 2012, LNCS 7731, pp. 1–14, 2013.
© Springer-Verlag Berlin Heidelberg 2013

In this paper we focus on anonymous authentication of mobile users accessing Location Based Services (LBS), such as point-of-interest services where a user sporadically queries an LBS provider to receive a nearby point of interest (*e.g.*, [12,15]) or people-locator services, where a watcher asks the LBS provider for the location of a target (*e.g.*, [14]). Typically, a user is requested to provide privacy-sensitive information to LBS service providers, such as location and itinerary, along with identifying information. The provision of both location and identification information to the network operator is generally considered acceptable: In a cell network, the operator already knows location and identity information of each subscriber in the network layer (using cell information and the IMEI/IMSI numbers). Otherwise, network connectivity is not possible. This however is considered acceptable, since the user is contracted with the network operator, who is subject to legal and regulatory constraints concerning users' privacy. From the service provider side, the collaboration with a mobile operator can provide a major resource of clients. Also the LBS provider can outsource the billing and accounting to the operator and in this way they can have a mutual economic interest. Evidently however, the provision of privacy-sensitive information to LBS providers raises privacy concerns, since they may be able to create and misuse user profiles. Moreover, LBS providers can be located anywhere world-wide, making it hard to impose regulatory and audit controls.

An efficient and "fair" anonymous authentication protocol could be trivially constructed if we considered the network operator as a trusted credential issuer. An LBS provider would provide access only if the anonymous credential was validated by the issuer. In case of dishonest behavior the issuer would be able to revoke the anonymity of a user. This solution however, has two major drawbacks: First, it is easy for users to transfer their credentials to others (thus violating non-transferability). Second, it is also easy for the operator together with the LBS provider, to fabricate transaction data that open to a user (thus violating non-frameability). In a fair system no entity should be fully trusted.

Our contribution. We propose an efficient anonymous authentication scheme for LBS services. In our scheme, each anonymous credential is cryptographically linked to a long-term certified public key of the user and is authenticated by the network operator. During the user access phase the use of the corresponding private key will be required, thus preventing a user from transferring credentials to others. Our scheme achieves fairness without reverting to strong (full-trust) assumptions: while the issuer in cooperation with an LBS provider are able to establish accountability and revoke credentials of a misbehaving user, they are not able to frame legitimate users. The scheme also fulfills other fundamental requirements of anonymous authentication such as unlinkability and untraceability of mobile users from LBS providers. We provide formal security proofs based on the intractability of the Divisible Computational Diffie Hellman assumption [1]. Our scheme is efficient for mobile devices, since it requires from the user 5 exponentiations for each credential issuing and 7 for each anonymous access. In Section 2 we describe the system setup and our threat model. In Section 3 we present our scheme, while in Section 4 we provide a proof of security. In Section

5 we review related work in comparison with our scheme and we conclude in Section 6.

2 Setup and Threat Model

We consider a typical mobile network (such as GSM or UMTS infrastructure), which includes the mobile operator $\mathcal{I}$ and a number of users subscribed with $\mathcal{I}$. The users may also access LBS services of independent service providers. For simplicity, we consider a user $\mathcal{U}$ and a provider $\mathcal{SP}$, although it is easy to extend the setup for multiple users and providers. Each user is connected to the network using a mobile device, identified uniquely by the mobile operator at the network layer (IMEI/IMSI). In order to prevent the $\mathcal{SP}$ from linking the location of $\mathcal{U}$ with its real identity, the operator will act as an issuer of anonymous credentials. Each user will be able to obtain multiple one-show credentials validated by $\mathcal{I}$ for a particular provider $\mathcal{SP}$, to anonymously authenticate to $\mathcal{SP}$.

Threat model. We consider both external and internal adversaries. An external adversary may attempt to eavesdrop and intercept the communication between the system entities in order to trace users, retrieve valid user credentials, or to obtain information on whether a credential was accepted. To deal with external adversaries, we assume that the communication channels between $\mathcal{U}$ and $\mathcal{I}$ and between $\mathcal{I}$ and $\mathcal{SP}$ are encrypted and two-way authenticated[1]. The communication between $\mathcal{U}$ and $\mathcal{SP}$ is encrypted and authenticated from $\mathcal{SP}$ to $\mathcal{U}$.

Internal adversaries are constructed by malicious ($\mathcal{U}$ and $\mathcal{SP}$) and semi-trusted ($\mathcal{I}$) internal entities. We distinguish the following cases. An authentication adversary $\mathcal{A}^{auth}$ models a malicious user (or collusion of users) and has access to all the users' credentials. The goal of $\mathcal{A}^{auth}$ is to transfer a usable credential to another user or to generate a new valid credential, and is only limited not to reveal the long-term private key of the user. A tracing adversary $\mathcal{A}^{trace}$ models a malicious service provider (or collusion of them), having access to all the secret information of $\mathcal{SP}$ and the history of all the user access instances. The goal of $\mathcal{A}^{trace}$ is to trace and/or link users by combining all available information. We emphasize that the issuer is not allowed to participate in $\mathcal{A}^{trace}$. Also, we assume that $\mathcal{A}^{trace}$ cannot link/trace users at lower layers (data-link or IP) or by using application content or context to trace/link users (we leave out of scope query content attacks). A framing adversary $\mathcal{A}^{frame}$ models a collusion of a malicious service provider and a semi-trusted issuer. The goal of $\mathcal{A}^{frame}$ is to frame a legitimate user by creating a transaction that opens to the user. $\mathcal{I}$ is semi-trusted since it is allowed to collude with $\mathcal{SP}$ in $\mathcal{A}^{frame}$, but is trusted not to collude with $\mathcal{SP}$ in $\mathcal{A}^{trace}$. Finally, we assume that all the adversaries are polynomially bounded and do not have the ability to break the computational assumptions of the underlying cryptographic assumptions. We also assume that a Public Key Infrastructure (PKI) for certificate management is already in place.

---

[1] This can be achieved by combining certified signature keys with the TLS protocol.

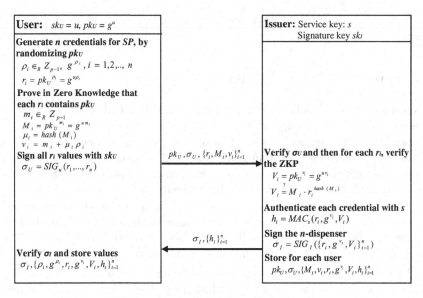

Fig. 1. The credential issuing protocol

3   A Fair, Anonymous Authentication Scheme for LBS

Let $\mathcal{I}$ denote the network operator responsible to issue, update and revoke anonymous user credentials, used to anonymously access an LBS provider $\mathcal{SP}$. We will use a discrete logarithm setting. Let p, q be two sufficiently large primes such that $q|p-1$ and let g be a generator of a multiplicative group G of order p (unless stated otherwise, all operations are done modulo p). Let $sk_U = u$, $pk_U = g^u$ be a certified signature key pair of $\mathcal{U}$ in a discrete log setting (*e.g.*, an ElGamal key pair) with the same generator g. Let sk_I, sk_{SP} be the certified signing keys of $\mathcal{I}$ and $\mathcal{SP}$ respectively, using any signature scheme. Finally, let s be a secret service key, shared between $\mathcal{I}$ and $\mathcal{SP}$.

3.1   Credential Issuing

The credential issuing protocol is executed between $\mathcal{U}$ and $\mathcal{I}$ (Fig. 1). Initially $\mathcal{U}$ chooses n random values $\rho_1, \rho_2, ..., \rho_n \in_R Z_{p-1}^*$ and computes n randomizations of his/her public key as: $r_i = (pk_U)^{\rho_i} \equiv g^{u\rho_i}$, $i = 1, ..., n$. Then, $\mathcal{U}$ will compute n zero-knowledge proofs of knowledge that the values r_i are correctly formed, *i.e.*, that they contain $\mathcal{U}$'s public key g^u. An efficient *non-interactive* proof can be constructed by using the approach in [11]. Specifically, $\mathcal{U}$ chooses a value $m_i \in_R Z_{p-1}^*$, computes $M_i = (pk_U)^{m_i} \equiv g^{um_i}$, then $\mu_i = hash(M_i)$, where *hash* is a cryptographic hash function, and $\mathrm{v}_i = m_i + \mu_i\rho_i$. For accountability purposes, $\mathcal{U}$ also computes a signature σ_U over the concatenation of $r_1, ..., r_n$. Finally, $\mathcal{U}$ sends to $\mathcal{I}$ the values pk_U, σ_U and $\{r_i, M_i, \mathrm{v}_i\}_{i=1}^n$.

On receiving these, $\mathcal{I}$ will first verify the signature σ_U and then will verify the zero-knowledge proofs M_i, v_i for each r_i. To do this, $\mathcal{I}$ computes $V_i = (pk_U)^{\mathrm{v}_i}$ and

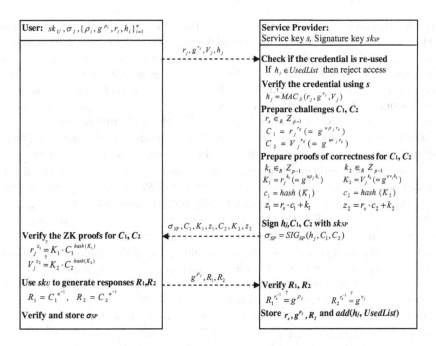

Fig. 2. The user access protocol

checks if $V_i \equiv M_i \cdot r_i^{hash(M_i)}$. If the verifications are successful, $\mathcal{I}$ authenticates each triplet $\{r_i, g^{v_i}, V_i\}$ by computing n Message Authentication Codes (MAC) with the service secret key s (shared only with $\mathcal{SP}$) as: $h_i = MAC_s(r_i, g^{v_i}, V_i)$, $i = 1, ..., n$. Then, $\mathcal{I}$ signs with its private signature key sk_I the concatenation of all the values $\{r_i, g^{v_i}, V_i\}_{i=1}^n$, and returns to $\mathcal{U}$ the credential authenticators h_i. At the same time, $\mathcal{I}$ stores, the public key pk_U, the signature σ_U and the n tuples $\{M_i, v_i, r_i, g^{v_i}, V_i, h_i\}_{i=1}^n$, to be used for possible accountability and/or revocation purposes. $\mathcal{U}$ verifies the signature σ_I and stores it along with the credential values $\{r_i, g^{v_i}, V_i, h_i\}$, and the secret random values ρ_i, and g^{ρ_i}, $i = 1, 2, .., n$. Note that the values g^{ρ_i} are also secret from the issuer and will be later used for non-frameability purposes.

3.2 User Access

The registered user will anonymously access the service provider $\mathcal{SP}$, for n unlinkable transactions, by using his private key $sk_U = u$, a different anonymous credential $\{r_i, g^{v_i}, V_i, h_i\}_{i=1}^n$ and the corresponding value g^{ρ_i} (Fig. 2).

For each access, $\mathcal{U}$ sends a different credential r_j, g^{v_j}, V_j, h_j to $\mathcal{SP}$. The $\mathcal{SP}$ will first verify if the credential has been already used, by checking whether it belongs to the list *UsedList*. If $h_j \in UsedList$ the access is rejected. Else the anonymous authentication continues by verifying (with the secret key s) that h_j is a valid MAC. If the credential is valid, the $\mathcal{SP}$ wants to be assured that it is only used by the legitimate user, who knows the secret key sk_U that corresponds to the public key used during credential issuing. To do this, the $\mathcal{SP}$ prepares two challenges C_1 and C_2, which the anonymous user can respond properly only if he uses the correct key $sk_U = u$. The $\mathcal{SP}$ chooses a random number r_s and computes $C_1 = r_j^{r_s} \equiv g^{u\rho_j r_s}$ and $C_2 = V_j^{r_s} \equiv g^{uv_j r_s}$. The challenge for $\mathcal{U}$ is to remove from C_1, C_2 the correct user's private key u, i.e., the one that corresponds to the public key used to construct r_j, V_j during the registration phase.

Note that a misbehaving $\mathcal{SP}$ could cheat $\mathcal{U}$ by sending a challenge C_1 (resp. C_2) that does not include r_j (resp. V_j). In that case, the $\mathcal{SP}$ would be able to remove all the exponents from the user's response, get $g^{u^{-1}}$ and link all the transactions of a user. In order to prevent this, the $\mathcal{SP}$ must also prepare zero-knowledge proofs that the challenges C_1, C_2 indeed contain the values r_j and V_j respectively. The $\mathcal{SP}$ chooses random numbers $k_1, k_2 \in_R Z_{p-1}$ and prepares $K_1 = r_j^{k_1} \equiv g^{u\rho_j k_1}$ and $K_2 = V_j^{k_2} \equiv g^{uv_j k_2}$. Then, the $\mathcal{SP}$ computes the hash values $c_1 = hash(K_1)$, $c_2 = hash(K_2)$. Finally, the $\mathcal{SP}$ computes the values $z_1 = r_s \cdot c_1 + k_1$, and $z_2 = r_s \cdot c_2 + k_2$. The $\mathcal{SP}$ also signs the challenges C_1, C_2 along with the used credential h_j using the key sk_{SP} as $\sigma_{SP} = SIG_{SP}(h_j, C_1, C_2)$. The server sends to $\mathcal{U}$ the values $\sigma_{SP}, C_1, K_1, z_1, C_2, K_2, z_2$.

On receiving these, $\mathcal{U}$ first verifies σ_{SP}, and then verifies that C_1, C_2 contain r_j and V_j, by checking that $r_j^{z_1} \equiv K_1 \cdot C_1^{hash(K_1)}$ and $V_j^{z_2} \equiv K_2 \cdot C_2^{hash(K_2)}$. If the verifications are successful, $\mathcal{U}$ can safely use his/her private key u and generate the responses: $R_1 = C_1^{u^{-1}}$ and $R_2 = C_2^{u^{-1}}$, without leaking additional information. The user $\mathcal{U}$ stores σ_{SP} (along with h_j, C_1, C_2) in its local store and sends to $\mathcal{SP}$ the responses g^{ρ_j}, R_1 and R_2.

Finally, the $\mathcal{SP}$ will verify that $(R_1)^{r_s^{-1}} \equiv g^{\rho_j}$ and $(R_2)^{r_s^{-1}} \equiv g^{v_j}$, where g^{v_j} is contained in the authenticated credential h_j. We note that showing g^{ρ_j} only during the user access for the verification of C_1 provides the non-frameability property: if g^{ρ_j} was known to $\mathcal{I}$ from the registration phase, it would be possible for $\mathcal{I}$ and $\mathcal{SP}$ to simulate a user access and frame a user (see Section 4.3 for a security proof). The second challenge provides non-transferability (see Section 4.4). If the responses are valid, $\mathcal{U}$ is allowed to anonymously access the requested service. The $\mathcal{SP}$ will store for future reference the values r_s, g^{ρ_j} associated to h_j and will add the credential to the $UsedList$.

Extending the scheme for many LBS providers. This only requires that $\mathcal{I}$ shares a different secret service key s_ℓ for each provider $\mathcal{SP}_\ell$.

3.3 Anonymity Revocation and Credential Revocation

Anonymity revocation. If $\mathcal{SP}$ has convincing arguments of service abuse for a particular access, then $\mathcal{SP}$ securely transfers the particular instance of the access protocol $\{r_j, g^{v_j}, V_j, h_j\}$ to $\mathcal{I}$. From user registration, $\mathcal{I}$ has stored in its database, $pk_U, \sigma_U, \{r_i, g^{v_i}, V_i, h_i\}$, $i = 1, 2, .., n$. The issuer will first verify that $\{r_j, g^{v_j}, V_j, h_j\}$ is indeed a valid credential. Then it will search in its user database, to find in which user's $\widetilde{\mathcal{U}}$ n-dispenser the credential in question is contained. The user $\widetilde{\mathcal{U}}$ will be identified as the misbehaving user. The user cannot deny that the misused credential belongs to him, since during the issuing phase the user has signed with σ_U all the values r_i used in each credential.

Credential revocation. In order to revoke all the credentials of a user, $\mathcal{I}$ manages a revocation list $revList$, which contains the credentials that had been issued to users that are no longer authorized. To revoke a user $\widetilde{\mathcal{U}}$, $\mathcal{I}$ simply appends to $revList$ all the n credentials that were issued to $\widetilde{\mathcal{U}}$, signs and publishes the list to $\mathcal{SP}$. The updated list is: $revList \leftarrow (revList, \{r_i, g^{v_i}, V_i, h_i\}_{i=1}^n)$. The $\mathcal{SP}$ will reject a user access request, if the credential is in $revList$. Note that in order to prevent $\mathcal{SP}$ from linking past transactions of a revoked user, the revocation list should be initialized with random values and then, for each new revoked credential added, the list should be randomly re-ordered. In this way a curious $\mathcal{SP}$ would not be able to link adjacent values within the revocation list.

3.4 Global Accountability / Non-frameability

Say that $\mathcal{SP}$ contacts $\mathcal{I}$ for a possible illegal user access and $\mathcal{I}$ runs the anonymity revocation protocol of Section 3.3 in order to reveal the identity of the user $\widetilde{\mathcal{U}}$ for a particular anonymous access. However, if $\mathcal{I}$ and $\mathcal{SP}$ are able to simulate all the messages of the user, it is possible that they have framed the user $\widetilde{\mathcal{U}}$, and thus the anonymous access scheme cannot provide global accountability. The question here is how to prove to a legal authority (*e.g.*, a Judge) that it is indeed $\widetilde{\mathcal{U}}$ who performed the transaction. For global accountability, the following protocol will be initiated by the global verifier (Judge). The Judge will ask from the parties involved, to provide the following: The $\mathcal{SP}$ gives the disputed user access instance (r_j, g^{v_j}, V_j, h_j), the random value r_s used to randomize the challenges and the response R_1 along with the value g^{ρ_j}, provided by the user during the user access. The issuer $\mathcal{I}$ provides $pk_{\widetilde{U}}, \sigma_{\widetilde{U}}$ for the user $\widetilde{\mathcal{U}}$ in question. Finally, $\widetilde{\mathcal{U}}$ is asked to provide σ_I, σ_{SP} and the value $\widetilde{\rho}_j$, that he/she used for the construction of his j-th credential. The Judge will execute the following protocol:

1. Check whether $\{r_j, g^{v_j}, V_j\} \in \sigma_I$, (*i.e.* this is a valid credential signed by $\mathcal{I}$).
2. Check if $r_j \in \sigma_{\widetilde{U}}$, (*i.e.*, $\widetilde{\mathcal{U}}$ has committed to r_j during the issuing phase).
3. Check if $C_1 \equiv r_j^{r_s}$, *i.e.*, r_s is the correct random value that was used by the $\mathcal{SP}$ during the generation of the challenges for this user access instance. Recall that the $\mathcal{SP}$ has committed to the values h_j, C_1, C_2 with σ_{SP} and thus will provide the correct random value.
4. Check that $(pk_{\widetilde{U}})^{\widetilde{\rho}_j} \equiv r_j$, *i.e.* $\widetilde{\mathcal{U}}$ cannot lie for $\widetilde{\rho}_j$, since $r_j \in \sigma_U$.
5. Check if $R_1^{r_s^{-1}} \equiv g^{\rho_j} \equiv g^{\widetilde{\rho}_j}$, where g^{ρ_j} was given to the Judge by the $\mathcal{SP}$ and $\widetilde{\rho}_j$ was given by $\widetilde{\mathcal{U}}$.

If the last check is true, then $\widetilde{\mathcal{U}}$ has performed the user access, since $\mathcal{I}$ and $\mathcal{SP}$ could not present the correct value g^{ρ_j} otherwise (see Section 4.3). If the check is false, this is a framing attempt. Recall that during the issuing phase the user only provides the proof of correctness that r_i contains his public key and not the values ρ_i or g^{ρ_i} used in $r_i = g^{u\rho_i}$. Finally, note that the signature σ_{SP} prevents the

$\mathcal{SP}$ from reusing g^{ρ_j} in order to frame a user. Since the user verifies σ_{SP} before responding to C_1, C_2, if the $\mathcal{SP}$ reused the opened value g^{ρ_j}, the user would provide two signatures $\sigma_{SP} = SIG_{SP}(h_j, C_1, C_2)$ and $\sigma'_{SP} = SIG_{SP}(h'_j, C'_1, C'_2)$, both linked to $g^{\widetilde{\rho}_j}$ and the Judge would be convinced that $\mathcal{SP}$ is framed.

3.5 Efficiency Analysis

Computation. The computation cost for the user for the credential issuing is: $5n + 2$ exponentiations *i.e.* almost 5 exponentiations per credential. The issuer performs $2n+2$ exponentiations. For each anonymous access, the user performs 7 exponentiations and the provider also performs 7 exponentiations. In total, the user performs 12 exponentiations for each anonymous access. The cost is feasible for mobile devices. If the user runs the issuing protocol from a typical computer and then load the mobile device with the issued credentials, then the cost for the mobile devices can be reduced only to the user access phase.

Bandwidth. Allowing for 128 bytes for public-key operations, 10 bytes for random number selection and 20 bytes for hashing operations, the communication cost of the credential issuing protocol (Fig. 1) is, $542n + 384$, for issuing n credentials. Similarly, the communication cost during a user access (Fig. 2) is 1566 bytes.

4 Security Analysis

4.1 Preliminaries and Notations

The size of a finite set $\mathbf{S}$ is denoted as $|\mathbf{S}|$. The term $s \in_R \mathbf{S}$ denotes the assignment of a uniformly chosen element of $\mathbf{S}$ to a variable s. Let A be a p.p.t algorithm. Then $A(x_1, ..., x_n) = y$ means that on input $x_1, ..., x_n$, the algorithm outputs a value that is assigned to variable y. Let E be some event, such as the result of a security experiment, then $Pr[E]$ denotes the probability that E occurs. The probability $\epsilon(l)$ is called negligible (in l), if for all polynomials f it holds that $\epsilon(l) \leq 1/f(l)$, for all sufficiently large l. In that case, the probability $1 - \epsilon(l)$ is called overwhelming.

Definition 1 (Divisible Computation Diffie-Hellman assumption.). *Let $l_p \in \mathbb{N}$ be a security parameter, $\mathbb{G}$ be a group of large prime exponent $p \approx 2^{l_p}$. Let g be an element of $\mathbb{G}$ of prime order p. Let $x, y \in_R Z_p^*$ and $X = g^x \mod p$, $Y = g^y \mod p$ and $Z \in_R Z_p$. The DCDH assumption is that every p.p.t adversary $\mathcal{A}^{DCDH}$ has negligible advantage (in l_p):*
$$Adv_{\mathcal{A}}^{DCDH} = |Pr[\mathcal{A}(p, g, X, Y) = g^{x/y}]|.$$

Definition 2 (Decisional Divisible Computation Diffie-Hellman assumption.). *Let $l_p \in \mathbb{N}$ be a security parameter, $\mathbb{G}$ be a group of large prime exponent $p \approx 2^{l_p}$. Let g be an element of $\mathbb{G}$ of prime order p. Let $x, y \in_R Z_p^*$ and $X = g^x \mod p$, $Y = g^y \mod p$ and $Z \in_R Z_p$. The DDCDH assumption is that every p.p.t adversary $\mathcal{A}^{DCDH}$ has negligible advantage (in l_p):*
$$Adv_{\mathcal{A}}^{DDCDH} = |Pr[\mathcal{A}(p, g, X, Y, g^{x/y}) = 1] - Pr[\mathcal{A}(p, g, X, Y, Z) = 1]|.$$

4.2   Proof of Untraceability and Unlinkability

The tracing adversary $\mathcal{A}^{trace}$ (described in Section 2) should not be able to trace the identity of a user running the anonymous access protocol of Section 3.2. This implies that the protocol messages generated by a user $\mathcal{U}$, should not leak information that will allow $\mathcal{A}^{trace}$ to trace $\mathcal{U}$. The only value that could trace the identity of $\mathcal{U}$, is the long-term public key g^u, used during the credential issuing. Let $\mathbf{U}$ be the set of all the users' public keys. Let $\pi_j^{g^u}$ denote an instance of the anonymous access protocol, in which the j-th credential of a user $\mathcal{U}$ was used. Since every key $g^{\tilde{u}} \in \mathbf{U}$ is publicly known, the goal of $\mathcal{A}^{trace}$ is to decide if, an anonymous access instance $\pi_j^{g^u}$ is linked or not, with each public key $g^{\tilde{u}} \in \mathbf{U}$.

We formalize anonymous access by a security experiment $\mathrm{Exp}_\mathcal{A}^{tr}$, where $\mathcal{A}^{trace}$ interacts with an oracle $\mathcal{O}^{trace}$ that takes as input, the public parameters p, g, the secret key $sk_{\mathcal{SP}}$ an instance $\pi_j^{g^u}$ of the anonymous access protocol of Section 3.2 and a test public key $g^{\tilde{u}} \in \mathbf{U}$ and outputs: $b = 1$ if $g^u = g^{\tilde{u}}$ or $b = 0$ if $g^u \neq g^{\tilde{u}}$.

Now we must define the information learned from each instance $\pi_j^{g^u}$ of the access protocol (Section 3.2). This information will be given as input to the adversary. Each user credential used by $\mathcal{U}$ contains $r_j = g^{u\rho_j}$, g^{v_j}, $V_j = g^{uv_j}$ and h_j. The value h_j is a hash of the above and thus does not provide additional information. During the response, the user also sends $g^{u\rho_j}$ and R_1, R_2. We examine what information is leaked during this step. The response to the challenges $C_1 = g^{u\rho_j r_s}$ and $C_2 = g^{uv_j r_s}$ does not provide additional information to the adversary, other than g^{ρ_j} and g^{v_j}. This is assured by the proofs of correctness K_1, z_1 and K_2, z_2 respectively. By verifying these proofs, $\mathcal{U}$ is assured that the challenge C_1 (resp. C_2) is a randomization of $g^{u\rho_j}$ (resp. g^{uv_j}). Thus the information learned in each anonymous user access protocol instance of $\mathcal{U}$ is: $\pi_j^{g^u} = (g^{u\rho_j}, g^{v_j}, g^{uv_j}, g^{\rho_j})$.

Definition 3 (Untraceability of our scheme.). *The anonymous authentication protocol described in Section 3.2 achieves untraceability, if every p.p.t adversary $\mathcal{A}^{trace}$ has negligible (in l_p) advantage:*
$$Adv_\mathcal{A}^{tr} = |Pr[\mathrm{Exp}_\mathcal{A}^{tr}(p, g, sk_{\mathcal{SP}}, \pi_j^{g^u}, g^u) = 1] - Pr[\mathrm{Exp}_\mathcal{A}^{tr}(p, g, sk_{\mathcal{SP}}, \pi_j^{g^u}, g^{\tilde{u}}) = 1].$$

Theorem 1. *The anonymous authentication scheme achieves unlinkability under the Decisional Divisible Computation Diffie-Hellman assumption.*

Proof. Assume by contradiction that the advantage of $\mathcal{A}^{trace}$ is non-negligible, *i.e.* the adversary can distinguish whether a public key $g^{\tilde{u}}$ and the access protocol instance $\pi_j^{g^u}$ given as input to the oracle $\mathcal{O}^{trace}$ are linked. Give to the oracle: the public parameters g, p, the provider's secret key $sk_{\mathcal{SP}}$, the access protocol instance of a user $\pi_j^{g^u} = (g^{v_j}, g^{uv_j}, g^{\rho_j}, g^{u\rho_j})$, and a public key $g^{\tilde{u}}$. The oracle will output $b = 1$, if the input public key $g^{\tilde{u}} = g^u$ (i.e. it is the public key used in $\pi_j^{g^u}$), and $b = 0$ otherwise.

Now the adversary $\mathcal{A}^{trace}$ can be used as a subroutine to break the DDCDH assumption of Definition 2. The adversary $\mathcal{A}^{DDCDH}$ will give to the oracle $\mathcal{O}^{trace}$

of the adversary $\mathcal{A}^{trace}$: g^{v_j} (as $X = g^x$), g^{uv_j} (as $Y = g^y$) and $g^{\tilde{u}}$ (as Z). Now $\mathcal{A}^{DDCDH}$ will check the output b of the oracle to decide the Decisional Divisible Computational Diffie-Hellman problem with non-negligible probability. If the oracle $\mathcal{O}^{trace}$ outputs $b = 0$, then $Adv_{\mathcal{A}}{}^{DDCDH}$ can decide that $g^{\tilde{u}} = g^{x/y}$. Else it decides that $g^{\tilde{u}} \neq g^{x/y}$. $\mathcal{A}^{DDCDH}$ can also use g^{ρ_j} as X and $g^{u\rho_j}$ as Y with the same advantage.

It is easy to prove that the protocol also provides unlinkability under the DD-CDH assumption. In that case, the adversary would take as input two different protocol instances and a public key. The output b of the oracle would be 1 if the *two* protocol instances are linked with the public key and 0 otherwise.

4.3   Proof of Non-frameability

The adversary $\mathcal{A}^{frame}$ (described in Section 2) should not be able to simulate a user access protocol instance $\pi_j^{g^u}$, that will open to user's public key g^u, if the global accountability protocol of Section 3.4 is run. We formalize a framing attempt by a security experiment $\text{Exp}_{\mathcal{A}}^{frame}$, where $\mathcal{A}^{frame}$ interacts with an oracle $\mathcal{O}^{frame}$ that takes as input: the public parameters p, g, the j-th instance of the credential issuing protocol (Section 3.1) of the user $\mathcal{U}$, denoted as $\varpi_j^{g^u}$, the combined secret information of $\mathcal{I}$ and $\mathcal{SP}$ (*i.e.* the private keys sk_{SP}, sk_I and s and the randomness r_s used for the challenges C_1, C_2) and outputs a valid user response of the anonymous access protocol $\pi_j^{g^u}$.

The input information given to $\mathcal{O}^{frame}$ from each instance $\varpi_j^{g^u}$ contains g^u, $r_j = g^{u\rho_j}$, M_j, v_j. Since M_j is only used for the zero knowledge proof of correctness of r_j, it does not provide additional information to the adversary. Thus, for the experiment $\text{Exp}_{\mathcal{A}}^{frame}$, the information given to the adversary oracle for each credential issuing protocol instance is: $\varpi_j^{g^u} = (g^u, g^{u\rho_j}, v_j)$. In order to simulate a user, $\mathcal{O}^{frame}$ must output all the information generated by the target user $\mathcal{U}$, during the user access protocol of Section 3.2. Thus the output of the oracle is: $\pi_j^{g^u} = (r_j, g^{v_j}, V_j, h_j, g^{\rho_j}, R_1, R_2)$.

Definition 4 (Non-frameability of our scheme.). *The accountability protocol of Section 3.4 will always trace a simulated framing anonymous access instance of the protocol of Section 3.2, if every p.p.t adversary $\mathcal{A}^{frame}$ has negligible (in l_p) advantage:*

$$Adv_{\mathcal{A}}^{frame} = |Pr[\text{Exp}_{\mathcal{A}}^{frame}(p, g, \varpi_j^{g^u}, sk_{SP}, sk_I, s, r_s) = \pi_j^{g^u}].$$

Theorem 2. *The anonymous authentication scheme achieves non-frameability under the Divisible Computation Diffie-Hellman assumption.*

Proof. Assume by contradiction that the advantage of $\mathcal{A}^{frame}$ is non-negligible. $\mathcal{A}^{frame}$ gives as input to the oracle, the public parameters g, p, an instance of the credential issuing protocol of Section 3.1 for a target user $\mathcal{U}$, $\varpi_j^{g^u} = (g^u, g^{u\rho_j}, v_j)$, the private keys sk_{SP}, sk_I and s and the randomness r_s used for the challenges $C_1 = g^{u\rho_j r_s}$, $C_2 = g^{uv_j r_s}$. The oracle outputs a simulated instance of the anonymous access protocol $\pi_j^{g^u} = (r_j, g^{v_j}, V_j, h_j, g^{\rho_j}, R_1, R_2)$ $= (g^{u\rho_j}, g^{v_j}, g^{uv_j}, h_j, g^{\rho_j}, g^{\rho_j r_s}, g^{v_j r_s})$, which is indistinguishable from a protocol instance run by the real user $\mathcal{U}$.

Now the adversary $\mathcal{A}^{frame}$ can be used as a subroutine to break the DCDH assumption of Definition 1. The adversary $\mathcal{A}^{DCDH}$ will give to the oracle $\mathcal{O}^{frame}$ as input: $g^{u\rho_j}$ (as $X = g^x$) and g^u (as $Y = g^y$) and v_j. The oracle will output $\pi_j^{g^u}$ as follows: $r_j = g^{u\rho_j}$ (already given in the input), $g^{v_j}, V_j = g^{uv_j}$ (using the input values v_j and g^u), h_j (using the key s), g^{ρ_j}, and $R_1 = g^{\rho_j r_s}, R_2 = g^{v_j r_s}$, (using g^{ρ_j}, g^{v_j} and r_s). However, the output value $g^{\rho_j} \equiv g^{x/y}$, which contradicts the DCDH assumption. Note that possible replay attacks based on an previously received g^{ρ_j} are not possible, due to the use of the signature σ_{SP}, as described in Section 3.4. It is easy to see that the scheme also provides exculpability.

4.4   Proof of Non-transferability

Although the response g^{ρ_j}, R_1 of the challenge C_1 provides non-frameability, it does not prevent a user from transferring one or more credentials to a non-registered user. For example, $\mathcal{U}$ could transfer his j-th credential by giving to another user $\mathcal{U}'$ the values $\rho_j, (\alpha \cdot u^{-1}), g^{\rho_j \alpha}$, for some α. Then $\mathcal{U}'$ would be able to respond C_1, by sending to $\mathcal{SP}$ the response $R_1' = C_1^{(\alpha \cdot u^{-1})}$ and $g^{\rho_j \alpha}$. The verification would work, the long term private key u would not be revealed and the credential transfer would be revealed only if the accountability protocol of Section 3.4 was run. This however is executed only in case of disputes, while non-transferability should be verified for each anonymous access. To avoid, this, the second challenge C_2 is used. The response R_2 is verified against g^{v_j}, which is authenticated with the MAC h_j and thus cannot be manipulated.

We formalize a credential transferring attempt by a security experiment $\text{Exp}_{\mathcal{A}}^{auth}$, where the adversary $\mathcal{A}^{auth}$ (described in Section 2) interacts with an oracle $\mathcal{O}^{auth}$ that takes as input: the public parameters p, g, all the private information related with the j-th user credential $cred_j$ and possible one-way transformations of u, but *not* the long-term private key u of the user, and outputs a valid user response of the anonymous access protocol $\pi_j^{g^u} = (g^{u\rho_j}, g^{v_j}, g^{uv_j}, h_j, g^{\rho_j}, R_1, R_2)$. The input information given to $\mathcal{O}^{auth}$ with $cred_j$ includes the public key g^u the credential $g^{u\rho_j}, g^{v_j}, g^{uv_j}$, the authenticator h_j, and the values v_j and ρ_j. The oracle also gets as input any one-way transformation of the user's private key u denoted as $f_\alpha(u)$, for every $\alpha \neq r_s$, as well as an one-way transformation of α (this will allow $\mathcal{O}^{auth}$ to simulate the response to the first challenge, without revealing u to $\mathcal{O}^{auth}$). We also give to the oracle, the one-way transformation $f_\alpha(u) = \alpha \cdot u^{-1}$ and g^α. The value $\alpha \in_R Z_p$ is kept secret from $\mathcal{O}^{auth}$, since otherwise the oracle could compute u. Thus for the experiment $\text{Exp}_{\mathcal{A}}^{auth}$, the input information $cred_j$ contains: $cred_j = (g^{u\rho_j}, g^{v_j}, g^{uv_j}, h_j, \rho_j, v_j, f_\alpha(u) = \frac{\alpha}{u}, g^\alpha)$.

Definition 5 (Non-transferability of our scheme.). *The anonymous authentication scheme of Section 3.2 achieves non-transferability, if every p.p.t adversary $\mathcal{A}^{auth}$ has negligible (in l_p) advantage:*

$$Adv_{\mathcal{A}}^{auth} = |Pr[\text{Exp}_{\mathcal{A}}^{auth}(p, g, g^u, g^{u\rho_j r_s}, g^{uv_j r_s}, cred_j) = \pi_j^{g^u}].$$

Theorem 3. *The anonymous authentication scheme achieves non-transferability under the Divisible Computation Diffie-Hellman assumption.*

Proof. Assume by contradiction that the advantage of $\mathcal{A}^{auth}$ is non-negligible. The oracle $\mathcal{O}^{auth}$ outputs a simulated instance of the anonymous access protocol $\pi_j^{g^u} = (g^{u\rho_j}, g^{v_j}, g^{uv_j}, h_j, g^{\rho'_j} = g^{\alpha\rho_j}, R'_1 = g^{\rho'_j r_s}, R_2 = g^{v_j r_s})$, which is indistinguishable from a protocol instance run by the real user $\mathcal{U}$. Recall that during the user access protocol the verifier receives both parts of response that verifies the first challenge C_1. It is easy for the oracle to provide $g^{u\rho_j}, g^{v_j}, g^{uv_j}, h_j$ and $g^{\rho'_j}$, using its input values. This however is not possible for the second response, which the verifier will accept only if it matches with the value g^{v_j}, which is authenticated through h_j. Since the advantage of $\mathcal{A}^{auth}$ is non-negligible, we assume that the oracle's output contains the correct value $R_2 = g^{v_j r_s}$. Now $\mathcal{A}^{DCDH}$ can use $\mathcal{A}^{auth}$ as a subroutine to break DCDH assumption. The adversary $\mathcal{A}^{DCDH}$ gives to the oracle $\mathcal{O}^{auth}$ the values $C_2 = g^{uv_j r_s}$ (as $X = g^x$), g^u (as $Y = g^y$) and the oracle outputs $R_2 = g^{v_j r_s} \equiv g^{x/y}$. This however contradicts the DCDH assumption. It is easy to see that non-transferability also implies unforgeability and user-coalition resistance.

5   Related Work

Anonymous authentication is an extensively studied field and can be categorized in two main frameworks. A first line of works is based on Brands [4] and Chaum's blind signatures [10], and has been implemented in Microsoft's U-Prove technology [20]. Credentials of this category are inherently one-show (*i.e.*, linkable when used more than once), however they are suitable in cases where a single credential needs to be traced or when a credential can only be used once. The second line of works is based on the framework of Camenish and Lysyanskaya (the CL framework) [7,8], proposed in [2] in the standard model and extended in [19,22], while a variation of the technology is implemented as the Idemix system [16]. Credentials of this category are multi-show with built-in unlinkability. Schemes of this category are inherently less efficient than the Brands' framework.

Both of these categories of work are focusing on anonymous authentication systems with a much wider scope than our scheme, which focuses on anonymity of mobile users from LBS services. The first scheme for mobile anonymity that makes use of the network operator as the credential issuer is the lightweight scheme of [23]. This scheme is efficient, since it transforms the RSA-based direct anonymous attestation scheme [5] to an elliptic curve scheme and pairings. The scheme of [23] only requires 5 scalar multiplications, which is the computation-intensive operation in their setting. Our scheme is more expensive but is feasible for mid-range modern mobile devices, since it requires 12 exponentiations for each anonymous access (including both credential issuing and user access). However, in the scheme of [23] credential non-transferability is based on the existence of embedded hardware, which is not required in our scheme. Moreover, our scheme improves system fairness, by providing user non-frameability.

Another view of anonymity in LBS is privacy-preserving access control for LBS services. Two frameworks can be considered in this area: (a) TTP-based schemes, which adopt a centralized model for privacy in LBSs, where online and/or offline TTPs are employed for either protecting the location information of users (*i.e.*, TTP spatial k-anonymity [13], TTP cloaking/obfuscation (*e.g.*, [15])), or for protecting the link between location information and user identity (*i.e.*, identity privacy with simple pseudonyms [14] or multiple, unlinkable pseudonyms [17,23]). (b) TTP-free solutions: Here trust assumptions are very weak or completely removed. The category contains *client-server* architectures based on the (inefficient) PIR cryptographic primitive (*e.g.*, [12]), where communication takes place between a user and an untrusted LBS provider, as well as fully-distributed or *collaborative* settings (*e.g.*, [21]), where trust is distributed among a set of system peers that form ad-hoc networks and collaborate to achieve privacy against a set of untrusted entities (*i.e.*, the LBS provider, and/or mobile peers or even the network operator). The main problems in both frameworks are the strong assumptions made by most TTP-based schemes and the high computation and communication costs of TTP-free schemes [18].

6   Conclusions

In this paper we proposed an efficient, secure and fair anonymous authentication scheme for mobile devices accessing LBS services. As future work, we plan to transform our scheme into a formal and general-use, fair anonymous authentication scheme, which will provide non-frameability and other fundamental properties in an efficient manner. We also plan to build a system prototype, and empirically measure the efficiency of our scheme.

References

1. Bao, F., Deng, R.H., Zhu, H.: Variations of Diffie-Hellman Problem. In: Qing, S., Gollmann, D., Zhou, J. (eds.) ICICS 2003. LNCS, vol. 2836, pp. 301–312. Springer, Heidelberg (2003)
2. Belenkiy, M., Chase, M., Kohlweiss, M., Lysyanskaya, A.: P-signatures and Noninteractive Anonymous Credentials. In: Canetti, R. (ed.) TCC 2008. LNCS, vol. 4948, pp. 356–374. Springer, Heidelberg (2008)
3. Bethencourt, J.: Cryptographic Techniques for Privacy Preserving Identity. Ph.D. thesis, EECS Department, University of California, Berkeley (May 2011), http://www.eecs.berkeley.edu/Pubs/TechRpts/2011/EECS-2011-58.html
4. Brands, S.A.: Rethinking Public Key Infrastructures and Digital Certificates: Building in Privacy. MIT Press, Cambridge (2000)
5. Brickell, E.F., Camenisch, J., Chen, L.: Direct anonymous attestation. In: Atluri, V., Pfitzmann, B., McDaniel, P.D. (eds.) ACM Conference on Computer and Communications Security, pp. 132–145. ACM (2004)
6. Burmester, M., Desmedt, Y., Wright, R.N., Yasinsac, A.: Accountable Privacy. In: Christianson, B., Crispo, B., Malcolm, J.A., Roe, M. (eds.) Security Protocols 2004. LNCS, vol. 3957, pp. 83–95. Springer, Heidelberg (2006)

7. Camenisch, J., Lysyanskaya, A.: An Efficient System for Non-transferable Anonymous Credentials with Optional Anonymity Revocation. In: Pfitzmann, B. (ed.) EUROCRYPT 2001. LNCS, vol. 2045, pp. 93–118. Springer, Heidelberg (2001)

8. Camenisch, J., Lysyanskaya, A.: Signature Schemes and Anonymous Credentials from Bilinear Maps. In: Franklin, M.K. (ed.) CRYPTO 2004. LNCS, vol. 3152, pp. 56–72. Springer, Heidelberg (2004)

9. Camenisch, J., Neven, G.: Saving On-Line Privacy. In: Bezzi, M., Duquenoy, P., Fischer-Hübner, S., Hansen, M., Zhang, G. (eds.) IFIP AICT 320. IFIP AICT, vol. 320, pp. 34–47. Springer, Heidelberg (2010)

10. Chaum, D.: Blind signatures for untraceable payments. In: Chaum, D., Rivest, R.L., Sherman, A.T. (eds.) CRYPTO 1982, pp. 199–203. Plenum Press (1982)

11. Fiat, A., Shamir, A.: How to Prove Yourself: Practical Solutions to Identification and Signature Problems. In: Odlyzko, A.M. (ed.) CRYPTO 1986. LNCS, vol. 263, pp. 186–194. Springer, Heidelberg (1987)

12. Ghinita, G., Kalnis, P., Khoshgozaran, A., Shahabi, C., Tan, K.L.: Private queries in location based services: anonymizers are not necessary. In: Wang, J.T.L. (ed.) SIGMOD Conference, pp. 121–132. ACM (2008)

13. Gruteser, M., Grunwald, D.: Anonymous usage of location-based services through spatial and temporal cloaking. In: MobiSys 2003, pp. 31–42. ACM, New York (2003)

14. Hauser, C., Kabatnik, M.: Towards privacy support in a global location service. In: IFIP Workshop on IP and ATM Traffic Management, WATM/EUNICE 2001 (2001)

15. Hengartner, U.: Location privacy based on trusted computing and secure logging. In: SecureComm 2008: Proceedings of the 4th International Conference on Security and Privacy in Communication Networks, pp. 1–8. ACM (2008)

16. IBM: IDentity Mixer - Idemix, http://www.zurich.ibm.com/~pbi/identityMixer_gettingStarted/, (accessed March 18, 2012)

17. Kölsch, T., Fritsch, L., Kohlweiss, M., Kesdogan, D.: Privacy for Profitable Location Based Services. In: Hutter, D., Ullmann, M. (eds.) SPC 2005. LNCS, vol. 3450, pp. 164–178. Springer, Heidelberg (2005)

18. Magkos, E.: A survey of cryptographic approaches for privacy preservation in location-based services. International Journal of Information Technologies and the Systems Approach (IJITSA) 4(2), 48–69 (2011)

19. Nguyen, L., Safavi-Naini, R.: Dynamic k-Times Anonymous Authentication. In: Ioannidis, J., Keromytis, A.D., Yung, M. (eds.) ACNS 2005. LNCS, vol. 3531, pp. 318–333. Springer, Heidelberg (2005)

20. Paquin, C., Thompson, G.: U-prove ctp white paper. Microsoft Corporation (2010)

21. Solanas, A., Martínez-Ballesté, A.: Privacy Protection in Location-Based Services Through a Public-Key Privacy Homomorphism. In: López, J., Samarati, P., Ferrer, J.L. (eds.) EuroPKI 2007. LNCS, vol. 4582, pp. 362–368. Springer, Heidelberg (2007)

22. Teranishi, I., Sako, K.: k-Times Anonymous Authentication with a Constant Proving Cost. In: Yung, M., Dodis, Y., Kiayias, A., Malkin, T. (eds.) PKC 2006. LNCS, vol. 3958, pp. 525–542. Springer, Heidelberg (2006)

23. Wachsmann, C., Chen, L., Dietrich, K., Löhr, H., Sadeghi, A.-R., Winter, J.: Lightweight Anonymous Authentication with TLS and DAA for Embedded Mobile Devices. In: Burmester, M., Tsudik, G., Magliveras, S., Ilić, I. (eds.) ISC 2010. LNCS, vol. 6531, pp. 84–98. Springer, Heidelberg (2011)

Enhancing Privacy in LTE Paging System Using Physical Layer Identification

Tuan Ta and John S. Baras

Institute for Systems Research
University of Maryland, College Park, MD 20742, USA
{tta,baras}@umd.edu

Abstract. User location privacy is a growing concern in cellular networks. It has been recently shown that the paging architecture in GSM networks leaks user location information. In this paper, we first prove theoretically that LTE networks also have the same vulnerability. We then propose a solution making use of a novel signal processing technique, physical layer identification. The idea is to embed users' unique tags onto the downlink paging signal waveforms so that the tags are stealthy and robust. We show that our scheme not only improves users' privacy, but also saves system bandwidth.

Keywords: LTE, location privacy, physical layer identification, paging.

1 Introduction

In all cellular networks, mobile stations (MS) mostly run on battery. To prolong the operational time of the MSs, the network architecture allows them to go into idle mode after being inactive for a certain period of time. In idle mode, the MSs do not sustain a connection with the serving base stations (BS). When there is a need to create a connection with an idle MS, e.g. voice calls, data, or system information updates, the BS sends out a notification to the MS in the form of a paging message. The location of an idle MS may have changed since the last time it was in communication. Therefore, the network maintains a tracking area for each idle MS. A tracking area consists of several cells. The MS has to report if it moves out of the assigned tracking area. In general, paging messages are sent without any confidentiality protection. As a result, everybody can listen to those messages. The privacy of those who are being paged is provided through the use of temporary IDs. Those are IDs which only have meaning in the context of the idle MS and the serving network within the tracking area. Recently, Kune *et al.* have shown that despite the use of temporary IDs, the location of a user's cellphone in a GSM network can still be leaked [1]. In particular, they show that an attacker can check if a user's cellphone is within a small area, or absent from a large area, without the user's awareness. As the authors highlighted, such vulnerability can lead to serious consequences. For example, in an oppressive regime, locations of dissidents are revealed to suppressive agents without cooperation from reluctant service providers. Another example is that a thief,

R. Di Pietro et al. (Eds.): DPM 2012 and SETOP 2012, LNCS 7731, pp. 15–28, 2013.

who attempts a break-in, can use the knowledge of the absence of the target to reduce the threat of encounter.

To perform this location attack, the attacker in [1] requires 2 capabilities:

- Cause paging request messages to appear on the GSM *Paging Control Channel* (PCCH)
- Listen on the GSM PCCH broadcast channel

In GSM networks, paging messages are sent on dedicated time-division channels. The *Temporary Mobile Subscriber Identity* (TMSI) is used for paging messages. The idea behind the location attack is that the adversary initiates a connection request to the user cellphone (this of course assumes that he knows the target's number), which results in a paging message being sent in the user's tracking area. By observing the paging channel, the adversary obtains a set of possible temporary IDs for the target user. Repeating this procedure several times, the adversary collects several sets of possible temporary IDs, from which he can do set intersection to get the temporary ID associated with the user's cellphone. Practical experiments on T-Mobile and AT&T GSM networks show that after 2 or 3 repetitions, the adversary can pinpoint the temporary ID of a user's cellphone [1]. To keep the user unaware of the attack, the connection request to his cellphone has to be terminated before a connection is established, but after the paging message is sent out. In [1], the authors, through experiments, show that by calling the target's number and hanging up within 5 seconds, a paging message would be sent out, but the user's phone would not ring. Another way of achieving this goal is to send "silent SMS", a controversial method used by German and French police to track people [4], [5].

After reviewing the paging architecture in LTE and proving that the same attack is possible in LTE networks, we propose a solution using physical layer identification tags. Most security measures operate on the bit level and above. We go further down, to the physical level of electromagnetic transmissions. Our method does not rely on cryptographic primitives. Addressing the attack, the mitigations in [1] either require additional control signaling (sending paging messages out to several tracking areas, changing TMSI more frequently), or introduce delay in response to users' requests. Our solution requires neither. In fact, it requires less signaling than the current standard. However, it does require additional signal processing steps and therefore needs to be incrementally deployed. We want to emphasize that even though the additional signal processing is not in the standard, it is not computationally expensive. Therefore the effect on power consumption of the UEs is minimal. Our technique is inspired by the physical layer authentication scheme in [2], [3]. In those works, Yu *et al.* describe a stealthy authentication technique in which the authenticating entity's credential is embedded as a watermark in the transmitted physical waveform. The authenticator detects the presence of the tag in the received waveform, and decides whether the waveform was transmitted by the legitimate transmitter or not. We extend this technique to the LTE paging system by assigning to each user equipment (UE) a unique tag. These tags are superimposed onto the paging transmitted waveform if the corresponding UEs are paged. The tags are transmitted with very low power such that they càn only be *detected*, and not *decoded*. By detecting the presence of its tag, a UE learns that it is paged. Because of the stealth property of the tags, an eavesdropper observing the paging waveform learns nothing about who are being paged.

The paper is structured as follows. In Section 2, we review the LTE paging system and show that it has the same vulnerability as the GSM system. Next, in Section 3, we describe our scheme. In Section 4, we evaluate the performance of our scheme through simulations. We finish with some conclusions and remarks.

2   LTE Paging System

In this section, we highlight some technical specifications of LTE which allow us to conclude that the location attack in [1] can be performed in an LTE network. We will use these details in the analysis of our scheme in subsequent sections.

Control Signaling: In contrast to the GSM architecture, in LTE there is no dedicated resource for paging. Instead, the paging messages are delivered in the same frequency band as normal data; and the existence of such paging messages in each subframe (1ms) is indicated in the control channel. In normal operation mode, at the beginning of each LTE downlink subframe, there are up to 4 (out of 14) OFDM symbols used to transmit control data. These *Downlink Control Information* (DCI) messages carry resource allocation information, Hybrid-ARQ, system information and paging indicator among others. Each control message is encapsulated in a *Physical Downlink Control Channel* (PDCCH) message. The DCI can be targeted to a specific user equipment (UE), or a group of UEs as in the case of a paging indicator. If the DCI is for a specific UE, the 16-bit CRC generated for that DCI will be XORed with the last 16 bits of the temporary ID of the targeted UE (e.g. *Cell Radio Network Temporary Identifier* C-RNTI). If the DCI is for a group of UEs, its CRC will be masked with one of the predefined IDs for group control information. The paging indicator ID, P-RNTI, is *FFFE* (in hexadecimal) [8].

UE Decoding: The UEs do not know a priori which PDCCH in the control region of a subframe is intended for them. Therefore they perform *blind decoding*, in which they try all possible sizes of PDCCH. The list of such allowable sizes can be found in [7]. If after unmasking the CRC of a possible PDCCH message with either a common ID or the UE's temporary ID, the CRC check returns true, then the UE knows that it has successfully decoded a valid PDCCH message. To reduce the number of PDCCH the UEs have to try to decode, each UE is given a *search space*. The search space is all possible starting positions of a PDCCH. There are UE-specific search spaces and common search spaces. The latter are locations which all UEs have to try decoding from. Group control information, including paging indicator, is sent on the common search space. Due to the requirement that broadcast control information has to reach users with poor channel conditions, group PDCCH have bigger sizes than other PDCCH, which allows for lower code rates to be used. Two allowable sizes for these PDCCH are

72 and 144 *resource elements* [7]. Resource element is the smallest resource unit
in LTE, comprising of 1 subcarrier in 1 OFDM symbol. All control information
are modulated with QPSK, therefore the paging PDCCH can have either 144 or
288 bits.

The DCI format for paging indicator is either 1A or 1C [7]. Depending on the
system bandwidth (1.4 - 20 MHz), DCI format 1A, and 1C can have 36 - 44, and
24 - 31 bits respectively [10]. This DCI has the location of the paging record in
the data portion of the subframe. The UE decodes that location in the *Physical
Downlink Shared Channel* (PDSCH) to get the record. The paging record contains a list of IDs of UEs being paged, which can be either *System Architecture
Evolution TMSI* (S-TMSI) or *International Mobile Subscriber Identity* (IMSI)
[9]. In normal cases, the temporary ID S-TMSI is used instead of the permanent
ID IMSI. If the UE sees its ID in the list, it knows that it is paged. Figure 1 illustrates an example of paging PDCCH and PDSCH positions in an LTE downlink
subframe.

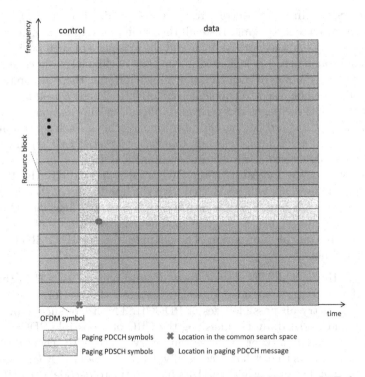

Fig. 1. An example of positions of paging PDCCH and PDSCH in an LTE downlink
subframe. Pilots and other types of physical channels are omitted for clarity.

Attacker Model: We will use an analogous attacker model as [1]. The only
difference is that our attacker is capable of causing paging request messages in
LTE networks and listen on LTE paging channels. While the first capability of
the attacker remains the same as in the original paper, the above procedure

serves to justify the practicality of the second capability. The attacker can listen on the control channel, and unmask PDCCH with P-RNTI. Once he decodes a paging indicator, he can go the specified location in PDSCH to obtain the list of paged IDs. In [1], Kune *et al.* use an open source GSM baseband software implementation [12] to read the TMSI of paged MSs. While an equivalent open source software for LTE baseband is not available at this moment, it is reasonable to expect that one will be developed in the future. We therefore conclude that the same location attack is feasible in LTE, and security measures should be taken proactively.

3   Privacy-Enhanced Paging Messages

To combat the vulnerability in the LTE paging system described in Section 2, we propose to use a UE's temporary ID as an input to create a tag unique to that UE. If a UE is paged during a subframe, its tag is embedded onto the paging PDCCH. The only requirement for the tags is that tags from 2 different UEs are uncorrelated. Here "embed" means that the tag is superimposed onto the PDCCH QPSK symbols. To be backward compatible with older user equipment, the content of the paging indicator is left unchanged. A simple scenario where one old UE (Alice) and one new UE (Bob) are paged in the same subframe is illustrated in Figure 2. If the tag embedding does not cause too much degradation to the PDCCH signal quality, Alice is still able to decode the control information and follow the standard procedure to see if she is paged. Bob, however, can determine if he is paged just by detecting the presence of his unique tag in the PDCCH. Therefore he does not need to decode the PDSCH, which saves battery considering that most UEs which expect paging messages are in idle mode. Listening on the paging channel, Eve can obtain Alice's temporary ID, but she cannot get Bob's tag. As will be shown later, Bob's tag is transmitted

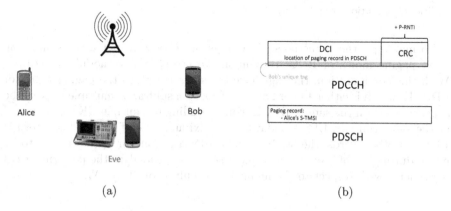

(a)   (b)

Fig. 2. (a) Simple scenario with one old UE (Alice) and one new UE (Bob) being paged at the same subframe. The eavesdropper, Eve, can listen on the paging broadcast channel and analyze the PDCCH waveform; (b) PDCCH and PDSCH paging messages.

with very low power so that nobody (including Bob) can decode it. Bob, however, can detect the presence of his tag in the paging PDCCH. Another benefit of this scheme comes in the form of downlink data bandwidth increase. Since Bob's ID is no longer needed to be transmitted in PDSCH, that bandwidth can be used for data transmission. The new UE capability as well as paging mechanism can be negotiated with the base station (eNodeB in LTE terms) at connection establishment. The operations at the eNodeB and UE are shown in Figure 3.

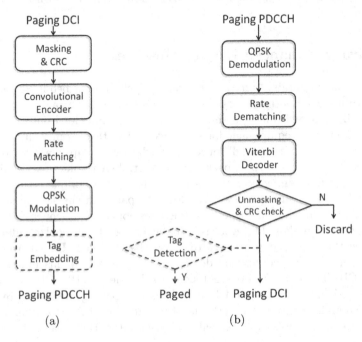

Fig. 3. Flow charts for (a) eNodeB and (b) User Equipment. Dashed boxes are additional operations required by the scheme.

To maximize the robustness of the tags, we choose to put a tag symbol on every paging indicator PDCCH symbol. We use QPSK to modulate the tags. With this configuration, the tags have the same length as the paging indicator PDCCH, which is either 144 or 288 bits. During a subframe, multiple tags can be superimposed on the same PDCCH, corresponding to multiple UEs being paged at the same time. In LTE standard, the maximum size of the paging record is 16 [9]. In other words, the 3GPP standard leaves room for up to 16 UEs to be paged during 1 subframe. In subsequent sections, we analyze the performance of our scheme with respect to the number of simultaneous tags, N_t.

3.1   eNodeB Operations

Let $\mathbf{b}$ be the paging DCI. The PDCCH symbols that encapsulate this DCI are $\mathbf{s} = f_e(\mathbf{b})$. Here $f_e(\cdot)$ is the encoding function, which includes CRC, convolutional encoding, rate matching, and QPSK modulation. Let $\mathbf{k}_i, i = 1, \ldots, N_t$, be the ith paged UE's ID. Generate the tag $\mathbf{t}_i = g(\mathbf{k}_i)$. As mentioned above, the functionality of the generator function $g(\cdot)$ is to create uncorrelated tags. The elements of $\mathbf{b}$ and $\mathbf{k}_i$ are in bits; while the elements of $\mathbf{s}$ and $\mathbf{t}_i$ are in QPSK symbols $\{\pm 1, \pm i\}$. The tags are superimposed onto the PDCCH to create the transmitted message

$$\mathbf{x} = \rho_s \mathbf{s} + \frac{\rho_t}{\sqrt{N_t}} \sum_{i=1}^{N_t} \mathbf{t}_i \tag{1}$$

Let $\mathbf{s} = (s^{(1)}, \ldots, s^{(L)})$, i.e. there are L QPSK symbols in the PDCCH signal. For paging indicators, $L = 72$ or 144. Assuming that each symbol of the PDCCH signal and of the tag has zero-mean and unit variance, we have

$$E[s^{(k)}] = 0, E\left[|s^{(k)}|^2\right] = 1 \quad \text{for} \quad k = 1, \ldots, L$$

$$E[t_i^{(k)}] = 0, E\left[|t_i^{(k)}|^2\right] = 1 \quad i = 1, \ldots, N_t \tag{2}$$

Since the tags are uncorrelated among themselves and independent of the PDCCH symbols,

$$E[\mathbf{s}^H \mathbf{t}_i] = 0, \quad i = 1, \ldots, N_t \tag{3}$$

$$E[\mathbf{t}_i^H \mathbf{t}_j] = 0, \quad i, j = 1, \ldots, N_t, \quad i \neq j \tag{4}$$

In (1), ρ_s and ρ_t are system parameters controlling the amount of power allocated to the signal and the tags, respectively. The power constraint is

$$\rho_s^2 + \rho_t^2 = 1 \tag{5}$$

From (1) - (5), we have

$$E[\mathbf{s}] = E[\mathbf{t}_i] = E[\mathbf{x}] = 0$$

$$E[|\mathbf{s}|^2] = E[|\mathbf{t}_i|^2] = E[|\mathbf{x}|^2] = L, \quad i = 1, \ldots, N_t \tag{6}$$

3.2   User Equipment Operations

Decode DCI. Assuming a frequency selective fading channel, the received signal at the UEs is

$$\mathbf{y} = \mathbf{Hx} + \mathbf{w} \tag{7}$$

where $\mathbf{H}$ is a diagonal matrix, with the elements being the attenuations at each subcarrier frequency. $\mathbf{w}$ is thermal noise at the transmitter and receiver circuitry. In LTE, pilot symbols are transmitted on fixed resource elements to help in channel estimation at the receivers [6]. There are many techniques that the receiver can use to perform channel estimation, e.g. LMMSE [11]. In general, the channel estimate can be written as

$$\hat{\mathbf{H}} = \mathbf{H} + \nu \tag{8}$$

where ν is the estimation error.

Let $\hat{H}^{(k)}, k = 1, \ldots, L$ be the diagonal elements of $\hat{\mathbf{H}}$, the receiver estimates the message symbols as

$$\hat{x}^{(k)} = \frac{\hat{H}^{(k)*}}{|\hat{H}^{(k)}|^2} y^{(k)}$$

$$= x^{(k)} - \frac{\nu^{(k)} x^{(k)}}{\hat{H}^{(k)}} + \frac{w^{(k)}}{\hat{H}^{(k)}} \tag{9}$$

It then decodes the DCI

$$\hat{\mathbf{b}} = f_d(\hat{\mathbf{x}}) \tag{10}$$

Here $f_d(\cdot)$ is the decoding function, which maps QPSK symbols to bits, undoes rate matching, performs Viterbi decoding, and removes CRC. After unmasking with the paging ID (*FFFE*), the CRC check returns true if the DCI is successfully decoded.

Tag Detection. The UE regenerates the message symbols from the decoded DCI, $\hat{\mathbf{s}} = f_e(\hat{\mathbf{b}})$, and subtracts it from the received signal to get the residue

$$\mathbf{r} = \frac{1}{\rho_t} (\hat{\mathbf{x}} - \rho_s \hat{\mathbf{s}}) \tag{11}$$

Assuming that the UE performs perfect channel estimation, we have

$$\mathbf{r} = \frac{1}{\sqrt{N_t}} \sum_{i=1}^{N_t} \mathbf{t}_i + \frac{1}{\rho_t} \hat{\mathbf{H}}^{-1} \mathbf{w} \tag{12}$$

It then checks for the presence of its tag, $\mathbf{t}$, by performing hypothesis testing on the statistic

$$\tau = \mathbf{t}^H \mathbf{r} \tag{13}$$

The hypotheses are

$$H_0 : \quad \mathbf{t} \text{ is not present in } \mathbf{r} \qquad \text{(null hypothesis)}$$
$$H_1 : \quad \mathbf{t} \text{ is present in } \mathbf{r} \qquad \text{(alternative hypothesis)}$$

The statistic under null hypothesis:

$$\tau | H_0 = \frac{1}{\sqrt{N_t}} \sum_{i=1}^{N_t} \mathbf{t}^H \mathbf{t}_i + \frac{1}{\rho_t} \mathbf{t}^H \hat{\mathbf{H}}^{-1} \mathbf{w} \tag{14}$$

Condition on $\mathbf{t}$, the second term in (14) is the sum of L Gaussian random variables

$$\eta_2 = \frac{1}{\rho_t}\mathbf{t}^H\hat{\mathbf{H}}^{-1}\mathbf{w} = \frac{1}{\rho_t}\sum_{k=1}^{L}\frac{t^{(k)^*}w^{(k)}}{\hat{H}^{(k)}} \tag{15}$$

The resulting Gaussian random variable has mean zero and variance

$$\sigma_{\eta_2}^2 = \frac{1}{\rho_t^2}\sum_{k=1}^{L}\frac{\sigma_w^2}{|\hat{H}^{(k)}|^2} = \frac{1}{\rho_t^2}\sum_{k=1}^{L}\frac{1}{\gamma^{(k)}} \tag{16}$$

where $\gamma^{(k)}$ is the SNR of the kth subcarrier.

The first term in (14) can be written as

$$\eta_1 = \frac{1}{\sqrt{N_t}}\sum_{i=1}^{N_t}\mathbf{t}^H\mathbf{t}_i = \frac{1}{\sqrt{N_t}}\sum_{i=1}^{N_t}\sum_{k=1}^{L}t^{(k)^*}t_i^{(k)} \tag{17}$$

η_1 is the sum of N_tL i.i.d. symbols from the set $\{\pm 1, \pm i\}$. According to the Central Limit Theorem, it can be approximated by a Gaussian random variable with zero-mean and variance $\sigma_{\eta_1}^2 = L$.

From (14) - (17), we have

$$\tau|H_0 \sim \mathcal{N}\left(0, L + \frac{1}{\rho_t^2}\sum_{k=1}^{L}\frac{1}{\gamma^{(k)}}\right) \tag{18}$$

The statistic under alternative hypothesis: Without loss of generality, let $\mathbf{t} = \mathbf{t}_1$. The statistic is

$$\tau|H_1 = \frac{1}{\sqrt{N_t}}\left(|\mathbf{t}_1|^2 + \sum_{i=2}^{N_t}\mathbf{t}_1^H\mathbf{t}_i\right) + \frac{1}{\rho_t}\mathbf{t}_1^H\hat{\mathbf{H}}^{-1}\mathbf{w} \tag{19}$$

Condition on $\mathbf{t}_1$, the term inside the parentheses in (19) can be approximated as a Gaussian random variable with mean $|\mathbf{t}_1|^2 = L$ and variance $(N_t - 1)L$. Therefore

$$\tau|H_1 \sim \mathcal{N}\left(\frac{L}{\sqrt{N_t}}, \frac{N_t-1}{N_t}L + \frac{1}{\rho_t^2}\sum_{k=1}^{L}\frac{1}{\gamma^{(k)}}\right) \tag{20}$$

The UE performs a threshold test on τ to determine the presence of its tag in the residue.

$$H = \begin{cases} H_0 & \text{if } \tau \leq \tau^0 \\ H_1 & \text{if } \tau > \tau^0 \end{cases} \tag{21}$$

In making the comparison in (21), we use only the real part of τ. The imaginary parts of $\tau|H_0$ and $\tau|H_1$ have very similar statistic, and therefore do not provide much information. By abuse of notation, we still call the real part τ.

The threshold τ^0 is a value between $[0, L/\sqrt{N_t}]$. The greater τ^0 is, the higher the probability of miss detection; whereas the smaller τ^0 is, the higher the probability of false alarm. We choose $\tau^0 = L/2\sqrt{N_t}$ for good performance in both criteria. With this choice of the threshold, the probability of missing a tag is

$$P_m = \Phi\left(\frac{-\frac{L}{2\sqrt{N_t}}}{\left(\frac{N_t-1}{N_t}L + \frac{1}{\rho_t^2}\sum_{k=1}^{L}\frac{1}{\gamma^{(k)}}\right)^{1/2}}\right) \qquad (22)$$

where $\Phi(\cdot)$ is the standard Gaussian cumulative distribution function. To get an idea of the theoretical performance of the scheme, let us look at a special case where the channel is flat fading with SNR = 10dB. Assume 10% of the transmitted power is allocated to tags, i.e. $\rho_t^2 = 0.1$; and 288 bits are used for PDCCH message, i.e. $L = 144$. When 4 users are paged simultaneously, i.e. $N_t = 4$, we have $P_m = 0.01$. So we can see under that condition, the tags are detected 99% of the time.

4   Simulations

As mentioned in Section 2, the PDCCH messages are designed to be very robust. In particular, convolutional code with low rate (1/3) is used. In addition, the paging DCI message can have 24 - 44 bits. Together with a 16-bit CRC, the size of the message before convolutionally encoded ranges from 40 to 60 bits. Thus the size of the message after convolutionally encoded ranges from 120 to 180 bits. When the PDCCH size is 144 bits, puncture may occur during rate matching. When the PDCCH size is 288 bits, redundant encoded bits are transmitted, which effectively increases the SNR at the receiving UEs. In order to evaluate the effect of our embedded tags on the probability of successfully decoding the DCI, we first simulate the DCI decoding performance with respect to different SNR levels. The result is shown in Figure 4. Here we use the energy per bit to noise power spectral density (EbNo) as the metric for SNR. Also shown is BER of the PDCCH message at the same EbNo levels. Figure 4 gives us a clear intuition of the PDCCH BER requirements for various DCI decoding performances. For instance, with PDCCH size of 288 bits, we can see that the probability of unsuccessfully decoding a paging DCI decreases rapidly from 0.4 at EbNo = -1 to 10^{-5} at EbNo = 5. Thanks to the convolutional encoder, the BER requires for PDCCH to achieve 10^{-5} DCI error rate is only 0.03. When the size of PDCCH is 144 bits, the UEs need an additional 1dB in SNR to get equivalent performance.

Next we want to see the effect of allocating part of the transmission power to the tags on the PDCCH BER. As long as the resulting BER conforms to the requirement obtained above, our scheme will not have negative effect on the DCI decoding performance. Figure 5 shows the BER of PDCCH message for various tag powers. We can see that the effect of tag embedment is minimal for $\rho_t^2 \leq 0.02$. When the channel condition is good, e.g. EbNo = 10dB, 20% of the

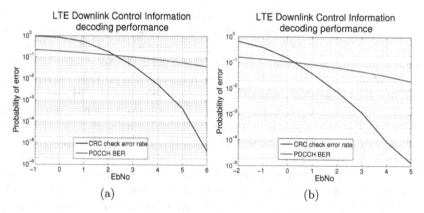

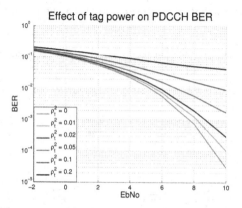

Fig. 4. DCI decoding performance as a function of SNR. Here the DCI size is 44 bits. The PDCCH size is (a) 144 bits, (b) 288 bits

Fig. 5. PDCCH BER for various values of tag power allocation. Here the PDCCH size is 288 bits, 16 tags are embedded.

power can be allocated to tags, which results in BER of 0.04. Referring back to Figure 4, this BER corresponds to a DCI decoding error rate of 10^{-4}.

After confirming that we can indeed allocate part of the transmission power to the identification tags, we evaluate the tag detection performance under various system settings. In particular, we alter 3 parameters: tag length, tag power and number of simultaneous tags. We expect the detection performance to increase with tag length and decrease with number of simultaneous tags. Referring back to (18) and (20), we see that the variance of the test statistic decreases monotonically with increased tag power, and therefore the detection performance will increase monotonically with increased tag power. However, we also know that increasing tag power degrades DCI decoding performance. If that degradation causes the UEs to fail to decode the paging PDCCH then the tags will be useless. Referring to Figure 5, we choose tag power allocation $\rho_t^2 = 0.05$ to be conservative.

Figure 6 shows the probability of detecting that the unique tag for a UE is present in 2 cases: the UE is being paged, and the UE is not being paged (misdetection). We can see a clear superior performance when 288-bit PDCCH is used. Let us consider a rather bad channel condition, EbNo = 2dB, 4 UEs are paged simultaneously. Figure 6 shows that our scheme still provides tag detection rate of 90% and false alarm rate of 2% if we use 288-bit PDCCH and allocate 5% of the transmission power for the tags. A natural question would be how this performance compares to the current paging system's. Both schemes rely on the successful decoding of the paging PDCCH. After this stage, our scheme's performance ties directly to the detection probability of the tags; whereas the current scheme's performance depends on the success of decoding the paging PDSCH. Since these are apples and oranges, a meaningful comparison can only be done through experiments. We are certainly interested in pursuing them in our future work. For now, it is worth noticing that the constellation size and code rate used for data channels are a lot more aggressive than those used for control channels. Therefore it is expected that decoding performance of data channels are worse than that of control channels in the same SNR condition.

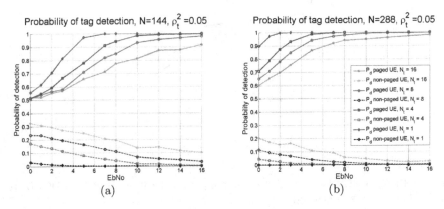

Fig. 6. Probability of tag detection for PDCCH size (a) 144 bits, (b) 288 bits

The idea behind the physical layer identification technique is to make use of channel noise to obfuscate the tags at the eavesdropper. Assuming that the eavesdropper, Eve in Figure 2(a), successfully decodes the paging PDCCH, regenerates the signal **s** in (1), and subtracts it from her received waveform. What she has left is the sum of the superimposed tags and the channel noise. Since the individual tags are modulated as QPSK symbols $\{\pm 1, \pm i\}$, the normalized sum of multiple tags will have the constellation as in Figure 7. The identity of a UE's tag, say Bob's, is hidden under 2 layers. First, the channel noise limits Eve to only partial information about the normalized sum of the tags. Second, since the tags are uncorrelated, the sum of them does not reveal any information about

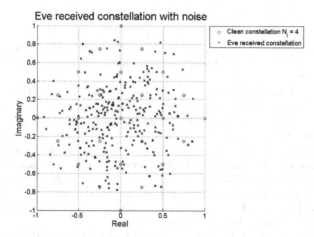

Fig. 7. Eavesdropper's received constellation at SNR = 20dB, $N_t = 4$

Bob's tag to Eve. We conclude that Eve has no reliable way of obtaining Bob's tag, and thus she cannot perform the location attack described in Section 1.

5   Conclusions

In this paper we have proposed a novel method to page user equipments in LTE network while protecting their privacy. The proposed method makes use of physical layer identification tags, which are designed to be robust and stealthy. Our scheme protects the privacy of paged users by hiding their ID in the transmitted waveforms. Using channel noise to our advantage, the scheme prevents an attacker from decoding the paged user's tag. As a result, attacks on the open nature of paging channel, e.g. [1], are no longer a threat. The scheme also provides bandwidth saving by not requiring the actual user IDs to be transmitted. Here we analyze our technique specifically for an LTE network; however, our technique is also applicable to other cellular networks such as GSM, WCDMA, WiMAX.

Acknowledgment. This material is based upon work partially supported by the Defense Advanced Research Projects Agency (DARPA) and the Semiconductor Research Corporation Focused Center Research Program through contract award number SA00007007, by the Army Research Office through MURI grant award W911-NF-0710287, by the AFOSR through MURI grant award FA9550-10-1-0573, and by the NSF through grant award CNS1018346.

Any opinions, findings and conclusions or recommendations expressed in this paper are those of the authors and do not necessarily reflect the views of any of the funding agencies mentioned.

References

1. Kune, D.F., Koelndorfer, J., Hopper, N., Kim, Y.: Location leaks over the GSM air interface. In: Proc. 19th Annual Network and Distributed System Security Symposium (2012)
2. Yu, P., Baras, J.S., Sadler, B.: Physical-Layer Authentication. IEEE Trans. on Information Forensics and Security 3, 38–51 (2008)
3. Yu, P., Baras, J.S., Sadler, B.: Multicarrier authentication at the physical layer. In: WoWMoM (2008)
4. Nohl, K., Munaut, S.: GSM Sniffing, http://events.ccc.de/congress/2010/Fahrplan/attachments/1783_101228.27C3.GSM-Sniffing.Nohl_Munaut.pdf
5. F-Secure: 440,783 "Silent SMS" Used to Track German Suspects in 2010 (2010), http://www.f-secure.com/weblog/archives/00002294.html
6. 3GPP TS 36.211: Evolved Universal Terrestrial Radio Access (E-UTRA); Physical channels and modulation (version 10.4.0) (2011)
7. 3GPP TS 36.213: Evolved Universal Terrestrial Radio Access (E-UTRA); Physical layer procedures (version 10.4.0) (2011)
8. 3GPP TS 36.321: Evolved Universal Terrestrial Radio Access (E-UTRA); Medium Access Control (MAC); Protocol specification (version 10.4.0) (2011)
9. 3GPP TS 36.331: Evolved Universal Terrestrial Radio Access (E-UTRA); Radio Resource Control (RRC); Protocol specification (version 10.4.0) (2011)
10. Baker, M., Moulsley, T.: Downlink Physical Data and Control Channels. In: LTE The UMTS Long Term Evolution, ch. 9, pp. 189–214 (2011)
11. Edfors, O., Sandell, M., van de Beek, J.J., Wilson, S.K., Borjesson, P.O.: OFDM channel estimation by singular value decomposition. IEEE Trans. on Communications 46, 931–939 (1998)
12. The OsmocomBB project - Open source GSM baseband software implementation, http://bb.osmocom.org/

Post-hoc User Traceability Analysis in Electronic Toll Pricing Systems

Xihui Chen[1,*], David Fonkwe[1], and Jun Pang[2]

[1] Interdisciplinary Centre for Security, Reliability and Trust, University of Luxembourg
[2] Faculty of Sciences, Technology and Communication, University of Luxembourg

Abstract. Electronic Toll Pricing (ETP), a location-based vehicular service, allows users to pay tolls without stopping or even slowing down their cars. User location records are collected so as to calculate their payments. However, users have privacy concerns as locations are considered as private information. In this paper, we focus on user traceability in ETP systems where anonymous location records are stored by the service providers. Based on user toll payment information, we propose a post-hoc analysis of user traceability, which aims at computing a user's all possible traces. Moreover, we propose several methods to improve the effectiveness of the analysis by combining other contextual information and propose a number of optimisations to improve its efficiency as well. We develop a prototype and evaluate the effectiveness of the analysis by conducting extensive experiments on a number of simulated datasets.

1 Introduction

Electronic Toll Pricing (ETP) systems, by collecting tolls electronically, aim to reduce users' delay at toll gates and thus to increase the throughput of public transportation networks. Cars are automatically identified when passing check points. The locations of the check points and the passing time are collected and stored by toll servers in the form of location records, which are used to calculate users' payments afterwards. Nowadays, the free access to civilian Global Navigation Satellite Systems (GNSS) has upgraded ETP into a more sophisticated service. Compared to location sensing techniques, e.g., number plate recognisers, GNSS positioning covers a much wider area. This leads to smart pricing and "Pay-As-You-Drive" (PAYD), binding a user's insurance to the roads he has actually travelled [1]. Meanwhile, this also causes more privacy concerns as more user records are collected by the system. For instance, by processing location records, the toll server can learn users' home addresses or medical information [2]. User mobility pattens can also be extracted [3], which are useful to construct user profiles.

In the last few years, protecting location privacy in ETP and PAYD systems has been widely studied [1, 4–9]. The general idea is to anonymise users' records and hide the links among them. In other words, ETP systems do not leak either the owner of a location record (*unlinkability*) or the fact that two records belong to the same user (*untraceability*). In general, privacy-preserving ETP systems can be divided into two categories based on whether users' locations are stored on user devices or the toll server. The first

* This author was supported by the FNR Luxembourg under project SECLOC 794361.

R. Di Pietro et al. (Eds.): DPM 2012 and SETOP 2012, LNCS 7731, pp. 29–42, 2013.

type of ETP systems, e.g., see [6], where users do not send locations to toll servers, offer better privacy protection. Whereas, the introduction of sophisticated cryptographic techniques such as zero-knowledge proofs usually imposes heavy computation overheads on user devices. By contrast, the second type of ETP systems (e.g., see [5, 7]), where location records are anonymised, have less computation overheads on user devices and can also support other applications, e.g., traffic monitoring and control. However, as such ETP systems focus on protecting a user's privacy and enforcing correct toll calculation, we notice that they usually tend to ignore the threats after user payment information has been calculated or collected by the server. Once users' payment information becomes part of the adversary's knowledge, the claimed user location privacy can be reduced or even nullified. For example, if in a given user's collected location records, there is only one combination of locations which have the same cost as his tolls, then the user's privacy is completely broken. In this paper, we focus on a user's untraceability, which is considered as a stronger requirement than unlinkability. We describe a user's traceability by a set of possible traces he might have travelled, and compute or *de-anonymise* such sets in a certain period (called a *toll session*) based on users' payments and other available contextual information.

Related Work. De-anonymisation has been applied in many areas, e.g., datasets [10] and social networks [11, 12]. The idea of de-anonymisation is to find the correlation of two elements by utilising background information. Narayanan and Shmatikov show that visitors of a website can be identified by combining their group membership information in social networks [11]. They also demonstrate that information from different data sources can be combined to de-anonymise a user in large sparse datasets [10].

With respect to location privacy, Gruteser et al. explore the technique of multi-target tracking to link location records of a user [13, 14]. After learning one of a user's locations, the user's whole trace can thus be obtained with a high probability. However, in the context of ETP, to the best of our knowledge, this paper is the *first attempt* to investigate threats on privacy by de-anonymising users' traces based on toll payments.

Our Contributions. We study the threats on user traceability in the ETP systems collecting anonymised location records. A *post-hoc user traceability analysis* using user toll payment information and such anonymised location records is proposed from the view of the adversary. We show that its effectiveness can be improved by taking into account additional information which is easily obtained, e.g., maps. For the sake of efficiency, we propose several optimisations to make the analysis more practical. We develop a prototype and evaluate the analysis on a number of simulated datasets.

Structure of the Paper. After introducing our framework, the adversary model and the notion of traceability sets (Sect. 2), we first propose an algorithm calculating users' traceability sets based on the fact that a user's trace in a toll session should cost the same as his toll payment (Sect. 3). Subsequently, we explore two types of contextual information that can help the adversary to reduce the size of the traceability set. One is about temporal and spatial constraints between location records (i.e., *reachability* and *connectivity*) while the other concerns users' repetitive behaviour patterns (i.e., *session similarity*) (Sect. 4). To improve the efficiency of our algorithm, we propose three optimisations in Sect. 5. The experimental results show that our analysis is effective (Sect. 6). We conclude the paper in Sect. 7 with some research directions for the future.

2 Preliminaries

2.1 Formal Framework

Let $\mathcal{U}$ be the set of users who register an ETP service and $\mathcal{L}$ be the set of all locations that can be passed by users. In practice, time is always discrete with minutes or seconds as the minimum unit. We use $\mathcal{T}$ to denote the totally ordered set of all discrete time points whose granularities are determined by applications.

Using a location, in the scenario of ETP, we can identify the corresponding road segment between two intersections. We call this segment a *link* and denote it by a pair $\langle \ell_1, \ell_2 \rangle$, where ℓ_1 and ℓ_2 are the two end locations. When two links shared one end location, we say they are *consecutive*. Formally, let $\ell k_1 = \langle \ell_1, \ell_2 \rangle$ and $\ell k_2 = \langle \ell'_1, \ell'_2 \rangle$ be two links. If $\ell_2 = \ell'_1$ or $\ell'_2 = \ell_1$, then they are consecutive, denoted as $\ell k_1 \sim \ell k_2$. Given a map, we use $\mathcal{LK} \subseteq \mathcal{L} \times \mathcal{L}$ to denote the set of all links on it.

A typical anonymised location record collected by toll servers can be abstracted in the form of $\langle \ell, t \rangle$, indicating that a user passed location ℓ at time t. As a user's location records transmitted on a link can be easily linked to each other, we consider links as the smallest units in our further analysis. Thus, instead of location records, we have link records, e.g., $\langle \ell k, t_e, t_x \rangle$ where t_e denotes the time the user entered ℓk and t_x is the time the user exited ℓk. To calculate users' tolls, toll servers first assign fees to link records based on a charging policy. The charging policy can be modelled as a function $f : \mathcal{LK} \times \mathcal{T} \to \mathbb{R}$, calculating the fee of a link according to the time a user entered the link, e.g., t_e.

Tracking technologies proposed in the last few years (e.g., see [14, 15]) allow us to make a further abstraction. As the adversary is able to link a user's link records together with a relatively high confidence when the user does not stop his car, these link records construct a *trip*. A *trip* is a sequence of link records a user continuously transmitted from one place to another. The order between links is determined by their time stamps. Suppose tr is a trip, denoted by $(\langle \ell k_1, t_{e_1}, t_{x_1} \rangle, \ldots, \langle \ell k_n, t_{e_n}, t_{x_n} \rangle)$ and t_δ is the minimum stay time of users before travelling on the next link. Then we have $\ell k_i \sim \ell k_{i+1} \wedge 0 < (t_{e_{i+1}} - t_{x_i}) \le t_\delta$ for $1 \le i < n$. We use $tr.startLink$ and $tr.startTime$ to denote its starting link, i.e., ℓk_1 and the corresponding entering time t_{e_1} of a trip tr. Similarly, we have $tr.endLink = \ell k_n$ and $tr.endTime = t_{x_n}$. The length of tr, the number of links in the trip, is denoted as $len(tr)$. Using link fees, we can calculate the corresponding fee for a given trip tr, i.e., $fee(tr) = \sum_{0 < i \le len(tr)} f(\ell k_i, t_{e_i})$. For two trips tr_1 and tr_2 with $tr_1.startTime < tr_2.startTime$, the distance between them, i.e., $d(tr_1, tr_2)$ is computed as the length of the shortest path connecting $tr_1.endLink$ and $tr_2.startLink$. In the following discussion, we fix a toll session and use $\mathcal{TR}$ to represent the set of trips transmitted by all users.

During a toll session, a user's real trace can thus be represented as a set of his trips stored in $\mathcal{TR}$. We call this set a *trace*. Suppose Tr_u be the real trace of user u in a toll session. The amount of tolls that u has to pay is $cost_u$ which equals to $\sum_{tr \in Tr_u} fee(tr)$.

Example 1. Fig. 1 shows a fraction of a map. There are five locations $\ell_1, \ldots, \ell_5$, which are the positions of five intersections. We also have four links $\ell k_1, \ldots, \ell k_4$ where $\ell k_i = \langle \ell_i, \ell_{i+1} \rangle$ $(i = 1, \ldots, 4)$. Suppose a user moves from ℓ_1 to ℓ_5 with one-hour stay at ℓ_3

and t_{ℓ_i} is the time the user passes ℓ_i. Then he has two trips with t_δ being 30 minutes – $(\langle \ell k_1, t_{\ell_1}, t_{\ell_2} \rangle, \langle \ell k_2, t_{\ell_2}, t_{\ell_3} \rangle)$ and $(\langle \ell k_3, t_{\ell_3}, t_{\ell_4} \rangle, \langle \ell k_4, t_{\ell_4}, t_{\ell_5} \rangle)$.

The notations used in this paper are summarised in Tab. 1.

Table 1. Notations

$\mathcal{U}$	set of users
$\mathcal{L}$	set of locations
$\mathcal{T}$	set of time points
$\mathcal{LK}$	set of links
$\mathcal{TR}$	set of trips
$fee(tr)$	trip tr fee
$cost_u$	user u's toll payment
Tr_u	a trace of user u
$d(tr_1, tr_2)$	distance between tr_1 and tr_2

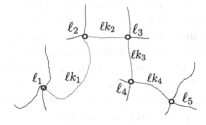

Fig. 1. An example of a user's trips

2.2   Adversary Model

The adversary has the motivation to obtain users' travel history (i.e., traces), because extracting traces is an essential preliminary step towards further data inference, e.g., trajectory pattern mining [3], location-based recommendation, car pooling and friend finder [16, 17]. In this paper, we assume that toll servers are malicious and collude with the adversary, which makes users' location records and toll payment information part of the adversary's knowledge. This assumption is realistic as the servers may sell their databases to, e.g., advertising companies, to have additional revenues. In the sequel, we focus on *post-hoc analysis*, meaning that the adversary analyses users' traces after users' toll payment information has been calculated and agreed by the users.

Besides, we assume the adversary has access to some common knowledge such as maps, the maximal speeds of cars, etc. Such information is easy to obtain, and the adversary can extract further information from it. For example, using maps, for any two links, the adversary can learn their distance. Such information is useful for the adversary to reduce their uncertainty on users' traces.

2.3   Traceability Sets

In the last few years, a number of measurements for location privacy have been proposed (e.g., see [14, 18]). As the adversary's aim is to trace users, inspired by the notion of anonymity sets by Chaum [19], we propose *traceability sets* to measure users' traceability. A traceability set consists of all traces that are possibly linked to a given user from the adversary's point of view, including the user's real trace. We use $AS_{TR}(u)$ to denote user u's traceability set.

Without considering extra information such as maps, i.e., the adversary only has access to users' anonymous trips $\mathcal{TR}$ and users' toll payments, the initial traceability set for a user u in the given toll session can be computed as follows:

$$AS_{TR}(u) = \{ Tr \subseteq \mathcal{TR} \mid \sum_{tr \in Tr} fee(tr) = cost_u \},$$

based on the fact that a user's trace should cost the same as his toll payment.

3   An Algorithm for Computing Traceability Sets

In this section, we propose an algorithm to construct users' initial traceability sets, which is inspired by a solution to the *subset sum problem* (SSP). The subset sum problem can be formulated as follows [20]: *Given a finite set $\mathcal{A}$, a weight function, $w : \mathcal{A} \to \mathbb{N}$, and a constant $s \in \mathbb{N}$, determine whether or not there exists a subset $B \subseteq \mathcal{A}$ such that $\sum_{a \in B} w(a) = s$.* This 'yes/no' decision problem has been proved to be NP-hard [21] and has no polynomial time solution so far. However, to the SSP with certain restrictions, polynomial time solutions have been proposed in the last few decades [22]. An optimal solution is proposed by Pisinger [23], which has linear computation time when each element in $\mathcal{A}$ is positive and bounded with the same constant. Let N be the size of $\mathcal{A}$ and W be the upper bound. The elements in $\mathcal{A}$ are ordered and then processed one after another. For each value in $[s-W, s+W]$, the algorithm maintains the corresponding *dominating* subset the summation of whose elements is equal to the value. The algorithm returns 'yes' if s has such a subset. In this way, the size of the intermediate set remains $2W$ and the computation complexity is thus $\mathcal{O}(NW)$.

As we have mentioned before, a user's initial traceability set is composed of the traces whose cost equals the user's toll payment and the adversary's aim is to further reduce the size of the set. Thus to compute a user's traceability set is essential for the adversary. This computation can be reduced to the SSP, thus it is also NP-hard and the corresponding computation time is exponential in users' payments. However, inspired by Pisinger's algorithm, we design an algorithm which has a good efficiency. The trips are non-increasingly ordered according to their fees and processed one after another. The algorithm maintains an intermediate set to store the subsets of earlier trips which are possible to construct a trace using the further trips to be processed. Similar to Pisinger's algorithm, the size of this intermediate set determines the number of operations needed. Therefore, we should keep it as small as possible to accelerate the computation of traceability sets.

More specifically, we take the following heuristics: (1) if the cost of the trips in a subset is larger than the user's payment, then the subset is removed as all fees are positive and the cost will never be reduced to the user's payment; (2) if the future trip with the minimum fee is added into a subset and the total cost of the resulted subset is larger than the payment, the subset can also be removed; (3) if all future trips are added into a subset and the new subset's cost is still less than the payment, then it is also removed. Alg. 1 shows the algorithm in more details.

The set U is the intermediate set which consists of all plausible subsets up to the current trip and initially it only consists of the empty set. For any trip in $\mathcal{TR}$, before adding to a subset $S \in U$, the algorithm checks the plausibility of U first with heuristics (2) and (3) (line 12). Note that *restFee* is the cost of the future trips that have not been processed and *minFee* is the minimum fee among all trips. After the trip is added, if the cost of the new subset equals $cost_u$, the set is added to the result $AS_{\mathcal{TR}}(u)$. It is added into the set T when the corresponding cost is smaller than $cost_u$ and removed, otherwise. At the end of each loop, U is updated by unionising T and *restFee* is subtracted by the trip's fee. After obtaining $AS_{\mathcal{TR}}(u)$, the adversary starts to reduce it by using additional contextual knowledge, which is discussed in the following section.

Algorithm 1. An algorithm to build an initial traceability set for a user u.

```
 1: FUNCTION: buildTraceSet
 2: INPUT: TR, cost_u
 3: OUTPUT: AS_TR(u);
 4: sort(TR, non-increasing);
 5: minFee = min_{tr∈TR} fee(tr);
 6: restFee = Σ_{tr∈TR} fee(tr);
 7: AS_TR(u) = ∅;
 8: U ← {∅};
 9: for all tr ∈ TR do
10:     T = ∅;
11:     for all S ∈ U do
12:         if restFee + Σ_{tr'∈S} fee(tr') < cost_u ∨ minFee + Σ_{tr'∈S} fee(tr') > cost_u then
13:             U = U/{S};
14:         else
15:             if fee(tr) + Σ_{tr'∈S} fee(tr') = cost_u then
16:                 AS_TR(u) = AS_TR(u) ∪ {S ∪ {tr}};
17:             else
18:                 if fee(tr) + Σ_{tr'∈S} fee(tr') < cost_u then
19:                     T = T ∪ {S ∪ {tr}};
20:                 end if
21:             end if
22:         end if
23:     end for
24:     U = U ∪ T; restFee = restFee − fee(tr);
25: end for
26: return AS_TR(u);
```

4   Reducing Traceability Sets

Once the adversary explores more information, he can improve the post-hoc analysis of a user's traceability by reducing the traceability sets.

4.1   Reachability and Connectivity

A user's real trace in a toll session has certain constraints among trips, which can be used to remove traces in his traceability set. We discuss two of such constraints – *reachability* and *connectivity*.

Both of the constraints benefit from maps, which are easy to obtain, especially after free high-precision maps such as Google maps become accessible to ordinary users. Given two positions, the adversary can compute the distance between them. Combining with users' maximum speed, we have the first constraint – reachability between trips. Intuitively, given two trips, if along the moving direction, users cannot move to the starting point of the later trip from the ending point of the earlier trip even with his maximum speed, then the later trip is considered not reachable from the earlier one. We use $maxSpeed_u$ to denote the maximum speed allowed by user u's vehicle. Recall that $d(tr_1, tr_2)$ is the distance between two trips.

Definition 1 (Reachability). *Let tr_1 and tr_2 be two trips in $\mathcal{TR}$ and $tr_1.endTime <$ $tr_2.startTime$. We say tr_2 is reachable for user u from tr_1 (denoted as $tr_1 \rightsquigarrow tr_2$) if and only if*

$$tr_2.startTime - tr_1.endTime > \frac{d(tr_1, tr_2)}{maxSpeed_u}.$$

This relation is reflexive, transitive but not symmetric because the connection between two trips may be unidirectional.

The second constraint is connectivity which is defined on two *successive trips*. Two trips are successive if in a trace, there are no other trips started between their starting time. For any two successive trips, they are *connected* if the earlier trip's ending point coincides with the other trip's starting point. In practice, due to the errors from positioning devices, even two positions from a static user may be different. Furthermore, it is possible that some vacant time exists between two trips before the first location record of the later trip is sent to the server. Therefore, we introduce a tolerance parameter d_δ to indicate the maximum distance allowed between two connected points.

Definition 2 (Connectivity). *Let tr_1 and tr_2 be successive trips and $tr_1.endTime <$ $tr_2.startTime$. We say tr_1 is connected to tr_2 (denoted as $tr_1 \rightarrow tr_2$) if and only if*

$$d(tr_1, tr_2) < d_\delta.$$

In practice, we cannot expect any two successive trips are connected because the tolling road sections are not always connected. Therefore, we define a metric called *connection rate* to measure the proportion of connected trips in a user's trace. Given a trace Tr, its connection rate $cr(Tr)$ can be calculated as follows:

$$cr(Tr) = \frac{|\{\langle tr_i, tr_j \rangle \mid tr_i \in Tr, tr_j \in Tr \text{ s.t. } tr_i \rightarrow tr_j\}|}{|Tr| - 1}.$$

Let c be the pre-defined minimal connection rate. Making use of the above two constraints, i.e., trip reachability and connectivity, the adversary can further reduce a user u's traceability set $AS_{TR}(u)$ to

$$\{Tr \subseteq \mathcal{TR} \mid (\forall_{\{tr_i, tr_j\} \subseteq Tr} tr_i \rightsquigarrow tr_j \lor tr_j \rightsquigarrow tr_j) \land cr(Tr) > c \land \sum_{tr \in Tr} fee(tr) = cost_u\}.$$

4.2 Session-to-Session Similarity

Users tend to have regular mobility patterns, which has been greatly discussed in the literature (e.g., see [2, 3]). This implies that a user's traces in different sessions should also have some similarity. Our aim is to show how the adversary can explore the similarity between toll sessions to reduce his uncertainty on users' traces. As users' daily activities are fixed to some extent, the places they linger are also fixed and in fact contained among the starting links and the ending links of trips. Since users' real stay places occur repetitively from session to session, this makes them have higher occurrence frequencies in sessions compared to other places. Our idea is to rank traces in a traceability set based on links' *similarity degrees* determined by their occurrence in sessions.

Given a link ℓk, we say that ℓk has appeared in a trace Tr denoted as $\ell k \in Tr$ if there exists a trip $tr \in Tr$ such that $tr.startLink = \ell k \lor tr.endLink = \ell k$.

Definition 3 (A Link's Similarity Degree). *Let* $AS_{TR1}, \ldots, AS_{TRn}$ *be a user* u's *traceability sets in* n *sessions and* ℓk *be a link appearing in at least one trace in any traceability set. The* similarity degree *for the link* ℓk *(i.e.,* $sim(\ell k)$*) is measured as:*

$$sim(\ell k) = \mid \{AS_{TRj} \mid \exists Tr \in AS_{TRj} \text{ s.t. } \ell k \in Tr\} \mid .$$

It is easy to see that $1 \leq sim(\ell k) \leq n$. For a traceability set, we can evaluate the similarity degree of each trace in it by the average similarity degree of the links appearing in the trace as follows:

$$S(Tr) = \frac{\sum_{\ell k \in Tr} sim(\ell k)}{\mid Tr \mid}.$$

For the traces in a traceability set, the adversary can thus have an approximate distribution over them based on their similarity degrees. This distribution represents the probabilities of the user to travel on each trace in the set. Given a user u and AS_{TRi}, we use $p_u(T_i = Tr)$ to denote the probability of trace Tr being u's real trace in session i, which is computed as follows:

$$p_u(T_i = Tr) = \frac{S(Tr)}{\sum_{Tr' \in AS_{TRi}} S(Tr')}.$$

This distribution enables the adversary to have a better guess on the user' real trace.

5 Improving Efficiency of the Post-hoc Analysis

From the above discussion, we can see that the initial traceability set is essential for the subsequent analysis. Although in Alg. 1, we have used the methodology of dynamic programming to improve its efficiency, Alg. 1 is still time-consuming as the computation complexity remains exponential in users' payments. Recall that we can keep the intermediate set U in Alg. 1 as small as possible to reduce the calculation time. Along this direction, we propose three optimisations – *on_the_fly trip non-overlapping detection* (OTF), *weak_user_first* (WUF) and *parallel_traversing* (PTR).

OTF. This optimisation explores a relation between trips – *non-overlapping*. Intuitively, as users never travel at two trips at the same time, in a trace, any two trips should be generated one after another and their travel periods should not overlap.

Definition 4 (Non-overlapping). *Let* tr_1 *and* tr_2 *be two trips in* $\mathcal{TR}$. *Trip* tr_1 *and* tr_2 *do not overlap (denoted as* $tr_1 * tr_2$*) if and only if:*

$$tr_1.endTime \leq tr_2.startTime \ \vee \ tr_2.endTime \leq tr_1.startTime.$$

This relation is irreflexive and symmetric, but not transitive.

From the definitions of reachability and non-overlapping, we can see for any two trips tr_1 and tr_2, if $tr_1 \leadsto tr_2$ then $tr_1 * tr_2$ as the time interval between two reachable trips can never be negative. However, compared with reachability check, non-overlapping detection is more efficient as only the simple comparison between time stamps is involved. Whereas, the distance between two trips has to be calculated to verify reachability, which is time-consuming especially in the case when the number of trips is large. Therefore, due to its efficiency, we add non-overlapping as another condition when deciding whether to add a new subset into the intermediate set or the traceability set (line 15 and 18).

WUF. As mentioned before, the time to compute a user's traceability set will become unacceptable when his payment is big.[1] However, if users with small fees (called *weak users*) are processed first, then users with large payments can be processed based on the trip set with weak users' traces removed. A smaller input $\mathcal{TR}$ in Alg. 1 thus results in less computation time and less memory consumption. Moreover, if we calculate a user's traceability set starting from the weakest user, a set of partitions of the trip set is obtained, each of whose blocks corresponds to a user's trace. A user's traceability set can then be constructed by all his traces occurring in those partitions. Alg. 2 gives more details of this calculation.

Algorithm 2. Weak_user_first Algorithm.

1: **PROCEDURE** WUF
2: **INITIAL:** $\forall u \in \mathcal{U}, AS_{TR}(u) = \emptyset$;
3: **INPUT:** $\mathcal{TR}, P = (u_1, \ldots, u_n)$
4:
5:   $AS = \text{buildTraceSet}(\mathcal{TR}, cost_{u_1})$;
6: **for all** $Tr \in AS$ **do**
7:     $\forall i > 1, AS(i)_{old} = AS_{TR}(u_i)$
8:     WUF$(\mathcal{TR}/Tr, (u_2, \ldots, u_n))$);
9:     **if** $\exists i \leq n, AS(i)_{old} \neq AS_{TR}(u_i)$ **then**
10:       $AS_{TR}(u_1) = AS_{TR}(u_1) \cup \{Tr\}$;
11:     **end if**
12: **end for**
13: return;

Users are first ordered in a sequence P according to their payments where users with smaller payments are put in front of the sequence. The algorithm takes $\mathcal{TR}$ and sequence P as input and its termination implies the accomplishment of the calculation of all users' traceability sets. Users' traceability sets are initially set empty. The weakest user u_1's traceability set AS is first calculated based on our algorithm discussed in Sect. 3 (line 5). Then for each trace $Tr \in AS$, we update the rest of the users' traceability sets by recursively calling the algorithm but with the set of trips not contained in Tr. The increment of one of the other users' traceability sets indicates that Tr is a trace that can be included in a partition of $\mathcal{TR}$. It is also added into $AS_{TR}(u_1)$ (line 7-11). When all traces in AS of the weakest user have been tested, all users' traceability sets are computed and the whole algorithm terminates.

PTR. In Alg. 1, for each trip in $\mathcal{TR}$, the set U is traversed sequentially from the beginning to the end (line 11 in Alg. 1) and updated at the end of the loop. So the computation time grows linearly with the size of U, which increases exponentially in the number of trips processed. However, we find the order of the subsets in U has no impact on the

---

[1] In some extreme cases, the algorithm may run out of the memory.

update of U at line 24. This observation allows us to process multiple subsets in U at the same time and leads to a parallel implementation.

Let $\{c_1, \ldots, c_k\}$ be the set of available processors with shared memory, where k is the number of processors. At the beginning of each loop (line 9 in Alg. 1), we split the intermediate set U evenly into sets $U_1, \ldots, U_k$. Processor c_i is then assigned with U_i, executes the operations at line 11-24 with U_i as input and returns the updated U_i as output, denoted as U_i'. Afterwards, we update U as $\bigcup_{i \in \{1, \ldots, k\}} U_i'$, which will be used in the next loop. Although ideally we can accelerate the algorithm by around k times, due to communication and task scheduling overhead we cannot achieve this in practice.

6   Experimental Results

We have conducted experiments to evaluate our analysis. First, we evaluate the optimisations and show that their combination has the best performance. Then we evaluate the methods to reduce users' traceability sets.

Setting of the Experiments. The experiments are performed on synthetic datasets generated by SUMO, a tool simulating urban mobility [24]. Users travel in Luxembourg city with an area of 51.46 km^2. There exist public real trajectory databases such as the one in [25, 26], but we cannot perform comprehensive analysis, e.g., similarity and connectivity due to the lack of user profiles and the incompleteness of location records. Furthermore, as our purpose is to test the effectiveness of the proposed post-hoc analysis, synthetic mobility databases are sufficient.

For each user, we automatically generate a profile including his places of interest and whether he has kids. Users' daily activities are generated based on such profiles by adding some randomness. SUMO takes such activity sequences as input and produces users' real traces according to factors such as real-time traffic and vehicle types. In general, the datasets used in our experiments consist of the trips of 50 users for 10 days, with each day as a toll session. On average, a user's real trace on a specific day has about five trips. The minimum stay time t_δ is set to 30 minutes. We implement a prototype in Python and run the experiments on a computation cluster of nodes with 12 2.26GHz Intel Xeon Cores, sharing 24GB memory.

Efficiency of the Optimisations. We start with evaluating the optimisations. Fig. 2 shows the computation time used to construct users' traceability sets based on datasets belonging to different number of users. We have four settings in terms of whether optimisations OTF, WUF and PTR are implemented. If no optimisations are implemented, in about 12 hours, the algorithm can only handle 10 users while using the optimisation OTF the algorithm can compute the traceability sets for 14 users. The improvement by WUF is more obvious. A dataset with 16 users is analysed. In our prototype, we simplify PTR by splitting the intermediate set (i.e., U in Alg. 1) only when its size first reaches 60,000 instead of in every loop due to the restriction of Python. This does not give us the best efficiency but still saves more than half of the computation time further. In the following experiments, we use the algorithm with all optimisations implemented.

Effectiveness of the Reducing Methods. We proceed to show the performance of the reducing methods as discussed in Sect. 4. We start with reachability and connectivity.

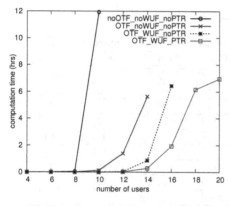

Fig. 2. Evaluation of the optimisations

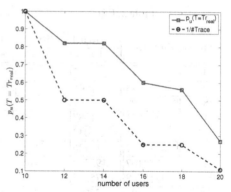

Fig. 3. Session-to-session similarity

Both of these two methods need to calculate the distance between successive trips. However, reachability is verified for each pair of successive trips while connectivity check relies on connection rates that can only be obtained after all pairs have been processed. Thus, we can perform reachability check first to reduce total check time. This is because the traces violating reachability can be immediately removed and there is no need to check connectivity on them any more. As in our datasets, users are always simulated to start the next connected trip from the ending link of the previous trip, thus the parameter d_δ is set to zero.

Tab. 2 summarises the results of running our algorithm on datasets with increasing sizes. Reachability check and connectivity check with connection rates 0.3 and 0.7 are executed sequentially. We use *reduction rate* to measure the number of traces removed from initial traceability sets by each check in addition to the previous one. We use '#init-Trace' to denote the number of traces in the initial traceability sets (without performing any checks), and '#Trace' and '#Reduc' to represent the number of traces left and the reduction rate after each check. Specifically, using reachability check, the proportion of removed traces stays around 15% when the number of users is larger than 14. Connectivity check removes most of the redundant traces. When the connection rate is 0.3, an average of 65% of the traces are removed while the connection rate of 0.7 will further reduce 13.5% of the traces on average. Although a large proportion of traces can be removed, we can see that more traces are calculated when the datasets have more users. This also leads to more remaining traces. Thus, we can conclude that when more traces are involved in an ETP system, it provides better privacy protection to users.

To show the effectiveness of session similarity, we fix a user and put him in groups with increasing sizes. We compare the size of his traceability set in a session. The similarity degree is calculated based on ten toll sessions. Let Tr_{real} be the user's real trace in the given session. Tab. 3 shows the size of the user's traceability set and the corresponding posterior probabilities of his real trace. Fig. 3 depicts the changes of the real trace's probability before and after session similarity is explored by the adversary. Session similarity does reduce the adversary's uncertainty about the real trace. For instance, the real trace has a probability 60% in 4 traces which is much larger than the uniform probability 25% (see the column where the number of users is 16). It is also

Table 2. Effectiveness of reachability and connectivity analysis

#user	#initTrace	Reachability		Connectivity 0.3		Connectivity 0.7	
		#Trace	%Reduc	#Trace	%Reduc	#Trace	%Reduc
4	17	17	0%	8	53%	4	24%
6	48	48	0%	16	67%	5	23%
8	99	97	2%	25	73%	7	18%
10	1501	1387	8%	180	80%	14	11%
12	9801	9043	8%	943	83%	49	9%
14	12757	11726	8%	1175	83%	53	9%
16	234167	195750	16%	13706	78%	246	6%
18	1158788	975397	16%	61753	79%	712	5%
20	3800390	3276691	14%	189302	81%	3378	5%
22	6085206	5269807	13%	282897	82%	4268	5%

Table 3. Effectiveness of toll session similarity

	#User=10	User=12	#User=14	#User=16	#User=18	#User=20
#Trace	1	2	2	4	4	9
$p_u(T = Tr_{real})$	100%	82%	82%	60%	56%	27%

clear that the datasets with more users provide better privacy protection as the size of the traceability set grows from 1 to 9 when the group size increases from 10 to 20.

7 Conclusion and Future Work

In this paper, we presented a post-hoc analysis of users' traceability based on toll payment information within ETP systems with central toll servers collecting anonymous travel records. As far as we know, this has not been addressed in the literature.

We first proposed an algorithm based on Pisinger's solution to the subset sum problem to compute traceability sets. Then we presented methods to reduce the sizes of traceability sets using reachability and connectivity of trips. Subsequently, we specified how to utilise users' mobility pattern among toll sessions, i.e., session-to-session similarity, to reduce the adversary's uncertainty about users' real traces. To improve the efficiency, we have developed three optimisations. We have also implemented a prototype to evaluate the effectiveness of our analysis on simulated user traces. The experimental results have shown that the post-hoc analysis is effective to trace users.

There are still several ways to improve our work. First, the design of mobility datasets has limitations. For instance, users have a fixed set of places of interest in different sessions. This simplifies our calculation especially when checking connectivity. The influence of similarity between user profiles is another future work. The results can help a user to choose groups which offer him better privacy protection. Other information can be used to further improve the effectiveness of our analysis as well, e.g., the frequency of paths taken to a public place. So far, the prototype is only implemented to show how effective the analysis is. We plan to further improve its efficiency.

References

1. Troncoso, C., Danezis, G., Kosta, E., Preneel, B.: PriPAYD: privacy friendly pay-as-you-drive insurance. In: Proc. ACM Workshop on Privacy in the Electronic Society (WPES), pp. 99–107. ACM (2007)
2. Ma, Z., Kargl, F., Weber, M.: Measuring long-term location privacy in vehicular communication systems. Computer Communications 33(12), 1414–1427 (2010)
3. Giannotti, F., Nanni, M., Pinelli, F., Pedreschi, D.: Trajectory pattern mining. In: Proc. 13th ACM SIGKDD Conference on Knowledge Discovery and Data Mining (KDD), pp. 330–339. ACM (2007)
4. de Jonge, W., Jacobs, B.: Privacy-Friendly Electronic Traffic Pricing via Commits. In: Degano, P., Guttman, J., Martinelli, F. (eds.) FAST 2008. LNCS, vol. 5491, pp. 143–161. Springer, Heidelberg (2009)
5. Popa, R.A., Balakrishnan, H., Blumberg, A.J.: VPriv: Protecting privacy in location-based vehicular services. In: Proc. 18th USENIX Security Symposium, pp. 335–350. USENIX Association (2009)
6. Balasch, J., Rial, A., Troncoso, C., Geuens, C.: PrETP: Privacy-preserving electronic toll pricing. In: Proc. 19th USENIX Security Symposium, pp. 63–78. USENIX Association (2010)
7. Chen, X., Lenzini, G., Mauw, S., Pang, J.: A group signature based electronic toll pricing system. In: Proc. 7th Conference on Availability, Reliability and Security (ARES). IEEE CS (to appear, 2012)
8. Garcia, F., Verheul, E., Jacobs, B.: Cell-Based Roadpricing. In: Petkova-Nikova, S., Pashalidis, A., Pernul, G. (eds.) EuroPKI 2011. LNCS, vol. 7163, pp. 106–122. Springer, Heidelberg (2012)
9. Meiklejohn, S., Mowery, K., Checkoway, S., Shacham, H.: The phantom tollbooth: Privacy-preserving electronic toll collection in the presence of driver collusion. In: Proc. 20th USENIX Security Symposium. USENIX Association (2011)
10. Narayanan, A., Shmatikov, V.: Robust de-anonymization of large sparse datasets. In: Proc. 29th IEEE Symposium on Security and Privacy (S&P), pp. 111–125. IEEE CS (2008)
11. Narayanan, A., Shmatikov, V.: De-anonymizing social networks. In: Proc. 30th IEEE Symposium on Security and Privacy (S&P), pp. 173–187. IEEE CS (2009)
12. Wondracek, G., Holz, T., Kirda, E., Kruegel, C.: A practical attack to de-anonymize social network users. In: Proc. 31st IEEE Symposium on Security and Privacy (S&P), pp. 223–238. IEEE CS (2010)
13. Gruteser, M., Hoh, B.: On the Anonymity of Periodic Location Samples. In: Hutter, D., Ullmann, M. (eds.) SPC 2005. LNCS, vol. 3450, pp. 179–192. Springer, Heidelberg (2005)
14. Hoh, B., Gruteser, M., Xiong, H., Alrabady, A.: Preserving privacy in GPS traces via uncertainty-aware path cloaking. In: Proc. 14th ACM Conference on Computer and Communications Security (CCS), pp. 161–171. ACM (2007)
15. Shokri, R., Theodorakopoulos, G., Boudec, J.Y.L., Hubaux, J.P.: Quantifying location privacy. In: Proc. 32nd IEEE Symposium on Security and Privacy (S&P), pp. 247–262. IEEE CS (2011)
16. Trasarti, R., Pinelli, F., Nanni, M., Giannotti, F.: Mining mobility user profiles for car pooling. In: Proc. 17th ACM SIGKDD Conference on Knowledge Discovery and Data Mining (KDD), pp. 1190–1198. ACM (2011)
17. Zheng, Y., Zhang, L., Ma, Z., Xie, X., Ma, W.: Recommending friends and locations based on individual location history. ACM Transactions on the Web 5(1), 5 (2011)
18. Chen, X., Pang, J.: Measuring query privacy in location-based services. In: Proc. 2nd ACM Conference on Data and Application Security and Privacy (CODASPY), pp. 49–60. ACM (2012)

19. Chaum, D.: The dining cryptographers problem: Unconditional sender and recipient untraceability. Journal of Cryptology 1(1), 65–75 (1988)
20. Pérez-Jiménez, M.J., Riscos-Núñez, A.: Solving the subset-sum problem by P systems with active membranes. New Generation Computing 23(4), 339–356 (2005)
21. Garey, M., Johnson, D.: Computers and Intractability: A Guide to the Theory of NP-Completeness. W. H. Freeman & Co. (1990)
22. Oltean, M., Muntean, O.: Solving the subset-sum problem with a light-based device. Natural Computing 8(2), 321–331 (2009)
23. Pisinger, D.: Linear time algorithms for knapsack problems with bounded weights. Journal of Algorithms 33(1), 1–14 (1999)
24. Behrisch, M., Bieker, L., Erdmann, J., Krajzewicz, D.: Sumo - simulation of urban mobility: An overview. In: Proc. 3rd Conference on Advances in System Simulation (SIMUL), pp. 63–68 (2011)
25. Xiao, X., Zheng, Y., Luo, Q., Xie, X.: Finding similar users using category-based location history. In: Proc. 18th ACM SIGSPATIAL Symposium on Advances in Geographic Information Systems (GIS), pp. 442–445. ACM (2010)
26. Yuan, J., Zheng, Y., Zhang, C., Xie, W., Xie, X., Sun, G., Huang, Y.: T-drive: Driving directions based on taxi trajectories. In: Proc. 18th ACM SIGSPATIAL Symposium on Advances in Geographic Information Systems (GIS), pp. 99–108. ACM (2010)

An Efficient and Secure Coding-Based Authenticated Encryption Scheme

Mohammed Meziani[1] and Rachid El Bansarkhani[2]

[1] CASED – Center for Advanced Security Research Darmstadt,
Mornewegstrasse 32, 64293 Darmstadt, Germany
mohammed.meziani@cased.de
[2] Technische Universität Darmstadt
Fachbereich Informatik
Kryptographie und Computeralgebra,
Hochschulstraße 10
64289 Darmstadt, Germany
elbansarkhani@cdc.informatik.tu-darmstadt.de

Abstract. An authenticated encryption (AE) scheme is a better way to simultaneously provide privacy and authenticity. This paper presents a new and efficient two-pass AE scheme, called SCAE, which is different from previously proposed ones based on number theoretic problems such as factoring and discrete logarithm problem or block ciphers. The proposed scheme is based on coding theory and is the first AE scheme of this type. Its security is related to the hardness of the regular syndrome decoding problem. The security requirement of privacy and that of authenticity are also proved. Additionally, the performance of SCAE is comparable to that of the other efficient schemes from the theoretical point of view. A software or hardware implementation of the proposed scheme is left open as future work to show its speed in practice.

Keywords: Authenticated encryption scheme, Provable security, Syndrome decoding.

1 Introduction

Authenticated encryption (AE) schemes are symmetric cryptographic primitives that provide simultaneous privacy and authenticity (integrity) protection for transmitted data. They are used in popular internet protocols like SSL [19] (or TLS [15]). The input of an authenticated encryption is the plain text, the secret key, and some public information, called nonce. Its output consists of the cipher text, and MAC tag, both are transmitted over an unsecured public channel to the receiver, which has to verify the validity of this tag, being confident that the plain text is authentic. In general, authenticated encryption systems can be classified into two main categories: one-pass and two-pass modes. The former provides both privacy and authenticity only in one step, while the latter requires two steps to achieve these properties.

There exist many methods to construct AE schemes. A traditional approach is the generic composition paradigm which consists in combining an encryption

R. Di Pietro et al. (Eds.): DPM 2012 and SETOP 2012, LNCS 7731, pp. 43–60, 2013.

algorithm and a message authentication code (MAC). A detailed analysis of such constructions is given in [8]. Such constructions are two-pass modes and make use of two separate secret keys and hence they are however quite slow. In addition to the previous approach, several attempts have been made to design authenticated encryption schemes directly from dedicated block ciphers. Notable examples in this direction include the works [24,23,26,33]. Most of these proposals are one-pass schemes and have been patented, causing serious problems in their usage. For that reason, novel two-pass modes have been appeared such as CCM [37], EAX [9], CWC [25] and GCM [2]. Like the generic compositions, such proposals process the plain text in two stages but they require only one key instead of two independent keys. However, these proposals are inefficient as generic compositions. In addition to the previous methods, there exist a new recently-developed approach to achieve AE schemes by using stream ciphers as underlying primitives, for example Helix [17] and SOBER [31]. The AE schemes based on this approach actually are apparently very fast compared with the previous one, but their security is a matter of opinion, because designing provably secure and efficient stream ciphers remains a big challenge, as reported during the eSTREAM project [1].

As far as we know, the most provably secure authenticated encryption schemes proposed come with a rigorous proof of security via a reduction the underlying cryptographic primitive, and there exists no reduction to the well-known problems. Therefore, it is desirable to have provably secure AE constructions, whose security is grounded on hard problems. One of such problem is the decoding of random linear codes, called also the syndrome decoding (SD) problem. Unlike the number-theoretic problems such as factoring and discrete logarithm problem [35], this problem is NP-complete [10] and is believed to resist quantum algorithms (certainly for properly chosen parameters). The fastest algorithm [6] for solving this problem has an exponential running time. In addition to that, SD-based systems enjoy the benefits of having fast encryption and decryption algorithms; they only use simple operations like shifts and XORs making them one of the promising candidates for post-quantum cryptography [11].

Our Contribution. The present work presents an efficient and provably secure two-pass authenticated encryption scheme, called SCAE, based on coding theory. To the best of our knowledge it is the first proposal of this type. Its design is inspired from the sponge approach and its security depends on the hardness of the regular syndrome decoding problem. Furthermore, the security proofs for SCAE are simple and straightforward. The security requirement, privacy and authenticity, are proved. Additionally, the proposed scheme enjoys nice computational properties. Its performance is comparable to that of the other efficient schemes. Different parameters are also proposed for SCAE allowing a trade-off between performance and security.

Outline. Section 2 introduces notations and basic facts about code-based cryptography. Section 3 briefly explains related work. Our proposed authenticated encryption scheme, called SCAE, is described in detail in Section 4. Its security proofs are given in Section 5. A short performance comparison between SCAE and some other AE proposals, as well as concrete parameters for SCAE are presented in Section 6. Finally, Section 7 concludes and gives some future work.

2 Coding Theory Background

This section introduces notations and some backgrounds from coding theory.

2.1 Notations

$|x|$: the length in bits of a string x.

$\mathtt{wt}(x)$: the Hamming weight of a string x, defined as the number of its non-null coordinates.

$x^{\top}$: the transpose of a string x.

$x \parallel y$: the concatenation of two strings of x and y.

$\mathsf{X} \parallel \mathsf{Y}$: the concatenation of two matrices X and Y.

$x \oplus y$: the bitwise XOR of two strings x and y, having the same size.

$x \xleftarrow{\$} S$: choosing an element x from a finite set S at random and assigning it to x.

$\mathcal{W}_{n,w}$: the set of binary strings having length n and weight w.

$\langle z \rangle_l$: the l-bit representation of z.

d_z : the decimal value of the binary string z.

2.2 Linear Codes

In general, an $[n, w, k]$ binary linear code $\mathcal{C}$ is a k-dimensional subspace of an n-dimensional vector space over a finite field $\mathbb{F}_2$, where k and n are positive integers with $k < n$. Elements of $\mathbb{F}_2^n$ are called words and elements of $\mathcal{C}$ are called codewords. The integer $b = n - k$ is called the co-dimension of $\mathcal{C}$. The weight of a word x, denoted by $w = \mathtt{wt}(x)$, is the number of non-zero entries in x. If the quotient n/w is a power of two, then a word x of length n and weight w is called regular if it consists of w blocks of length n/w, each with a single non-zero entry. The sum of two regular words is called a 2-regular word. A generator matrix G of $\mathcal{C}$ is a $k \times n$ matrix whose rows form a basis of $\mathcal{C}$, .i.e. $\mathcal{C} = \{x \cdot G : x \in \mathbb{F}_2^k\}$. A parity check matrix H of $\mathcal{C}$ is an $b \times n$ matrix, which is defined by $\mathcal{C} = \{x \in \mathbb{F}_2^n : H \cdot x^{\top} = 0\}$ and generates the code's dual space.

2.3 Some Hard Problems

The security of the most code-based cryptographic primitives is related to the hardness of the following problems.

Problem 1 (Syndrome decoding (SD)): *Given a $b \times n$ random binary matrix H, a binary vector $y \in \mathbb{F}_2^b$, and an integer $w > 0$, find a word $x \in \mathbb{F}_2^n$ of weight $wt(x) = w$, such that $H \cdot x^{\top} = y$.*

This problem is proven NP-complete in [27] and decades of research in coding theory indicate that it is hard in the average case [5]. A special case of this problem is called the regular syndrome decoding (RSD) problem, which only has solutions in the set of regular words. This is proven NP-complete in [3], and reads as follows.

Problem 2 (Regular Syndrome Decoding (RSD)): *Given a $b \times n$ random binary matrix H, a binary vector $y \in \mathbb{F}_2^b$, and an integer $w > 0$, find a regular word $x \in \mathbb{F}_2^n$ of weight $wt(x) = w$, such that $H \cdot x^T = y$.*

Problem 3 (2-Regular Null Syndrome Decoding (2-NRSD)): *Given a $b \times n$ random binary matrix H, a binary vector $y \in \mathbb{F}_2^b$, and an integer $w > 0$, find a 2-regular word $x \in \mathbb{F}_2^n$ of weight $wt(x) \leq 2w$, such that $H \cdot x^T = 0$.*

This problem has also been proven to be NP-Complete in [3]. All currently known algorithms to solve the above problems have an exponential running time. The most efficient one is recently presented in [6].

The most famous systems based on the SD problem, are the McEliece and Niederreiter cryptosystems [27,29], which are equivalent from the security point of view. The Niederreiter cryptosystem uses a parity check matrix of size instead of a generator matrix. Its plaintext domain is $\mathcal{W}_{n,w}$, while $\mathbb{F}_2^r$ forms its cipher text space. If plain texts contain some random padding bits, then the system is called the *randomized* Niedderreiter cryptosystem [30]. This variant is the major ingredient of our construction described later.

3   Related Work

The construction presented in this work is inspired from the sponge construction [20][1]. This construction is a mode of operation, which uses random transformations or permutations and a padding rule to design a mapping that takes strings of variable length input and returns strings of variable length. This mapping, called a sponge function, is used to construct cryptographic primitives such as hash functions [13,4,22], pseudo-random number generators [12], and authenticated encryption schemes [14]. The main idea behind the sponge construction is to iteratively apply the underlying permutation or random transformation (denoted here F), to a internal state of length b bits, called the width, which is composed of the c-bit capacity and the r-bit bitrate ($b = c + r$). All the bits of the initial state are set to some fixed value.

In the context of cryptographic hash functions, the hashing process is depicted in Figure 1 and consists of two phases: the absorbing and the squeezing phase. After applying an appropriate padding rule and splitting the message P into r-bit chunks, i.e. $P = (P_1, P_2, \cdots, P_l)$, the absorbing step consists in iteratively processing all r-bit message chunks P_i by combining them (usually by XOR) to the bitrate part of the internal state and then applying the underlying permutation or transformation. Then it follows the squeezing phase, where the bitrate parts are (may be successively extracted and) returned as blocks h_i of

---

[1] See http://sponge.noekeon.org/

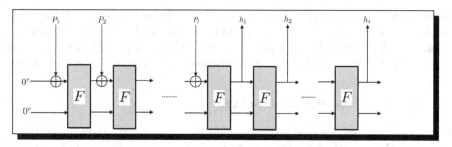

Fig. 1. A graphical illustration of the sponge-based hashing

the final hash value of length ℓ, interleaved with applications of the permutation or transformation. The number of hash blocks is determined by the user.

4 A Code-Based Authenticated Encryption

4.1 Formal Definitions

Before describing our proposal, we introduce the following definitions.

Definition 1. An authenticated encryption (short AE) scheme consists of three algorithms $\Pi = (\mathcal{G}; \mathcal{E}; \mathcal{D})$ described as follows. Let $\mathcal{K}$, $\mathcal{M}$, and $\mathcal{N}$ be three finite sets defining the key, the plain text, and the nonce space, respectively.

1. The key generation algorithm $\mathcal{G}$ is a randomized algorithm that takes as argument the empty set $\emptyset$ and outputs a key K from $\mathcal{K}$; we denote this process as

$$\mathcal{G}(\emptyset) = K \in \mathcal{K}.$$

2. The encryption algorithm $\mathcal{E}$ is a deterministic algorithm that takes a secret key K, a nonce N and a plaintext pair M as input and returns a ciphertext C and a tag T; for the sake of convenience we write $\mathcal{E}_K(\cdot, \cdot) = \mathcal{E}(K, \cdot, \cdot)$. This process can be expressed as

$$\mathcal{E}_K(N, M) = \mathcal{E}(K, N, M) = (C, T).$$

3. The decryption algorithm $\mathcal{D}$ is a deterministic algorithm that takes a tuple (K, N, C, T) as input and returns a plaintext M or a fail symbol $\perp$ indicating that T is not valid and therefore the transmitted message has been modified. As before we denote $\mathcal{D}(K, \cdot, \cdot, \cdot) = \mathcal{D}_K(\cdot, \cdot, \cdot)$. This procedure is defined by

$$\mathcal{D}_K(C, T, N) = \begin{cases} M & \text{if T is valid} \\ \perp & \text{otherwise} \end{cases}$$

The authenticated encryption scheme is said to be correct if $\mathcal{D}_K(\mathcal{E}_K(N, M), T, N) = M$.

Definition 2. An authenticated encryption scheme with associated data (AEAD) is an AE scheme, which takes an extra data (called header) H as input together with a secret key K, a nonce N and a plaintext pair M, and produces a ciphertext C and a tag T. Its formal definition is similar to that stated above.

4.2   The Proposed Protocol: SCAE

In what follows, we describe a construction for an authenticated scheme based on coding theory, called SCAE, which stands for Sponge-like Code-based Authenticated Encryption scheme.

The key idea behind our construction is to use the randomize-then-combine paradigm, introduced by Bellare and Micciancio [7], inside the sponge-like construction in order to obtain a code-based authenticated encryption scheme. Unlike sponge construction, a counter is used to modify the c-bit part using XOR operation during the encryption/decryption process.

Parameters. Consider five positive integers n, w, c and r satisfying $\frac{n}{w} = 2^\alpha$ for some $\alpha > 0$, and $b = w \cdot \alpha = r + c$. To use our scheme one has to specify a random binary matrix $\mathbf{A}$ of size $b \times n$. Let $\mathcal{K} = \{0,1\}^{\frac{b}{2}}$ be the set of possible keys. Given these parameters, one defines an encryption function $E : \mathcal{K} \times \{0,1\}^b \to \{0,1\}^b$, where each $E(K,\cdot) = E_K(\cdot)$ is a one-to-one transformation over $\{0,1\}^b$. Formally, for a random secret key $K \in \mathcal{K}$, we first define

$$f(y) = \bigoplus_{i=1}^{w} A_i[d_{\langle y_i \rangle_\alpha}], \ y = (y_1, \cdots, y_i, \cdots, y_w) \in \{0,1\}^b \text{ s.t. } \langle y_i \rangle_\alpha \in \{0,1,\ldots,2^\alpha-1\}, \quad (1)$$

where $A_i[j] \in \mathbb{F}^b$ for $j \in \{0,1,\ldots,2^\alpha-1\}$, are the columns of a random binary matrix $\mathbf{A}$ of size $b \times n$. The integer values $d_{\langle y_i \rangle_\alpha}$ indicate which columns of $\mathbf{A}$ have to be combined using the bitwise XOR-operator.

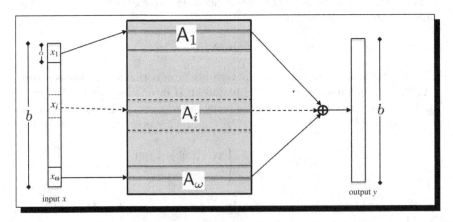

Fig. 2. An graphical illustration of the core function f used to build E_K

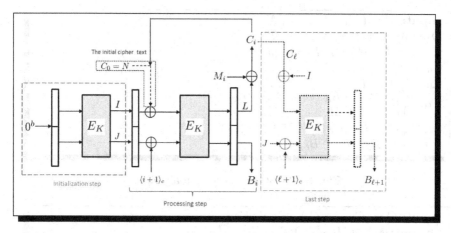

Fig. 3. A schematic diagram of the proposed authenticated encryption scheme

Now we define our encryption functions as

$$E_K(z) = f((K|z_1) \oplus f(z_2|K)), \quad z = (z_1, z_2) \in \{0,1\}^{\frac{b}{2}} \times \{0,1\}^{\frac{b}{2}}. \qquad (2)$$

Remark 1. We emphasize that the function f is similar to that of the mapping g firstly introduced in [21] and recently modified in [28].

Description of SCAE: A graphical illustration of SCAE is shown in Figure 3 including the following conditions on nonces and tags.

Nonces. Like other authenticated encryption schemes, our proposal uses a nonces N of length r bits, which is required for the encryption and decryption process. Each nonce should be non-repeating and selected by the party who want to encrypt. Every new message is associated with a single nonce.

Tags. The tag is an c-bit string and consists of a number of unknown "local" tags having the same length. By trivial means, it implies that the probability to forge a valid ciphertext has to be 2^{-c}.

Our construction consists of the following steps:

- Key Generation: Select randomly a secret key K of length $b/2$ bits from $\mathcal{K}$, and binary random matrix $\mathbf{A}$ of size $b \times n$ to construct the encryption function $E_K(\cdot)$ defined by equation (2). The key K is then secretly transmitted to two parties who want to encrypt and decrypt in order to authenticate their messages, while the matrix $\mathbf{A}$ is made public.

- Encryption: To encrypt a plaintext $M \in \{0,1\}^*$ using key $K \in \{0,1\}^{\frac{b}{2}}$ and nonce $N \in \{0,1\}^r$, obtaining a ciphertext C and a tag T, do the following. Let $\ell = \lceil \frac{|M|}{r} \rceil$, and denote $M = (M_1, \cdots, M_\ell)$ the message to be encrypted. If $|M_\ell| < r$ then prepend one "1" followed by $r - |M_\ell|$ zeros to M_ℓ to obtain an r-bit block. As in the sponge construction, initialize the

Input: $M = (M_1, \cdots, M_\ell)$, N, K
Output: $C = (C_1, \cdots, C_\ell)$, T
$(I, J) \leftarrow E_K(0^b)$ $//$ $|I| = r$, $|J| = c$
$C_0 \leftarrow N$
for $i \leftarrow 1$ **to** ℓ
  do $\begin{cases} (L, B_i) \leftarrow E_K (C_{i-1} \oplus I \parallel \langle i \rangle_c \oplus J) \\ C_i \leftarrow L \oplus M_i \end{cases}$
$(L, B_{\ell+1}) \leftarrow E_K (C_\ell \oplus I \parallel \langle \ell + 1 \rangle_c \oplus J)$
$T \leftarrow B_1 \oplus B_2 \oplus \cdots \oplus B_{\ell+1}$

Fig. 4. The SCAE encryption algorithm

Input: $C = (C_1, \cdots, C_\ell)$, T, N, K
Output: $M = (M_1, \cdots, M_\ell)$ or $\bot$
$(I, J) \leftarrow E_K(0^b)$ $//$ $|I| = r$, $|J| = c$
$C_0 \leftarrow N$
for $i \leftarrow 1$ **to** ℓ
  do $\begin{cases} (L, B_i) \leftarrow E_K (C_{i-1} \oplus I \parallel \langle i \rangle_c \oplus J) \\ M_i \leftarrow L \oplus C_i \end{cases}$
$(L, B_{\ell+1}) \leftarrow E_K (C_\ell \oplus I \parallel \langle \ell + 1 \rangle_c \oplus J)$
$T' \leftarrow B_1 \oplus B_2 \oplus \cdots \oplus B_{\ell+1}$
if $T' = T$
  then Output $M = (M_1, \cdots, M_\ell)$
  else Output $\bot$

Fig. 5. The SCAE decryption algorithm

system with 0^b at the beginning. Compute $(I, J) = E_K(0^b)$ with $|I| = r$ and $|J| = c$. For $i = 1, \cdots, \ell$, produce ciphertexts C_i as follows: $C_0 = N$, $(L, B_i) = E_K (C_{i-1} \oplus I \parallel \langle i \rangle_c \oplus J)$, and $C_i = L \oplus M_i$, where $|L| = r$ and $|B_i| = c$. Then compute $(L, B_{\ell+1}) = E_K (C_\ell \oplus I \parallel \langle \ell + 1 \rangle_c \oplus J)$. Finally, compute a tag $T = B_1 \oplus B_2 \oplus \cdots \oplus B_{\ell+1}$. The "local" tags $B_1, \cdots, B_{\ell+1}$ are never made directly visible to the attacker, but only their XOR-sum is returned. Figure 4 algorithmically illustrates the encryption procedure.

- Decryption and verification: Given $C = (C_1, \cdots, C_\ell)$, T and N, the receiver knowing the secret key K executes the following in order to recover plaintext $M = (M_1, \cdots, M_\ell)$. First compute $(I, J) = E_K(0^b)$ with $|I| = r$ and $|J| = c$. Then for $i = 1$ to ℓ, do the following: $C_0 = N$, $(L, B_i) = E_K (C_{i-1} \oplus I \parallel \langle i \rangle_c \oplus J)$, and $M_i = L \oplus C_i$, where $|L| = r$ and $|B_i| = c$. Then compute $(L, B_{\ell+1}) = E_K (C_\ell \oplus I \parallel \langle \ell + 1 \rangle_c \oplus J)$. To verify whether the received tag T is valid, compute $T' = B_1 \oplus B_2 \oplus \cdots \oplus B_{\ell+1}$. If T and T' match, then accept the plaintext $M = (M_1, \cdots, M_\ell)$, otherwise output a fail symbol $\bot$ indicating that the message is not authentic. The whole decryption/verfication process is presented in Figure 5.

Extending SCAE into SCAE with Associated Data (SCAE-AD): The above described construction can be easily converted into SCAE with Associated Data (SCAE-AD). This can be achieved by applying the generic conversions proposed in [34]. The main idea in [34] briefly works as follows: the first step consists in constructing an SCAE scheme with arbitrary length nonces (denoted here SCAE$^+$) from the original SCAE by using a collision resistant hash function $h : \{0,1\}^* \to \{0,1\}^r$, whose output length is r bits. The security of SCAE$^+$ is directly reducible to the security of SCAE. The second step is to convert the resulting SCAE$^+$ into SCAE-AD by replacing (N, H) in SCAE-AD by the combination $N \parallel H$ in SCAE$^+$. As pointed out in [34] the only problem in this conversion is to find a collision hash function outputting hash values of length r bits. To fix this issue, one can use, for instance the SHA-3 finalist Keccack hash function [13], to produce the desired hash length.

5 Security Analysis of SCAE

This section discusses the security analysis of our SCAE from both theoretical and practical points of view. We first give the formal definitions of privacy and authenticity, then we state the main assumptions needed to prove the security of SCAE.

5.1 Security Notions

An authenticated encryption is designed to provide two security goals: privacy and authenticity. Following the security model in [32], these notions are formally defined as follows. An adversary $\mathcal{A}$ as a probabilistic algorithm having access to an encryption oracle $\mathcal{E}_K(\cdot,\cdot)$ selects nonce-message pairs $(N^1, M^1), \cdots, (N^q, M^q)$ and obtains the corresponding ciphertexts $\mathcal{C}^i = (C^i, T^i) = \mathcal{E}_K(N^i, M^i)$, $i = 1, \cdots, q$. The adversary must be nonce-respecting meaning that it is not allowed to repeat a nonce in its queries to the encryption oracle, i.e., $N^i \neq N^j$, for all $i \neq j$. In order to attack the privacy notion, $\mathcal{A}$ is either given access to the real encryption $\mathcal{E}_K(\cdot,\cdot)$, or to a fake oracle $\mathcal{O}(\cdot,\cdot)$, that take as input (N^i, M^i) and output random ciphertexts $\mathcal{O}(N^i, M^i)$ having the same length as the real ciphertexts $(C^i, T^i) = \mathcal{E}_K(N^i, M^i)$. The attacker has to make a distinction between both oracles. Formally, this can be defined as follows. An authenticated encryption Π is said to be ϵ-*privacy secure*, if for all nonce-respecting adversaries $\mathcal{A}$, it holds

$$\mathbf{Adv}_\Pi^{priv} = \Pr[K \xleftarrow{\$} \mathcal{K} | \mathcal{A}^{\mathcal{E}_K(\cdot,\cdot)}(\cdot) = 1] - \Pr[\mathcal{A}^{\mathcal{O}(\cdot,\cdot)} = 1] \leq \epsilon \quad (3)$$

In an authenticity attack, the adversary $\mathcal{A}$ first asks queries $(N^1, M^1), \cdots,$ (N^q, M^q), obtains the corresponding ciphertexts $\mathcal{C}^i = (C^i, T^i) = \mathcal{E}_K(N^i, M^i)$, and finally constructs a ciphertext $\mathcal{C}$ and a nonce N. It is said to successfully *forge* if $\mathcal{C} \notin \{\mathcal{C}^1, \cdots, \mathcal{C}^q\}$ and $\mathcal{D}_K(\mathcal{C})$ is valid. This can be formulated as follows. An authenticated encryption Π is said to be ϵ-*authenticity secure*, if for all nonce-respecting adversaries $\mathcal{A}$, it holds

$$\mathbf{Adv}_\Pi^{auth} = \Pr[K \xleftarrow{\$} \mathcal{K} | \mathcal{A}^{\mathcal{E}_K(\cdot,\cdot)} \text{ outputs a forgery}] \leq \epsilon \quad (4)$$

5.2   Cryptographic Assumptions

We state our complexity assumptions below.

Assumption 1: For properly chosen parameters (n, w, b) there is no polynomial time algorithm which can distinguish the underlying $b \times n$ binary matrix from a random matrix of the same size with non-negligible probability.

The second assumption states that it is hard to solve an instance of the (regular) syndrome decoding problem when the parameters (n, w, b) are chosen properly.

Assumption 2: The Regular Syndrome Decoding problem with parameters (n, w, b) is hard for every polynomial time algorithm.

Remark 2. The first assumption is trivially fulfilled as we use random linear codes, rather restricted families like Goppa codes for an efficient decoder is known, and whose parity check (or generator) matrices can be distinguished from random ones as demonstrated in [16]. These two assumption have been used as a basic building block of security of several code-based schemes such as Fisher-Stern's pseudorandom number generator [18], and Stern's identification scheme [36].

Next we specify some properties that the core encryption function E_K fulfils.

5.3   Some Properties of E_K

The underlying encryption function enjoys some interesting features:

1. **Security reduction.** Consider the encryption function E_K defined earlier.

   $$E_K(x) = f((K|x_1) \oplus f(x_2|K)), \ x = (x_1, x_2) \in \{0,1\}^{\frac{b}{2}} \times \{0,1\}^{\frac{b}{2}}, \ K \in \{0,1\}^{\frac{b}{2}}.$$

   We want to show that $E_K(x)$ for some $x \in \{0,1\}^b$ can be rewritten as $\mathbf{A} \cdot y^\top$, where y is an unknown regular word derived from x and K. To this end, let $\mathbf{A} = A_1|\ldots|A_w$, where A_i is a binary random submatrix of size $b \times 2^\alpha$. For $y = (y_1, \ldots, y_w)$, $f(y) = \bigoplus_{i=1}^{w} A_i[d_{\langle y_i \rangle_\alpha}]$. Thus, we can associate y with a value t whose decimal notation is $(t_1, \ldots, t_w)$ such that $t_i = (y_i + 1) + (i - 1)2^\alpha$. The reverse transformation of y to t is obtained by $t_i \equiv y_i - 1 \pmod{2^\alpha}$, for $i = 1, \cdots, w$. By doing so, one can straightforward check that $\mathbf{A} \cdot t^\top = f(y)$. Since E_K is a function of f, we conclude that $E_K(x)$ can be rewritten as product of $\mathbf{A}$ by a regular word $s_{x,K}$ coming from x and K, i.e., $E_K(x) = \mathbf{A} \cdot s_{x,K}^\top$. Hence the hardness of inverting $x \to E_K(x)$ is reducible to the hardness of solving an instance of the regular syndrome decoding problem. As shown in [28], the running time of all the best-known algorithms (including the fastest one proposed recently in [6]) for inverting f (and also implicitly E_K) is still exponential.

2. **Pseudorandomness.** Here, we want to show that the function E_K, where K is random, is pseudorandom, meaning that its outputs are indistinguishable

from random string. To do so, it is sufficient to prove that the output $f(x)$ is pseudo-random for some uniformly random input x. This indeed follows from the fact that $x \to f(x)$ can be regarded as $\mathbf{A} \cdot y_x^\top$, where y_x is random regular word corresponding to x, as shown previously. Consequentially, if some fixed part of y_x is made random then we obtain an instantiation of the randomized Niederreiter's system [30][1], where the plaintext space is the set of all regular words of length n and weight w. Thus, as in [30], assuming that the above assumptions hold, we conclude that the ciphertexts $f(x)$, for some randomized input x, are pseudorandom. Therefore the function E_K is also pseudorandom, as it calls f as subroutine.

5.4 Security Arguments

Now we present theorems showing that our protocol is secure in the sense that it provides the privacy and authenticity property. For doing so, as explained before we consider a chosen plaintext scenerio attacks, where an nonce-respecting adversary $\mathcal{A}$ chooses q queries of nonce-message pairs $(N^1, M^1), \cdots, (N^q, M^q)$, where $M^i = (M_1^i, \cdots, M_{\ell_i}^i)$, $N^i = C_0^i$ for $i = 1, \cdots, q$ and $t = \sum_{i=1}^q \ell_i$, and gets the corresponding ciphertexts $(C^1, T^1), \cdots, (C^q, T^q)$, with $C^i = (C_1^i, \cdots, C_{\ell_i}^i)$. Furthermore, we call an "inner" collision for SCAE each pair of inputs (X_{k-1}^i, X_{k-1}^j) that are equal, i.e., $X_{k-1}^i = X_{k-1}^j$, where $1 \leq i < j \leq q$, $k \in \{1, \cdots, \min\{\ell_i, \ell_j\}\}$, and X_{k-1}^i is defined by $X_{k-1}^i = (C_{k-1}^i \oplus I, k \oplus J)$. By definition, we have $X_{k-1}^i = X_{k-1}^j$ implies $C_{k-1}^i = C_{k-1}^j$.

Based on this definition, we now state the following Lemmas, which will help us to prove the security of our proposal.

Lemma 1. *Let denote* $E_K(x) = (y, z)$, *and* $E_K(x') = (y', z')$, *where* $x, x' \in \{0,1\}^b$, $y, y' \in \{0,1\}^r$, *and* $z, z' \in \{0,1\}^c$. *The probability to have* $y = y'$ *provided that* $x \neq x'$ *is approximately equal to* $2^{-\frac{r}{3.3}}$.

Proof. As mentioned above, $E_K(x)$ can be rewritten as product of a $b \times n$ random binary matrix $\mathbf{A}$ by a regular word $s_{x,K}$ coming from x and K, i.e., $E_K(x) = \mathbf{A} \cdot s_{x,K}^\top$. Having $x \neq x'$ such that $y = y'$ can be interpreted as a solution of an instance of the 2-NSRD problem with parameters (n, w, r). As shown in [3], the success probability to find this solution roughly amounts to $2^{-\frac{r}{3.3}}$

∎

Lemma 2. *For the authenticated encryption SCAE based on the function* $E_K(\cdot)$, *the probability to produce an inner collision by a nonce-respecting adversary making* q *queries is upper bounded by* $\frac{(q-1)t}{2^{\frac{r}{3.3}}}$.

Proof. It is clear that for $k = 0$ there is no inner collision due to $C_0^i = N^i \neq N^j = C_0^j$ (nonce-respecting assumption). Hence, we consider $k \geq 1$. We want to prove that if $X_{k-1}^i \neq X_{k-1}^j$, then $\Pr[X_k^i = X_k^j] \leq 2^{-\frac{r}{3.3}+1}$. Indeed, we have

---

[1] The proofs given for the randomized Niedderreiter's cryptosystem are inspired from [18] under the same assumptions we use in this paper.

$$\Pr[X_k^i = X_k^j] = \Pr[C_k^i = C_k^j]$$
$$= \Pr[L^i \oplus M_k^i = L^j \oplus M_k^i]$$
$$= \Pr[(L^i \oplus M_k^i = L^j \oplus M_k^i) \cap (M_k^i = M_k^i)] + \Pr[(L^i \oplus M_k^i = L^j \oplus M_k^i) \cap (M_k^i \neq M_k^i)]$$
$$= \Pr[L^i = L^j] + \Pr[(L^i \oplus M_k^i = L^j \oplus M_k^j) \cap (M_k^i \neq M_k^j)]$$
$$= \Pr[L^i = L^j] + \Pr[(L^i \oplus L^j = M_k^i \oplus M_k^j) \cap (M_k^i \neq M_k^j)]$$

where L^i and L^j are defined by $(L^i, B_k^i) = E_K\left(X_{k-1}^i\right)$ and $(L^j, B_k^j) = E_K\left(X_{k-1}^j\right)$. Since $X_{k-1}^i \neq X_{k-1}^j$, applying Lemma 1 delivers

$$\Pr[L^i = L^j] \approx 2^{-\frac{r}{3.3}}$$

On the other hand, the term $L^i \oplus L^j$ is approximately uniformly distributed over $\{0,1\}^r$. Thus the probability to successfully get $L^i \oplus L^j = M_k^i \oplus M_k^j$ is at most $\frac{1}{2^r}$. i.e.,

$$\Pr[(L^i \oplus L^j = M_k^i \oplus M_k^j) \cap (M_k^i \neq M_k^j)] \leq 2^{-r}$$

Consequently, we obtain

$$\Pr[X_k^i = X_k^j] \leq 2^{-\frac{r}{3.3}} + 2^{-r} \leq 2^{-\frac{r}{3.3}+1}$$

Furthermore, there exit $\frac{(q-1)t}{2}$ triples (i,j,k) with $1 \leq i < j \leq q$ and $k \in \{1, \cdots, \min\{\ell_i, \ell_j\}\}$. Thus the probability to find at least a colliding triple is less that equal $\frac{(q-1)t}{2} \cdot \frac{1}{2^{\frac{r}{3.3}-1}} = \frac{(q-1)t}{2^{\frac{r}{3.3}}}$

∎

From the previous Lemma we derive the following theorems.

Theorem 1 (Privacy property). *The SCAE scheme based on the function $E_K(\cdot)$ is ϵ-privacy secure, against all nonce-respecting adversaries, where $\epsilon = \frac{(q-1)t}{2^{\frac{r}{3.3}}}$, i.e.*

$$Adv_{SCAE}^{priv} \leq \frac{(q-1)t}{2^{\frac{r}{3.3}}} \tag{5}$$

Proof. If there exist no inner collisions, then all the inputs of $E_K(\cdot)$ are distinct, and due to the pseudo-randomness property of $E_K(\cdot)$, the corresponding outputs are indistinguishable from random bit sequences. That means, the distribution of the outputs from the "real" encryption and the fake oracle are equal, and to differentiate the two oracle, a nonce-respecting adversary has to find an inner collision, which occurs with a probability upper bounded by $\frac{(q-1)t}{2^{r+1}}$. This demonstrates our claim.

∎

The next theorem states the security argument of our proposal regarding the authenticity property.

Theorem 2 (Authenticity property). *The SCAE scheme based on the function $E_K(\cdot)$ is ϵ-authenticity secure with respect to all nonce-respecting adversaries, where $\epsilon = \frac{(q-1)t}{2^{\frac{r}{3.3}}} + \frac{1}{2^c}$, i.e.*

$$Adv_{SCAE}^{auth} \leq \frac{(q-1)t}{2^{\frac{r}{3.3}}} + \frac{1}{2^c} \tag{6}$$

Proof. It is sufficient to prove that without having inner collisions the upper bound of success probability of forging a plaintext is $\frac{1}{2^c}$. We will use the same notations as before. By construction, an adversary is given the following system of linear equations defined over $\{0,1\}^c$

$$\begin{cases} T^1 = B_1^1 \oplus B_2^1 \oplus \cdots \oplus B_{\ell_1}^1 \\ T^2 = B_1^2 \oplus B_2^2 \oplus \cdots \oplus B_{\ell_2}^2 \\ \cdots \quad \cdots \quad \cdots \quad \cdots \quad \cdots \\ T^q = B_1^q \oplus B_2^q \oplus \cdots \oplus B_{\ell_q}^q \end{cases}$$

Where T^i are known, while B_k^i $(i = 1, \cdots q; k = 1, \cdots \ell_i)$ are unknown and uniformly distributed independent numbers in $\{0,1\}^c$ because of the pseudo-randomness of E_K and the absence of inner collisions. In addition to that, the values B_1^i are statistically independent because all N^i are different (nonce-respecting assumption), and therefore all q equations are linearly independent. In a forgery attack, an adversary is said to be successful if he could build (N, C) and a tag T with $N = C_0$ and $C = (C_1, \cdots, C_\ell)$ meeting the following conditions:

$$C \neq C^i, \ \forall i \in \{1, \cdots, q\} \tag{7}$$
$$T = B_1 \oplus B_2 \oplus \cdots \oplus B_\ell \tag{8}$$

In order to prove the claimed theorem it is sufficient to show that the equation (8) is linearly independent from all the equations given above. As a result, the value of T should be a random number in $\{0,1\}^c$, and therefore the probability to correctly guess it equals to $\frac{1}{2^c}$. This amount to proving that the sum of equation (8) with any subsystem derived from the above equations will certainly contain a set of unknowns variables B_k or B_k^i. We have to consider two cases:

- If $X_0 \neq X_0^i$, $\forall 1 \leq i \leq q$, then B_1 will not vanish and thus the claimed assumption holds.
- For the sake of simplicity, suppose that $X_0 = X_0^1$. In this case, we get $C_0 = C_0^1$, which implies $B_1 = B_1^1$ (by construction). Consequently, the sum of T with T^1 (denoted by S) becomes

$$S = T \oplus T^1 = (B_2 \oplus \cdots \oplus B_\ell) \oplus (B_2^1 \oplus \cdots \oplus B_{\ell_1}^1). \tag{9}$$

In general, if $X_k = X_k^1$ for some k, the values $B_k = B_k^1$ will be disappeared from S. In the contrary case, to determine S, we have to count the number of B_k and B_k^1 provided that $X_k \neq X_k^1$ by defining the following set:

$$\Lambda = \{X_k \ \text{s.t.} \ X_k \neq X_k^1\}_{2 \leq k \leq \ell} \cup \{X_k^1 \ \text{s.t.} \ X_k \neq X_k^1\}_{2 \leq k \leq \ell_1} \tag{10}$$

By doing so, the equation (9) becomes $S = T \oplus T^1 = \bigoplus_{\lambda \in \Lambda} \lambda$.

Obviously the set Λ is non-empty because $C \neq C^i$, and therefore for $i > 1$ adding T^i to S will insert a value T_1^i , which cannot be canceled out. This proves our claim about the linear independence of the equation (8) from all the equations listed above.

■

6   Performance and Comparison

Estimated Cost for Evaluating E_K. Computing $E_K(x)$ for some $x \in \{0,1\}^b$ requires two evaluations of the function f plus one XOR-operation. The evaluation of f can be done only by XORs. Indeed each call of f needs $w - 1$ XORs of bit strings of length b bits, which in total results in $(2w - 1)b$ binary xor-operations to calculate $E_K(x)$. This quantity does not depend on n. So for small values of w and b we will theoretically get a high performance in our construction. For instance, using $w = 32$, and $b = 256$, one evaluation of E_K requires about 2^{14} binary operations. Note that one can decrease the number of binary operations needed to evaluate E_K by xoring $\frac{w}{2}$ columns of matrix A in advance. Actually, the knowledge of K (by the communicating parties) allows to compute the XOR-sum of $\frac{w}{2}$ columns selected from sub-matrices $A_{\frac{w}{2}}, \ldots, A_w$, respectively. That implies that, the overall complexity for evaluating E_K becomes $(\frac{3w}{2} - 1)b$ instead of $(2w - 1)b$. In addition, this complexity could be further decreased in practice due to the incremental property of the core function f. If an input x is slightly modified to a new input x', then it should be quickly to produce the output of the modified message x'. This is done by computing the new output, z', from the old output value z in contrast to conventional functions that have to recompute the the new output, z', from scratch, which requires a longer time.

A Short Comparison with Some Other AE Schemes. Table 1 gives a brief overview on basic features of SCAE compared to some other proposals. As we can see, in particular, the theoretical cost (measured by the number of the underlying function calls) required to handel a $|M|$-bit plaintext approximately amounts to $\lceil \frac{|M|}{b} \rceil + 2$. As a result, SCAE runs at the same speed as OCB mode, and only is a bit slower than remaining schemes. Furthermore, SCAE possesses smaller and correlated tags and nonces, allowing a trade-off between the security and the performance in contrast to OCB, EAX, and GCM.

Concrete Parameters. The main parameters of SCAE depend on α and w because of $b = w\alpha$, $n = w2^\alpha$, and $b = r + c$. Adjusting these two parameters allows to trade off performance versus security. As shown earlier, the security of SCAE is related on the hardness of two problems: the RSD and the 2-NRSD problem. Inverting the core function f implies solving an instance of RSD with parameters (n, w, b), while the level of privacy and authenticity is related to the hardness of solving an instance of RSD with parameters (n, w, r) and the parameters c. As a result, to get good privacy and authenticity, we have to carefully select α and w. Table 2 presents different parameters for our proposal including the tag size,

Table 1. A comparison of basic characteristics of SCAE with some other schemes. The input size of the underlying block cipher or pseudo-random function (PRF) is equal to b bits while the tag length is c bits with $c < b$. The cost is given in terms of the number of the underlying block cipher or PRF calls. In order to get a reasonable comparison, the costs given here for EAX, OCB, and GCM modes do not include the cost to process the associated data (AD).

	With AD	Tag size c (bits)	Nonce size r (bits)	repeating nonce	Verify-Then-Decrypt	Cost
EAX [9]	yes	$\leq b$	any	no	yes	$\lceil \frac{|M|}{b} \rceil + 1$
OCB [33]	yes	$\leq b$	b	no	no	$\lceil \frac{|M|}{b} \rceil + 2$
GCM [2]	yes	$\leq b$	any	yes	no	$\lceil \frac{|M|}{b} \rceil + 1$
SCAE	no	$\leq c$	$\leq b - c$	no	no	$\lceil \frac{|M|}{b} \rceil + 2$

Table 2. Some concrete parameters for SCAE. The security levels are estimated according to the best known attack [6]

Parameters (n,w,b) $b=r+c$	Tag size c (bits)	Nonce/Block size r (bits)	# Queries q	# Blocks t	Upper bound for priv. $\approx \frac{qt}{2^{\frac{b}{3.3}}}$	Upper bound for auth. $\approx \frac{qt}{2^{\frac{b}{3.3}}} + \frac{1}{2^c}$	Complexity of solving $\mathrm{RSD}(n,w,b)$
$(8192, 32, 256)$	16	240	2^{10}	2^{16}	$\approx 2^{-46}$	$\approx 2^{-16}$	90
	32	224	2^{10}	2^{32}	$\approx 2^{-25}$	$\approx 2^{-25}$	
	64	192	2^{10}	2^{30}	$\approx 2^{-18}$	$\approx 2^{-18}$	
$(8192, 48, 384)$	16	368	2^{10}	2^{16}	$\approx 2^{-85}$	$\approx 2^{-16}$	120
	32	352	2^{20}	2^{32}	$\approx 2^{-64}$	$\approx 2^{-32}$	
	64	320	2^{20}	2^{64}	$\approx 2^{-12}$	$\approx 2^{-12}$	
$(8192, 64, 512)$	16	496	2^{40}	2^{16}	$\approx 2^{-94}$	$\approx 2^{-16}$	200
	32	480	2^{40}	2^{32}	$\approx 2^{-73}$	$\approx 2^{-32}$	
	64	448	2^{40}	2^{64}	$\approx 2^{-31}$	$\approx 2^{-31}$	

the nonce/block, and the upper bounds for privacy and authenticity as a function of the number of queries and blocks. Note that the upper bound on the plaintext length for SCAE is $r(2^c - 3)$ bits, which approximately gives 2^c blocks .

7 Conclusion

In this paper, we presented a new two-pass authenticated encryption scheme, called SCAE, based on linear codes. This is the first proposal of this type. The security of the scheme is based on the hardness of a variant of the syndrome decoding problem. The privacy and authenticity properties are proved in the sense of information-theoretical context. In addition to that, the performance of our proposal is comparable to that of the other existing work, such as OCB and EAX, from the theoretical point of view. A software or hardware implementation of the proposed scheme is left open as future work to show its speed in practice.

References

1. http://www.ecrytp.eu.org/stream
2. NIST Special Publication 800-38A. Recommendation for block cipher modes of operation-methods and techniques (2001),
   http://csrc.nist.gov/publications/nistpubs/800-38a/sp800-38a.pdf/
3. Augot, D., Finiasz, M., Sendrier, N.: A Family of Fast Syndrome Based Cryptographic Hash Functions. In: Dawson, E., Vaudenay, S. (eds.) Mycrypt 2005. LNCS, vol. 3715, pp. 64–83. Springer, Heidelberg (2005)
4. Aumasson, J.-P., Henzen, L., Meier, W., Naya-Plasencia, M.: QUARK: A Lightweight Hash. In: Mangard, S., Standaert, F.-X. (eds.) CHES 2010. LNCS, vol. 6225, pp. 1–15. Springer, Heidelberg (2010)
5. Barg, A.: Complexity issues in coding theory, vol. 1, pp. 649–754. Elsevier Science, Amsterdam (1998)
6. Becker, A., Joux, A., May, A., Meurer, A.: Decoding Random Binary Linear Codes in $2^{(n/20)}$: How $1 + 1 = 0$ Improves Information Set Decoding. In: Pointcheval, D., Johansson, T. (eds.) EUROCRYPT 2012. LNCS, vol. 7237, pp. 520–536. Springer, Heidelberg (2012)
7. Bellare, M., Micciancio, D.: A New Paradigm for Collision-Free Hashing: Incrementality at Reduced Cost. In: Fumy, W. (ed.) EUROCRYPT 1997. LNCS, vol. 1233, pp. 163–192. Springer, Heidelberg (1997)
8. Bellare, M., Namprempre, C.: Authenticated Encryption: Relations among Notions and Analysis of the Generic Composition Paradigm. J. Cryptol. 21(4), 469–491 (2008)
9. Bellare, M., Rogaway, P., Wagner, D.: Eax: A conventional authenticated-encryption mode (2003), http://eprint.iacr.org/
10. Berlekamp, E., McEliece, R., van Tilborg, H.: On the inherent intractability of certain coding problems. IEEE Transactions on Information Theory 24(2), 384–386 (1978)
11. Bernstein, D.J., Buchmann, J., Dahmen, E.: Post Quantum Cryptography. Springer (2008)
12. Bertoni, G., Daemen, J., Peeters, M., Van Assche, G.: Sponge-Based Pseudo-Random Number Generators. In: Mangard, S., Standaert, F.-X. (eds.) CHES 2010. LNCS, vol. 6225, pp. 33–47. Springer, Heidelberg (2010)
13. Bertoni, G., Daemen, J., Peeters, M., Van Assche, G.: The keccak sha-3 submission. Submission to NIST (Round 3) (2011)

14. Bertoni, G., Daemen, J., Peeters, M., Van Assche, G.: Duplexing the Sponge: Single-Pass Authenticated Encryption and Other Applications. In: Miri, A., Vaudenay, S. (eds.) SAC 2011. LNCS, vol. 7118, pp. 320–337. Springer, Heidelberg (2012)

15. Dierks, T., Allen, C.: The TLS Protocol Version 1.0 (1999)

16. Faugère, J.-C., Gauthier, V., Otmani, A., Perret, L., Tillich, J.-P.: A distinguisher for high rate mceliece cryptosystems. IACR Cryptology ePrint Archive, 331 (2010)

17. Ferguson, N., Whiting, D., Schneier, B., Kelsey, J., Lucks, S., Kohno, T.: Helix: Fast Encryption and Authentication in a Single Cryptographic Primitive. In: Johansson, T. (ed.) FSE 2003. LNCS, vol. 2887, pp. 330–346. Springer, Heidelberg (2003)

18. Fischer, J.-B., Stern, J.: An Efficient Pseudo-random Generator Provably as Secure as Syndrome Decoding. In: Maurer, U.M. (ed.) EUROCRYPT 1996. LNCS, vol. 1070, pp. 245–255. Springer, Heidelberg (1996)

19. Freier, A.O., Karlton, P., Kocher, P.C.: The SSL protocol v3. Netscape Communications Corp. (1996), http://home.netscape.com/eng/ssl3/ssl-toc.html

20. Peeters, M., Bertoni, G., Daemen, J., Van Assche, G.: Sponge Functions. In: ECRYPT Hash Workshop 2007 (2007)

21. Gaborit, P., Laudaroux, C., Sendrier, N.: SYND: a Very Fast Code-Based Cipher Stream with a Security Reduction. In: IEEE Conference, ISIT 2007, Nice, France, pp. 186–190 (July 2007)

22. Guo, J., Peyrin, T., Poschmann, A.: The PHOTON Family of Lightweight Hash Functions. In: Rogaway, P. (ed.) CRYPTO 2011. LNCS, vol. 6841, pp. 222–239. Springer, Heidelberg (2011)

23. Jutla, C.S.: Encryption modes with almost free message integrity. J. Cryptology 21(4), 547–578 (2008)

24. Katz, J., Yung, M.: Unforgeable Encryption and Chosen Ciphertext Secure Modes of Operation. In: Schneier, B. (ed.) FSE 2000. LNCS, vol. 1978, pp. 284–299. Springer, Heidelberg (2001)

25. Kohno, T., Viega, J., Whiting, D.: Cwc: A high-performance conventional authenticated encryption mode (2003), http://eprint.iacr.org/

26. Matsui, M. (ed.): FSE 2001. LNCS, vol. 2355. Springer, Heidelberg (2002)

27. McEliece, R.J.: A public-key cryptosystem based on algebraic coding theory. DNS Progress Report, 114–116 (1978)

28. Meziani, M., Hoffmann, G., Cayrel, P.-L.: Improving the Performance of the SYND Stream Cipher. In: Mitrokotsa, A., Vaudenay, S. (eds.) AFRICACRYPT 2012. LNCS, vol. 7374, pp. 99–116. Springer, Heidelberg (2012)

29. Niederreiter, H.: Knapsack-type cryptosystems and algebraic coding theory. Problems of Control and Information Theory. Problemy Upravlenija i Teorii Informacii 15, 159–166 (1986)

30. Nojima, R., Imai, H., Kobara, K., Morozov, K.: Semantic security for the mceliece cryptosystem without random oracles. Des. Codes Cryptography 49, 289–305 (2008)

31. Hawkes, P., Rose, G.G.: Primitive specification for sober-128. IACR Cryptology ePrint Archive, 81 (2003)

32. Rogaway, P.: Authenticated-encryption with associated-data. In: ACM Conference on Computer and Communications Security, pp. 98–107 (2002)

33. Rogaway, P., Bellare, M., Black, J.: Ocb: A block-cipher mode of operation for efficient authenticated encryption. ACM Trans. Inf. Syst. Secur. 6(3), 365–403 (2003)

34. Sarkar, P.: A Simple and Generic Construction of Authenticated Encryption with Associated Data. ACM Trans. Inf. Syst. Secur. 13(4), 33:1–33:16 (2010)
35. Shor, P.W.: Algorithms for Quantum Computation: Discrete Logarithms and Factoring. In: SFCS 1994: Proc. of the 35th Annual Symposium on Foundations of Computer Science, pp. 124–134. IEEE Computer Society (1994)
36. Stern, J.: A New Identification Scheme Based on Syndrome Decoding. In: Stinson, D.R. (ed.) CRYPTO 1993. LNCS, vol. 773, pp. 13–21. Springer, Heidelberg (1994)
37. Whiting, D., Housley, R., Ferguson, N.: Counter with CBC-MAC, CCM (2003)

Proposal of Non-invasive Fingerprint Age Determination to Improve Data Privacy Management in Police Work from a Legal Perspective Using the Example of Germany

Ronny Merkel[1], Matthias Pocs[2], Jana Dittmann[1], and Claus Vielhauer[1,3]

[1] Research Group Multimedia and Security, Otto-von-Guericke University of Magdeburg,
Universitätsplatz 2, 39106 Magdeburg, Germany
[2] Project Group Constitutionally Compatible Technology Design, University of Kassel,
Pfannkuchstraße 1, 34109 Kassel, Germany
[3] Department of Informatics and Media, Brandenburg University of Applied Sciences,
Magdeburger Straße 50, 14770 Brandenburg an der Havel, Germany
{merkel,dittmann}@iti.cs.uni-magdeburg.de,
matthias.pocs@uni-kassel.de, claus.vielhauer@fh-brandenburg.de

Abstract. Innovation in sensors and pattern recognition technologies impacts on our society. Recent improvements in capturing techniques allow for the application of high-resolution contactless image sensors to the lifting of latent fingerprints, potentially replacing classical contact based techniques such as powdering and sticky tape lifting in the future. This technology might help police authorities to identify criminals, but it also poses privacy concerns due to its ability to capture large amounts of fingerprints. Therefore, one has to give special consideration to data privacy management. One way of promoting data privacy could be to determine the age of fingerprints in advance and to not capture fingerprints left at times irrelevant for a crime. Another way could be to determine the age of fingerprints in parallel to the investigation and securely delete fingerprint data as soon as it is found to be of age different to the crime. To this end, we explore the possible future technology of fingerprint age determination and its use for data privacy protection in a repressive application scenario at the crime scene as well as a preventive one at the airport. This will be analyzed from a technical-legal point of view in order to promote legal criteria of the German and European privacy and data protection laws.

Keywords: Data protection, data minimization, fingerprint age determination, privacy by design, digital fingerprint collection, legality of technology.

1 Introduction

Data privacy protection is an essential requirement in many countries for working with personal data [1]. Especially the capturing, storage and processing of latent fingerprints, which is a widely accepted technique in the scope of criminal investigations, is subject to many laws and regulations. In recent years, common fingerprint enhancement and lifting techniques have been extended and might even be replaced

R. Di Pietro et al. (Eds.): DPM 2012 and SETOP 2012, LNCS 7731, pp. 61–74, 2013.
© Springer-Verlag Berlin Heidelberg 2013

in the future by modern contactless optical and non-invasive capturing devices, allowing for higher resolutions and faster, semi-automated fingerprint acquisition [2-3]. Such new techniques impact the practical police work in many different ways. One of the major advances of such new contactless scanners can be seen in the age determination of fingerprints, specifying the time a print has remained on an object before being lifted by a forensic expert. Recent work [4-5] has shown promising tendencies to finally solve this long researched challenge. The method would add very important information to the investigation of crimes, while at the same time offers numerous new possibilities to enhance the privacy protection of fingerprints in daily police work, in comparison to previous manual lifting, storing and processing methods.

In general, police work is divided into two types: **repressive** and **preventive** (see Article 70 of [6]). **Repressive** police work describes the **investigation of committed crimes** and contactless fingerprint lifting techniques might be applied here by determining the age of a fingerprint from a crime scene prior to its complete capture, allowing for a pre-selection of traces. **Preventive** application scenarios are designed to prevent crimes and are represented here using the example of an **airport luggage handling** use case [7]. It proposes the identification of suspicious luggage directly before being loaded onto the aircraft using age determination. If the age of a print is younger than the check-in time of the luggage owner, the print can be considered suspicious and the luggage is investigated in more detail. Contactless fingerprint scanners might allow for the acquisition of such large amounts of prints in the near future and therefore would enable the general application of **preventive** scenarios.

The contribution of this paper can be seen in the following points:

- We investigate the implications of contactless, non-invasive fingerprint age determination to promote data protection laws using the example of Germany and the EU.
- We distinguish between two exemplary use cases, which are a **repressive** crime scene investigation and a **preventive** airport luggage handling scenario [7] and discuss the different implications of such cases.
- We introduce possible methods to use fingerprint age determination for the significant enhancement of data privacy management of latent fingerprints and discuss their limitations.
- We point out where additional laws are required to adjust the legal system to the new technological advances, especially for **preventive** application scenarios.

The remainder of this paper is structured as follows: In section 2, a brief overview over current age estimation proposals and the general potential of such technique in the near future is given, followed by a summary of existing legal aspects of classical fingerprint lifting techniques concerning data privacy (section 3). Section 4 gives an overview over common principles for the work with personal data and the design of new technologies, derived from the German data protection law [8]. Privacy improvements, which might be achieved using age estimation of fingerprints, are suggested and discussed in section 5 and are put into context of the data protection principles of section 4. Section 6 concludes the paper and summarizes subjects of future work.

2   Current Proposals and General Possibilities of Fingerprint Age Determination

The age of a latent fingerprint might be described as the time which has passed from the initial application of the print until its lifting by forensic experts. The determination or at least estimation of such age can provide many benefits to a forensic investigation, such as the determination of the sequence in which certain events took place or the sequencing of overlapped fingerprints [9]. However, most important are its implications to the realization of data protection laws, since the age of a fingerprint provides information whether the print is related to a certain time period of interest (e.g. the time of a crime). Fingerprints laid at other times should not be lifted or identified.

Solving the challenge of determining a fingerprints age is therefore very attractive to forensic investigators since several decades and substantial efforts were made to solve it, such as [10-14]. Despite such efforts, no reliable age estimation schemes could be developed. Main reasons seem to lie in the complex network of influences on the aging process (e.g. sweat composition, environmental impact, different surfaces, application characteristics or scan settings), which lead to a high variability in the aging tendency [4]. Furthermore, the often contact-based lifting techniques (e.g. sticky tape lifting) and pre-treatment with different substances (such as powdering, ninhydrin bathing or cyanoacrylate fuming) often destroy or at least heavily alter the fingerprint in a physical way as well as change its chemical composition. Such methods prevented the creation of time series, which can capture a fingerprint in regular intervals over a certain time period and would enable the systematic investigation of characteristic changes when aging.

In recent years, significant improvements were achieved in the area of non-invasive image sensors, such as surface measurement devices, microscopes or spectroscopes. Such improvements create a new potential for the age determination, since they allow for a systematic investigation of fingerprint changes when aging using time series. Chemical changes are investigated in [15-16] using spectroscopy, complemented by the examination of changes in the fingerprint image contrast using a Chromatic White Light (CWL) sensor [4], leading to a first classification of fingerprints into two well defined time classes. Additional time classes, features and images sensors are also possible and are currently investigated.

Taking into account that the presented conditions are based on first investigations and that many more aging features, image sensors and fusion approaches are currently explored, we assume the following conditions to be possible already or realistic for the near future (but are not yet applied to practical crime scene investigations):

1) The age estimation of latent fingerprints (full, partial or smeared) with the minimum scan settings of a measured area of 4 x 4 mm and a dot distance of 20 μm is already possible to a certain extend [4], leading to a classification accuracy of 70 - 80% for a separation of fingerprints into those younger as or older than five hours. Such settings can depict approximately 9 - 11 fingerprint ridges with a maximum length of about 4 mm and are therefore not sufficient for an

identification of the print, according to dactyloscopic experts from our research partner from the State Police Office. In the near future, such age estimation approach is expected to be applicable to specific, application-dependent time intervals with an increased accuracy (which is unlikely to reach 100%, but provides a certain degree of reliability).

2) The capturing time of a single fingerprint is less than three minutes in [4]. Due to the creation of time series of ten temporal samples, with a time offset of one hour, the total processing time is approximately 10 hours. However, such procedure is not optimized yet and age estimation times of a few minutes up to a few hours are expected in the near future, with the ability of several fingerprints being processed in parallel (according to [4], up to 20 fingerprints can be processed in parallel at this point in time using a single capturing device, if they can be fitted to the measurement table).

3) Fingerprint age estimation was performed in [4] for an indoor crime scene and the fingerprint aging behavior was investigated for ten different surfaces in [4] and [5] (glass, veneer, scissor blade, car door, mobile phone, socket cover, smooth furniture surface, 5 Euro-Cent coin, CD-case and hard disk platter). In the near future, application scenario specific age estimation approaches are expected, determining the age of fingerprints under specific environmental conditions (e.g. indoor vs. outdoor) and for different surface types.

4) Time spans of up to 24 hours were examined in [4] for the age estimation. However, preliminary tests show changes in the fingerprint contrast over at least one year and possibly longer, which might be used in future work to estimate a fingerprints age also for several weeks, month or years.

5) Additional image sensors capturing physical as well as chemical fingerprint traits are currently investigated and are expected to lead to a combined age estimation approach. Consequently, age estimation should not be seen as a sensor specific technique, but rather as independent from the underlying contactless fingerprint scanner.

3   Existing Legal Aspects of Classical Fingerprint Lifting and Processing

This section describes the existing legal aspects of protecting personal data, which apply to all types of fingerprint lifting techniques, from common methods of chemical or physical enhancement and subsequent sticky tape lifting or photographing to modern high-resolution, contactless capturing devices. It furthermore applies to all types of applications, in **repressive** as well as **preventive** scenarios. The specific legal requirements for data protection in the police sector are different from country to country. However, the results presented in this paper for the Federal Republic of Germany are also useful for other European countries since there are common legal traditions in the European Union (EU).

In Germany, the Data Protection Act [8] is the most important law protecting the personality of citizens. Furthermore, article 1(1) and 2(1) of the German constitution [6] proclaim the so-called right to "informational self-determination". Whenever there is a deep impact on the personality of individuals, one has to apply the legal principles of the

Data Protection Act in a strict way. In particular, the Act is divided into three parts: a general part, one for the public sector and one for the private sector. The police is part of the public sector. In its general part and the specific parts the Act defines the principles of data protection. For our assessment, the following principles of the Data Protection Act are relevant: system suitability (§ 4), use limitation (§§ 13 and 14), data security (§ 9), transparency and accountability (§§ 4, 4d - 4g, 6 and 19 - 21), data minimization (§§ 3a and 6a), false hit rate (§§ 3a, 6a and 20) as well as distinction between individuals (§ 3a).

Concerning other European countries, there are similar data protection requirements. The EU has recognized the "right to data protection" in Article 8 of the European Fundamental Rights Charter [17]. There is a European law on this fundamental right planned, which will harmonize the police law in a few years' time. Currently, there is a draft law on data protection in the police sector [18]. This law specifies the same principles as the German Data Protection Act: system suitability (Article 7), use limitation (Article 4(b)), data security (Article 27), transparency and accountability (Articles 10 - 16 and 18), data minimization (Article 19), false hit rate (Articles 4(d), 9 and 19) as well as distinction between individuals (Articles 5 and 6). This law is comparable to the German Data Protection Act and will harmonize the law across the EU. Therefore, the results in this paper do not only apply to Germany, but also to other EU countries.

For fingerprint scanning devices, technology designers have to apply the principles of the data protection laws in a strict way because the devices pose several specific risks for the fundamental rights. Fingerprints contain sensitive data about an individual's health and ethnic origin and they are uniform personal identifiers that can be used to connect several databases. There is a risk of statistic errors when comparing biological characteristics as well as erroneous operation of the fingerprint system by police officers and other operators. Senior police officers could urge parliaments to pass laws to use the system for punishing minor offences or taking measures against non-criminals like witnesses, contact persons, etc. This risk is often referred to as function creep. Apart from that, there is also the risk of procuring and using a scanning system of a producer who only pretends to have applied the data protection principles. There is also the risk of attacks on the fingerprint system which belongs to the field of IT security. Finally, the technology designers need to apply the data protection principles in a strict way to prevent disproportionate follow-up police measures, such as arresting individuals without reasonable suspicion.

Whenever a police uses technology that poses specific risks for fundamental rights, the law requires the legislator to enact a legal basis that gives the police specific instructions on how to use such technology, concretizing the Data Protection Act. In the scope of this paper, we discuss two examples of such regulations for the Federal Republic of Germany. This is sufficient because the specific regulations are of rather legal interest and have only few impact on the technology design. The main impact can be seen in the legal principles outlined earlier, which are comparable to those of other EU countries. The examples of regulations used in this paper are the German Code of Criminal Procedure [19] and the different state police laws of Germany (e.g. [20]), which regulate the collection of personal data. While the federal government of Germany is responsible for the instructions concerning **repressive** police work, the federal states are responsible for the respective **preventive** part. This requires two different types of laws regulating the use of fingerprint scanners, one for its use at the crime scene, and another one for its use at the airport.

For the **repressive** scenario of lifting fingerprints at crime scenes, §§ 163(1) and 161 of the German Code of Criminal Procedure [19] are relevant, which state: "The authorities and officers of police service must explore crimes and give orders [...] to prevent the affair from becoming obscure," respectively, "the public prosecutor has the power [...] to conduct on his own or make authorities and officers of the police service conduct investigations of all kind." However, it is important to mention that the legal basis needs to be specified. §§ 163(1) and 161 do not give specific details about the semi-automated, contactless capture of fingerprints. This is due to the fact that the legislator enacted §§ 163(1) and 161 considering classical, manual methods of fingerprint collection. Hence, it is unclear whether or not §§ 163(1) and 161 are specific legal bases on how to use contactless fingerprint scanners. However, both paragraphs do not only allow, but also require police officers to acquire all information relevant for the investigation of the crime. This applies also to the age of fingerprints, if it provides additional information for solving the crime and if the corresponding evaluation methods exist.

For the specific instructions concerning **preventive** police work, the police laws of the 16 federal states regulate the collection of personal data. For example, the police law of Hesse provides in § 13(1) [20]: "The police authorities may collect personal data to fulfill their tasks if it is necessary to prevent a danger [...]". The use of fingerprint scanners in a **preventive** airport scenario seems to have no legal regulations in place at the moment. It might therefore be necessary in the future to enact police laws concerning the fingerprint collection at airports. Such rules need to be designed very carefully, to be consistent to the constitutional laws. In case of non-conformity, they might be cancelled by constitutional courts.

In order to remove any doubts about the legality of new contactless fingerprint lifting techniques in a **repressive** as well as a **preventive** application, it is significant for technology designers and police authorities to consider the general data protection principles described in the Data Protection Act. For fingerprint scanners, this means that the design of a scanner and the related systems as well as the organization of the police department and the data management should promote such principles.

4   Principles of Data Protection Laws for the Design of Systems Acquiring and Processing Personal Data

As mentioned in the previous section, the data protection laws are relevant for the use of contactless fingerprint scanners and for their legality it is crucial to promote these laws by technology and application design and data privacy management. The data protection laws share common principles, which are specified in the Data Protection Act and are outlined in this section. Such principles apply to **repressive** and **preventive** applications in the same way in respect to German as well as European laws. They will serve as the basis for assessing to what extent the use of age determination might improve the legality of contactless fingerprint scanners used at crime scenes and airports.

System suitability: The first data protection principle is that the system needs to be able to achieve the stated goal, which is, identifying criminals. To do so one has to consider the technical possibility as well as the economic reasonability. Concerning the technical possibility, one has to focus on the actual performance of the fingerprint scanner. This means that the fingerprints have to be available to the police when they need them and to the right police department(s).

Use limitation: Another data protection principle is that the system needs to limit the data use to the stated purpose. This criterion disables the legislator to permit secondary uses of the IT systems procured for the fight against crime. With biological characteristics such as fingerprints there are specific risks of secondary use. On one hand, one can gain health and ethnic data from fingerprints [21]. These types of data are subject to special protection by the law, such as Article 8 of the European Data Protection Directive [1]. On the other hand, the fingerprints can be used as identifiers to connect several databases that are used for different purposes to a personality profile. In this case, the captured data would be used as so-called uniform personal identifier, which is prohibited according to the case law of the German Federal Constitutional Court and is subject to strict regulation of the European data protection law. This means that the fingerprint scanner should prevent fingerprints from being used as uniform personal identifiers and from gaining health and ethnic data from them.

Data security: The system needs to be secured by technological means considering access control and the state of the art of cryptography. This is also a new requirement of Art. 27 of the Directive Proposal for Police Data Protection [18] (it enshrines a list of access controls as legal requirements). This means that the fingerprint system should be secured against attacks and other unauthorized access.

Transparency and accountability: Another data protection principle is transparency and accountability. On one hand, the system needs to be designed in a way that enables courts and supervisory authorities to understand when and which police department used certain data in the past. On the other hand, the system user needs to demonstrate that he has taken measures to ensure compliance with the data protection principles. Furthermore, the user must implement mechanisms for auditors to verify the effectiveness of these measures. It means that the fingerprint scanning system needs to be able to log when and where fingerprints are scanned and who collects them. Furthermore, the system operator needs to be able to demonstrate the source and other information to ensure that the technology design required by the law and its actual realization correspond.

Data minimization and "data frugality": The system has to be designed in a way that unneeded personal data is not collected or is pseudo-/anonymized. This principle of data minimization, more precisely, "data avoidance and data frugality" is laid down in § 3a of the Federal Data Protection Act. This principle removes or at least reduces all the specific risks (of using sensitive data, uniform identifiers, function creep, IT security, and follow-up measures). The principle of data minimization includes the requirement to reduce the number of false hits and to limit the hits or matches to dangerous persons and criminals.

The principle of data frugality obliges the data controller to design and select technology, which is oriented towards the goal of processing no personal data or as little personal data as possible (so far, all fingerprints found at a crime scene are lifted for analysis). In particular, the provision lays down that minimization should be achieved by means of "pseudo-/anonymization as far as this is possible and the effort involved is reasonable in relation to the desired level of protection." According to § 3(6) of the Data Protection Act, anonymization is defined as "changing personal data in a way that they can no longer, or only with a disproportionately large amount of time, costs and work be assigned an identified or identifiable natural person." Although it refers to anonymi-"zation" instead of anonymi-"ty", the provision does not mean that one can only de-personalize data after having them already collected and stored. It is clear that also the collection of personal data falls within the scope of the principle of data frugality. Hence, the goal is also to enable starting a transaction anonymously [22].

False hit rate: As a part of data frugality, the system needs to be designed in a way that false hits are reduced. Hence, people are more likely to be treated as nonsuspects.

Distinction between individuals: As another element of data frugality, the system must distinguish between individuals so that the hits or matches are reduced to dangerous persons and criminals. One has to distinguish between people having committed minor offences and serious crimes, between suspects and nonsuspects as well as between people suspected on the basis of mere assumptions and facts. The police focus is to identify serious criminals and should not expose any other person that is known to the police to follow-up measures.

The principles of data protection promote fundamental rights, in particular, the right to informational self-determination as well as privacy and data protection. In addition, it promotes human dignity if fingerprints are used as uniform identifiers by state authorities for treatment of data subjects as mere "objects"; the special protection of sensitive data (Article 8 Data Protection Directive [1]) such as health and ethnic information contained in fingerprints; as well as the right to travel and the freedom of movement, in case that subjects are tracked and continuously monitored in different places. Finally, they promote property as a fundamental right (in case of confiscation), the right to innocence until proven guilty (if the system or its design suffer from errors), the right to judicial review (in non-transparent systems), and the prohibition of arbitration (in case of unspecified purpose of use).

5   Privacy Improvements Using Fingerprint Age Determination

Using the data protection principles as a benchmark, we discuss in this section to what extent the use of fingerprint age determination might improve the data protection and data privacy management of contactless captured fingerprints in respect to the two defined scenarios. Many legal implications of fingerprint age determination follow directly from the conditions under which age determination schemes operate or might operate in the near future, as described in section 2.

One of the most important advantages of the age determination of fingerprints using contactless scanning devices can be seen in the fact that age determination can be performed without creating the possibility of identification. If the minimum scan settings of a measured area size of 4 x 4 mm and a dot distance of 20 μm as described in section 2 are used, the captured fingerprint images are comprised of approximately 9 - 11 ridge lines, each with a length of a maximum of 4 mm, which is inadequate for identification. Therefore, fingerprint age determination can be seen as a technique not capturing personal data being protected by the Data Protection Act. This creates the possibility of a fingerprint selection prior to its complete capturing and can therefore improve the privacy protection in different ways.

System suitability: Concerning the data protection principle of system suitability, age determination can enhance the suitability of a fingerprint scanning application by providing additional information about the estimated time a fingerprint was left. Such information can be used for a more specific selection of only relevant fingerprints, in a **repressive** application scenario (only fingerprints laid at the approximated time of the crime are of relevance) as well as a **preventive** scenario (only fingerprints laid at suspicious times are of interest, e.g. a fingerprint applied to a piece of luggage after check-in might be suspicious [7]). Furthermore, such a pre-selection of fingerprints supports the economic reasonability, since fewer fingerprints have to be captured in the following detailed scan. A limitation of the age determination might be the required time, which is estimated in section 2 to be a few minutes up to a few hours in the near future. Such capturing time seems to be reasonable for crime scenes, where common enhancement techniques (such as ninhydrine bathing or cyanoacrylate fuming) also require a certain processing time. However, in a **preventive** luggage handling scenario at airports, luggage cannot be scanned for minutes or even hours before being loaded onto an aircraft, requiring very short age estimation times.

Use limitation: The secondary use of scanned fingerprints for other purposes poses a threat for both **repressive** as well as **preventive** application scenarios. Since a fingerprint cannot be identified during age determination, a secondary use is limited to a significant extent. Furthermore, since the captured area size and resolution is smaller than in a complete fingerprint scan, also the extraction of health and ethnic information is significantly limited in comparison to a full captured fingerprint. Several studies, e.g. from Buković et al. [23], Gupta et al. [24] and Sangita et al. [25] have investigated the correlation of specific ridge patterns (such as loop, whorl or arch) to certain diseases, such as ovarian cancer, bronchial asthma or pulmonary tuberculosis. When determining the age of a fingerprint trace, the captured area is in most cases too small to identify the general ridge pattern of the print, effectively preventing the extraction of such health-related information. This is a great advantage in comparison to the lifting of complete fingerprints. It can therefore be concluded that the risk of a secondary use of age determination scans is significantly smaller than in the case of (contactless or contact based) lifting of the full fingerprint. However, the general possibility of a secondary use of captured fingerprints with common as well as modern lifting techniques has not been subject to very detailed investigations so far and therefore remains an issue for future work.

Data security: Data security is a general issue for all personal captured, stored or processed data at police authorities, in **repressive** as well as **preventive** scenarios. Age information of fingerprints is non-identifiable and therefore has an inherent protection against misuse. However, we recommend applying exactly the same security measures used for the capture, storage and processing of all other fingerprint data.

Transparency and accountability: Age determination can be seen as a well suited tool to ensure transparency and accountability, if the accuracy is sufficiently high. For example, in a **repressive** application scenario, a police officer might be required by the technical design of a fingerprint storage database to specify the time interval of relevance to his investigation. Only fingerprint traces left within such time interval will be handed to him. Secure logging might furthermore provide the means for courts or supervisory authorities to understand which fingerprints where used by which police officer and which time intervals were requested. In a **preventive** application at airports, suspicious time periods should be specified in advance and all fingerprints not falling into such time period should automatically be skipped by the capturing device. An exemplary secure log can provide transparency to what time periods are specified as being suspicious.

Data minimization and "data frugality": The most significant advantage of fingerprint age determination can be seen in the realization of the data frugality principle, which is one of the most important principles of data privacy protection. No mechanism can protect fingerprints better than not capturing them. In a **repressive** application, currently all fingerprints found at crime scenes are lifted, investigated and the corresponding people identified. A prior age determination would limit such lifting and identification to people who have been at the crime scene during the time of the crime and can therefore effectively prevent the identification of people not being involved in the crime, even if they have been at the scene (see fig. 1). Such method would pose a major improvement to the realization of the Data Protection Act, since it can prevent the identification and false accusation of people having been at the crime scene but not being involved in the crime, which is a very important issue considering the temporal imprisonment or loss of reputation of such people when falsely accused.

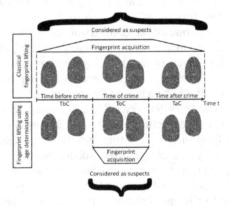

Fig. 1. Data minimization improvements using fingerprint lifting with age determination in comparison to classical fingerprint lifting (prints were generated using SFinGe [26])

The method can be formalized by dividing time into the three disjunctive intervals *TbC* (time before crime), *ToC* (time of crime) and *TaC* (time after crime), where $TbC < ToC < TaC$. During age determination, a latent fingerprint is assigned to a time interval *AoF* $[t_1,t_2|t_1 \leq t_2]$, with a probability of correctness *PoC (AoF [t1,t2])*. For each fingerprint found at the crime scene, the age interval *AoF* of the print is determined. If the intersection of the fingerprint age interval and the time of the crime is not empty (i.e. *AoF* $\cap$ *ToC* $\neq \emptyset$), the full fingerprint needs to be captured and identified, because it is related to the time of the crime. In case the intersection is empty (i.e. $AoF \cap ToC = \emptyset$), the fingerprint has been left before or after the time of the crime and should therefore be discarded. However, the probability of correctness PoC indicates that a certain probability of error PoE exists when determining the age of a fingerprint ($PoE = 1 - PoC$). Therefore, the severity of crime SoC needs to be balanced against the probability of error PoE. In case the crime is of great severity (SoC is high) and the value of PoE exceeds a certain threshold, additional fingerprints might have to be captured as well, to minimize the risk of missing relevant traces.

Lifting fingerprints for **preventive** purposes is a very strongly debated topic. The lifting and identification of the fingerprints of large amounts of people is an ethically questionable process, which is forbidden by the constitution for most cases. Fingerprint age determination can successfully prevent the lifting and identification of large amounts of fingerprints while still allowing for a **preventive** analysis of them. The age determination of large amounts of fingerprints is not critical, since no identification is possible. The age of a fingerprint can then be compared to specific time intervals and fingerprints laid at suspicious times can be further investigated, while all others are not lifted at all. Concerning the introduced luggage handling scenario at airports, fingerprints laid after check-in might be a result of tampering with the luggage and can therefore be considered suspicious. The capturing and further investigation of such fingerprints is legally justified and can be used to effectively prevent crimes.

False hit rate: Fingerprint age determination trivially decreases the false hit rate in a **repressive** as well as a **preventive** application, since many prints can be excluded prior to a full fingerprint scan. However, also the accuracy of the age determination needs to be considered, if fingerprints are excluded from further investigations on the basis of their age. At the moment, the accuracy of the age determination is not yet high enough to be applicable in practice. First results have shown accuracies of 70 – 80% for distinguishing fingerprints into those younger as or older than five hours [4]. However, taking into account that the age determination is a challenge, which has been researched since many decades, the improvements made in recent years are quite remarkable. It is therefore expected that the performance of age estimation schemes will rise significantly in the near future.

Distinction between individuals: Age determination of fingerprints supports the distinction between individuals being at a certain place at the time of a crime (**repressive** scenario) or at a suspicious time (**preventive** scenario) from those being at such places at other points in time. A pre-selection of potential suspects by time is very effective, however, cannot be used alone for identifying dangerous people or to distinguish between minor offences and serious crimes. Therefore, additional information needs to be taken into account, such as the type of object the fingerprint is found on (e.g. a murder weapon vs. a stolen pack of cigarettes in a **repressive** application or a fingerprint on a bag containing weapons vs. a fingerprint on a bag containing daily items). If such additional information indicates a minor offense or even and error in the age estimation, the full fingerprint should not be captured.

From the fact that all of these data protection principles are promoted, it follows that applying age determination also promotes the German Code of Criminal Procedure, which focuses mainly on **repressive** application scenarios. According to the exemplary chosen paragraphs §§ 163(1) and 161, police officers are obliged to "conduct investigations of all kind" to "prevent the affair from becoming obscure". This implies a capture of all important traces without delay, including a fingerprints age. So far, criminal experts decide at the crime scene, which traces have to be captured and which are irrelevant for the investigation. Also, they decide which aspects of the trace are examined, which are often mutually exclusive (e.g. the DNA contained in a fingerprint might be captured, altering the fingerprint and preventing the capture of its ridge pattern). Such selection leads in most cases to a certain loss of information and even errors, which is comparable to abstraction processes in digital forensics (see also [27]). In such case, the forensic expert decides, which information is preferred. With classical acquisition techniques, the age information of fingerprints is an example of such loss, since age estimation is not possible after lifting the print. Using contactless fingerprint scanners, the age of a trace can be performed in addition to lifting the print and therefore extends the amount of information available.

Determining the age of fingerprints prior to their lifting might introduce a delay of a few minutes up to a few hours (see section 2). However, it also allows for a pre-selection, which saves time and resources when lifting prints. Furthermore, classical contact-based enhancement techniques (e.g. ninhydrine bathing or cyanoacrylate fuming) and manual processing require a substantial amount of operational steps and processing time. It is therefore expected for most cases that a future contactless age determination does not take more time than the classical enhancement techniques. In addition to such use of age estimation for a very strong data protection, also adaptive methods might be used, e.g. for large crime scenes with a high amount of fingerprints. In such case, fingerprints might be lifted from the crime scene and processed in the usual manner, while an age determination is performed in parallel. Once prints are determined to be of ages different from the specific time interval under investigation, the fingerprint data is erased immediately in a forensically secure way. Such method would offer a compromise between a maximum data privacy protection and time constraints for large crime scenes.

In case of a **preventive** application, no regulations exist so far. The emerging technology of automated contactless fingerprint acquisition devices enables the **preventive** investigation of large amounts of fingerprints. To avoid misuse of such techniques, new regulations are required in the near future. The legislator has to design these future police laws carefully, to avoid cancellation by the constitutional courts. It is decisive whether or not fingerprint scanning devices have sufficient safeguards for the protection of data privacy in place. Since age determination is such a safeguard, this technology is a factor that can help to justify the use of contactless fingerprint scanner at airports with future police laws.

6   Conclusion and Future Work

In this paper, we proposed the usage of non-invasive fingerprint age determination to improve data privacy management in police work, in respect to a repressive as well as a preventive application scenario. Taking the upcoming use of contactless fingerprint scanners as well as current data protection laws of the Federal Republic of Germany and the EU into account, we summarized legal design requirements for new technology capturing personal data. Proposing and discussing new methods for the privacy-enhanced capture of fingerprints, we showed how contactless new fingerprint scanners can be used for police work while at the same time increasing the data privacy protection by means of age estimation. We have furthermore shown that the use of age determination might even be demanded by the requirement of the law to asses all available information and can be used either prior to lifting fingerprints (maximum privacy protection) or in parallel to the investigation with subsequent deletion of print data being determined as not belonging to the crime (maximum time efficiency).

We conclude that incorporating age estimation approaches into the design of modern fingerprint scanners as well as into forensic procedures improves data privacy management and is decisive for compliance of such devices with the law in repressive application scenarios. We furthermore point out that age estimation improves data privacy management and is decisive for a privacy-conform usage of latent fingerprints in preventive applications. However, almost no regulations exist in this field, requiring an increased attention of the legislative authorities and a design of new laws.

Forensic methods are in the process of significant changes. Contactless fingerprint scanners are about to be implemented in daily police work, requiring additional laws, guidelines and policies. A very important requirement for future work can therefore be seen in the data privacy conform design of such new systems and the inclusion of age estimation schemes into them. Furthermore, laws have to be designed to legitimate and regulate the use of such new devices, especially concerning the emerging possibility of preventive fingerprint acquisition. Concerning age estimation techniques, further improvements of capturing time and accuracy are the most important requirements.

Acknowledgments. The work in this paper has been funded in part by the German Federal Ministry of Education and Science (BMBF) through the Research Programme under Contract No. FKZ: 13N10816, FKZ: 13N10818 and FKZ: 13N10820.

References

1. Directive 95/46/EC of the European Parliament and of the Council on data protection. Official Journal of the European Union L 281, p. 31 (1995)
2. Leich, M., Kiltz, S., Dittmann, J., Vielhauer, C.: Non-destructive forensic latent fingerprint acquisition with chromatic white light sensors. In: Proc. SPIE 7880, 78800S (2011)
3. Crane, N.C., Bartick, E.G., Schwartz Perlman, R., Huffman, S.: Infrared Spectroscopic Imaging for Noninvasive Detection of Latent Fingerprints. Journal of Forensic Science 52(1) (2007)
4. Merkel, R., Gruhn, S., Dittmann, J., Vielhauer, C., Bräutigam, A.: On non-invasive 2D and 3D Chromatic White Light image sensors for age determination of latent fingerprints. Forensic Sci. Int. (2012), http://dx.doi.org/10.1016/j.forsciint.2012.05.001
5. Merkel, R., Bräutigam, A., Kraetzer, C., Dittmann, J., Vielhauer, C.: Evaluation of binary pixel aging curves of latent fingerprint traces for different surfaces using a chromatic white light (CWL) sensor. In: Proceedings of the Thirteenth ACM Multimedia Workshop on Multimedia and Security, pp. 41–50 (2011)
6. The German constitution (Grundgesetz) as amended in the German law gazette (Bundesgesetzblatt), I 944 (2010)

7. Hildebrandt, M., Pocs, M., Dittmann, J., Ulrich, M., Merkel, R., Fries, T.: Privacy Preserving Challenges: New Design Aspects for Latent Fingerprint Detection Systems with Contact-Less Sensors for Future Preventive Applications in Airport Luggage Handling. In: Vielhauer, C., Dittmann, J., Drygajlo, A., Juul, N.C., Fairhurst, M.C. (eds.) BioID 2011. LNCS, vol. 6583, pp. 286–298. Springer, Heidelberg (2011)

8. German Federal Data Protection Act (Bundesdatenschutzgesetz) as amended in the Bundesgesetzblatt I 2814 (2009)

9. Kärgel, R., Giebel, S., Leich, M., Dittmann, J.: Separation and sequence detection of overlapped fingerprints: experiments and first results. In: Proc. SPIE 8189, 81890U (2011)

10. Popa, G., Potorac, R., Preda, N.: Method for Fingerprints Age Determination (May 15, 2012), http://www.rjlm.ro/doc/127849931710-methodforfingerprintsagedetermination.pdf

11. Baniuk, K.: Determination of Age of Fingerprints. Forensic Science International 46, 133–137 (1990)

12. Aehnlich, J.: Altersbestimmung von daktyloskopischen Spuren mit Hilfe der Laser-Fluoreszenzspektroskopie, Diploma Thesis, University of Hannover (2001)

13. Wolstenholme, R., Bradshaw, R., Clench, M.R., Francese, S.: Study of latent fingermarks by matrix-assisted laser desorption/ionisation mass spectrometry imaging of endogenous lipids. Rapid Commun. Mass Spectrom. 23, 3031–3039 (2009)

14. De Paoli, G., Lewis, S.A., Schuette, E.L., Lewis, L.A., Connatser, R.M., Farkas, T.: Photo and Thermal-Degradation Studies of Select Eccrine Fingerprint Constituents. Journal of Forensic Science 55(4), S962–S969 (2010)

15. Antoine, K.M., Mortazavi, S., Miller, A.D., Miller, L.M.: Chemical Differences are Observed in Children's Versus Adults' Latent Fingerprints as a Function of Time. Journal of Forensic Science 55(2) (2010)

16. Williams, D.K., Brown, C.J., Bruker, J.: Characterization of children's latent fingerprint residues by infrared microspectroscopy: Forensic implications. Forensic Science International 206(1), 161–165 (2011)

17. Charter of Fundamental Rights of the European Union, Official Journal of the European Union 2007 C 303, 1 (2007)

18. EU Commission: Proposal for a Directive of the European Parliament and of the Council on data protection in the police sector. COM (2012) 10 final (January 25, 2012)

19. German Code of Criminal Procedure (Strafprozessordnung) as amended in the Bundesgesetzblatt I 3044 (2011)

20. Act of Hesse concerning the Public Security and Order (Hessisches Gesetz über die öffentliche Sicherheit und Ordnung) as amended in the law gazette for acts and ordinances of the state of Hesse (Gesetzes- und Verordnungsblatt) I 14 (2005)

21. Article 29 Working Party on Data Protection (European Board of Data Protection Authorities), Opinion on Biometrics (WP83) no. 3.7 (2003)

22. Roßnagel, A.: Das Gebot der Datenvermeidung und -sparsamkeit als Ansatz wirksamen technikbasierten Persönlichkeitsschutzes? In: Eifert, Hoffmann-Riem (eds.) Innovation, Recht und öffentliche Kommunikation, Duncker und Humblot, p. 51 (2011)

23. Buković, D., Persec, Z., Buković, N., Martinac, P.: Qualitative dermatoglyphic traits in ovarian cancer patients: a case-control study. Coll. Antropol. 23(2), 641–644 (1999)

24. Gupta, U.K., Prakash, S.: Dermatoglyphics: a study of finger tip patterns in bronchial asthma and its genetic disposition. Kathmandu University Medical Journal (KUMJ) 1(4), 267–271 (2003)

25. Babu, S.S., Powar, B.P., Khare, O.N.: Palmar Dermatoglyphics in Pulmonary Tuberculosis. J. Anat. Soc. India 54(2), 1–9 (2005)

26. Cappelli, R.: Synthetic fingerprint generation. In: Maltoni, D., Maio, D., Jain, A.K., Prabhakar, S. (eds.) Handbook of Fingerprint Recognition, 2nd edn. Springer (2009)

27. Carrier, B.: Defining Digital Forensic Examination and Analysis Tools Using Abstraction Layers. International Journal of Digital Evidence 1(4), 1–12 (2003)

Differential Privacy in Tripartite Interaction: A Case Study with Linguistic Minorities in Canada

Arnaud Casteigts[1,3], Marie-Hélène Chomienne[1], Louise Bouchard[2], and Guy-Vincent Jourdan[3]

[1] Institut de Recherche de l'Hôpital Montfort, Ottawa
[2] Institute of Population Health, University of Ottawa
[3] School of Electrical Engineering and Computer Science, University of Ottawa

Abstract. This paper relates our venture to solve a real-world problem about official language minorities in Canada. The goal was to enable a form of linkage between *health* data (hosted at ICES – a *provincial* agency) and *language* data from the 2006 census (hosted at Statistics Canada – a *federal* agency) despite a seemingly impossible set of legal constraints. The long-term goal for health researchers is to understand health data according to the linguistic variable, shown to be a health determinant. We first suggested a pattern of tripartite interaction that, by design, prevents collection of residual information by a potential adversary. The suggestion was quickly set aside by Statistics Canada based on the risk of collusion an adversary could exploit among these entities. Our second suggestion was more involved; it consisted in adapting differential privacy mechanisms to the tripartite scheme so as to control the level of leakage in case of collusion. While not being rejected and even receiving enthousiastic interest *per se*, the solution was considered an option only if other simpler (but also less promising) alternatives are first, and methodically ruled out.

1 Introduction

1.1 The Context

Research in population health consists in studying the impact of various factors (*determinants*) on health, with the long-term objective of yielding better policies, programs, and services. Determinants of health are many, and researchers of Official Language Minority Communities (OLMCs) focus specifically on those related to speaking an official language in a minority context, such as English in Quebec, or French in the rest of Canada. (The setting for our study is the case of Francophone minorities in Ontario where English is the predominant official language.) Investigations of this type require, at the very minimum, the possibility of associating health data to linguistic information, whether at an individual or community level. Unfortunately, the largest health databases in Ontario, held at the Institute for Clinical Evaluative Sciences (ICES), do not include a linguistic variable to date.

R. Di Pietro et al. (Eds.): DPM 2012 and SETOP 2012, LNCS 7731, pp. 75–88, 2013.

High-quality language variables from the 2006 Census exist at Statistics Canada (SC). Linking to the Census variables in the context of a punctual study is possible, and has already been done in Manitoba [1], but every such operation needs to satisfy a prescribed review and approval process [2]; it must also take place over a limited time, and requires to move the external data to be linked (health data, in our case) from its original source to SC, which may not be achievable repeatedly.

We are interested in finding ways to exploit linguistic data from the 2006 Census on a regular and automated basis, by enabling its linkage to ICES health data in a dynamic way. It must be clear that we do not consider here a traditional type of linkage, in which data from both parts are matched to produce a somewhat larger amount of information of an individual nature (whether nominatively or anonymously). The linkage we consider is intrinsically transient and aggregated: it consists in allowing ICES to learn interactively how many Francophones are present in a given sample of individuals. This simple operation, referred to as a *count query*, can reveal a powerful building block to answer more complex questions about OLMCs, as we will see. Count queries are actually a particular type of *tabulation*, an operation already practiced at SC but that requires a manual process of verification. Turning it into something automated poses a number of challenges that we address here. A preliminary version of this paper also appeared in a technical report by the same authors [3].

We are concerned with ensuring privacy for both health and linguistic data. We suggested two possible mechanisms to enable dynamic count queries. The first consisted in a circular workflow between the three involved entities: health researchers, ICES, and SC. The workflow is initiated by the researcher through the submission of health criteria to ICES. A representative sample of individuals matching these criteria is then generated and sent to SC, which performs the count query. The result of the query is finally returned to the researcher. The privacy in this mechanism comes from the fact that the researcher does not know the sample details, SC does not know the health criteria that were used to generate that sample, and ICES does not know the final answer. This however assumes that no additional exchange of information occurs between the entities (no collusion). In particular, the assumption that ICES and the health researchers do not collude was rejected by SC, which considers by policy anything external as one and a single entity.

The second solution we proposed strives to prevent colluded attacks by means of adding noise to the queries answers. We found basic techniques in early literature on differential privacy [4, 5, 6, 7, 8, 9, 10, 11] that fitted well our needs (more recent works have been done, but these seminal papers essentially contained all we needed). Differential privacy is concerned with understanding the precise impact of adding noise in privacy data analysis. We adapted these results to characterize what leakage is precisely at play in our scenario, and what parameters are involved in the tradeoff between leakage and utility. These results allowed us to make the point that using census data was technically feasible, which was well received by the SC establishment (and the subject of a talk we gave at their annual event: the *Health Data Users Conference 2011*). Of particular interest to them was the genericity of the approach and its potential to enrich provincial health databases more systematically with the range of federally available census data. After a short preamble introducing the main assumptions and basic problem, this paper describes both solutions and their applicability.

1.2   Assumptions

For the sake of clarity, we will make three assumptions. These assumptions will be used recurrently in the document, and relaxed (or discussed) in Section 4. They are:

1. The language of an individual can be fully described by a Boolean value {*Franco, Anglo*}. (This over-simplistic view is erroneous, since language is a *multi-dimensional* variable.)
2. The census data comprises this variable relative to each individual. (In fact, the unit of census is the *household*, not the individual.)
3. It is possible to generate, from the ICES database, a representative sample of individuals matching a given set of health criteria. (From our discussions with ICES representatives, this seems to be a fair assumption.)

1.3   Count Queries

Given a sample of individuals s, and a property p, a *count query* $q(s, p)$ consists of counting the number of individuals in s that satisfy p. We consider the basic count query illustrated on Figure 1.

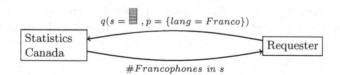

Fig. 1. A basic count query

As such, a sample of individuals is sent to SC, and SC answers back with the number of Francophones in that sample. To illustrate the potential of this simple query, let us consider the following questions:

1. In Ontario, what is the average angioplasty rate among Francophones? (vs. Anglophones)
2. In Ontario, what is the hospital utilization rate for 65+ seniors with type-2 diabetes? (Francophones vs. Anglophones)

As far as *language* is concerned, the use of count queries can answer these questions. In the first case, ICES would generate a representative sample of individuals having undergone angioplasty, then ask SC for a count query in that sample. By normalizing the resulting answer over the more general ratio of Francophones in Ontario (which is known), one can answer the initial question. We can apply a variation of this method to the second example, by using several samples in various ranges of utilization rates by 65+ diabetic patients. Hence, a single mechanism (count query) on a single variable (language) seems sufficient – as far as SC is concerned – to answer a variety of OLMC-related questions.

The problem: A malicious use of count queries, if unsupervised, could make it possible to identify the language of a given individual (say, Madame x). Consider the following attack: making a query with a sample s_1 that does not contain x; then making a second query with the same sample, plus x (see Figure 2). Obviously, if $answer(s_2) > answer(s_1)$, then Madame x is Francophone.

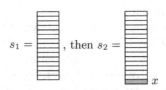

Fig. 2. Identifying the language of an individual by successive queries (basic example)

Even though language is supposedly not as 'sensitive' as other classes of information (e.g. health or income), SC's policy in regard of residual information is absolutely strict. Solutions to this problem are not trivial, even though one may think it suffices to prevent *this* particular scenario. More complex adversarial strategies could actually be designed. Our first solution avoids the problem by means of dataflow itself; while the second acknowledges the risk and characterizes what tradeoff is at play between leakage and utility with the addition of noise.

2   First Mechanism: Tripartite Interaction

The first (and simplest) mechanism aims at providing guaranties at the data workflow level. It consists of a *tripartite* interaction between researchers, ICES, and SC; each entity obtaining and contributing only the minimal amount of information required to carry out the count query. The workflow is depicted on Figure 3, and can be summarized in three chronological steps:

1. Researchers issue a set of criteria related to a research question (e.g., angioplasty rates, or hospital utilization rate in a 65+ type 2 diabetes population);
2. ICES generates a sample of individuals responding to the criteria and sends it directly to SC;
3. SC executes the language query on the generated sample, and answers directly to the researchers.

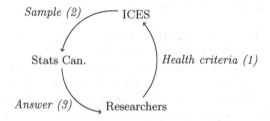

Fig. 3. Privacy by means of tripartite interaction

This scheme protects privacy by combining the three following facts:

1. SC does not know what health criteria the sample is associated with;
2. Health researchers do not know what sample is generated;
3. ICES does not know the result of the language query.

Privacy of ICES health data results from statements 1 and 2, whose combination implies that ICES remains at all times the only entity capable of associating individuals with the queried health criteria. Similarly, the combination of statements 2 and 3 implies that SC remains the only entity capable of associating a sample of individual with the number of Francophones within; such an association being necessary to collect residual information (and thus perform attacks like the one in Figure 2).

3   Second Mechanism: Noisy Count Queries

The first mechanism having been set aside by SC due to the possibility of identifying an individual's language if ICES and the health researchers collude as a single entity, we have proposed a more elaborate mechanism whereby random noise is added to the answers, as illustrated on Figure 4.

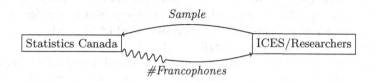

Fig. 4. Noisy count queries

As we will see in this section, this mechanism involves the interplay between three parameters: 1) the magnitude of the noise, 2) the level of statistical leakage tolerated by SC, and 3) the number of queries that can be performed (before shutting down the service). We have characterized this interplay mathematically, based on seminal results on differential privacy.

3.1   Overview of the Principle

What makes possible an attack like that of Figure 2 on page 78, and more generally the accumulation of residual information on individuals, is that the presence
or absence of these individuals inside the sample does impact the answer. Suppose the exact answers for s_1 and s_2 are respectively 586 and 587 (*i.e.*, Madame
x is Francophone) and consider adding or removing a small random number to
the answer before returning it – we call it *perturbing* the answer with some *noise*.
The resulting answers for s_1 and s_2 may be for example 589 and 584, or 583 and
587, or 585 and 585. Clearly, these answers do not leak Madame x's language,
and still, they are meaningful to a researcher.

There exist different types of noise, the most common of which are binomial,
Gaussian, or Laplacian noises (named after the distributions from which the
random number is drawn). As we will see, Laplacian noise has good properties
that makes it an appropriate choice in our case. We consider perturbing the
answer by adding a random number drawn from a Laplace distribution (see
the example on Figure 5). This distribution can be considered at various *scales*,
depending on how sharp or flat the probabilities are concentrated around the
true result.

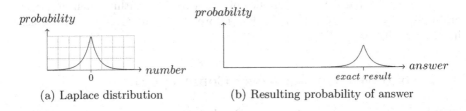

(a) Laplace distribution   (b) Resulting probability of answer

Fig. 5. Addition of Laplacian noise

Intuitively, performing a small number of *noisy queries* will not leak much
individual information, whereas repeating a similar operation many times could
eventually leak something substantial. In fact, *every query does leak a small
amount of statistical information*, the quantity of which depends on the noise
magnitude (scale of the Laplace distribution).

Consider again the example with s_1 and s_2, and two different scenarios, where
noise is added according to a small scale or a large scale, respectively. The
resulting probabilities of answers are represented on Figure 6. In a worst-case
scenario, assume the requester already knows the correct answer for s_1, and is
querying the system with s_2. It eventually obtains a random answer, say n.

Figure 6 shows intuitively how the leakage depends on the noise scale. On the
left, with an arbitrary small scale, answer n is approximately 6 times more likely
if Madame x is Francophone. Thus, obtaining answer n indirectly implies that
Madame x has ∼85.7 % chances to be Francophone. With the larger scale, on the
right, answer n is about 1.3 more likely to occur if Madame x is Francophone,

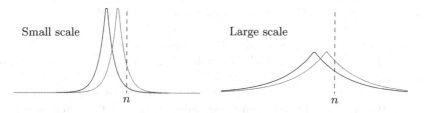

Fig. 6. Different magnitudes of noise. *The black and red curves in each picture represent the probability of answer if Madame x is non-Francophone or Francophone, respectively. The vertical bar represents a possible (and arbitrary) answer n.*

inducing "only" a belief of ∼56.5 % that she is Francophone. A convenient property of Laplacian noises is that the ratio between both curves does not depend on the exact position of n. If you choose n further right, zoom in and measure again the ratio, it remains the same. The left side of the curves behaves symmetrically; as for the middle section between both peaks, it exhibits a varying ratio, but its value necessarily remains smaller than those on the right and left sides.

It is therefore possible to *bound* the amount of leakage such a query induces by choosing a desired noise magnitude. Now, one should keep in mind that while larger magnitudes of noise mean safer data, they also mean less accurate answers to the researchers. There is actually a tripartite tradeoff between *noise, utility,* and the *number of queries* that the system can hold.

3.2   Detailed Principle

Private data analysis research is at the confluence of cryptology, statistics, and database systems. It focuses on statistical exploitation of privately held data by means of dedicated mechanisms. Adding noise to a query is one of these mechanisms, referred to as *output perturbation*. This topic has seen a resurgence of interest in the past five years, mainly due to a conceptual shift in the definition of privacy.

Differential privacy: Access to a statistical database should not enable one to learn anything about an individual, given that its data is in [the tested sample], that could not be learnt otherwise.

This definition should be understood as follows. Consider that we know that 1) Madame x underwent an angioplasty, and 2) 60 % of angioplasty patients are Francophones (from a count query at SC). The subsequent belief that Madame x has 60 % chances of being a Francophone should *not* be considered as a leakage over Madame x's language, because the same belief could have been inferred with or without her being in the tested sample. (Such information is precisely what OLMC researchers attempt to learn.)

Based on this definition, a new line of research was developed [4, 5, 6, 7, 8] around the question of how to limit the amount of information one can learn – *leakage* – about a specific individual that cannot be learned by means of an encompassing sample. The neighbor-sample setting discussed previously represents a worst-case scenario in this regard because the difference between both outputs can be attributed to a single individual; the leakage generated in this setting is therefore considered as an *upper bound* on the risk the database is more generally exposed to.

Relation between Noise and Leakage. Let us first imagine that *only one* query is performed over the whole lifetime of the system. (The extension to multiple queries is rather straightforward and discussed in a second step.) The main result from the field of differential privacy is to teach us how to generate the noise so as to observe a desired bound on the leakage, assuming this bound is expressed using the 'neighbor-sample' setting. Concretely, once this bound (let us note it *param*) is decided upon, differential privacy tells us how to generate the noise so as to ensure that

$$\frac{P[answer(s_1) = n]}{P[answer(s_2) = n]} \leq param \tag{1}$$

for any neighbor samples s_1, s_2 and any possible answer n. The scale of the noise is then determined based on *param* and on the *sensitivity* of the considered query; in our case, a *count* query. (The differential privacy framework is very general and applies to other types of queries; we will discuss some of them later in this document.)

Sensitivity: The sensitivity of a query, noted Δq, is defined as the maximal difference in output that two *neighbor* samples can induce. Two neighbor samples in our case cannot induce a difference larger than 1; thus, the sensitivity of count queries is 1. Note that the sensitivity does not depend on the size of the sample. This may appear counter-intuitive, but is actually consistent with generating the noise irrespective of the sample size.

The formula: The main result from [8], subsequently simplified in [4], tells us that differential privacy is guaranteed with a given leakage bound '*param*' if the noise added to each answer is generated according to a Laplace distribution of scale

$$b = (\Delta q)/log(param) \tag{2}$$

This is usually written $Noise \sim Lap(0, b)$, where the first parameter simply indicates that the noise will be *centered* on the true result.

Number of queries: This formula composes very well in the case of a sequence of queries. Indeed, the above papers tell us that, in order to maintain the same level of leakage for a sequence of queries, it suffices to generate the noise as if that sequence was a *single* query whose sensitivity is the count of all the sensitivities. When all queries are of a same type, this comes to considering the scale

$$b = (\#q\Delta q)/log(param), \tag{3}$$

where $\#q$ is the number of queries in the sequence and Δq is the sensitivity of every individual query. A convenient consequence is that the database holder can think of choosing *'param'* irrespective of the number of queries.

Choosing the Leakage Parameter. A minimum of leakage is necessary for utility. If for instance $param = 1$, which implies that the probability of answer must be exactly the same for any neighbor samples s_1 and s_2, the problem that arises is that any *non*-neighbor pair of samples can be indirectly connected through a *chain* of neighbor samples. By transitivity, choosing $param = 1$ therefore implies that the sample has no impact on the answer, which is nonsense. How to choose *param* is context-specific, and generally not discussed in the above papers. We explore this question in the context of language queries at Statistics Canada.

Belief: From the point of view of SC, the easiest way to formulate an 'acceptable' level of leakage is to specify the maximal belief allowed on the language of an individual. Say, for example, that this limit is 80 % (*i.e.,* we should never believe that Madame x has more than 80 % chances to be Francophone or Anglophone).

Worst case: We are interested in determining what value of *param* should be chosen under the worst possible assumptions (mostly unrealistic). These assumptions are:

1. The adversary has no interest in health research; its only purpose is to learn Madame x's language.
2. The adversary has sufficient access in order to waste *all* the 'capital' of queries offered by SC in that sole purpose.
3. The adversary is able to build samples in which the language of each individual but Madame x is known.
4. SC applies no filter on the queries.

Consider the same attack scenario as discussed in Section 3.1, based on two neighbor samples s_1 and s_2 (the second being equal to the first, plus Madame x). Because of point 3, the adversary already knows the *exact* answer for s_1, and can therefore use all the credit of queries to play and replay s_2. Assume it eventually gets a final answer n. Whether n corresponds to an average, a count, or any other combination of all the answers does not matter: differential privacy tells us that this answer cannot be *param* times more likely for s_2 than for s_1, which is the only thing that matters here.

Three cases are considered, depending on the position of n with respect to the two probability peaks: if n is on the right of the right peak, then Madame x is *param* more likely to be Francophone than non-Francophone; and symmetrically, if n is on the left of the left peak, she is *param* more likely to be Anglophone. In the middle section, she could be up to *param* more likely – but not more, as already discussed – to be either. Let us assume that n is on the right of the right peak, while keeping in mind that the following reasonning applies symmetrically. This implies that

$$\frac{P[x \ is \ Francophone]}{P[x \ is \ not \ Francophone]} \leq param$$

$$\implies \frac{P[x \ is \ Francophone]}{1 - P[x \ is \ Francophone]} \leq param$$

$$\cdots$$

$$\implies P[x \ is \ Francophone] \leq param/(1 + param) \tag{4}$$

This formula can be used to decide what value of *param* corresponds to the maximal belief allowed by policy; in the case of our 80%-example above, this corresponds to *param* = 4. We now combine Equations 3 and 4 to represent the 3D tradeoff between maximal belief, noise scale, and number of queries allowed. A meaningful cut of this volume is shown on Figure 7(a).

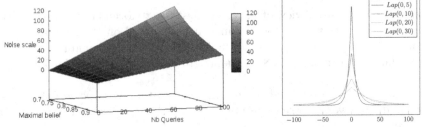

(a) Tradeoff between noise scale, number of queries, and maximal belief (multiply by 100 for percentage).

(b) Examples of noise scales.

Fig. 7. Choice of parameters

The right picture (Figure 7(b)) represents several examples of noise scales. Essentially, it gives the intuition that the precision of an answer deteriorates quickly with the scale parameter. How this affects the quality of the results for a researcher depends on how large the samples are. If samples are large (say, larger than 10000), then a scale of 30, or even 50, may not be a problem. If, on the other hand, the samples sizes are in the order of 1000, then any scale larger than 20 or 30 will induce meaningless answers. (This also depends on the specific question investigated and how deep it involves the language determinant.)

To close this illustrative discussion, let us consider that researchers require a scale no larger than 30, and SC tolerates a maximal belief of 80%, the tradeoff on Figure 7(a) tells us that up to ~50 queries are still possible. This is not a lot, but keep in mind that this tradeoff represents a totally unrealistic worst-case scenario, where a single adversary can (and decides to) play *all* the credit of queries on a *single* sample, in which the language of *all* individuals but Madame x's is already known.

3.3   Discussion

What could be the consequences of relaxing some of the worst-case assumptions listed above? A first observation is that in our case, the researchers do not generate the samples directly; they do it through health criteria that are submitted to ICES (e.g. Figure 3), and the content of these samples is not known to the researchers. This implies that Assumption 3 is mostly unrealistic, and a given noisy answer will actually correspond to possibly more than two exact results. Further mathematical investigations are required to understand these implications precisely, but we can reasonably think that it would drastically lower the leakage that a query can possibly generate.

Another important aspect is to determine whether SC considers the couple ICES/researchers to be itself the adversary, or to be the potential victim of an external adversary. Put differently, does SC fear a direct misuse of the system, or a leak in data resulting from a normal-use? This point is crucial because the samples played in the context of a normal use are likely to generate much less leakage (intuitively, to the extent of a different order of magnitude).

As a third observation, Statistics Canada could easily filtrate the queries (Assumption 4) to prevent large intersection between the samples, and thereby drastically reduce the potential leakage of query combinations. Again, further mathematical investigation could be appropriate to explore, e.g., the correspondance between the size of intersection and the leakage. We believe that although difficult in the general case, this type of characterization remains reasonably feasible in the particular case of language-based count queries. We will contribute towards this direction if the option is concretely considered.

In regards to all these considerations, it is not senseless to believe that the number of possible count queries could actually jump to several thousands, while keeping the leakage below any reasonable level, *e.g.,* much lower than a belief of 80 %. If unfortunately these somewhat optimistic observations are not considered by the involved players (desiring to stick to the worst-case model), then there will still be a way to satisfy all the parts. The solution would consist in deploying a *non*-bounded service, in which the cumulated leakage is progressively computed as the queries are performed, and the service is shutdown when the leakage has reached a given threshold.

4   Relaxing the Three Initial Assumptions

Language: We assumed heretofore that the language of an individual could be described by a boolean value {*Franco, Anglo*}. Language is actually more subtle and requires looking at several aspects. In particular, the census data at SC includes the following variables: Mother tongue (for 100 % of the population); Knowledge of official languages, Knowledge of non-official languages, First official language spoken, Language spoken at home, and Language of work (for 20 % of the population). Also, some of these variables may include other options than French and English, as well as a possible combination of several languages. It is clear that a mere *count query* cannot precisely render the ratio of "Francophones" in a given sample; at the most it could for example count the number of persons who report French as mother tongue and *not* English (the census form allows to report several mother tongues). Fortunately, the differential privacy framework can easily be applied to more complex queries such as *histograms*, at the price of a slightly higher sensitivity per query [4].

Linkage technicalities: So far, we have assumed that a correspondence was *technically* feasible between an individual and its language variables at Statistics Canada. In fact, the unit of census is not the individual, but the *household*. Both the short-form and the long-form census comprise a nominative field, but this field is apparently optional and is known to contain, occasionally, some exotic answers like 'Mickey Mouse'. Three options are possible here: 1) Assume that the persons living in a same household share similar language profiles, and then build the query samples based on postal addresses; 2) Rely on the cleaning operation that is currently performed on the census data at Statistics Canada, and which recently allowed to reach the level of 15 % of records linkable nominatively (all from the long-form subset); or 3) Set up a complementary linkage, housed at SC, between the census data and the minimal amount of administrative data allowing to associate insurance numbers with the corresponding census records. (Note that this represents only a subset of what was done for Manitoba as part of a larger linkage including health data directly at SC [1].)

Generation of the samples at ICES: Health information is highly-sensitive, and ICES has a strong policy of confidentiality in this regard (see [12]). Concretely, the database held at ICES is sanitized by replacing all nominative information by anonymous identifiers. Whether these identifiers can technically and lawfully be reversed to the original information is a question we are starting to investigate. It is likely that ICES maintains somewhere a private table with such associations. Thus, we believe that it is at least *technically* feasible. Such an operation should however be considered with utmost care. The feasibility also depends on what level of trust ICES grants to SC, even though SC does not need to know what health data is associated with a query (this is actually one of the advantages of the proposed mechanism). If need be, the body of research on cryptography techniques can be explored and leveraged. For instance, recent encryption methods have been proposed for the specific problem of querying databases using confidential inputs and criteria [13], that is in our case, preventing SC to learn what sample a given query is about.

5   Concluding Remarks

While not being rejected and even receiving enthousiastic interest *per se*, our second solution based on differential privacy was judged too difficult to deploy in the short term. Since other options exist that involve different (though less accurate) linguistic data, we were advised to explore these alternatives first and consider our solution only once the quality of these alternatives is shown insufficient for OLMC studies. In particular, efforts are being carried out at ICES to receive linguistic information from Ontario's Ministry Of Health And Long-Term Care (MOHLTC). Unfortunately, this information corresponds to the language individuals select for correspondence with the Ministry, which has potential for several biases and is not considered as reliable by OLMC researchers (in addition to being unidimensional). We are currently running an independent project to assess the quality of this variable, which, in case of negative results, will justify the deployment of stronger solutions like the one proposed here.

Acknowledgments. We are grateful to a number of persons that helped (and are still helping) us in this study. In particular, we want to thank Mariette Chartier, professor at the University of Manitoba, for her insightful comments and for sharing feedback on Manitoba experiments; Simone Dahrouge, scientist at C.T. Lamont primary health care center, for valuable information on ICES protocols and databases; Richard Trudeau, head of the health division at SC, for all the information on Statistics Canada rules and for mentioning the existence of tabulations; Michael Wolfson, formerly assistant chief statistician at SC (now professor at the University of Ottawa), for clarifying SC's point of view regarding the uniqueness of the ICES/researchers entity; Doug Manuel, Adjunct Scientist at ICES, for information on anonymization of health data; and Jean-Marie Berthelot, VP of Programs at the Canadian Institute for Health Information, for considerable insights about the diversity of parameters to take into account, and the possibly larger scope of this work. Finally, this study was made possible thanks to the financial support of the Ontarian Ministry of Health and Long-Term Care (through the AHRNI initiative and the RRASFO network), and the *Institut de Recherche de l'Hôpital Montfort*.

References

1. Houle, C., Berthelot, J.M., David, P., Wolfson, M.C., Mustard, C., Roos, L.: Matching census database and Manitoba health care files. In: Proc. of International Workshop on Record Linkage Techniques, p. 305. National Academies (1997)
2. Statistics Canada Website. Policy on record linkage (fetched September 2010), `http://www.statcan.gc.ca/record-enregistrement/policy4-1-politique4-1-eng.html`
3. Casteigts, A., Chomienne, M.-H., Bouchard, L., Jourdan, G.-V.: Enabling Dynamic Linkage of Linguistic Census Data at Statistics Canada. Institut de Recherche de l'Hôpital Montfort, Technical report (March 2011)
4. Dwork, C., McSherry, F., Nissim, K., Smith, A.: Calibrating Noise to Sensitivity in Private Data Analysis. In: Halevi, S., Rabin, T. (eds.) TCC 2006. LNCS, vol. 3876, pp. 265–284. Springer, Heidelberg (2006)
5. Nissim, K., Raskhodnikova, S., Smith, A.: Smooth sensitivity and sampling in private data analysis. In: Proc. of 39th ACM Symposium on Theory of Computing (STOC), pp. 75–84 (2007)
6. Dwork, C.: Ask a Better Question, Get a Better Answer – A New Approach to Private Data Analysis. In: Schwentick, T., Suciu, D. (eds.) ICDT 2007. LNCS, vol. 4353, pp. 18–27. Springer, Heidelberg (2006)

7. Dwork, C., Nissim, K.: Privacy-Preserving Datamining on Vertically Partitioned Databases. In: Franklin, M. (ed.) CRYPTO 2004. LNCS, vol. 3152, pp. 528–544. Springer, Heidelberg (2004)
8. Blum, A., Dwork, C., McSherry, F., Nissim, K.: Practical privacy: the SuLQ framework. In: Proc. of ACM Symposium on Principles of Database Systems (PODS), pp. 128–138 (2005)
9. Hardt, M., Talwar, K.: On the geometry of differential privacy. In: Proc. of the 42nd ACM Symposium on Theory of Computing (STOC), pp. 705–714 (2010)
10. Smith, A.: Privacy-preserving statistical estimation with optimal convergence rates. In: Proc. of the 43rd ACM Symposium on Theory of Computing (STOC), pp. 813–822 (2011)
11. Kifer, D., Machanavajjhala, A.: No free lunch in data privacy. In: Proc. of the 2011 Intl. Conf. on Management of Data, pp. 193–204 (2011)
12. Privacy at ICES (fetched March 2011), http://ices.queensu.ca/privacy.html
13. Stolfo, S.J., Tsudik, G. (eds.): IEEE Security & Privacy Magazine, SI on Privacy-Preserving Sharing of Sensitive Information. IEEE Computer Society (July-August 2010)

EsPRESSo: Efficient Privacy-Preserving Evaluation of Sample Set Similarity

Carlo Blundo[1], Emiliano De Cristofaro[2], and Paolo Gasti[3]

[1] Università di Salerno, Italy
[2] PARC
[3] UC Irvine

Abstract. In today's digital society, electronic information is increasingly shared among different entities, and decisions are made based on common attributes. To address associated privacy concerns, the research community has begun to develop cryptographic techniques for controlled (privacy-preserving) information sharing. One interesting open problem involves two mutually distrustful parties that need to assess the *similarity* of their information sets, but cannot disclose their actual content. This paper presents the first efficient and provably-secure construction for privacy-preserving evaluation of sample set similarity, measured as the *Jaccard* similarity index. We present two protocols: the first securely computes the Jaccard index of two sets, the second approximates it, using MinHash techniques, with lower costs. We show that our novel protocols are attractive in many compelling applications, including document similarity, biometric authentication, genetic tests, multimedia file similarity. Finally, we demonstrate that our constructions are appreciably more efficient than prior work.

1 Introduction

The availability of electronic information is increasingly essential to the functioning of our communities and, in numerous circumstances, data needs to be shared between parties without complete mutual trust. This naturally raises commensurate privacy concerns with respect to the disclosure, and long-term safety, of sensitive contents. One interesting problem occurs whenever two or more entities need to evaluate the similarity of their information, but are reluctant to disclose data wholesale. This task faces three main technical challenges: (1) how to identify a meaningful metric to estimate similarity, (2) how to compute a measure of it such that no private information is revealed during the process, and (3) how to do so efficiently. We denote this problem as *Privacy-preserving Evaluation of Sample Set Similarity* and we motivate it below, vis-à-vis a few relevant applications.

Document Similarity: Two parties need to estimate the similarity of their documents (or collections thereof) – in many settings, documents contain sensitive information and parties may be unwilling, or simply forbidden, to reveal their content. For instance, program chairs of a conference may want to verify that none of submitted papers is also under review in other conferences or journals, but, naturally, they are not allowed to disclose papers in submission. Likewise, two law enforcement authorities (e.g., the FBI and the local police), or two investigation teams with different clearance levels,

R. Di Pietro et al. (Eds.): DPM 2012 and SETOP 2012, LNCS 7731, pp. 89–103, 2013.
© Springer-Verlag Berlin Heidelberg 2013

might need to share documents pertaining suspect terrorists, but they can do so only conditioned upon a clear indication that content is relevant to the same investigation.

Iris Matching: Biometric identification and authentication are increasingly used due to fast and inexpensive devices that can extract biometric information from a multitude of sources, e.g., voice, fingerprints, iris, and so on. Clearly, given its utmost sensitivity, biometric data must be protected from arbitrary disclosure. Consider, for instance, an agency that needs to determine whether a given biometric appears on a government watch-list. As agencies may have different clearance levels, privacy of biometric's owner needs to be preserved if no matches are found, but, at the same time, unrestricted access to the watch-list cannot be granted.

Genetic Paternity/Ancestry Testing: Advances in DNA sequencing technologies will soon yield ubiquitous and low-cost full sequencing of human genomes [9]. This will stimulate the deployment of algorithms that perform, *in computation*, various genomic tests, such as genetic *paternity* and *ancestry* testing. Since individuals tied by parent-child or ancestry relationships carry almost identical genomes, an attractive technique to establish such ties is to measure the genomes' similarity. However, it is well-known that (human) genomic information is extremely sensitive, as a genome not only uniquely identifies an individual, but it also reveals information about, e.g., ethnic heritage, disease predispositions, and many other phenotypic traits [12].

Multimedia File Similarity: Digital media, e.g., images, audio, video, are increasingly relevant in today's computing ecosystems. Consider two parties that wish to evaluate similarity of their media files, e.g., for plagiarism detection: sensitivity of possibly unreleased material (or copyright issues) may prevent parties from revealing actual contents.

All examples above exhibit some common features: neither party can reveal its information in its entirety. What they are willing to reveal is limited to a metric that assesses their similarity. This paper presents the design of efficient cryptographic techniques for privacy-preserving evaluation of sample set similarity. Such techniques do not only appeal to examples above, but to any setting where parties need to evaluate similarity of sets, independently of their nature. It is relevant to a wide spectrum of applications, for instance, in the context of privacy-preserving sharing of information and/or recommender systems, e.g., to privately assess similarity of social network profiles, social interests, network traces, attack logs, healthcare information, and so on.

1.1   Technical Roadmap and Contributions

Our first step is to identify a *metric* for effectively evaluating similarity of sample sets. While several measures have been proposed, such as, cosine similarity (for vectors), Hamming and Levenshtein distances (for strings), Euclidean, Manhattan, or Minkowski similarity (for geometric objects), Pearson coefficient (for statistical data), we focus on a well-known, widely used, measure: the *Jaccard Similarity Index* [15]. It quantifies the similarity between two sets A and B, and is a rational number between 0 and 1. Experimental and analytical results indicate that high values of the Jaccard index capture well the informal notion of "roughly the same" [4] and can be used, e.g., to find near duplicate records [32] and similar documents [4], for web-page clustering [29], data mining [30], and genetics [11,26]. As sample sets can be relatively large, in distributed settings, an approximation of the index is oftentimes preferred to its exact calculation. To this end, *MinHash* techniques [4] are used to estimate the Jaccard index, with remarkably lower computation and communication costs (see Sec. 2.1).

In this paper, we define and instantiate a cryptographic primitive geared for *privacy-preserving evaluation of sample set similarity*. We design two efficient protocols, allowing two interacting parties to compute (resp., approximate) the Jaccard index of their private sets, without reciprocally disclosing any information about their content (or, at most, an upper bound on their size). Our main cryptographic building block is Private Set Intersection Cardinality (PSI-CA) [13], introduced in Sec. 2.2. Specifically, we use PSI-CA to privately compute the magnitude of set intersection and union, and derive the value of the Jaccard index. As fast (linear-complexity) PSI-CA protocols become available, this can be done efficiently, even on large sets. Nonetheless, our work shows that, using MinHash approximations, one can obtain an estimate of the Jaccard index with remarkably increased efficiency – i.e., reducing the size of input sets, thus, the number of (costly) cryptographic operations.

Privacy-preserving evaluation of sample set similarity is appealing in many real-world scenarios. We focus on document similarity and show that privacy is attainable with low overhead, while *we defer to the extended version of the paper [3] for other applications, such as, iris matching and multimedia file similarity*. Our experiments demonstrate that our generic technique – while not bounded to specific applications – is appreciably more efficient than state-of-the-art protocols that only focus on one specific scenario, while maintaing comparable accuracy. Finally, in the process of reviewing related work, we identify limits and flaws of some prior results.

Organization. The rest of this paper is structured as follows. Next section introduces building blocks, then Sec. 3 presents our construction for secure computation of Jaccard index and an even more efficient technique to (privately) approximate it. Then, Sec. 4, presents our constructions for privacy-preserving document similarity evaluation. The paper concludes in Sec. 5. (Note that the extended version of the paper [3] also includes constructions for privacy-preserving similarity evaluation of irises and multimedia contents, as well as a very fast protocol to privately approximate set intersection cardinality, that additionally hides set sizes.)

2   Preliminaries

2.1   Jaccard Similarity Index and MinHash Techniques

Jaccard Index. One of the most common metrics for assessing the similarity of two sets (hence, of data they represent) is the Jaccard index [15]. It measures the similarity between two sets A and B as $J(A, B) = |A \cap B|/|A \cup B|$. High values of the index suggest that two sets are very similar, whereas, low values indicate that A and B are almost disjoint. The Jaccard index of A and B can be rewritten as a mere function of the *intersection*: $J(A, B) = |A \cap B|/(|A| + |B| - |A \cap B|)$.

MinHash Techniques. Computing the Jaccard index incurs a complexity linear in set sizes. Thus, in the context of a large number of big sets, its computation might be relatively expensive. In fact, for each pair of sets, the Jaccard index must be computed from scratch, i.e., no information used to calculate $J(A, B)$ can be re-used for $J(A, C)$. (That is, similarity is not a transitive measure.) As a result, an *approximation* of the Jaccard index is often preferred, as it can be obtained at a significantly lower cost, e.g., using MinHash techniques [4]. Informally, MinHash techniques extract a small representation $h_k(S)$ of a set S through deterministic (salted) sampling. This representation has a constant size k, independent from $|S|$, and can be used to compute an approximation of the Jaccard index. The parameter k also defines the expected error with respect to the exact Jaccard index. Intuitively, larger values of k yield smaller approximation errors. The computation of $h_k(S)$ also incurs a complexity linear in set sizes, however, it must be performed *only once* per set, for *any* number of comparisons. Thus, with MinHash techniques, evaluating the similarity of any two sets requires only a constant number of comparisons. Similarly, the bandwidth used by two interacting parties to approximate the Jaccard index of their respective sets is also constant ($O(k)$).

There are two strategies to realize MinHashes: one employs multiple hash functions, while the other is built from a single hash function.[1]

MinHash with Many Hash Functions. Let $\mathcal{F}$ be a family of hash functions that map items from set U to distinct τ-bit integers. Select k different functions $h^{(1)}(\cdot), \ldots, h^{(k)}(\cdot)$ from $\mathcal{F}$; for any set $S \subseteq U$, let $h_{min}^{(i)}(S)$ be the item $s \in S$ with the smallest value $h^{(i)}(s)$. The MinHash representation $h_k(S)$ of set S is a vector $h_k(S) = \{h_{min}^{(i)}(S)\}_{i=1}^k$. The Jaccard index $J(A, B)$ is estimated by counting the number of indexes i-s, such that that $h_{min}^{(i)}(A) = h_{min}^{(i)}(B)$, and this value is then divided by k. Observe that it holds that $h_{min}^{(i)}(A) = h_{min}^{(i)}(B)$ exactly when the minimum hash value of $A \cup B$ lies in $A \cap B$.

This measure can be obtained by computing the cardinality of the intersection of $h_k(A)$ and $h_k(B)$, in the following way. Each element a_i of the vector $h_k(A)$ is encoded as $\langle a_i, i \rangle$. Similarly, $\langle b_i, i \rangle$ represents the i-th element of vector $h_k(B)$. An unbiased estimate of the Jaccard index between A and B is given by:

$$sim(A, B) = \frac{\left| \{\langle a_i, i \rangle\}_{i=1}^k \cap \{\langle b_i, i \rangle\}_{i=1}^k \right|}{k} \tag{1}$$

As discussed in [5], if $\mathcal{F}$ is a family of min-wise independent hash functions, then each value of a fixed set A has the same probability to be the element with the smallest hash value. Specifically, for each min-wise independent hash function $h^{(i)}(\cdot)$ and for any set S, we have that, for any $s_j, s_l \in S$, $\Pr[s_j = h_{min}^{(i)}(S)] = \Pr[s_l = h_{min}^{(i)}(S)]$. Thus, we also obtain that $Pr[h_{min}^{(i)}(A) = h_{min}^{(i)}(B)] = J(A, B)$. In other words, if r is a random variable that is 1 when $h_{min}^{(i)}(A) = h_{min}^{(i)}(B)$ and 0 otherwise, then r is an unbiased estimator of $J(A, B)$; however, in order to reduce its variance, such random variable must be sampled several times, i.e., $k \gg 1$ hash values must be used. In particular, by Chernoff bounds [7], the expected error of this estimate is $O(1/\sqrt{k})$.

Approximating (Jaccard) Similarity of Vectors without MinHash. If one needs to approximate the Jaccard index of two fixed-length *vectors* (rather than sets), one could

---

[1] This paper focuses on the former technique, thus, we defer the description of the latter to the full version of the paper [3], which also overviews possible MinHash instantiations.

use other (more efficient) techniques similar to MinHash. Observe that a vector $\overrightarrow{S}$ can be represented as a set $S = \{\langle s_i, i \rangle\}$, where s_i is simply the i-th element of $\overrightarrow{S}$. We now discuss an efficient strategy to approximate the Jaccard index of two vectors $A = \{\langle a_i, i \rangle\}_{i=1}^{n}$, $B = \{\langle b_i, i \rangle\}_{i=1}^{n}$ of length n, without using MinHash. The approach discussed here incurs constant ($O(k)$) computational and communication complexity, i.e., it is independent from vectors' length of the vectors being compared. First, select k random values $(r_1, \ldots, r_k)$, for r_i uniformly distributed in $[1, n]$, and compute $A_k = \{\langle a_{r_i}, r_i \rangle\}_{i=1}^{k}$ and $B_k = \{\langle b_{r_i}, r_i \rangle\}_{i=1}^{k}$, respectively. The value $\delta = |A_k \cap B_k|/k$ can then be used to assess the similarity of A and B. We argue that δ is an unbiased estimate of $J(A, B)$: for each $\alpha \in (A_k \cup B_k)$ we have that $\Pr[\alpha \in (A_k \cap B_k)] = \Pr[\alpha \in (A \cap B)]$ since $\alpha \in (A \cap B) \wedge \alpha \in (A_k \cup B_k) \Leftrightarrow \alpha \in (A_k \cap B_k)$. We also have $\Pr[\alpha \in (A \cap B)] = J(A, B)$, thus, δ is indeed an unbiased estimate of $J(A, B)$.

The above algorithm implements a perfect min-wise permutation for this setting: since elements $(r_1, \ldots, r_k)$ are uniformly distributed, for each $i \in [1, k]$ any element in A and B has the same probability of being selected. As such, similar to MinHash with many hash function, the expected error is also $O(1/\sqrt{k})$.

2.2 Cryptography Background

Private Set Intersection Cardinality (PSI-CA) is a cryptographic protocol involving two parties: Alice, on input $A = \{a_1, \ldots, a_w\}$, and Bob, on input $B = \{b_1, \ldots, b_v\}$, such that Alice outputs $|A \cap B|$, while Bob has no output. In the last few years, several PSI-CA protocols [13,31,20,10] have been proposed, that are secure in different security models and under different assumptions. We choose the protocol in [10] as it achieves communication and computation complexity linear in set sizes. As a result, throughout this paper, we use the PSI-CA construction from [10], which is secure, in the presence of semi-honest adversaries, under the DDH assumption in the Random Oracle Model (ROM). It requires $O(|A| + |B|)$ *offline* and $O(|A|)$ *online* modular exponentiations in $\mathbb{Z}_p$ with exponents from subgroup $\mathbb{Z}_q$. (Offline operations are computed only once, for any number of interactions and any number of interacting parties). Communication overhead amounts to $O(|A|)$ elements in $\mathbb{Z}_p$ and $O(|B|)$ – in $\mathbb{Z}_q$. Assuming 80-bit security parameter, $|q| = 160$ bits and $|p| = 1024$ bits. (PSI-CA from [10] is reviewed in the extended version of this paper [3].)

Adversarial Model: We use standard security models for secure two-party computation, which assume the adversary to be either semi-honest or malicious.[2] As per definitions in [14], protocols secure in the presence of *semi-honest adversary* assume that parties faithfully follow all protocol specifications and do not misrepresent any information related to their inputs, e.g., size and content. However, during or after protocol execution, any party might (passively) attempt to infer additional information about other party's input. Whereas, security in the presence of *malicious parties* allows arbitrary deviations from the protocol. Security arguments in this paper are made with respect to *semi-honest* participants.

---

[2] Hereafter, the term *adversary* refers to protocol participants. Outside adversaries are not considered, since their actions can be mitigated via standard network security techniques.

3   Privacy-Preserving Sample Set Similarity

3.1   Private Computation of Jaccard Index

We now present our first construction for privacy-preserving computation of Jaccard Index. We consider two parties, Alice and Bob, on input sets A and B, respectively. We show that parties can efficiently compute $J(A,B)$ in a privacy-preserving manner using protocol illustrated in Figure 1 below.

Privacy-preserving computation of $J(A,B)$
(Run by Alice and Bob, on input, resp., A,B)

---

1. Alice and Bob execute PSI-CA on input, resp., $(A,|B|)$ and $(B,|A|)$
2. Alice learns $c = |A \cap B|$
3. Alice computes $u = |A \cup B| = |A| + |B| - c$
4. Alice outputs $J(A,B) = c/u$

Fig. 1. Proposed protocol for privacy-preserving computation of set similarity

Complexity. The cost of protocol in Figure 1 is dominated by that incurred by the underlying PSI-CA protocol. As we select the PSI-CA construction of [10], which incurs linear communication and computational complexities, overall complexities of protocol in Figure 1 are also linear in the size of sets. If we were to compute the Jaccard index without privacy, asymptotic complexities would be same as our privacy-preserving protocol – i.e., linear. However, given the lack of cryptographic operations, constants hidden by the big $O()$ notation would be much smaller.

Security. Our main security claim is that, by running the protocol in Figure 1, parties do not reciprocally disclose the content of their private sets, but only learn similarity computed as the Jaccard index and the size of the other party's input (hence, the cardinality of set intersection and union). Therefore, security of protocol in Figure 1 relies on that of the underlying PSI-CA instantiation (DDH in ROM). In particular, Alice and Bob do not exchange any information besides messages related to the PSI-CA protocol. For this reason, a secure implementation of the underlying PSI-CA guarantees that neither Alice nor Bob learn additional information about the other party's set (thus, we omit detailed formal proofs to ease presentation).

Performance Evaluation. Our technique for secure Jaccard index computation can be instantiated using any PSI-CA construction. Nonetheless, to maximize efficiency, we choose the one in [10]. To assess the practicality of resulting construction, protocol in Figure 1 has been implemented in C (with OpenSSL and GMP libraries), using 160-bit random exponents and 1024-bit moduli to obtain 80-bit security.[3] We assume $|A| = |B| = 1000$ and set items to be hashed using SHA-1, thus, they are 160-bit. In this setting, protocol in Figure 1 would incur (i) about $0.5s$ total computation time on a single Intel Xeon E5420 core running at 2.50GHz and (ii) 276KB in bandwidth. We

---

[3] Source-code implementation of all protocols is available upon request.

omit running times for larger sets since, as complexities are linear, one can easily derive a meaningful estimate of time/bandwidth for any size.

We also implement an optimized prototype that further improves total running time by (1) pipelining computation and transmission and (2) parallelizing computation on two cores. We test the prototype by running Alice and Bob on two PCs equipped with 2 quad-core Intel Xeon E5420 processors running at 2.50GHz, however, we always use (at most) 2 cores. On a conservative stance, we do not allow parties to perform any pre-computation offline. We simulate a 9Mbps link, since, according to [24], it represents the current average Internet bandwidth in US and Canada.

In this setting, and again considering $|A| = |B| = 1000$, total running time of protocol in Figure 1 amounts to $0.23s$. Whereas, the computation of Jaccard index *without* *privacy* takes $0.018s$. Therefore, we conclude that privacy protection, in our experiments, only introduces a 12-fold slowdown, independently from set sizes.

Comparison to Prior Work. Performance evaluation above does not include any prior solutions, since, to the best of our knowledge, there is no comparable cryptographic primitive for privacy-preserving computation of the Jaccard index. The work in [28] is somewhat related: it targets private computation of the Jaccard index using Private Equality Testing (PET) [21] and deterministic encryption, however, it introduces the need for a non-colluding semi-honest *third party*, which violates our design model. Also, it incurs an impractical number of public-key operations, i.e., *quadratic* in the size of sample sets (as opposed to linear in our case). Finally, additional (only vaguely) related techniques include: (i) work on privately approximating dot product of two vectors, such as, [27,18], and (ii) probabilistic/approximated private set operations based on Bloom filters, such as, [18,19]. (None of this techniques, however, can be used to solve problems considered in this paper.)

3.2 Private Estimation of Jaccard Index Based on MinHash

The computation of the Jaccard index, with or without privacy, can be relatively expensive when (1) sample sets are very large, or (2) each set must be compared with a large number of other sets. Thus, MinHash techniques, introduced in Sec. 2.1, are often used to estimate the Jaccard index, trading off an expected error with appreciably faster computation. We now show how to privately approximate the similarity of two sample sets combining MinHash and PSI-CA. Our construction is general and does not assume any specific instantiation, given that it is a multi-hash MinHash.

Recall, from Sec. 2.1, that Jaccard index can also be approximated as $sim(A, B) = |\{\langle a_i, i \rangle\}_{i=1}^k \cap \{\langle b_i, i \rangle\}_{i=1}^k|/k$, where $a_i = h_{min}^{(i)}(A)$ and $b_i = h_{min}^{(i)}(B)$. Therefore, privacy-preserving estimation of the Jaccard index, using multi-hash MinHash, can be reduced to securely computing cardinality of set intersection above. The resulting protocol is presented in Figure 2 below.

It is easy to observe that, compared to the Jaccard index computation (Sec. 3), the use of MinHash leads to executing PSI-CA on smaller sets, as it holds $k \ll \text{Min}(|A|, |B|)$. Thus, communication and computation overhead depends on k, since inputs to PSI-CA are now sets of k items, independently from the size of A and B.

Private Jaccard index estimation $sim(A, B)$
(Run by Alice and Bob, on input, resp., A, B)

---

1. Alice and Bob compute, $\{\langle a_i, i \rangle\}_{i=1}^{k}$ and $\{\langle b_i, i \rangle\}_{i=1}^{k}$, resp., using multi-hash MinHash
2. Alice and Bob execute PSI-CA on input, resp., $(\{\langle a_i, i \rangle\}_{i=1}^{k}, k)$ and $(\{\langle b_i, i \rangle\}_{i=1}^{k}, k)$
3. Alice learns $\delta = |\{\langle a_i, i \rangle\}_{i=1}^{k} \cap \{\langle b_i, i \rangle\}_{i=1}^{k}|$
4. Alice outputs $sim(A, B) = \delta/k$

Fig. 2. Proposed protocol for privacy-preserving approximation of set similarity

Security and Extensions. Similar to the protocol in Sec. 3.1, the security of protocol in Figure 2 relies on the security of the underlying PSI-CA construction.

In this protocol, the Alice learns some additional information compared to the protocol in Sec. 3.1. In particular, rather than computing the similarity – and therefore the size of the intersection – of sets A and B, she determines how many elements from a particular subset of A (constructed using minhash) also appear in the subset selected from B. To overcome this limitation, Alice and Bob can construct their input sets (Step 1 in Figure 2) using a set of OPRFs rather than a set of hash functions: Alice and Bob engage in a multi-party protocol where Alice inputs her set $A = \{a_1, \ldots, a_v\}$ and learns a random permutation of $\text{OPRF}_{key_j}(a_1), \ldots, \text{OPRF}_{key_j}(a_v)$ for random keys key_j, $1 \leq j \leq k$. Alice constructs her input selecting the smallest value $\text{OPRF}_{key_j}(a_i)$ for each j. Bob constructs his input without interacting with Alice. While the cost of this protocol is linear in the size of the input sets, it is significantly higher than that of protocol Sec. 3.1.

Performance Evaluation. We also tested the performance of our construction for privacy-preserving approximation of Jaccard similarity, again using the PSI-CA from [10]. We used the same setting of Sec. 3.1, i.e., we selected sets with 1000 items, 1024-bit moduli and 160-bit random exponents, and ran experiments on two PCs with 2.5GHz CPU and a 9Mbps link. Selecting $k = 400$, thus, bounding the error to 5%, the total running time of protocol in Figure 2 amounts to $0.09s$ – less than half compared to the one in Figure 1. Whereas, in the same setting, the approximation of Jaccard index *without privacy* takes $0.007s$. Thus, the slow-down factor introduced by the privacy-protecting layer (similar to the protocol proposed in Sec. 3.1) is 12-fold. Again, note that times for different set sizes can be easily estimated since the complexity of the protocol is linear.

Prior Work. The estimation of set similarity through MinHash – whether privacy-preserving or not – requires counting the number of times for which it holds that $h_{min}^{(i)}(A) = h_{min}^{(i)}(B)$, with $i = 1, \ldots, k$. We have denoted this number as δ. Protocol in Figure 2 above attains secure computation of δ through privacy-preserving set intersection cardinality. However, it appears somewhat more intuitive to do so by using the approach proposed by [2] in the context of social-network friends discovery. Specifically, in [2], Alice and Bob compute, resp., $\{a_i\}_{i=1}^{k}$ and $\{b_i\}_{i=1}^{k}$, just like in our protocol. Then, Alice generates a public-private keypair (pk, sk) for Paillier's additively homomorphic encryption cryptosystem [25] and sends Bob $\{z_i = Enc_{pk}(a_i)\}_{i=1}^{k}$. Bob computes $\{(z_i \cdot Enc_{pk}(-b_i))^{r_i}\}_{i=1}^{k}$ for random r_i's and returns the resulting vector of ciphertexts after shuffling it. Upon decryption, Alice learns δ by counting the number of 0's. Nonetheless, the technique proposed by [2] actually incurs an increased complexity, compared to our protocol in Figure 2 (instantiated with PSI-CA from [10]). Assuming 80-bit security parameters, thus, 1024-bit moduli and 160-bit subgroups, and 2048-bit Paillier moduli, and using m to denote a multiplication of 1024-bit numbers, multiplications of 2048-bit numbers count for $4m$. Using square-and-multiply, exponentiations with q-bit exponents modulo 1024-bit count for $(1.5|q|)m$. In [2], Alice performs k Paillier encryptions (i.e., $2k$ exponentiations and k multiplications) and k decryptions (i.e., k exponentiations and multiplications), while Bob computes k exponentiations and multiplications. Therefore, the total computation complexity amounts to $(6 \cdot 4 \cdot 1.5 \cdot 1024 + 4 \cdot 4)km = 36,880km$. Whereas, our approach (even without pre-computation) requires both Alice and Bob to perform $4k$ exponentiations of 160-bit numbers modulo 1024-moduli and $2k$ multiplications, i.e., $(4 \cdot 1.5 \cdot 160 + 2)km = 962km$, thus, our protocol achieves a 38-fold efficiency improvement. Communication overhead is also higher in [2]: it amounts to $(2 \cdot 2048)k$ bits; whereas, using PSI-CA, we need to transfer $(2 \cdot 1024 + 160)k$ bits, i.e., slightly more than half the traffic.

4   Privacy-Preserving Document Similarity

After building efficient (linear-complexity) primitives for privacy-preserving computation/approximation of Jaccard index, we now explore their applications to a few compelling problems. We start with evaluating the similarity of two documents, which is relevant in many common applications, including copyright protection, file management, plagiarism prevention, duplicate submission detection, law enforcement. In last few years, the security community has started investigating privacy-preserving techniques to enable detection of similar documents without disclosing documents' actual contents. Below, we first review prior work and, then, present our technique for efficient privacy-preserving document similarity.

4.1   Related Work

The work in [16] (later extended in [23]) is the first to realize *privacy-preserving document similarity*. It realizes secure computation of the *cosine similarity* of vectors representing the documents, i.e., each document is represented as the list of words appearing in it, along with the normalized number of occurrences. Recently, Jiang and Samanthula [17] have proposed a novel technique relying on the Jaccard index and N-gram based document representation [22]. (Given any string, an N-gram is a substring of size N). According to [17], the N-gram based technique presents several advantages over cosine similarity: (1) it improves on finding *local similarity*, e.g., overlapping of pieces of texts, (2) it is language-independent, (3) it requires a much simpler representation, and (4) it is less sensitive to document modification. We overview it below.

Documents as Sets of N-grams. A document can be represented as a set of N-grams contained in it. To obtain such a representation, one needs to remove spaces and punctuation and build the set of successive N-grams in the document. An example of a sentence, along with its N-gram representation (for $N = 3$), is illustrated in Figure 3. The similarity of two documents can then be estimated as the *Jaccard index* of the two

> *the quick brown fox jumps over the lazy dog*
> $\downarrow$
>
> {azy, bro, ckb, dog, ela, equ, ert, fox, hel, heq, ick, jum, kbr, laz, mps, nfo, ove, own, oxj, pso, qui, row, rth, sov, the, uic, ump, ver, wnf, xju, ydo, zyd}

Fig. 3. Tri-gram representation

corresponding sets of N-grams. In the context of document similarity, experts point out that 3 results as a good choice of N [4].

To enable privacy-preserving computation of Jaccard index, and therefore estimation of document similarity, Jiang and Samanthula [17] propose a two-stage protocol based on *Paillier*'s additively homomorphic encryption [25]. Suppose Alice wants to privately evaluate the similarity of her document D_A against a list of n documents held by Bob, i.e., $D_{B:1}, \ldots, D_{B:n}$. First, Bob generates a global space, $|S|$, of tri-grams based on his document collection. This way, D_A as well as each of Bob's document, $D_{B:i}$, can be represented as binary vectors in the global space of tri-grams: each component is 1 if the corresponding tri-gram is included in the document and 0 otherwise. We denote with A the representation of D_A and with B_i that of $D_{B:i}$. Then, Alice and Bob respectively compute random shares a and b_i such that $a + b_i = |A \cap B_i|$. Next, they set $c = |A| - a$ and $d_i = |B| - b_i$. Finally, Alice and Bob, on input (a, c) and (b_i, d_i), resp., execute a Secure Division protocol (e.g., [6,1]) to obtain $(a + b_i)/(c + d_i) = |A \cap B_i|/|A \cup B_i| = J(A, B_i)$.

The computational complexity of the protocol in [17] amounts to $O(|S|)$ Paillier encryptions performed by Alice, and $O(n \cdot |S|)$ modular multiplications – by Bob. Whereas, communication overhead amounts to $O(n \cdot |S|)$ Paillier ciphertexts.

Flaw in [17]. Unfortunately, protocol in [17] *is not secure*, since Bob has to disclose his global space of tri-grams (i.e., the set of all tri-grams appearing in his document collection). Therefore, Alice can passively check whether or not a word appears in Bob's document collection. Actually, Alice can learn much more, as we show in Appendix A. We argue that this flaw could be fixed by considering the global space of tri-grams as the set of all possible tri-grams, thus, avoiding the disclosure of Bob's tri-grams set. Assuming that documents are stripped of any symbol and contain only lower-cased letters and digits, we obtain $S = \{a, b, \ldots, z, 0, 1, \ldots, 9\}^3$. Unfortunately, this modification would tremendously increase computation and communication overhead.

4.2 Our Construction

As discussed in Sec. 3, we can realize privacy-preserving computation of the Jaccard index using PSI-CA. To privately evaluate the similarity of documents D_A and any document $D_{B:i}$, Alice and Bob execute protocol in Figure 4. Function Tri-Gram($\cdot$) denotes the representation of a document as the set of tri-grams appearing in it.

Complexity. Complexity of protocol in Figure 4 is bounded by that of the underlying PSI-CA construction. Using the technique in [10], computational complexity amounts to $O(|A| + |B_i|)$ modular exponentiations, whereas, communication overhead – to

Alice (D_A)	Bob $(D_{B:i})$
$A \leftarrow$ Tri-Gram(D_A)	$B_i \leftarrow$ Tri-Gram$(D_{B:i})$

$$\left\{ \begin{array}{c} \longrightarrow \\ \longleftarrow \end{array} \right\}$$

$|A \cap B_i| \leftarrow$ PSI-CA(A, B_i)

Output Similarity as $J(A, B_i) = \dfrac{|A \cap B_i|}{|A| + |B_i| - |A \cap B_i|}$

Fig. 4. Privacy-preserving *evaluation* of document similarity of documents D_A and $D_{B:i}$

$O(|A| + |B_i|)$. Observe that, in the setting where Alice holds one documents and Bob a collection of n documents, complexities should be amended to $O(n|A| + \sum_{i=1}^{n} |B_i|)$. However, due to the nature of protocol in [10], Bob can perform $O(\sum_{i=1}^{n} |B_i|)$ computation *off-line*, ahead of time. Hence, total *online* computation amounts to $O(n|A|)$.

More Efficient Computation Using MinHash. As discussed in Sec. 2.1, one can approximate the Jaccard index by using MinHash techniques, thus, trading off accuracy with significant improvement in protocol complexity. The resulting construction is similar to the one presented above and is illustrated in Figure 5. It adds an intermediate step between the tri-gram representation and the execution of PSI-CA: Alice and Bob apply MinHash to sets A and B_i, respectively, and obtain $h_k(A)$ and $h_k(B_i)$. The main advantage results from the fact that PSI-CA is now executed on smaller sets, of constant size k, thus, achieving significantly improved communication and computational complexities. Again, note that the error is bounded by $O(1/\sqrt{k})$.

Performance Evaluation. We now compare the performance of our constructions to the most efficient prior technique, i.e., the protocol in [17] (that, unfortunately, is insecure). We consider the setting of [17], where Bob maintains a collection of n documents. Recall that our constructions use the PSI-CA in [10]. Assuming 80-bit security parameters, we select 1024-bit moduli and 160-bit random exponents. As [17] relies on Paillier encryption, it uses 2048-bit moduli and 1024-bit exponents. In the following, let m denote a multiplication of 1024-bit numbers. Multiplications of 2048-bit numbers count for $4m$. Modular exponentiations with q-bit exponents modulo 1024-bit count for $(1.5|q|)m$. The protocol in [17] requires $O(|S|)$ Paillier encryptions and $O(n \cdot |S|)$ modular multiplications. As pointed above, we need $|S| = 36^3 = 46,656$. Therefore, the total complexity amounts to $(4 \cdot 1.5 \cdot 1024 + 4n)|S|m = (6144 + 4n)|S|m \approx (2.9 \cdot 10^8 + 1.9 \cdot 10^5 n)m$.

Our construction above requires $(2 \cdot 1.5 \cdot 160n|A|)m$ for the computation of Jaccard index similarity and $(1.5 \cdot 160nk)m$ for its approximation. Thus, to compare performance of our protocol to that of [17], we need to take into account the dimensions of A, B_i, as well as n and k. To this end, we collected 393 scientific papers from the KDDcup dataset of scientific papers published in ArXiv between 1996 and 2003 [8]. The average number of different tri-grams appearing in each paper is 1307. Therefore, cost of our two techniques can be estimated as $(2 \cdot 1.5 \cdot 160 \cdot 1307n)m$ and $(1.5 \cdot 160 \cdot nk)m$, respectively. Thus, our technique for privacy-preserving document similarity is faster

Alice (D_A)	Bob $(D_{B:i})$
$A \leftarrow$ Tri-Gram(D_A)	$B_i \leftarrow$ Tri-Gram$(D_{B:i})$
$h_k(A) \leftarrow$ MinHash(A)	$h_k(B_i) \leftarrow$ MinHash(B_i)

$|h_k(A) \cap h_k(B_i)| \leftarrow$
    PSI-CA$(h_k(A), h_k(B_i))$

Output Similarity Approximation as: $sim(A, B_i) = \dfrac{|h_k(A) \cap h_k(B_i)|}{k}$

Fig. 5. Privacy-preserving *approximation* of document similarity of documents D_A and $D_{B:i}$

Table 1. Computation time of privacy-preserving document similarity

n	[17]	Figure 4	Figure 5	
			$k = 100$	$k = 40$
10	9.5 mins	6.3 secs	0.05 secs	0.05 secs
10^2	9.9 mins	63 secs	1.9 secs	1.9 secs
10^3	12.7 mins	10.4 mins	48 secs	19.2 secs
10^4	40.7 mins	1.74 hours	8 mins	3.2 mins
10^5	5.3 hours	17.4 hours	1.2 hours	32 mins

than [17] for $n < 2000$. Furthermore, using MinHash techniques, complexity is always faster (and of at least one order of magnitude), using both $k = 40$ and $k = 100$. Also, recall that, as opposed to ours, the protocol in [17] is *not* secure.

Assuming that it takes about $1\mu s$ to perform modular multiplications of 1024-bit integers (as per our experiments on a single Intel Xeon E5420 core running at 2.50GHz), we report estimated running times in Table 1 for increasing values of n (i.e., the number of Bob's documents).

We performed some statistical analysis to determine the real magnitude of the error introduced by MinHash, when compared to the Jaccard index without MinHash. Our analysis is based on the trigrams from documents in the KDDcup dataset [8], and confirms that the average error is within the expected bounds: for $k = 40$, we obtained an average error of 14%, while for $k = 100$ the average error was 9%. This is acceptable, considering that the Jaccard index actually provides a normalized *estimate* of the similarity between two sets, not a definite metric.

Remark: In the extended version of the paper [3], we also propose constructions for privacy-preserving similarity evaluation of irises and multimedia contents.

5   Conclusion

This paper introduced the first efficient construction for privacy-preserving evaluation of sample set similarity, relying on the Jaccard index measure. We also presented an efficient randomized protocol that approximates, with bounded error, this similarity index. Our techniques are generic and practical enough to be used as a basic building block for a wide array of different privacy-preserving functionalities, including document and multimedia file similarity, biometric matching, genomic testing, similarity of social profiles, and so on. Experimental analyses support our efficiency claims and demonstrate improvements over prior results. Source-code implementation of all proposed protocols and experiments is available upon request and will be released along with the final version of the paper.

Naturally, our work does not end here: additional applications and extensions require further investigation. Also, as part of future work, we plan to investigate privacy-preserving computation of other similarity measures.

References

1. Atallah, M.J., Bykova, M., Li, J., Frikken, K.B., Topkara, M.: Private collaborative forecasting and benchmarking. In: WPES (2004)
2. Baglioni, E., Becchetti, L., Bergamini, L., Colesanti, U., Filipponi, L., Vitaletti, A., Persiano, G.: A lightweight privacy preserving sms-based recommendation system for mobile users. In: RecSys (2010)
3. Blundo, C., De Cristofaro, E., Gasti, P.: EsPRESSo: Efficient Privacy-Preserving Evaluation of Sample Set Similarity, Extended Version (2012), http://arxiv.org/abs/1111.5062
4. Broder, A.: On the resemblance and containment of documents. In: Compression and Complexity of Sequences (1997)
5. Broder, A., Charikar, M., Frieze, A., Mitzenmacher, M.: Min-wise independent permutations. In: STOC (1998)
6. Bunn, P., Ostrovsky, R.: Secure two-party k-means clustering. In: CCS (2007)
7. Chernoff, H.: A measure of asymptotic efficiency for tests of a hypothesis based on the sum of observations. The Annals of Mathematical Statistics (1952)
8. Cornell Univ. KDDCUP Dataset, http://www.cs.cornell.edu/projects/kddcup/datasets.html
9. Davies, K.: The $1,000 genome: the revolution in DNA sequencing and the new era of Personalized Medicine. Free Press (2010)
10. De Cristofaro, E., Gasti, P., Tsudik, G.: Fast and Private Computation of Set Intersection Cardinality (2012), http://eprint.iacr.org/2011/141
11. Dombek, P., Johnson, L., Zimmerley, S., Sadowsky, M.: Use of repetitive DNA sequences and the PCR to differentiate Escherichia coli isolates from human and animal sources. Applied and Environmental Microbiology 66(6) (2000)
12. Fowler, J., Settle, J., Christakis, N.: Correlated genotypes in friendship networks. Proceedings of the National Academy of Sciences 108(5) (2011)
13. Freedman, M., Nissim, K., Pinkas, B.: Efficient Private Matching and Set Intersection. In: Cachin, C., Camenisch, J.L. (eds.) EUROCRYPT 2004. LNCS, vol. 3027, pp. 1–19. Springer, Heidelberg (2004)
14. Goldreich, O.: Foundations of cryptography. Cambridge Univ. Press (2004)
15. Jaccard, P.: Etude comparative de la distribution florale dans une portion des Alpes et du Jura (1901)
16. Jiang, W., Murugesan, M., Clifton, C., Si, L.: Similar document detection with limited information disclosure. In: ICDE (2008)
17. Jiang, W., Samanthula, B.K.: N-Gram Based Secure Similar Document Detection. In: Li, Y. (ed.) DBSec 2011. LNCS, vol. 6818, pp. 239–246. Springer, Heidelberg (2011)

18. Kantarcioglu, M., Nix, R., Vaidya, J.: An efficient approximate protocol for privacy-preserving association rule mining. In: KDD (2009)
19. Kerschbaum, F.: Outsourced Private Set Intersection Using Homomorphic Encryption. In: AsiaCCS (2012)
20. Kissner, L., Song, D.: Privacy-Preserving Set Operations. In: Shoup, V. (ed.) CRYPTO 2005. LNCS, vol. 3621, pp. 241–257. Springer, Heidelberg (2005)
21. Lipmaa, H.: Verifiable Homomorphic Oblivious Transfer and Private Equality Test. In: Laih, C.-S. (ed.) ASIACRYPT 2003. LNCS, vol. 2894, pp. 416–433. Springer, Heidelberg (2003)
22. Manber, U.: Finding similar files in a large file system. In: USENIX (1994)
23. Murugesan, M., Jiang, W., Clifton, C., Si, L., Vaidya, J.: Efficient privacy-preserving similar document detection. The VLDB Journal 19 (August 2010)
24. Ookla Net Metrics. Canada and US Source Data (2011), http://www.netindex.com/source-data/
25. Paillier, P.: Public-Key Cryptosystems Based on Composite Degree Residuosity Classes. In: Stern, J. (ed.) EUROCRYPT 1999. LNCS, vol. 1592, pp. 223–238. Springer, Heidelberg (1999)
26. Popescu, M., Keller, J., Mitchell, J.: Fuzzy measures on the gene ontology for gene product similarity. Transactions on Computational Biology and Bioinformatics (2006)
27. Ravikumar, P., Cohen, W., Fienberg, S.: A secure protocol for computing string distance metrics. In: PSDM (2004)
28. Singh, M., Krishna, P., Saxena, A.: A privacy preserving jaccard similarity function for mining encrypted data. In: TENCON (2009)
29. Strehl, A., Ghosh, J., Mooney, R.: Impact of similarity measures on web-page clustering. In: AAAI (2000)
30. Tan, P., Steinbach, M., Kumar, V., et al.: Introduction to data mining. Pearson (2006)
31. Vaidya, J., Clifton, C.: Secure set intersection cardinality with application to association rule mining. Journal of Computer Security 13(4) (2005)
32. Xiao, C., Wang, W., Lin, X., Yu, J.: Efficient similarity joins for near duplicate detection. In: WWW (2008)

A   Flaw in Private Document Similarity in [17]

In this section, we show that the protocol in [17] is not privacy-preserving (even in semi-honest model). In fact, Bob, in order to participate in the protocol, must disclose his global space of tri-grams. Given this information, Alice can efficiently check whether a word, e.g., w, appears in Bob's document collection. Indeed, Alice computes w's tri-gram based representation, then she checks whether all such tri-grams appear in Bob's public global space. If so, Alice learns that w appears in a document held by Bob with some non-zero probability. Technically, this probability is not 1 because Alice could have a *false positive*, i.e. w may not be in Bob's documents even though w's trigrams are in Bob's public global space. On the other hand, if at least one of the tri-grams of w is not in Bob's public global space, Alice learns that Bob's documents do not contain w. This, obviously, violates privacy requirements. If Alice and Bob include punctation and spaces in their tri-grams representation of their documents, the probability of *false positive* becomes negligible. We do not exploit "relations" between consecutive meaningful words in the sentence, which could potentially (further) aggravate information leakage about Bob's documents.

We now show yet another attack that lets Alice learn even more, since the N-grams representation *embeds* document's structure. From the global space of tri-grams $\mathcal{GS}$, we can construct a directed graph $G(V, E)$ representing relations between tri-grams in Bob's document collection. Any path in such a graph will lead to a textual fragment contained in some document held by Bob. A vertex in the graph represents a tri-gram; whereas, an edge between two vertices implies that the two corresponding tri-grams are consecutive tri-grams in a word. Given a trigram $x \in \mathcal{GS}$, with $x^{(i)}$ we denote the i-th letter in x. The directed graph $G(V, E)$ is constructed as follows. The vertex set is $V = \{V_x \mid x \in \mathcal{GS}\}$ and the edge set is $E = \{\langle V_x, V_y \rangle \mid x^{(2)} = y^{(1)} \wedge x^{(3)} = y^{(2)}\}$. A path $V_{x_1}, \ldots, V_{x_n}$ in G, will correspond to the string $x_1^{(1)} x_1^{(2)} x_2^{(3)} x_3^{(3)} \cdots x_n^{(3)}$. Such a string (or some of its substring) appears in some document in Bob's collection. By using algorithms based on Deep First Search visit of a graph, a vocabulary, and syntactic rules, we could extract large document's chunks. We did not explore further other techniques to extract "information" from the global space of tri-grams as we consider them to be out of the scope of this paper.

SlopPy: Slope One with Privacy

Sébastien Gambs and Julien Lolive

Université de Rennes 1 - INRIA / IRISA,
Avenue du Général Leclerc
35042 Rennes, France
sgambs@irisa.fr, julien.lolive@inria.fr

Abstract. In order to contribute to solve the personalization/privacy paradox, we propose a privacy-preserving architecture for one of state-of-the-art recommendation algorithm, Slope One. More precisely, we describe SlopPy (for *Slope One with Privacy*), a privacy-preserving version of Slope One in which a user never releases directly his personal information (*i.e*, his ratings). Rather, each user first perturbs locally his information by applying a Randomized Response Technique before sending this perturbed data to a semi-trusted entity responsible for storing it. While there is a trade-off to set between the desired privacy level and the utility of the resulting recommendation, our preliminary experiments clearly demonstrate that SlopPy is able to provide a high level of privacy at the cost of a small decrease of utility.

Keywords: Privacy, Recommender Systems, Collaborative Filtering, Randomized Response Technique.

1 Introduction

The advent of personalization is strongly tied to the development and rapid growth of Electronic Commerce during the last decade. Indeed, major Internet companies provide services that are tailored to the interests of their users, which in turn as lead to the collection of large amount of personal data and the construction of detailed profiles of these users. For instance, Google personalizes the news pushed towards a specific user according to the topics of the news that he had consulted in the past [4]. Another approach consists in using a *recommender system* that creates a user's profile and compare it to the profiles of other users in order to select in accordance with the tastes of similar users, the most relevant items (*e.g.*, advertisements, movies, . . .) for this particular user. For example, Amazon relies on a recommendation engine using an *item-based collaborative filtering* to propose suggestions to users about books that they might like [10].

The massive gathering of personal information generated by the development of personalized services is clearly at odds with the privacy rights of the users of these systems. More precisely, the two fundamental questions summarizing the interplay between personalization and privacy are the following [12]:

". . . (1) to what extent users have to disclose personal information in order to enjoy personalized and context-aware services in a user-controlled,

R. Di Pietro et al. (Eds.): DPM 2012 and SETOP 2012, LNCS 7731, pp. 104–117, 2013.
© Springer-Verlag Berlin Heidelberg 2013

privacy-preserving and trusted way, as well as (2) to find a reasonable balance between user-centric requirements and natural business interests of service providers and authorities, who offer and regulate such services."

While we recognize that the second issue is also fundamental, in this paper we focus mainly on addressing the first one. In particular, we believe that in order to protect the privacy of their users and limit the risks of privacy breaches, the recommender systems must integrate the privacy issues directly into the conception of their architecture, following the *privacy-by-design* paradigm. Indeed, while personalization and privacy may seem to be antagonist at first glance, privacy-preserving personalized services and architectures have been developed in the past few years that aim at reconciling these seemingly conflicting goals, in particular in the context of personalized target advertising systems [17,7].

In this paper, we present our approach towards this direction by proposing a privacy-preserving architecture for one of state-of-the-art recommendation algorithm, Slope One [9]. More precisely, we describe SlopPy (for *Slope One with Privacy*), a privacy-preserving version of Slope One in which a user *never* releases directly his personal information (*i.e*, his ratings) to a trusted third party. Rather, each user first perturbs locally his information by applying a *Randomized Response Technique* before sending this perturbed data to a semi-trusted entity responsible for storing it. Out of the perturbed ratings, the semi-trusted entity construct two matrices (*i.e.*, the deviation matrix and the cardinality matrix) following the standard Slope One algorithm. When a user needs a recommendation on a particular item (*i.e.*, a movie), he fetches particular information from these matrices through a *private information retrieval* scheme [13] hiding the content of his query (*i.e.*, the item he is interested in) to the semi-trusted entity. By combining the data retrieved with his true ratings (which are only stored locally on his machine), the user can then locally compute the output of the recommendation algorithm for this particular item. While there is often a trade-off to set between the desired privacy level (quantified in terms of the magnitude of the noise added) and the utility of the resulting recommendation (measured by the Mean Absolute Error and the Root Mean Squared Error), our experiments clearly demonstrate that SlopPy is able to provide a high level of privacy at the cost of a small decrease of utility.

The outline of the paper is the following. First, in Section 2, we give an overview of the background on the Slope One recommendation algorithm as well as local perturbation approaches such as Randomized Response Techniques. then in Section 3, we briefly review privacy-preserving versions of Slope One that have been developed in recent years. Afterwards, in Section 4, we describe SlopPy, which is both a privacy-preserving version of Slope One and a recommendation architecture built around this algorithm. Finally, in Section 5, we report on experimentations performed with SlopPy on the classical Movielens dataset before concluding with a discussion and some future work in Section 6.

2   Background

Slope One recommendation algorithm. While several approaches exist to recommendation such as collaborative filtering, item-based recommendation and content-based recommendation, thereafter we focus on Slope One [9], which is a collaborative filtering algorithm (*i.e.*, the recommendation is based on the tastes of similar users) designed by Lemire and Maclachlan.

Let us first fix the notation. For the rest of this paper, let the variable u refers to a specific user while i and j will be used as the indexes of particular items (such as movies). Let also r denotes a true rating that a user has really given to an item (*e.g.*, a movie he has seen), while $\hat{r}$ denotes a predicted rating, which is the effective prediction made by the recommendation algorithm (in our case Slope One or SlopPy) on an item that a user has never rated. For instance, $r_{u,i}$ corresponds to the rating given by user u on the item i while $\hat{r}_{u,j}$ is the prediction of the rating that user u will give to item j according to the recommendation algorithm. In general, the rating given to an item will be either an integer or a real value drawn from a finite range. For example, in the case of the Movielens dataset, the interval considered is $[1, 5]$ in which a rating of 5 is an excellent rating while a value of 1 corresponds to the worst possible one. Finally, the variable n denotes the total number of items in the domain considered (*e.g.*, the number of possible movies).

To predict the rating of a particular item i for a specific user u, the Slope One algorithm combines the information about all the items that u has rated with the information about the ratings of all users that have also rated i. First, Slope One constructs a *cardinality matrix* of size n by n containing the value of $\phi_{i,j}$, which corresponds to the number of users that have rated both items i and j. This can be done easily in a non-private version of the algorithm by having all users sending all their ratings to a central entity. Afterwards, Slope one computes a *deviation matrix* out of the ratings provided by users. More precisely, the (standard) deviation matrix of size n by n is constructed by computing the standard deviation $\overline{\delta_{i,j}}$ between each pair of items i and j by considering the subset of users that have rated *both* items i and j:

$$\overline{\delta_{i,j}} = \frac{\sum_u (r_{u,i} - r_{u,j})}{\phi_{i,j}} \qquad (1)$$

in which $r_{u,i}$ and $r_{u,j}$ are respectively the ratings of user u for the item i and j, while $\phi_{i,j}$ is the number of users that have rated both items i and j. Note that the construction of the cardinality and deviation matrices can be done in a time directly proportional to their sizes, which is $O(n^2)$ for n the number of items in the domain.

The standard (*unweighted*) version of Slope One relies only on the deviation matrix to perform a recommendation. More precisely, the following equation summarizes the formula used by unweighted Slope One to predict the rating (the sum is performed over the subset of items that have been rated by user u):

$$\mathsf{UnweightedSlopeOne}(u, j) = \frac{\sum_{i|i \neq j} (\overline{\delta_{i,j}} + r_{u,i})}{n_u} \qquad (2)$$

in which j is the item on which the rating will be predicted for the user u, $\overline{\delta_{i,j}}$ is the standard deviation between the pair of items i and j, $r_{u,i}$ is the rating given by user u to item i and n_u is the number of items that have been rated by user u. The *Weighted Slope One* is another variant of the Slope One algorithm also due to Lemire and Maclachlan [9]. In a nutshell, compare to the standard (*i.e.*, unweighted) version, the main difference is that the weighted version of Slope One considers that the pairs of items that are the most relevant for the prediction are the ones that have been rated by a large number of users. This is reflected by the following formula for the prediction:

$$\mathsf{WeightedSlopeOne}(u, j) = \frac{\sum_{i|i\neq j} (\overline{\delta_{i,j}} + r_{u,i})\phi_{i,j}}{\sum_{i|i\neq j} \phi_{i,j}} \tag{3}$$

in which j is the item on which the rating will be predicted for the user u, $\phi_{i,j}$ corresponds to the number of users that have rated both items i and j, $\overline{\delta_{i,j}}$ is the standard deviation between the pair of items i and j and $r_{u,i}$ is the rating given by user u to item i. Standard metrics for measuring the accuracy of a recommendation algorithm are the *Mean Absolute Error* (MAE) and the *Root Mean Square Error* (RMSE), which basically are two different ways to quantify the difference between the true rating r and the prediction one $\hat{r}$. Both prediction methods (*i.e.*, the weighted and the unweighted ones) have a computational cost of $O(n)$, for n the number of possible items of the domain as they basically require to use all the n entries of a row of the deviation matrix (and possibly also the cardinality matrix in case of Weighted Slope One).

A key observation to make is that the prediction of weighted Slope One is based on both local information (*i.e.*, $r_{u,i}$) that the user can store on his computer and global information that is retrieved out of the deviation and cardinality matrices (*i.e.*, $\overline{\delta_{i,j}}$ and $\phi_{i,j}$). Out of the different recommendation algorithms available, we have chosen to focus on the development of the privacy-preserving variant of Slope One, both because it has an accuracy that is closed to state-of-the-art algorithms (as measured by the MAE and the RMSE), and also because its structure, which decouples the local and global information needed for the recommendation, makes it natural to introduce privacy in its framework.

Local computation and Randomized Response Technique. Local computation consists in keeping the profile of a user under his control on his own machine and to perform all the computations (or at least the sensitive ones) needed for the personalization on the clients' side. With respect to privacy, the main advantage of this technique is that the information of the user never leaves his computer, thus limiting the risks of privacy leaks. For instance, in the case of a recommender system, the local computation can be done in a transparent manner to the user by a module directly integrated within his browser. Several systems based on this approach have been proposed in the recent years, in particular in the context of privacy-preserving targeted advertisement systems, such as Privad [7], Adnostic [17] and RePriv [6].

Randomized Response Technique (RRT) can be seen as a specific form of local perturbation method in which the user perturbs himself his data before releasing it. Originally, this technique was invented by Warner [18] in the 1960's as a survey tool enabling individuals to randomize their answer on questions that are deemed sensitive while still preserving global statistical properties of the sample. In privacy, RRT is a general term referring to any local perturbation technique in which the user locally perturbs his data independently of the data of other users (in contrast to other methods such as k-anonymity sanitizing the data in a global manner).

3   Related Work

RRT methods for recommendation algorithm. Within the context of recommendation systems, Polat and Du [16] have developed a multi-group scheme to randomize the items of a profile. Using this technique, each user partitions the items of his profile into groups of same size and then each group is perturbed independently with some predefined probability p. One of the limits of this approach is that if the adversary has some knowledge about a particular group then this may help him to de-randomize this part of the profile. For instance, if the adversary knows that the first item of the group should be 1, then depending on the value observed on the released data, it can detect whether this group was perturbed or not and then potentially retrieve the original data for this group (at least provided that each item is binary).

In general, one of the main difficulty for assessing the privacy offered by a perturbation method (such as a RRT) is to have a meaningful measure of the risk that the adversary is likely to de-randomize this method. More precisely, to reason about the privacy guarantees provided by such method requires to understand how the adversary might infer the true ratings out of the perturbed ones. For instance, a recent study of Pashalidis and Preneel [15] has evaluated the privacy/utility trade-off provided by different classes of obfuscation strategies in the context of personalized services.

Privacy-preserving variants of Slope One. Basu, Vaidya and Kikuchi have proposed in the recent years three variants of Slope One integrating privacy into the design of the recommendation algorithm [1,2,3]. These three privacy-preserving variants of Slope One rely on very different approaches. For instance, one of the approach achieves privacy through the arbitrary partition of matrices [2] while the second is based on the use of cryptographic techniques [3]. More precisely, the main objective of the protocols proposed in [3] is to compute in a secure and distributed manner the output of the Slope One algorithm (namely the deviation and cardinality matrices) from rating data that is split among several sites.

The third approach is the closest to our work as it also corresponds to a perturbation technique combined with the use of homomorphic encryption [1]. This method adds noise to the deviation matrix during the training phase (*i.e.*, the time at which the matrices are computed) and to the ratings themselves at prediction time. In a nutshell, the prediction query of the user representing the item in which he is interested is protected through the use of homomorphic encryption scheme, such as the Paillier's cryptosystem [14], that has been set up by the user and which allows to perform arithmetic operations (such as addition and/or multiplication) on encrypted values. More precisely, the true ratings of the user are encrypted homomorphically and then send to the server storing the deviation and cardinality matrices. The server then perform the necessary computations in order to generate an encrypted version of the prediction before sending back the result to the user. Finally, the user can decrypt the result in order to fetch the corresponding prediction. The privacy of this scheme is ensured through the use of the homomorphic encryption for which the user is the only one to know the secret key. The experiments conducted on the Movielens dataset shows that proposed method is still accurate compared to the standard version of the algorithm (as measured in terms of MAE).

4   SlopPy

In this section, we describe SlopPy (for *Slope One with Privacy*), a privacy-preserving version of Slope One in which a user *never* releases directly his personal information (*i.e*, his ratings). In the rest of this section, we give an overview of the general architecture of the system in Section 4.1 (due to space limitations we leave the details of the architecture to the full version of this paper) before describing the SlopPy recommendation algorithm in Section 4.2.

4.1   Overview of the SlopPy Architecture

SlopPy architecture. Figure 1 illustrates the architecture of the SlopPy recommender system. More precisely in SlopPy, each user first perturbs locally his data (Step 1) by applying a *Randomized Response Technique* (RRT) before sending this information to the entity responsible for storing this information through an *anonymous communication channel* (Step 2). This entity is assumed to be *semi-trusted*, also sometimes called *honest-but-curious* in the sense that it is assumed to follow the directives of the protocol (*i.e.*, it will not for instance corrupt the perturbed ratings send by a user or try to influence the output of the recommendation algorithm) but nonetheless tries to extract as much information as it can from the data it receives. Out of the perturbed ratings, the semi-trusted entity constructs two matrices (*i.e.*, the deviation matrix and the cardinality matrix) following the Weighted Slope One algorithm (Step 3). When a user needs a recommendation on a particular movie, he queries these matrices through a variant of a *private information retrieval* scheme [13] (Step 4) hiding the content of his query (*i.e.*, the item he is interested in) to the semi-trusted entity. By combining the data retrieved (Step 5) with his true ratings (which once again are only stored on his machine), the user can then locally compute the output of the recommendation algorithm for this particular item (Step 6).

Philosophy behind SlopPy. Overall, the philosophy of SlopPy is that users contribute to the common good (*i.e.*, the construction of the deviation and cardinality matrices that are needed to perform the recommendation) but still protect

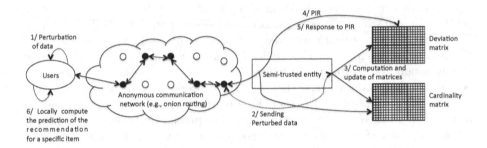

Fig. 1. Overview of the architecture of SlopPy

their privacy by not sending directly their true ratings but rather a perturbed version of it. The semi-trusted entity is responsible for administrating the common good in the sense of computing and storing the deviation and cardinality matrices, which are considered to be *public data* that any user should have the right to access[1]. On the other hand, the true ratings of a particular user are considered to be *private information* and are only stored locally on his machine. The computation of the prediction for a particular recommendation is done by the user querying the matrices through a *private information retrieval* scheme. In a nutshell, this technique allows a user to learn the content of a particular row of the matrix without the semi-trusted entity learning his query. One of the advantage of the centralized aspect of our system is that as the semi-trusted entity has access to all the perturbed ratings of the users, and therefore it can easily maintain and update the deviation and cardinality matrices.

Protection of privacy in SlopPy. In a recommender system, we believe that ensuring privacy amounts to design a system that can hide at least the three following information :

1. The true ratings of the user.
2. The identity of the user behind an action (*e.g.*, an action could be the submission of ratings during the training phase or a prediction request).
3. The content of the query itself (*i.e.*, the item the user is interested in).

In SlopPy, the ratings of the user are protected by randomizing them through the application of a RRT before they are released (see Section 4.2 for more details). In order to hide the identity of the user behind the submission of the ratings, the architecture of SlopPy relies on the use of an anonymous communication channel. This anonymous channel could be either implemented through the use of a proxy that is assumed to be independent of the semi-trusted entity

---

[1] We acknowledge that this assumption is not necessary compatible with a business model in which the knowledge of such matrices is considered as a business secret by the semi-trusted entity. In such situation, additional mechanisms should be used in order to limit the number of queries that a particular user can perform, for instance by relying on techniques such as oblivious transfer and anonymous e-cash.

(*i.e.*, not colluding with him) or through an anonymous communication network such as TOR (*The Onion Routing*) [5]. The advantage of the latter solution is that preservation of the identity of the user does not only rest on the shoulders of the single entity but rather the trust is spread among several nodes of the anonymous communication network. If the user needs to update his profile on a regular basis, it is possible to envision that the user can choose a long-term pseudonym. This pseudonym could be for instance the public verification key of a digital signature scheme that has been set up by the user. When the user needs to update his profile, he simply sends the ratings of new items that he has not rated previously through an anonymous communication channel along with a proof of his identity in the form of a signature on his updated profile. In particular, the user should not send another fresh randomized version of items that he has rated in the past. Otherwise, by observing several randomizations of the same rating, it may become possible for the server to de-randomize the ratings of a particular user by doing a simple average. Finally, the protection of the content of a query is ensured through a variant of a private information retrieval scheme based on homomorphic encryption scheme. This protocol allows to learn the content of a particular row of one of the matrices for an optimal communication cost of $\Theta(n)$, for n the number of items in the domain considered. We defer the details of this protocol as well as the detailed analysis of the architecture for the full version of the paper but overall the asymptotic complexity of SlopPy is the same as the Slope One algorithm. However, in practice the use of an anonymous channel as well as the use of homomorphic encryption induce an overhead that is likely to impact the performance in a non-negligible manner.

4.2   SlopPy Recommendation Algorithm

Randomization operator. The core of the SlopPy architecture is a recommendation algorithm, which is effectively a privacy-preserving variant of Weighted Slope One. The main modification of the algorithm consists in the participants sending a perturbed version of their ratings rather than their true ratings. More precisely, each participant applies a RRT on his profile in order to obtain the perturbed version. Only the perturbed version is released publicly to the semi-trusted third party responsible for constructing the deviation and the cardinality matrices while the true ratings are stored locally on the user's machine. We have constructed four different randomization operators for the RRT that we describe thereafter.

1. *Independent randomization.* With the method IndRand, each item in the profile is randomized in an independent manner with a probability p, which is an input parameter of the RRT method, and left untouched with the complementary probability $1 - p$. More precisely, if $p = 0$ then no randomization occurs (*i.e.*, the true ratings are unmodified) while a value of $p = 1$ means that *each* item of the profile is randomized. When a rating is randomized

then the perturbed rating is drawn uniformly at random among all the values except the original one. (Another possibility would have been to randomize over all possible values.)

2. *Deviation.* With the method Deviation, each rating is perturbed such that its value is likely to be slightly increased or decreased compared to the original value. This randomization operator is implemented by first drawing a random number a predefined interval chosen according to the rating scale and then generating a perturbed rate that corresponds to the addition of this random number to the original rating. If the generated rating is above or below the maximal (or minimal) possible rating then to ensure that this value remains within the set of possible rates by rounding it to the nearest integer within this set. For instance, in the Movielens dataset, the set of possible rates is $S = \{1, 2, 3, 4, 5\}$ and we choose to draw the random number in the interval $[-2, 2]$. In this setting, if the true rate had originally a value of 5 and the randomization should result in the rate being modified to 6 due to the rounding, instead the rating of 5 is chosen in order to remain within the set of possible values. We acknowledge that this method is not perfect in the sense that it makes some ratings more probable than others, which could be an issue with respect to privacy. In the future, we plan to investigate the potential risks for privacy induced by this method in order to better understand its limits.

3. *Deviation and randomization.* The method DevAndRand is simply composed of the application of the Deviation method on all ratings, followed by the application of the IndRand method on the ratings resulting from the previous method.

4. *Block randomization.* The method BlockRand decomposes the profile of the user into block of ratings of same size and then for each block, all the ratings of this block are randomized with probability p (as with the IndRand but with the difference that each rating is not randomized independently) or all left untouched. For the experiments reported in this paper, we have chosen to use a block size of 10 items for all users but of course other block sizes are possible (*e.g.*, block size of 5 or 15 items).

Prediction method. Beside the different randomization operators, we have also studied two different ways to predict a rating (both are based on Equation 3). The first method called PerturbedRec performs the recommendation by taking into account the perturbed version of the ratings while computing Slope One. On the other hand, the second method called OriginalRec injects the true ratings in the part of the Slope One algorithm that can be computed locally. This is made possible by the fact that all the users keep locally a copy of their true ratings. More precisely, using the method PerturbedRec means that the perturbed ratings generated during Step 1 will also be considered as the local input of the prediction during Step 6 while with the method OriginalRec the local inputs to Step 6 are the original ratings unmodified.

5   Experimental Results

In this section, we briefly report on the preliminary results we have obtained by testing the SlopPy algorithm. More precisely, we have tested the different randomization and prediction methods detailed in Section 4.2 on the Movielens dataset and compared the accuracy obtained for different parameters as well as against the "non-private" Weighted Slope One algorithm. The Movielens dataset contains 100 000 ratings provided by 943 users on 1682 different movies (*i.e.*, items), with an average number of ratings of 106 ratings per user but a high variance. Therefore, the number of items $n = 1682$ and the dataset is sparse in the sense that an overall of 100 000 ratings out of the 1 586 126 possible ratings corresponds to a density of 6.3%.

To evaluate the accuracy of the recommendation algorithm of SlopPy, we rely on two metrics: the standard Mean Absolute Error (MAE) and the Root Mean Squared Error (RMSE). The MAE measures the average absolute error between the true rating $r_{u,i}$ provided by user u on item i and the rating $\hat{r}_{u,i}$ predicted by the recommendation algorithm. More precisely, the MAE is generated by computing the absolute difference $\mid \hat{r}_{u,i} - r_{u,i} \mid$ for each user u and item i whose rating is known and then averaging by dividing by the total number of predictions. The smaller the MAE, the more accurate is the recommendation. Indeed, a MAE whose value is equal to zero would correspond to a recommendation algorithm making a perfect prediction, which is never observed in practice. Similarly to the MAE, the RMSE also quantifies the difference between a predicted rating $\hat{r}_{u,i}$ and a true rating $r_{u,i}$. More precisely, the RMSE corresponds to the square root of the sum of the squared difference between $(\hat{r}_{u,i} - r_{u,i})^2$ normalized by the total number of predictions. Like the MAE, a small RMSE is an indication of a good accuracy for the recommendation.

We compare SlopPy by using the standard Weighted Slope One algorithm as the baseline. On the Movielens dataset, the baseline displays a MAE of 0.68 and a RMSE of 0.85. As SlopPy perturbs the inputs provided to the recommendation algorithm by performing the RRT on the ratings used to build the deviation and cardinality matrices, we expect intuitively that the accuracy of the recommendation will be degraded as well, thus resulting in a higher MAE and RMSE. This intuition was confirmed by the results of experiments as demonstrated by Figures 2 and 3. Furthermore, Figure 3 clearly shows that predicting a rating while using the original ratings kept locally lead to a high accuracy even if the ratings transmitted have been perturbed heavily, which is not the case when the prediction is done by using also the perturbed ratings (*cf.* Figure 2). In addition, SlopPy seems to be robust as the MAE and the RMSE smoothly vary when the number of perturbed ratings increases. With respect to the Deviation method (which is equivalent to the DevAndRand method with a randomization probability $p = 0$), the MAE and the RMSE were respectively around 0.74 and 1.05 when PerturbedRec was used as a prediction method, and 0.70 (MAE) and 0.88 (RMSE) when relying on OriginalRec for the prediction. In terms of computational time, SlopPy (much like Slope One) is very efficient and running it

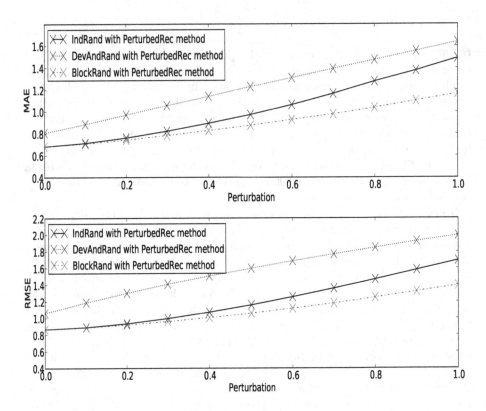

Fig. 2. Computation of the MAE and RMSE for the IndRand, DevAndRand and BlockRand randomization methods for the prediction method PerturbedRec. The x-axis indicates the *perturbation* in terms of the probability p. For instance, a perturbation of 0.9 means that on average 9 ratings out of 10 are randomized (or conversely that 1 rating out of 10 is left untouched).

on the whole Movielens dataset takes approximately two minutes on a MacBook Pro with a 2.4GHz Intel Core i7 and 4GB of RAM.

6   Discussion and Future Work

In the future, we would like to investigate other randomization operators such as an erasure/creation operator that will delete some true ratings and on the contrary also generate a random rating for a particular item when there was none. In particular, we would like to observe how this type of randomization affects the utility of the recommendation. We believe that the use of such an operator (possibly combined with other randomization operators) is one of the few ways to avoid linking attacks by which the adversary (which could be for instance the semi-trusted entity) uses some *a priori* knowledge to de-anonymize

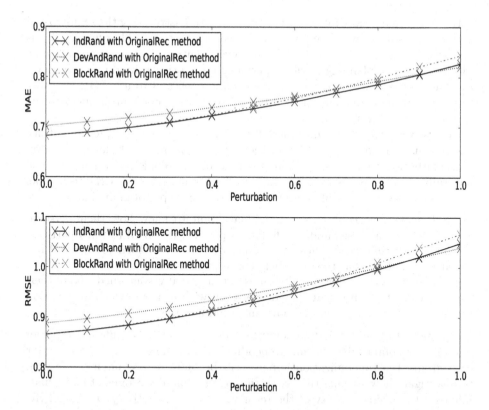

Fig. 3. Computation of the MAE and RMSE for the IndRand, DevAndRand and BlockRand randomization methods for the prediction method OriginalRec. The *x*-axis indicates the *perturbation* in terms of the probability *p*. For instance, a perturbation of 0.9 means that on average 9 ratings out of 10 are randomized (or conversely that 1 rating out of 10 is left untouched).

a particular dataset. For instance, if the adversary knows that a Alice has seen 3 movies among which two are quite uncommon, the combination of these 3 movies could act as quasi-identifiers and be potentially used to de-anonymize Alice when she submit her ratings to SlopPy even if she submit her records anonymously after having perturbed them. This type of inference attack is similar in spirit to the de-anonymization attack conducted by Narayanan and Shmatikov on the Netflix dataset [11].

With respect to the architecture, we would like to design a distributed version of the semi-trusted entity. Indeed in the current architecture, all the trust rests on the shoulders of this entity, which is assumed to follow the recipe of the Slope One algorithm and not to try to influence the outcome of the recommendation. This security assumption is not necessarily safe to make in some context in which the semi-trusted entity might be tempted to influence the recommendation in order for some items to be recommended more often (for instance the semi-trusted entity might make more money out of these items). Distributing the semi-trusted entity, for instance by relying on techniques such as threshold cryptography, is a possible approach to split the trust on several entities instead of a single one. Moreover, we are planning to run experimentally a private information retrieval to evaluate the practical efficiency of such approach and to use TOR as a way to simulate the anonymous channel by which a user can submit a query to the private information retrieval scheme.

We also want to study in more details the interplay between privacy and utility and how users might adjust their privacy level by themselves tailoring the level of perturbation that they apply to their needs. In SlopPy, this can be done naturally by allowing users to set up their level of noise for the RRT technique. For instance, Kobsa [8] differentiates between three types of individuals:

- *Extremely concerned.* These individuals want to know how their personal information are used and which data is possibly disclosed to third parties.
- *Somewhat concerned.* These individuals do care about their privacy but not at the same level as the extremely concerned.
- *Mildly concerned.* These individuals are not really concerned about their privacy in the sense that they do not even wish to know which information is collected about them and how this information is used.

We propose to adopt this taxonomy in order to model the different types of users of a recommender system. Depending on the chosen level of privacy for each group, the randomization applied will be more or less intense. We plan to investigate how varying the proportion of the different groups of individuals influence the overall quality of the recommendation. Intuitively, if most of the population is composed of the extremely concerned then it is to be expected to the accuracy of the recommendation will be lower than if the three populations are uniformly present but of course this intuition needs to be verified and quantified.

Finally, in order to give precise privacy guarantees we want to analyze the possible risks of de-randomization on the proposed methods by studying the distributions that they induced on the outputs (*i.e.*, ratings). Indeed, if the proposed randomized operator leads to distributions that are closed to each other whatever the original input then this means that the probability of de-randomizing a particular perturbed rating is small.

Acknowledgments. This research has been funded by the Quaero program and the Inria large scale project CAPPRIS (Collaborative Action on the Protection of Privacy Rights).

References

1. Basu, A., Vaidya, J., Kikuchi, H.: Perturbation Based Privacy Preserving Slope One Predictors for Collaborative Filtering. In: Dimitrakos, T., Moona, R., Patel, D., McKnight, D.H. (eds.) IFIPTM 2012. IFIP AICT, vol. 374, pp. 17–35. Springer, Heidelberg (2012)

2. Basu, A., Vaidya, J., Kikuchi, H.: Privacy preserving weighted Slope One predictor for item-based collaborative filtering. In: Proceedings of the International Workshop on Trust and Privacy in Distributed Information Processing (co-organized with IFIPTM 2011) (2011)

3. Basu, A., Vaidya, J., Kikuchi, H.: Efficient privacy-preserving collaborative filtering based on the weighted Slope One predictor. Journal of Internet Services and Information Security 1(4) (2011)

4. Das, A., Datar, M., Garg, A.: Google news personalization: Scalable online collaborative filtering. In: Proceedings of the 16th International Conference on World Wide Web (WWW 2007), pp. 271–280 (2007)

5. Dingledine, R., Mathewson, N., Syverson, P.: Tor: The second-generation onion router. In: Proceedings of the 13th USENIX Security Symposium, pp. 303–320 (2004)

6. Fredrikson, M., Livshits, B.: RePriv: Re-imagining content personalization and in-browser privacy. In: Proceedings of the 32nd IEEE Symposium on Security and Privacy, pp. 131–146 (2011)

7. Guha, S., Cheng, B., Francis, P.: Privad: practical privacy in online advertising. In: Proceedings of the 8th USENIX Symposium on Networks, System Design and Implementation (2011)

8. Kobsa, A.: Privacy-enhanced personalization. Communications of the ACM 50(8), 24–33 (2007)

9. Lemire, D., Maclachlan, A.: Slope One predictors for online rating-based collaborative filtering. In: Proceedings of the 2005 SIAM International Data Mining Conference (SDM 2005) (2005)

10. Linden, G., Smith, B., York, J.: Amazon.com recommendations item-to-item collaborative filtering. IEEE Internet Computing 7(1), 76–80 (2003)

11. Narayanan, A., Shmatikov, V.: Robust de-anonymization of large sparse datasets. In: Proceedings of the 29th IEEE Symposium on Security and Privacy, pp. 111–125 (2008)

12. Olesen, H., Noll, J., Hoffmann, M.: User profiles, personalization and privacy (2009)

13. Ostrovsky, R., Skeith III, W.E.: A Survey of Single-Database Private Information Retrieval: Techniques and Applications. In: Okamoto, T., Wang, X. (eds.) PKC 2007. LNCS, vol. 4450, pp. 393–411. Springer, Heidelberg (2007)

14. Paillier, P.: Public-Key Cryptosystems Based on Composite Degree Residuosity Classes. In: Stern, J. (ed.) EUROCRYPT 1999. LNCS, vol. 1592, pp. 223–238. Springer, Heidelberg (1999)

15. Pashalidis, A., Preneel, B.: Evaluating tag-based preference obfuscation systems. IEEE Transactions on Knowledge and Data Engineering 24(9), 1613–1623 (2012)

16. Polat, H., Du, W.: Achieving Private Recommendations Using Randomized Response Techniques. In: Ng, W.-K., Kitsuregawa, M., Li, J., Chang, K. (eds.) PAKDD 2006. LNCS (LNAI), vol. 3918, pp. 637–646. Springer, Heidelberg (2006)

17. Toubiana, V., Narayanan, A., Boneh, D., Nissenbaum, H., Barocas, S.: Adnostic: Privacy preserving targeted advertising. In: Proceedings of the Network and Distributed System Security Symposium, NDSS 2010 (2010)

18. Warner, S.L.: Randomized response: A survey technique for eliminating evasive answer bias. Journal of the American Statistical Association 60, 63–69 (1965)

A Semi-lattice Model for Multi-lateral Security

Florian Kammüller

Middlesex University, London and Technische Universität Berlin
f.kammueller@mdx.ac.uk, flokam@cs.tu-berlin.de

Abstract. In this paper, we present a new security model for distributed active objects. This model emphasizes the aspects of decentralisation and private data of objects. We consider principals as active objects thereby amalgamating subjects and objects into one concept providing a simple uniform security model based on visibility of objects and object local security specification of method accessibility. Decentralized security policies are possible in which every principal has some data that is inaccessible to others. We introduce this new security model algebraically as a semi-lattice contrasting it to the foundations of lattice-based security models similar to Denning's work. As a proof of concept we show how the model can be naturally interpreted for a calculus of active objects.

1 Introduction

Active objects enclose data and act by exchanging method calls with other active objects in a configuration. The central point of this investigation is how security and privacy relate to active objects. We present a security model that is tailored to them and is thus centered around the following two points. Instead of considering principals as "real" identities that are external to the system, we consider their representation in the system as active objects, thereby economizing a conceptual distinction between objects and subjects by commonly considering them as active objects. Secondly, we utilize the confinement property of objects to provide a language based concept for privacy. Consider Figure 1: multi-level security models support strict hierarchies like military organization (left); multi-lateral security is intended to support a decentralized security world where parties A to E share resources without a strict hierarchy (right). But all lattice-based security models actually achieve the middle schema: since a lattice has joins, there is a security class $A \sqcup B \sqcup C \sqcup D \sqcup E$ that has access to all classes A to E. For a truely decentralized multi-lateral security model this top element is considered harmful. Since joins and meets are the only tool available we solve the problem by using semi-lattices that omit joins.

Denning [10] first defined an algebraic model for Bell-LaPadula: multi-level security (MLS) combines total orders, e.g. unclassified ... top secret, with sets of compartments, e.g. {*personnel, sales*}, into a lattice of security classes. Those classes are used to contain subjects and objects (i.e., their identities) and allow access control decisions of information flow control based on the order. Twenty years later, Myers and Liskov define the Decentralized Label Model (DLM) [22]

R. Di Pietro et al. (Eds.): DPM 2012 and SETOP 2012, LNCS 7731, pp. 118–132, 2013.

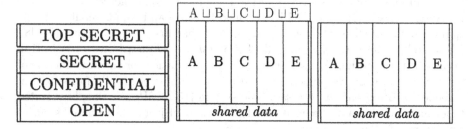

Fig. 1. Multi-level security[4, Ch. 8] and multi-lateral security: idea and reality

by simplifying hierarchy levels and compartments directly into a (powerset) lattice over principals' identities, e.g. Alice A and Bob B. They thus emphasize the user orientation (decentralization) and economize by labeling the system objects (program elements) directly. Now, we take that simplification trend further by additionally identifying the principals identities with active objects thus commonly treating subjects and objects. Consequently, our security classes are constituted as sets of active objects identities. The DLM merges the concept of read and write into the classification (owners and readers can be separately assigned to a class). While this allows considering confidentiality and integrity simultaneously, we prefer to leave this distinction out of the classification to make the concepts simpler. In this paper we only deal with confidentiality but as usual integrity can be simply achieved since it is given by duality.

The main contribution of this work is a security model for distributed active objects; analysis tools for the language concepts of active objects based on their visibility, and asynchronous communication with futures have been provided in a proof of concept for ASP_fun. The security model differs from the usual ones.

In this paper, we first introduce active objects by reviewing ASP_fun [15] providing a foundation for the further presentation of our new model (Section 2). The following section then presents the semi-lattice as our security model combining two classical lattices (Section 3) where the attacker is also an active object – like any other principal. Based on the security semi-lattice model, we then consider information flow for active objects (Section 4). We also provide a formal information flow predicate, a notion of noninterference, for active objects summarizing our technical underpinning of the suggested model in the formal framework ASP_fun which includes a type system for static analysis of security. We end the paper wrapping up with related work and conclusions (Section 5). Detailed proofs, formalizations, and example inferences are available online [19].

2   Active Objects

Active objects are like actors [2] but are closer integrated with the concepts of object-orientation. An object is an *active object* if it serves as an access point to its own methods and associated (passive) objects and their threads. Consequently, every call to those methods will be from outside. These remote calls are collected in a list of requests. A practical implementation of active objects is the ProActive system [7] a Java API developed by Inria and commercialized by its spin-off ActiveEON. A theory of active objects has first been given as ASP [8]. We introduce here ASP_{fun}, our calculus of *functional* distributed objects [15], because it is (a) designed to serve as a concise foundation for the introduction of new concepts for active objects and (b) because is has been fully formalized in Isabelle/HOL together with a safe type system [15]. ASP_{fun} is thus best suited to formally develop a new security model for active objects and a related security type system for the static analysis of security.

Activity. The ensemble of active object, passive objects and request list defines an *activity*. The entries in the list of requests can be accessed uniquely by futures.

Futures. A *future* can intuitively be described as a promise for the result of a method call. The concept of futures has been introduced in Mulitlisp [14] and enables asynchronous processing of method calls in distributed applications: on calling a method a future is immediately returned to the caller enabling the continuation of the computation at the caller side. Only if the method call's value is needed, a so-called wait-by-necessity may occur. Futures identify the results of asynchronous method invocations to an activity. Technically, we can see a future as a pair consisting of a future *reference* and a future *value*. The future reference points to the future value which is the instance of a method call in the request queue of a remote activity. In the following, we will use future and future *reference* synonymously for simplicity. Futures can be transmitted between activities. Thus different activities can use the same future.

2.1 A Simple Language of Active Objects

Let us use a slightly extended form of the simplest ς-calculus from the Theory of Objects [1] by distributing ς-calculus objects into activities. Our simple object calculus is functional because method update is realized on a copy of the object: there are no side-effects.

ς-*calculus.* Objects consist of a set of labeled methods $[l_i = \varsigma(y)b]^{i\in 1..n}$ (attributes are considered as methods not using the parameters). The calculus features method call $t.l(s)$ and method update $t.l := \varsigma(y)b$ on objects where ς is the binder for the method parameter y. Every method may also contain a "*this*" element representing the surrounding object. The this is classically expressed as a second parameter x but we use literally *this* to facilitate understanding. The ς-calculus is Turing complete, e.g. it can simulate the λ-calculus. We illustrate the ς-calculus by our example below.

Syntax of ASP_{fun}. ASP_{fun} is a minimal extension of the ς-calculus by one single additional primitive, the *Active*, for creating an activity. In the syntax (see Table 1) we distinguish between underlined constructs representing the static syntax

Table 1. ASP$_{\text{fun}}$ syntax

$$
\begin{array}{llr}
s, t ::= & y & \text{variable} \\
\mid & \underline{this} & \text{generic object reference} \\
\mid & \overline{[l_j = \varsigma(y_j)t_j]^{j \in 1..n}} & \text{object definition} \\
\mid & \overline{s.l_i(t)} & (i \in 1..n) \text{ method call} \\
\mid & \overline{s.l_i := \varsigma(y)t} & (i \in 1..n) \text{ update} \\
\mid & \overline{Active(s)} & \text{Active object creation} \\
\mid & \alpha & \text{active object reference} \\
\mid & f_i & \text{future}
\end{array}
$$

that may be used by a programmer, while futures and active object references are created at runtime.

We use the naming convention s, t for ς-terms, α, β for active objects, f_k, f_j for futures, Q_α, Q_β for request queues.

Configuration. A *configuration* of active objects is a set of activities

$$
C ::= \alpha_i [(f_j \mapsto s_j)^{j \in I_i}, t_i]^{i \in 1..p}
$$

where $\{I_i\}$ are disjoint subsets of $\mathbb{N}$. The unordered list $(f_j \mapsto s_j)^{j \in I_i}$ represents the request queue, t_i the active object, and $\alpha_i \in \text{dom}(C)$ the activity reference. A configuration represents the "state" of a distributed system by the current parallel activities. Computation is now the state change induced by the evaluation of method calls in the request queues of the activities. To keep our active object language semantics simple, we define active objects t_i to be immutable after their creation. However, since the configuration is changed *globally* by the stepwise computation of requests and the creation of new activities, we can easily simulate state change.

The constructor $Active(t)$ activates the object t by creating a new activity in which the object t becomes active object. Although the active object of an activity is immutable, an update operation on activities is provided. It performs an update on a freshly created copy of the active object placing it into a new activity with empty request queue; the invoking context receives the new activity reference in return. If we want to model operations that change active objects, we can do so using the update. Although the changes are not literally performed on the original objects, a state change can thus be implemented at the level of configurations (for examples see [15,17]). Efficiency is not the goal of ASP$_{\text{fun}}$ rather minimality of representation with respect to the main decisive language features of active objects while being fully formal.

Results, values, programs and initial configuration. A term is a result, i.e., a totally evaluated term, if it is either an object (like in [1]) or an activity reference. We consider values as results [15].

In a usual programming language, a programmer does not write configurations but usual programs invoking some distribution or concurrency primitives (in

ASP$_\text{fun}$ *Active* is the only such primitive). This is reflected by the ASP$_\text{fun}$ syntax given above. A "program" is a term s_0 given by this static syntax (it has no future or active object reference and no free variable). In order to be evaluated, this program must be placed in an initial configuration. The initial configuration has a single activity with a single request consisting of the user program:

$$initConf(s_0) = \alpha[f_0 \mapsto s_0, []]$$

Sets of data that can be used as *values* are indispensable if we want to reason about information flows. In ASP$_\text{fun}$, such values can be represented as results (see above) to any configuration either by explicit use of some corresponding object terms or by appropriate extension of the initial configuration that leads to the set-up of a data base of basic datatypes, like integers or strings.

Local semantics (the relation $\rightarrow_\varsigma$) and the *parallel* (configuration) semantics (the relation $\rightarrow_\parallel$) are informally described as follows.

- LOCAL: the local reduction relation $\rightarrow_\varsigma$ is based on the ς-calculus.
- ACTIVE: *Active(t)* creates a new activity α, with t as its active object, global new name α, and initially no futures; altogether we write this in our notation as $\alpha[\varnothing, t]$.
- REQUEST: *method call* $\beta.l(t)$ creates new future f_k for the method l of active object β; the future f_k can be used to refer to the future value $\beta.l(t)$ at any time.
- REPLY: *returns result*, i.e., replaces future f_k by the referenced result term, i.e., the future value resulting from some $\beta.l(t)$.
- UPDATE-AO: *active object update* creates a copy of the active object and updates the active object of the copy – the original remains the same (functional active objects are *immutable*).

2.2   Example: Private Sorting

As an example for a standard program consider the implementation of quick sort as an active object χ illustrated in Figure 2. The operations we use are :: for list cons, @ for list append, # for list length, *hd* for the list head, and a let construct (see [15] for details on their implementation).

$$
\begin{aligned}
&\chi[\varnothing, \\
&\quad [\text{qsort} = \varsigma(y) \text{ if } y = [] \text{ then } [] \\
&\qquad\qquad\quad \text{else let } (a :: l) = y \\
&\qquad\qquad\qquad\quad (l_1, l_2) = this.\text{part } (a, l) \\
&\qquad\qquad\qquad\quad l_1' = \text{if } \#l_1 \leq 1 \text{ then } l_1 \text{ else } this.\text{qsort}(l_1) \\
&\qquad\qquad\qquad\quad l_2' = \text{if } \#l_2 \leq 1 \text{ then } l_2 \text{ else } this.\text{qsort}(l_2) \\
&\qquad\qquad\quad \text{in } l_1'@[a]@l_2' \text{ end,} \\
&\quad \text{part} = \varsigma(p, y) \text{ if } y = [] \text{ then } ([], []) \\
&\qquad\qquad\quad \text{else let } (a :: l) = y \\
&\qquad\qquad\qquad\quad (l_1, l_2) = this.\text{part } (p, l) \\
&\qquad\qquad\quad \text{in if } p < (a.\text{ord}) \text{ then } (l_1, a :: l_2) \text{ else } (a :: l_1, l_2) \text{ end}] \\
&\quad]
\end{aligned}
$$

The quick sort algorithm in χ is parametric over a numerical order method "ord" used in method part assumed to be available uniformly in the target objects contained in the list that shall be sorted. The following controller object α holds a list of active objects (for now left out) using the quicksort algorithm provided by χ to sort this list on execution of the manage method.

$$\alpha\big[\varnothing, [\text{manage} = \varsigma(y)\,this.\text{sort}(this.\text{list}),$$
$$\text{sort} = \varsigma(y)\ \chi.\text{qsort}(y)$$
$$\text{list} = \dots]\big]$$

The target objects contained in $\alpha's$ (omitted) list are active objects of the kind of β below. Here, the n in the body of method ord is an integer specific to β and the field income shall represent some private confidential data in β.

$$\beta\big[\varnothing, [\text{ord} = \varsigma(y)n, \text{income} = \dots]\big]$$

If active objects of the kind of β represent principals in the system, it becomes clear what is the privacy challenge: the controller should be able to sort his list of β-principals without learning anything about their private data, here income.

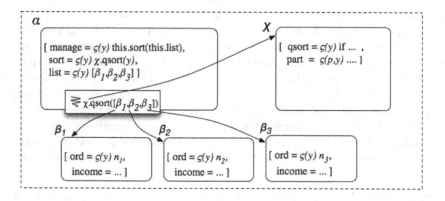

Fig. 2. Example configuration with three active objects $\beta_1, \beta_2, \beta_3$ in controller α's list

3   The Semi-lattice Security Model for Active Objects

The main differences of our model to classical models are that principals are identified with active objects and the model is a multi-lateral security model. Our model simply combines a security classification *local* to objects with a *global* security classification of objects. Each of these classifications is a classical security class lattice but together they are only a semi-lattice to avoid privacy breaches.

Confidentiality. A computation of active objects is an evaluation of a distributed set of mutually referencing activities. Principals, objects, programs and values are thus all contained in this configuration. There are no external inputs to this system – it is a closed system of communicating actors. The representation of active objects by remotely accessible activities is the key to confidentiality. Remote method calls are issued along these references, the resulting futures follow the same references, and consequently all information flows along them. We coin the name *visibility* for the relation spanned by the public activity references of a configuration (see Definition 1, Section 4.2). In order to judge admissible information flows, we use visibility as the flow relation of a concrete configuration (see Section 4). To define all possible security classes and their flow relation we construct the algebraic structure of a semi-lattice of activities and its partial order relation. These classes are assigned to activities of a concrete configuration by labeling (see below).

Attacker Model. We adopt a language based approach to security. Thus, we restrict the attacker to only have the means of the language to make his observations. Consequently, we can consider the attacker – as any other principal – as being represented by an activity. The attacker's knowledge is determined by all active objects he sees, more precisely their public parts. If any of the internal computations in inaccessible parts of other objects leak information, the attacker can learn about them by noticing differences in different runs of the same configuration. Inaccessible parts of other objects are their private methods or other objects that are referenced in these private parts. Our security model is considered below as the basis for a more formal definition of information flow security (see Section 4.2). Our information flow predicate is a noninterference property: a program is secure for a given security classification if the visible parts from the viewpoint of an attacker remain the same for all possible evaluations of the configuration. The attacker can be anyone leading to a general multi-lateral information flow predicate. Thus, the model also includes colluding attackers.

Semi-Lattice. The semi-lattice of security classes for active objects is a combination of global and local security lattices.

Local Classification and Global Classification. For every active object there is the public (L) and a private (H) level partitioning the set of this active object's methods. To remotely access active objects, the key is their identity. As a semantical representation of security classes for our principals, we thus chose sets of activity references. They form the *compartments* with respect to the Denning MLS terminology [10]. Sets of compartments, so-called *categories*, build the security classes, a lattice $\mathcal{P}(\mathcal{I})$.

$$(\mathcal{P}(\mathcal{I}), \cap, \cup, \subseteq, \varnothing, \mathcal{I})$$

In a concrete configuration, the assignment of principals to global classes results from visibility.

Combination of Lattices. The semi-lattice of security classes for active objects is a combination of global and local security lattices. The order relation of the global lattice is the visibility relation and the order relation of the local lattice is the relation $\leq$ defined on $\{L, H\}$ as $\{(L, L), (L, H), (H, H)\}$. Private methods of an object are not visible to any other than the object itself. To realize this exclusiveness, the combined security class ordering for active objects is defined such that a method class (H, δ) dominates (L, δ) but no other (X, δ_0) dominates (H, δ). The combination of local and global types into pairs gives a partial order

$$CL \equiv (\{L, H\} \times \mathcal{P}(\mathcal{I}), \sqsubseteq)$$

with

$$(S_0, I_0) \sqsubseteq (S_1, I_1) \equiv \left(\begin{matrix} S_0 <_S S_1 \vee S_0 = S_1 = L \\ I_0 \subseteq I_1 \end{matrix} \right)$$

where $<_S = \{(L, H)\}$ is the strict ordering on the local security classes. We use the vertical notation $\binom{\phi}{\xi}$ to abbreviate $\phi \wedge \xi$. Consequently, meets exist but no joins. The partial order CL is thus just a semi-lattice as seen in Figure 3.

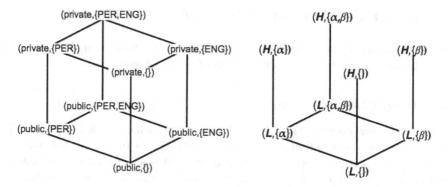

Fig. 3. Taking the top off MLS lattice (left example) leads to semi-lattice on the right

Practical Classification. The pairs in CL are the classes for methods. Since all methods in an object have the same global second component δ, we can factor out this global label of the object representing the object label by (a) each method l_i is labeled simply with L or H. (b) objects are labeled with a pair $([l_i = S_i]^{i=1..n}, \delta)$ where $S_i \in \{L, H\}$ is method l_i's label and δ is the object's global classification.

Labeling Example. To illustrate how activities are labeled in the semi-lattice model, consider the running example from Section 2.2 where we assume the list in controller to contain various active object references $[\beta_0, \ldots, \beta_n]$. We assign to each activity the global class containing its own identity and those of all its visible activities. For our example, the *global* class of controller would be the following.

$$\delta_{\text{controller}} = \{\text{controller}\} \cup \delta_\chi \cup \bigcup_{i=0..n} \delta_{\beta_i}$$

The global classes δ_{β_i} of the β_i objects and δ_χ in turn contain all their visible objects' classes. The practical labeling of an object is illustrated as follows by the label of the β_i objects specifying the method ord as public but income not.

$$(\{\text{ord} \mapsto L, \text{income} \mapsto H\}, \delta_{\beta_i})$$

The classifications are accurate if we assume that there is no "backward" visibility, i.e., from β_i to α for some $i \in 0..n$. Since the visibility relation is a partial order it is also antisymmetric. Consequently, in case of mutual visibility, the activities become assigned to the same class. Note, that in ASP$_{\text{fun}}$ this cannot happen: due to a *no cycle* property [15], no cyclic references can occur. Therefore, every global security class labels at most one activity. For generalization of the security model to arbitrary active object languages, cycles and the resulting commonality of security classes needs to be taken into account.

4   Information Flow of Distributed Active Objects

In the following we first recall the main concepts of information flow applying them to our system view of configurations of active objects.

4.1   Information Flow Control

Information flow control [11] technically uses an *information flow policy* which is given by the specification of a set of *security classes* to classify information and a *flow relation* on these classes that defines allowed information flows. System entities that contain information, for example variables x, y, are bound to security classes. Any operation that uses the value of x to calculate that of y, creates a flow of information from x to y. This operation is only admissible if the class of y dominates the class of x in the flow relation, formally written $\delta_x \sqsubseteq \delta_y$ where δ_e denotes the class of entity e. The concept of information flow classically stipulates that the security classes together with the flow relation as an order relation on the classes are a lattice [10,9]. We differ here.

Information Flow Control for Active Objects. Information is contained in data values which are here either objects or activity references (see Section 2). To apply the concept of information flow control to configurations of active objects, we need to interpret the above notions of security classes, their flow relation, and the entities that are assigned to the security classes: we identify the classes of our security model as the security classes of methods and the flow relation as the semi-lattice ordering on these classes. Flows of information local to objects are generated by local method calls between neighboring methods of the same object. These are regulated by the local L/H-classification of an object's methods. Global flows result from remote method calls between object's methods. The combined admissible flows have to be in accordance with a concrete configuration. We introduce in the following section the concept of visibility as the flow relation that provides such a combination.

Enforcing Legal Information Flows. To illustrate the task of controlling information flows, we first extend the intuition about information flow to configurations of active objects. An active object sees only other active objects that are directly referenced in its methods or those active objects that are indirectly visible via public methods of visible objects. From the viewpoint of one active object, information may flow into the object and out of the object. For each direction, there are two ways how information may flow: implicit or explicit flows. Information flows *explicitly into* an object by parameters passed to remote calls directed to the object's methods; it may also flow *implicitly into* the object simply if the choice of which method is called depends on the control flow of the calling object. Similarly, information flows *explicitly out* of an active object by parameters passed to remote method calls and *implicitly out* of it, if the choice depends on the object's own control flow. Some of these flows are illustrated on our running example below.

Information Flow Example. We will now finally illustrate the security model on the running example showing implicit information flows of active objects introduced above in Section 2.2. Let us assume that the implementation of the β-objects featuring in the controller's list had the following implementation.

```
β[∅,
   [ord = ς(y)ord',
    income = ... ,
    ord' = ς(y) if this.income − y ∗ 1000 > 0 then ord'(y + 1) else y]
   ]
```

Let us further assume that ord and ord' were public methods and income again the private field of β. We have here a case of an implicit information flow: since the guard of the if-command in ord' depends on the private field income, effectively the order number of a β-object is the income modulo 1K of β. Under our security model this control flow represents an illicit flow of information from a high level value in β to its public parts and is thus visible to the controller which should not be the case. It should thus be detectable by an information flow control analysis: we will show next how to detect it statically by a security type system.

4.2   Proof of Concept

To show that the security model for active objects provides a viable basis for security analysis of active object languages, we provide an instance of this model for the calculus of functional active objects ASP_{fun}. To provide this proof of concept, we first give a formal definition of visibility for ASP_{fun} followed by the definition of the information flow predicates α-noninterference and its generalization to multi-level security. We finally briefly summarize our work on a security type system based on this.

Visibility is defined formally in ASP_{fun} by Definition 1. This definition distinguishes the two cases how an active object name α can be visible to another active object β.

Definition 1 (Visibility). *Let C be a configuration with a security specification sec partitioning the methods of each of C's active objects locally into H and L methods. Then, the relation $\leq_{VI}$ is inductively defined on activities by the following two cases. The context variable E denotes a ς-term context [19].*

$$\begin{pmatrix} C(\beta) = \beta[Q_\beta, [l_i = \varsigma(y)t_i]^{i\in 1..n}] \\ sec(l_i) = L \wedge t_i = E[\alpha] \end{pmatrix} \Rightarrow \alpha \leq_{VI} \beta$$
$$\begin{pmatrix} C(\beta) = \beta[Q_\beta, [l_i = \varsigma(y)t_i]^{i\in 1..n}] \\ sec(l_i) = L \wedge t_i = E[\gamma] \wedge \alpha \leq_{VI} \gamma \end{pmatrix} \Rightarrow \alpha \leq_{VI} \beta$$

We then define the relation called visibility $\sqsubseteq_C^{sec}$ as the reflexive transitive closure over $\leq_{VI}$ for any C, sec. If the configuration C and security assignment sec are clear from context, we may omit C and sec. □

In ASP_{fun} active objects are created by activation, futures by method calls. Names of active objects and futures may differ in evaluations of the same configuration but this does not convey any information to the attacker. In order to express the resulting structural equivalence, we use typed bijections [6] that enable the definition of an isomorphism of configurations necessary to define indistinguishability. This technique of using the existence of "partial bijections" to define an isomorphism between configurations only serves to express equality of visible parts but is rather technical as it needs to provide differently typed bijections for the involved structure, e.g. futures, objects, and request lists. We therefore omit it here. It is in full contained in [19]. *Indistinguishability* must be read here simply as equal (up to names) from α's viewpoint.

To illustrate α-indistinguishability, consider the running example of Section 2.2 and its change to the β-objects in Section 4.1. Let in both instances ord be specified as L and income as H. In the first implementation of β in Section 2.2, $\beta's$ ord attribute is a fixed value n. For any run of the configuration containing χ, controller α, and various instances of β-objects, the controller perceives ord as the same n_i for any of the objects β_i. However, in the second implementation of β in the previous section, the controller sees a different value for ord if the income of an object β_i changes. Assuming controller α to be the attacker, he can make deductions about a change in the H-classified income of this β_i: an implicit information flow against the flow relation since income is H and ord and ord' are L thus visible to α. If none of those flows occurs – neither explicit nor implicit ones – the configuration is α-noninterfering.

Definition 2 (α-Noninterference). *If configuration C_0 is indistinguishable to any C_1 for α with respect to sec and the corresponding visibility and remains so* *under the evaluation of configurations* $\rightarrow_\|$, *then* C_0 *is noninterfering with respect to sec for* α.

$$\begin{pmatrix} C_0 \rightarrow_\| C_0' \\ C_0 \sim_\alpha C_1 \end{pmatrix} \Longrightarrow \exists\ C_1'.\begin{pmatrix} C_1 \rightarrow_\|^* C_1' \\ C_0' \sim_\alpha C_1' \end{pmatrix}$$

Our bisimulation based definition of noninterference relates C_0 simply to any arbitrary configuration C_1 not specifying a "common program". This is in accordance to our view of the program as a closed system where initial values are part of the configuration. This implicit use of "program" is unusual compared to other definitions. Our definition of noninterference thus entails H-compositionality: it does not presuppose that any H-parts need to be identical in the two configurations only the low (α-visible) parts.

The parameterization of the attacker as an active object α grants the possibility to adapt the noninterference predicate. If we universally quantify α in our definition of noninterference, we obtain a predicate where each object could be the attacker corresponding to multi-lateral security.

Definition 3 (Multi-Lateral Security). *If any two configurations* C_0, C_1 *are* α-*noninterfering for all* $\alpha \in \mathrm{dom}(C_0) \cup \mathrm{dom}(C_1)$ *then multi-lateral security holds.*

A general catch-22 problem exists for information flow control in object-orientation: a method call is an information flow to the remote object; its response flows information back. Therefore, method communication is trivially restricted to objects of one class. As a remedy we propose *functional* method calls, i.e., no side-effects in called remote objects. This is naturally given for $\mathrm{ASP}_{\mathrm{fun}}$ but can be implemented in the run-time for other languages.

4.3 Type System and Properties

We provide a type system for the $\mathrm{ASP}_{\mathrm{fun}}$ instance of our model. A technical paper containing the formal type system, its properties and the Isabelle/HOL formalization is available online at [19]. We provide here just a summary. The types of this type system correspond quite closely to the security classes introduced in Section 3: two dimensions, a local and a global one, are used to infer a hierarchy of visibility of a configuration. The global type determines objects' access and the local type partitions methods into public and private ones. The idea of the type system is to make statically decidable whether the local typing specification of all active objects is such that no information of the private parts is leaked into the public parts. Consequently, if that is the case, an attacker α cannot learn anything about them. The type system is formally given by an inductive definition combining two sets of rules in a mutually inductive way: one set of rules specifies a global typing relation that carries a current calling context (a kind of "program counter" already used in Fenton's data mark machine [12]). The local security specification of active objects' methods can be simply integrated by initial maps of existing active object names of the configuration to security types.

The type system guarantees a confinement property: any future contained in the request queue of an active object is the result of a call to an L-method of that active object. The classical safety property of the type system is preservation: a configuration type only changes conservatively, i.e., the type of all existing configuration elements remains the same but new elements are introduced. The main result for security is soundness: a configuration that can be typed in this type system has the noninterference property shown in the previous section.

For practical applications, the type system is a tool: it describes an algorithm that enables checking configurations before run-time for any inadmissible information flows. For example, the adaptation of the quicksort example in Section 4.1 that contains an implicit flow would be detected automatically since it leaks information from a high method to a low method that is remotely accessible.

5   Conclusion

Compared to other formal work on distributed security, like [21], the most important difference is that we specifically address active objects. Similar work applying classical noninterference models to actors, e.g. [16], is based on simple message passing models different to our high level language model. Another comparable work [5] addresses only direct information flows in active objects.

Another decisive difference is that the classification of activities to security classes results from the references in a configuration. Usually, the security classification is specified external to the system and then imposed on a program. The global classification of our approach thus corresponds to a kind of *computational noninterference* similar to Alpizar's work [3]. The visibility approach applies particularly well to active objects languages of the ASP-family. For other distributed languages, alternative mechanisms for modularity, in the style of import/export-lists or nodes as in Erlang, may well be used to implement visibility.

Our earlier work [18] used a hiding mechanism for ASP_{fun} to practically explore privacy. Based on a simpler flat security model, we proved that for delayed parameter passing via currying secure information flow can be verified. Using the above summarized security type system we can now statically prove security of this example even for the richer distributed security model (see [19] for details). Apart from technical advances, like a type system, the main progress of the current work is the security model tailored to active objects exploiting their natural structure to provide a natural implementation of multi-lateral security. As a practical precursor to our model, we have experimented with a reference monitor extension of our Erlang Active Objects implementation of ASP_{fun} [13].

Lattices, and also combinations of lattices are common practice for security models: for example Denning's multi-level security classes are constructed with categories built as sets of compartments. However, in Denning's model the resulting structure is a strictly hierarchical lattice unsuited for our distributed model where local private data and globally dominating entities may yet not be in flow relation. In brief, our model forbids some of the access paths that are possible in classical security lattices by changing the foundations from lattice to semi-lattice.

The specialty of our model is that it economizes the upper half of the usual security lattice in order to support "mathematically inbuilt" privacy: the H parts of each object are thus not accessible for anyone other than the active object itself. As discussed in the introduction, classical object-oriented models [22,20] do not support this "inbuilt privacy". The security specification local to an active object is at the discretion of this object whereas the global security specification is so only indirectly as a consequence of the configuration implementation. The abstract model conception is shown to be feasible by providing a formalization in the active object calculus ASP_{fun}. We additionally propose functional method calls with futures as a mechanism addressing the limitation we call catch-22 on secure object communication. It comes for free in ASP_{fun} but may simply be implemented also in other active object languages in the run-time systems.

The difference of our approach of moving the principals into the language manifests itself as well in the security definition. Our definition of security may seem weaker but provides an accurate way of formal expression of an attacker's view based on the means of the language. It therefore expresses clearly what are the observation means of any attacker.

References

1. Abadi, M., Cardelli, L.: A Theory of Objects. Springer, New York (1996)
2. Agha, G., Mason, I.A., Smith, S.F., Talcott, C.L.: Towards a Theory of Actor Computation (Extended Abstract). In: Cleaveland, W.R. (ed.) CONCUR 1992. LNCS, vol. 630, pp. 565–579. Springer, Heidelberg (1992)
3. Alpízar, R., Smith, G.: Secure Information Flow for Distributed Systems. In: Degano, P., Guttman, J.D. (eds.) FAST 2009. LNCS, vol. 5983, pp. 126–140. Springer, Heidelberg (2010)
4. Anderson, R.: Security Engineering – A Guide to Building Dependable Distributed Systems. Wiley (2001)
5. Attali, I., Caromel, D., Henrio, L., Aguila, F.L.D.: Secured information flow for asynchronous sequential processes. ENTCS 180(1), 17–34 (2007)
6. Banerjee, A., Naumann, D.A.: Stack-based access control for secure information flow. Journal of Functional Programming 15(2) (2003)
7. Caromel, D., Delbé, C., di Costanzo, A., Leyton, M.: ProActive: an integrated platform for programming and running applications on grids and P2P systems. Computational Methods in Science and Technology 12(1), 69–77 (2006)
8. Caromel, D., Henrio, L., Serpette, B.P.: Asynchronous and deterministic objects. In: Principles of Programming Languages, POPL 2004. ACM Press (2004)
9. Davey, B.A., Priestley, H.A.: Introduction to Lattices and Order, 2nd edn. Cambridge University Press (2002)
10. Denning, D.E.: Lattice model of secure information flow. Communications of the ACM 19(5), 236–242 (1976)
11. Denning, D.E., Denning, P.J.: Certification of programs for secure information flow. Communications of the ACM 20(7) (1977)
12. Fenton, J.S.: Information protection systems. PhD thesis, Univ. Cambridge (1973)
13. Fleck, A., Kammüller, F.: A security model for functional active objects with an implementation in erlang. In: Computational Informatics, Blue Herons (2011)

14. Halstead Jr., R.H.: Multilisp: A language for concurrent symbolic computation. ACM Transactions on Programming Languages and Systems 7(4), 501–538 (1985)
15. Henrio, L., Kammüller, F., Lutz, B.: Aspfun: A typed functional active object calculus. Science of Computer Programming 77(7-8), 823–847 (2012)
16. Hutter, D., Mantel, H., Schaefer, I., Schairer, A.: Security of multi-agent systems: A case study on comparison shopping. J. Applied Logic 5(2), 303–332 (2007)
17. Kammüller, F.: Using functional active objects to enforce privacy. In: 5th Conf. on Network Architectures and Information Systems Security, SAR-SSI 2010 (2010)
18. Kammüller, F.: Privacy Enforcement and Analysis for Functional Active Objects. In: Garcia-Alfaro, J., Navarro-Arribas, G., Cavalli, A., Leneutre, J. (eds.) DPM 2010 and SETOP 2010. LNCS, vol. 6514, pp. 93–107. Springer, Heidelberg (2011)
19. Kammüller, F.: Information Flow Control for Functional Active Objects (May 2012), http://user.cs.tu-berlin.de/~flokam/proofs.pdf
20. Kogan, B., Jajodia, S.: An audit model for object-oriented databases. In: 7th Annual Computer Security Applications Conf., ACSAC 1991, pp. 90–99 (1991)
21. Mantel, H., Sabelfeld, A.: A unifying approach to the security of distributed and multi-threaded programs. J. Computer Security 11, 2003 (2002)
22. Myers, A.C., Liskov, B.: A decentralized model for information flow control. In: SOSP 1997. ACM (1997)

Prioritized Execution of Privacy Policies*

Ilaria Matteucci, Paolo Mori, and Marinella Petrocchi

IIT - CNR, Pisa, Italy
`name.surname@iit.cnr.it`

Abstract. This paper addresses the issue of solving conflicts occurring in the authorization decision process among policies applicable to an access request. We propose a strategy for conflict resolution based on the evaluation of the specificity level of the elements constituting the policies. Operatively, the strategy is implemented by exploiting a well known decision making technique. Two practical examples of use in the healthcare scenario are given.

1 Introduction

Healthcare organizations provide medical services to their patients, such as various kind of examinations and diagnostics, and produce electronic documents concerning these services (*e.g.,* reservations, prescriptions, payments, and results of examinations). These documents are stored in the data centres of the organizations where they have been produced. The Electronic Patient Record (EPR) groups the documents related to the same patient in a single electronic object.

The availability of medical data is a fundamental requirement for guaranteeing appropriate and prompt medical care. Hence, the stakeholders of the various healthcare organizations should be able to access the patient's data, wherever these data are stored and whenever these data are needed. However, since medical documents include sensitive data, their sharing must be regulated in order to assure data privacy. This regulation can be enabled by adequate privacy policies.

The scenario we deal with in this paper is in line with the Italian Authority for data protection. The Authority states that, besides the privacy policies defined by the healthcare organizations where the data have been produced, and the ones defined by the national healthcare system, also the patients can impose some constraints on the data included in their EPRs. These three entities have their own rules regulating data sharing: since data involved in different policies may overlap, conflicts among such policies can arise. As an example, the patient P can decide that the document D, related to a given psychiatric examination, can be accessed by psychiatrists only. Instead, the policy defined by the national healthcare system could state that each general practitioner can access all the data of their patients. Obviously, the two policies are in conflict when the general practitioner of P tries to access D. In such a situation, it is important to have a strategy for *prioritizing* the application of one policy with respect to the other one.

---

* The research leading to these results received funding from the European Union 7th Framework Programme under grant n. 256980 (NESSoS) and from the IIT internal project MobiCare.

R. Di Pietro et al. (Eds.): DPM 2012 and SETOP 2012, LNCS 7731, pp. 133–145, 2013.

This paper proposes a strategy for conflict resolution between conflicting policies, based on a well-known approach for multi-criteria decision making. This strategy allows to decide which, between the conflicting policies, is more *relevant* within a specific scenario, according to a series of criteria. Throughout the paper, we deal with structured policies, whose elements include subjects, actions, data objects, and environmental conditions fixing the *context* within which those subjects can/cannot perform actions on objects. According to the policy structure, we identify different kind of conflicting policies. Then, we define a set of criteria over the policies' elements. The conflicting policies are then evaluated under these criteria, to prioritize the execution of one policy with respect to the other(s). Prioritization is done by applying the Analytic Hierarchy Process (AHP). This process is worldwide recognised as a comprehensive framework for structuring a decision problem, for representing and quantifying its elements, for relating those elements to overall goals, and for evaluating alternative solutions.

The setting proposed in this paper let the development of an automatic conflict resolutor an easy task, also in emergency scenarios, as we will discuss later on.

The paper is organized as follows. Section 2 recalls related work. Section 3 defines the structure of the privacy policies we deal with, and describes our reference scenario. Section 4 gives a definition of conflicting policies. In Section 5, the conflict resolution strategy and examples of application are presented. Finally, Section 6 draws the conclusion.

2   Related Work

In [1,2,3], we provide an analysis framework for detecting conflicts among privacy policies, without however providing a strategy for solving them. This paper could be considered a natural follow up, focusing on a strategy for the resolution of such conflicts.

In [4], the authors propose a conflict resolution strategy for medical policies, by presenting a classification of conflicts and suggesting a strategy based on high level features of the policy as a whole (such as the recency of a policy). If such characteristics are not sufficient for deciding which policy should be applied, the *default deny* approach is applied.

In the literature, there exists some work related to general conflict resolution methods for access control in various areas. The approach adopted by the eXtensible Access Control Markup Language (XACML) [5] is a very general one. In fact, XACML policies (or policy sets) must include a *combining algorithm* that defines the procedure to combine the individual results obtained by the evaluation of the rules of the policy (of the policies in the policy set). XACML defines standard rule-combining algorithms: Deny-Overrides, Permit-Overrides, First-Applicable, and Only-One-Applicable. As an example, the Deny-Overrides algorithm states that the result of the policy is Deny if the evaluation of at least one of the rules returns Deny.

A classification of anomalies that may occur among firewall policies is presented in [6]. In order to prevent the occurrence of conflicts, the authors develop an editing tool that allows a user to insert, modify, and remove, policy rules in order to avoid anomalies. Also, work in [7] proposes methods for preventing policy conflicts, more than a strategy for solving them when they occur.

Differently, in [8,9] the authors deal with the detection and resolution of conflicts. Work in [8] defines a policy precedence relationship that takes into account the following principles: *a)* Rules that deny the access have the priority on the others; *b)* Priorities could be explicitly assigned to policy rules by the system administrators; *c)* Higher priority is given to the rule whose distance with the object it refers to is the lowest, where a specific function should be defined to measure such distance; and *d)* Higher priority is given to the rule that is more specific according to the domain nesting criteria. The approach in [8,9] is extended in [10]. Indeed, the authors introduce the definition and employment of the precedence establishment principals in a context-aware-manner, *i.e.,* according to the relation among the specificity of the context. Also in this case the decision criterion is only one that group all the contextual conditions. In [9], the authors investigate policy conflict resolution in pervasive environments. They discussed different strategy for conflict detection but the part dedicated to the conflict resolution strategy just refer to quite standard strategies, *i.e.,* role hierarchies override and obligation precedence. Also in [11], four different strategies for solving conflicts are considered. They distinguish among solving conflicts at compile-time, at run-time, in a balanced way leaving to run-time only potential conflicts, or in ad-hoc way accordingly to the particular conflicts. In general they take into account the role of the requester for deciding which policy wins the conflict. Also in this case, the strategy is based only on one criterion.

With respect to the solutions proposed in the previously described papers, our approach aims at defining a finer grained strategy for conflict resolution, because it is based on a finer definition of the policy specificity. In particular, our approach firstly evaluates the specificity of the policy in identifying each element, namely: subject, object, action and environment. Then, it combines these values through a weighted sum, that allows us to assign more relevance to the specificity of the definition of one the policy element with respect to the others (*e.g.,* we could choose that the specificity in defining the subject is 2 times more relevant than the specificity in defining the object).

3   Structured Privacy Policies

This section firstly defines a structure for the privacy policies considered later on, and then depicts a plausible set of policies regulating the controlled exchange of medical information. Privacy policies are expressed in terms of the following elements: *subject*, *object* (or resource), *action*, and *environment*. Furthermore, policies are divided into two main classes, according to their effect:

- **Authorizations**: they express the actions that a subject is *allowed* to perform on an object within an environment.
- **Prohibitions**: they express the actions that a subject is *not allowed* to perform on an object within an environment.

It is worth noticing that the above assumptions are not restrictive. For example, XACML relies on similar assumptions. Hence, we consider a privacy policy as a set of rules that are evaluated for each access request to decide whether a given subject is allowed to perform a given action on a given resource in a given environment. The features of the policy elements, *i.e.,* subjects, objects, actions, and environment, are expressed through *attributes*. Policy rules include conditions on the value of these attributes to determine which rule can be applied to each access request. In the rest of the paper, we will consider the following attributes (for the sake of simplicity, a restricted set of attributes is considered):

Subject. The attributes for subjects are: ID, Role, and Organization.
- ID expresses an unique identifier of the subject, *e.g., "abcde*123".
- Role specifies the functions and the capabilities of a subject. As an example:
  - *general practitioner* has a general view of the patient medical history;
  - *psychiatrists, orthopedists . . .* identify doctors that are highly specialised;
  - *rescue team member* retrieves the first information at the incident location.
- Organization represents the organization the subject belongs to, *e.g.,* the "Red Cross"

Object. The attributes for objects are: ID, Issuer, and Category.
- ID is a code that expresses the identifier of the object, *e.g., "xyz"*.
- Issuer is the entity that produces that object, *e.g.,* the doctor that writes it;
- Category is *medical*, including documents that collect medical information about the patient, and *administrative*, including documents collecting personal information, as the patient's name, surname, address, . . .

Action. We consider their IDs only, *e.g.,* "Read", "Print", "Write", "Modify" . . .

Environment. The attributes of the environment are: Time, Location, and Status. The last attribute specifies the exceptionality of a situation, such as an emergency one.

We imagine a set of Authorization and Prohibition policies emitted by the National Healthcare System (NHS) and by the patients, such as Mr. Paul Red. We recall that, in a real scenario, a wider set of attributes will be used.

NHS A1 Subjects having the role "General Practitioner" can read/print the documents having category "medical" of their patients;

A2 Subjects having the role "General Practitioner" can read/print the documents having category "administrative" of their patients;

A3 Subjects having the role "Rescue Team Member" and belonging to the organization "Red Cross" can read/print the documents having category "medical" of a patient in an emergency situation;

A4 Subjects having the role "Emergency Doctor" can read/print the documents having category "medical" of a patient in an emergency situation;

A5 Subjects having the role "Administrative Personnel" can read/print the documents having category "administrative";

A6 Subjects can read/print/modify the documents they have issued;

Mr. Paul Red P1 Subjects not having the role "Psychiatrist" cannot read/print the document with ID *xyz* before 31/12/2020.

P2 Subject with ID dr12345 cannot read/print the document with ID *xyz*;

Some notes on the above policies follow. The prohibition policies have been written by the patient, Mr. Paul Red, because the document with ID *xyz*, issued by a Psychiatrist, is a drug prescription and the patient does not want to disclose it to anyone but Psychiatrists. Dr. Jack Brown, whose unique ID is dr12345, is the General Practitioner of Mr. Paul Red, and he is also a Psychiatrist, but the patient does not want to disclose that document to Dr. Jack Brown, for some reason that is immaterial here.

3.1 Classification of Attributes

To support the decision process, we define an ordering among the attributes related to the same policy element. This ordering expresses how including in a policy a condition on a given attribute contributes to make the policy more specific. Roughly speaking, attribute $a1$ of element e is more *specific* than attribute $a2$ of the same element if a condition on this attribute is likely to identify a more homogeneous and/or a smaller set of entities within e. Let the reader consider two policies, one saying that subjects with role *general practitioner* are allowed to access objects of category *medical*, the other saying that the subject with ID dr12345 (*i.e.,* Dr. Jack Brown, who is a *general practitioner*), is not allowed to read the object with ID *xyz*, which is a *medical* document. Quite obviously, the second policy is more specific than the first one, since attribute ID identifies one subject and one object only, while the conditions on the attributes in the first policy identify a larger set of subjects and objects (*i.e.,* the set of the NHS general practitioners and a generic set of medical documents).

Aiming at evaluating the specificity of a policy, we propose to classify the policy attributes as follows:

Subject Attributes. ID is more relevant than Role and Organization. Role and Organization have the same relevance.

Object Attributes. ID is more relevant than Issuer that is more relevant than Category.

Environment Attributes. Status is more relevant than Time and Location. Time and Location have the same relevance.

Since many attributes can be defined in real scenarios, ordering them according to their specificity is a non trivial task. However, in our approach, the task is eased since attributes can be compared in a pairwise fashion, as clarified in the following.

4   Classification of Conflicting Policies

Conflicts can arise between authorization and prohibition policies when they are going to be applied for allowing (or not allowing) the access to some resources. Similar to [4], we distinguish the following kind of conflicting policies:

Contradictions. Two policies are *contradictory* if one allows and the other denies the right to perform the same action by the same subject on the same object under the same environment. The policies are exactly the same, except for their effect.

Exceptions. One policy is an exception of another one, if they have different effects (allow and deny) on the same action, but one policy is a "subset" of the other one, *i.e.,* the subject (and/or the object, and/or the environment) is specified with more specific attributes than those of the other. Let the reader consider Authorization A1 and Prohibition P2:

A1 Subjects having the role "General Practitioner" can read/print the documents having category "medical" of their patients;

P2 Subject with ID dr12345 cannot read/print the document with ID *xyz*;

P2 is an exception of A1, since the subject with ID dr12345, *i.e.,* Dr. Jack Brown, cannot access the document with ID *xyz* even if that document is related to one of his patients.

Correlations. Two policies are correlated if they have different effects (allow and deny) and the attribute set of a policy intersects the attribute set of the other one.

As an example, the following policies are correlated:

A5 Subjects having the role "Administrative Personnel" can read/print the documents having category "administrative";

P3 Subjects having the role "Administrative Personnel" cannot read/print the documents having category "administrative" until 31/12/2020;

Both the policies exploit the attribute role of the subject and the attribute category of the object, but the second one also exploits the environmental attribute Time.

Differently from [4], we consider also attributes on the environment, *e.g.,* time, location, and status, providing, to some extent, a context-aware classification of conflicts.

5   Conflict Resolution Strategy

This section shows how to apply the Analytical Hierarchy Process to prioritize the execution of a privacy policy with respect to a conflicting one.

5.1   The Analytical Hierarchy Process

The Analytic Hierarchy Process (AHP) [12,13] is a multi-criteria decision making technique, which has been largely used in several fields of study. Given a decision problem, within which different *alternatives* can be chosen to reach a *goal*, AHP returns the *most relevant* alternative with respect to a set of *criteria*. This approach requires to subdivide a complex problem into a set of sub-problems, equal in number to the chosen criteria, and then computes the solution (*i.e.,* choose the most relevant alternative) by properly merging all the local solutions for each sub-problem.

We give a simple example of the basic steps of AHP. Let the reader suppose to have as *goal* "choosing a restaurant for dinner". The possible alternatives are a Japanese sushi bar, a French *brasserie*, and an Italian *trattoria*. The problem must be structured as a hierarchy, as shown in Figure 1, linking goal and alternatives through a set of criteria. In the proposed example, appropriate *criteria* could be: cost, food, and staff.

Furthermore, AHP features the capability to further refine each criterion in subcriteria. In the dinner example, two possible sub-criteria for food are quality and variety, whereas two possible sub-criteria for staff are kindness and expertise.

Once the hierarchy is built, the method performs pairwise comparison, from the bottom to the top, in order to compute the relevance, hereafter called *local priority*: i) of each alternatives with respect to each sub-criteria, ii) of each sub-criterion with respect to the relative criterion, and finally, iii) of each criterion with respect to the goal. Note

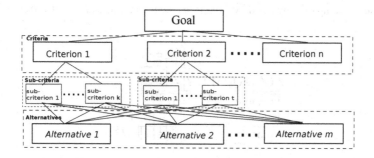

Fig. 1. Generic AHP hierarchy

Table 1. Fundamental Scale for AHP

Intensity	Definition	Explanation
1	Equal	Two elements contribute equally to the objective
3	Moderate	One element is slightly more relevant than another
5	Strong	One element is strongly more relevant over another
7	Very strong	One element is very strongly more relevant over another
9	Extreme	One element is extremely more relevant over another

that, in case of a criterion without sub-criteria, the local priority of each alternative is computed with respect to the criterion.

Comparisons are made through a scale of numbers typical to AHP (see Table 1) that indicates how many times an alternative is *more relevant* than another.

Pairwise comparison matrices and computation of local priorities. Pairwise comparisons are expressed in a matricial form, called *pairwise comparison matrix*. A pairwise comparisons matrix M is a square matrix which has positive entries and it is reciprocal, *i.e.,* for each element a_{ij}, $a_{ij} = \frac{1}{a_{ji}}$. The following notion of *consistency* has been defined for a pairwise comparison matrix: it is consistent if $a_{i,j} \cdot a_{j,l} = a_{i,l}$, $\forall (i,j,l)$. The satisfaction of this last property implies that if x is more relevant than y, and y is more relevant than z, then z cannot be more relevant x. In practice, building a perfectly consistent matrix is not possible, since the judgements are left to humans. As Saaty shows in [14], inconsistency of a reciprocal matrix $w \times w$ can be captured by the so called *Consistency Index*: $\text{CI} = \frac{\lambda_{max} - w}{w - 1}$, where λ_{max} is the maximum eigenvalue of M. For a consistent matrix $CI = 0$, whilst a matrix is considered semi-consistent if $CI < 0.1$. If this last condition does not hold, then the comparison values must be re-evaluated.

Given a comparison matrix, local priorities are computed as the normalized eigenvector associated with the largest eigenvalue [15].

Table 2 shows the comparison matrix for the *quality of food* sub-criterion of the three restaurants example and their local priorities. Indeed, the vector of local priorities for this sub-criterion is reported on the right side of the matrix, and it expresses that the

Table 2. Example Comparisons Matrix: Restaurants vs Quality of Food(CI=0.007)

FOOD QUALITY	Japanese	Italian	French	Loc. Prio.
Japanese	1	$\frac{1}{7}$	$\frac{1}{5}$	0.08
Italian	7	1	2	0.59
French	5	$\frac{1}{2}$	1	0.33

italian restaurant is the more advised among the three alternatives since it has the best quality of food (0.59 is the higher local priority).

The same procedure is repeated to compare the restaurants with respect to the cost criterion, the sub-criterion *variety*, the other sub-criteria of staff, and to compare the sub-criteria with respect to the relative criterion, obtaining other comparisons matrices that we do not report for the sake of brevity.

Computation of global priorities. Once all local priorities are computed, the following formula computes the global priorities. For the sake of simplicity, we have in mind a hierarchy tree where the leftmost $n1$ criteria have a set of sub-criteria each, while the rightmost $n2$ criteria have no sub-criteria below them, and $n1 + n2 = n$ is the number of total criteria.

$$P_g^{a_i} = \sum_{w=1}^{n1} \sum_{k=1}^{q(w)} p_g^{c_w} \cdot p_{c_w}^{sc_k^w} \cdot p_{sc_k^w}^{a_i} + \sum_{j=1}^{n2} p_g^{c_j} \cdot p_{c_j}^{a_i} \tag{1}$$

$q(w)$ is the number of sub-criteria for criterion c_w, $p_g^{c_w}$ is the local priority of criterion c_w with respect to the goal g, $p_{c_w}^{sc_k^w}$ is the local priority of sub-criterion k with respect to criterion c_w, and $p_{sc_k^w}^{a_i}$ is the local priority of alternative a_i with respect to sub-criterion k of criterion c_w. $p_{c_w}^{sc_k^w}$ and $p_{sc_k^w}^{a_i}$ are computed by following the same procedure of the pairwise comparisons matrices illustrated above.

Finally, it is worth noticing that comparisons between pairs of elements are either based on concrete data, or they come from judgements of experts in the field, or from personal disposition of the decision makers, *e.g.,* the system administrators that define the security policies in our scenario. Whatever the nature of the comparison is, the strength of AHP is that it converts them to numerical priorities.

5.2   An AHP instance for Conflict Resolution

We propose the AHP hierarchy in Fig. 2 for instantiating a conflict resolution strategy.
The elements of the hierarchy are as follows:

- The *goal* is ranking two conflicting policies.
- The *alternatives* are the conflicting policies.

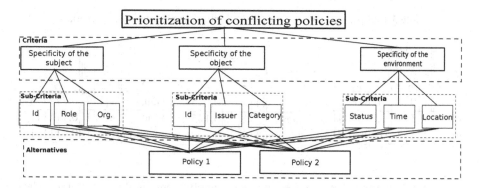

Fig. 2. AHP Hierarchy for Policy Conflict Resolution

- The *criteria* are the following:

  Specificity of the subject. This criterion evaluates the attributes exploited in the two policies to identify the subject, to determine which of the policies define a more specific set of subjects.

  Specificity of the object. This criterion evaluates the attributes exploited in the two policies to identify the object.

  Specificity of the environment. This criterion evaluates the attributes to identify the environment.

- Each criterion has a set of *subcriteria* that are the attributes of the criterion:

  Subcriteria for subject: ID, role, and organization.

  Subcriteria for object: ID, category, and issuer.

  Subcriteria for environment: status, time, and location.

The above list is not exhaustive, since the methodology allows the insertion of other criteria and subcriteria that may be helpful to evaluate the alternatives.

AHP requires to make pairwise comparisons between entities at one level of the hierarchy with respect to the entities at the upper level. We propose to instantiate such comparisons as follows.

First, we quantify how the three criteria are relevant for achieving the goal of solving conflicts. Without loss of generality, we hypothesize that all the criteria equally contribute to meet the goal. In this straightforward case, the pairwise comparison matrix is a 3x3 matrix with all the elements equal to 1, and the local priorities of the criteria with respect to the goal are simply 0.33 each ($p_g^{c_j} = 0.33$, $j = 1,\ldots,3$).

Then, we quantify how subcriteria are relevant with respect to the correspondent criteria. The comparisons are made with the help of the classification of attributes proposed in Section 3.1. In particular, in our example we use the matrices in Table 3, with the local priorities shown in the last column of each matrix. In the matrix that compares the subject's attributes (the left-most one in Table 3), we write $a_{12} = 9$ since we think that the subject ID allows to identify the subject *extremely* better than the subject role. Indeed, the subject ID exactly identifies one subject. For the same reason, we put $a_{13} = 9$ (ID *vs* the organization the subject belongs to).

Table 3. Comparison matrices and local priorities for subcriteria w.r.t. criteria

SUBJ	ID	role	organiz.	$\bar{p}_{Subj}$	OBJ	ID	issuer	category	$\bar{p}_{Obj}$	ENV	status	time	location	$\bar{p}_{Env}$
ID	1	9	9	0.818182	ID	1	5	7	0.7454	status	1	7	7	0.777778
role	$\frac{1}{9}$	1	1	0.0909091	issuer	$\frac{1}{5}$	1	$\frac{4}{3}$	0.1454	time	$\frac{1}{7}$	1	1	0.111111
org	$\frac{1}{9}$	1	1	0.0909091	category	$\frac{1}{7}$	$\frac{3}{4}$	1	0.1091	location	$\frac{1}{7}$	1	1	0.111111

We remark that the values in these matrices simply represent the perception of the authors on the relative relevance of the attributes. Other values could have been chosen.

Finally, the conflicting policies Policy1 and Policy2 are evaluated with respect to subcriteria. In particular, we need k 2x2 matrices, where k is the number of subcriteria (in our case, k=9). The matrices are built according to a very simple approach, based on the presence of the attributes in the policies:

- Policy1 and Policy2 contain (or do not contain) attribute A: then $a_{12} = a_{21} = 1$.
- If only Policy1 contains A, than $a_{12} = 9$, and $a_{21} = \frac{1}{9}$.
- If only Policy2 contains A, than $a_{12} = \frac{1}{9}$, and $a_{12} = 9$.

We do not consider as a decisional criterion the specificity of the action. This is because we evaluate the action only according to its ID, always present in a policy. So the evaluation of the alternative policies with respect to the criterion *action* is constant, and it does not add any meaningful information for taking the final decision.

5.3 Example

Let us suppose that a car accident that involves Mr. Paul Red happens. A rescue team member, before administering a given drug to the patient, needs to access his medical history, to check for possible incompatibilities with drug therapies that the patient could have in progress. Hence, the rescue team member also needs to access document with ID *xyz* that, in fact, is a drug prescription that a Psychiatrist gave to the patient. The medical information of the people involved in the accident should be immediately available to the rescuers, that could have to take decisions quickly. On the one hand, the required information are sensitive, so its unfolding is regulated by privacy policies, possibly established by different organizations. On the other hand, data protection should not affect the possibility of saving the patient life. It is important to have a procedure for solving conflicts occurring between policies that simultaneously may be applied.

When the rescue team member tries to access the document with ID *xyz*, a conflict occurs among the policy A3 and the policy P1 (see Section 3).

A3 Subjects having the role "Rescue Team Member" and belonging to the organization "Red Cross" can read/print the documents having category "medical" of a patient in an emergency situation;

P1 Subjects not having the role "Psychiatrist" cannot read/print the document with ID *xyz* before 31/12/2020.

Indeed, the subject that is trying to access the data has role Rescue Team Member and (s)he is member of Red Cross; also, the status of the environment is set to "Emergency", given that an accident with victims has occurred. According to policy A3, issued by NHS, the subject can access the object. However, according to P1, issued by the victim, the same subject cannot access that object, since s(he) is not a psychiatrist.

We recall that the local priorities of the uppermost two levels of the AHP hierarchy in Fig. 2 are stitched to the policies themselves. They are defined according to the scenario when the policies are created, and they do not change until the policies change. In our case, we hypothesize that, for the uppermost level, the local priorities are all equal to 0.33, while the local priorities for the middle level have been specified in Table 3.

Instead, the local priorities of the lowest level are evaluated at runtime, when someone tries to access the data. The evaluation is simply based on the presence, or the absence, of an attribute in the conflicting policies. In our example, we have that:

- A3 identifies the subject through role and organization, while P1 through the role.
- A3 identifies the object through category and P1 through the object ID.
- A3 identifies the environment through status and P1 through time.

Table 4 shows an example of the simple 2x2 matrix that compares A3 and P1 w.r.t. the presence of the attribute ID of the element object. Since P1 specifies the object through the ID, while A3 does not, we give 9 to P1 and $\frac{1}{9}$ to A3.

Table 4. A3 and P1 evaluated w.r.t. the presence of the attribute ID of the object

ID_{Obj}	A3	P1	$\bar{p}_{ID_{Obj}}$
A3	1	$\frac{1}{9}$	0.1
P1	9	1	0.9

Similar 2x2 matrices are built for evaluating A3 and P1 w.r.t. all the sub-criteria (we have 9 matrices). The global priorities are calculated according to Expr. 1 in Sec. 5.

$$P_g^{A3} = 0.33 \cdot ((p_{Subj}^{ID} \cdot p_{ID}^{A3}) + (p_{Subj}^{Role} \cdot p_{Role}^{A3}) + (p_{Subj}^{Org} \cdot p_{Org}^{A3})) +$$

$$0.33 \cdot ((p_{Obj}^{ID_{Obj}} \cdot p_{ID_{Obj}}^{A3}) + (p_{Obj}^{Iss} \cdot p_{Iss}^{A3}) + (p_{Obj}^{Cat} \cdot p_{Cat}^{A3})) +$$

$$0.33 \cdot ((p_{Env}^{Stat} \cdot p_{Stat}^{A3}) + (p_{Env}^{Time} \cdot p_{Time}^{A3}) + (p_{Env}^{Loc} \cdot p_{Loc}^{A3})) = 0.52$$

where $\bar{p}_{Subj}^{(\cdot)}$, $\bar{p}_{Obj}^{(\cdot)}$, and $\bar{p}_{Env}^{(\cdot)}$ are the vectors of local priorities shown in Figure 3 (rightmost column of each matrix), while p_{ID}^{A3}, p_{Role}^{A3}, ... are the local priorities of policy A3 against all the subcriteria, as the result of the nine 2x2 matrices. For example, $p_{ID_{Obj}}^{A3} = 0.1$, see Table 4. Complementary, for policy P1 we obtain $P_g^{P1} = 0.48$. Hence, the result of the decision strategy shows a slight preference for the execution of policy A3.

In order to validate our approach, we show another example, in which one of the conflicting policies is clearly more specific than the other (thus, in accordance with our philosophy, the application of this policy should obtain the highest priority).

Let us suppose that Dr. Jack Brown, with role General Practitioner and ID dr12345, tries to access the medical document with ID *xyz* of his patient Mr. Paul Red. An exception conflict raises between policies A1 and P2 (see Section 4):

A1   Subjects having the role "General Practitioner" can read/print the documents having category "medical" of their patients;

P2   Subject with ID dr12345 cannot read/print the document with ID *xyz*;

Intuitively, P2 is much more specific than A1, since it identifies both the subject and the object through IDs. Applying AHP, we obtain what we expected: the global priority of P2 is 0.7, while the one of A1 is 0.3.

Finally, we remark that all the matrices that we have computed for our examples are consistent or nearly consistent: this assures the consistency of the comparisons and the plausibility of the priorities.

6   Conclusions and Future Work

This paper presented a strategy for solving conflicts that could arise in the authorization decision process between two (or more) policies applicable to an access request. We relied on some existing conflict detection procedures (like the ones proposed in our earlier work [1,2,3]) and we focused on conflict resolution.

Our approach evaluates how much a policy is specific in identifying the subject, the object, and the environment to which it is applicable. The basic idea is that policies that are applicable to smaller set of subjects, objects, and environmental conditions should have the priority on the others. To determine the specificity of a policy, we consider which attributes are used to identify the elements to which the policy is applicable. Operatively, the approach has been implemented by exploiting AHP, a well known decision making technique. Two practical examples of use in the healthcare scenario have been given. The methodology works as expected for these two examples, but this does not necessarily means that it will work for any possible scenario. Thus, it could be worth to test the methodology on a richer set of examples, possibly taken from the real world, with real data and real reported conflicts.

Also, there could be the unlucky case in which the conflicting policies are contradictory (see Section 4) and they exploit exactly the same set of attributes. In this case, following our approach would lead to a priority of 0.5 for both the policies, giving no meaningful information on which policy should be enforced. A future investigation for improving the evaluation of the policy specificity could try to evaluate the cardinality of the sets of elements determined by the conditions that the policies define on these attributes. However, defining these cardinalities appears a really challenging task.

We are currently working on the development of a software component implementing the proposed strategy, that can be easily automatized. In particular, the priorities for criteria (*i.e.,* the relevance of the specificity of each element: subject, object, and environment, see Figure 2) and of the sub-criteria (*i.e.,* for each element, the mutual relevance of attributes) are computed when the policies are written, because all the required data (*i.e.,* the judgments of the system administrators) are already available at that time. Instead, the local priorities of the policies with respect to each sub-criterion can be computed at run-time only, when a conflict between policies is detected. This last step is very simple and fast, because it simply consists of checking, for each attribute, whether it is used in any, one, .., or all the conflicting policies. This conflict resolution software component will be integrated within the policy analyser presented in [1,2,3], that performs conflict detection.

Finally, we remark that both the policy attributes and the pairwise comparisons suggested in the paper are merely examples to explain how the strategy works. A different set of attributes and a different values for pairwise comparisons could be adopted in a real scenario.

Acknowledgments. We thank the anonymous reviewers of DPM 2012 for valuable comments that allow us to improve the paper.

References

1. Matteucci, I., Petrocchi, M., Sbodio, M.L., Wiegand, L.: A Design Phase for Data Sharing Agreements. In: Garcia-Alfaro, J., Navarro-Arribas, G., Cuppens-Boulahia, N., de Capitani di Vimercati, S. (eds.) DPM 2011 and SETOP 2011. LNCS, vol. 7122, pp. 25–41. Springer, Heidelberg (2012)
2. Martinelli, F., Matteucci, I., Petrocchi, M., Wiegand, L.: A Formal Support for Collaborative Data Sharing. In: Quirchmayr, G., Basl, J., You, I., Xu, L., Weippl, E. (eds.) CD-ARES 2012. LNCS, vol. 7465, pp. 547–561. Springer, Heidelberg (2012)
3. Matteucci, I., Mori, P., Petrocchi, M., Wiegand, L.: Controlled data sharing in E-health. In: Socio Technical Aspects in Security and Trust, pp. 17–23. IEEE (2011)
4. Jin, J., Ahn, G.J., Hu, H., Covington, M.J., Zhang, X.: Patient-centric authorization framework for electronic healthcare services. Computers & Security 30(2-3), 116–127 (2011)
5. OASIS: eXtensible Access Control Markup Language (XACML) Version 3.0 (2010)
6. Al-Shaer, E.S., Hamed, H.H.: Firewall policy advisor for anomaly discovery and rule editing. In: IFIP/IEEE Integrated Network Management, pp. 17–30 (2003)
7. Hall-May, M., Kelly, T.: Towards conflict detection and resolution of safety policies. In: Intl. System Safety Conf. (2006)
8. Lupu, E.C., Sloman, M.: Conflicts in policy-based distributed systems management. IEEE Trans. Softw. Eng. 25(6), 852–869 (1999)
9. Syukur, E.: Methods for policy conflict detection and resolution in pervasive computing environments. In: Policy Management for Web (WWW 2005), pp. 10–14. ACM (2005)
10. Masoumzadeh, A., Amini, M., Jalili, R.: Conflict detection and resolution in context-aware authorization. In: Security in Networks and Distributed Systems, pp. 505–511. IEEE (2007)
11. Dunlop, N., Indulska, J., Raymond, K.: Methods for conflict resolution in policy-based management systems. In: Enterprise Distributed Object Computing, pp. 98–109. IEEE (2003)
12. Saaty, T.L.: Decision-making with the AHP: Why is the principal eigenvector necessary. European Journal of Operational Research 145(1), 85–91 (2003)
13. Saaty, T.L.: Decision making with the Analytic Hierarchy Process. International Journal of Services Sciences 1(1), 83–98 (2008)
14. Saaty, T.L.: How to make a decision: The Analytic Hierarchy Process. European Journal of Operational Research 48(1), 9–26 (1990)
15. Saaty, T.L.: A scaling method for priorities in hierarchical structures. Journal of Mathematical Psychology 15(3), 234–281 (1977)

What Websites Know About You[*]
Privacy Policy Analysis Using Information Extraction

Elisa Costante[1], Jerry den Hartog[1], and Milan Petković[1,2]

[1] Eindhoven University of Technology, The Netherlands
{e.costante,j.d.hartog,m.petkovic}@tue.nl
[2] Philips Research Europe, High Tech Campus, The Netherlands
milan.petkovic@philips.com

Abstract. The need for privacy protection on the Internet is well recognized. Everyday users are asked to release personal information in order to use online services and applications. Service providers do not always need all the data they gather to be able to offer a service. Thus users should be aware of what data is collected by a provider to judge whether this is too much for the services offered. Providers are obliged to describe how they treat personal data in privacy policies. By reading the policy users could discover, amongst others, what personal data they agree to give away when choosing to use a service. Unfortunately, privacy policies are long legal documents that users notoriously refuse to read. In this paper we propose a solution which automatically analyzes privacy policy text and shows what personal information is collected. Our solution is based on the use of Information Extraction techniques and represents a step towards the more ambitious aim of automated grading of privacy policies.

1 Introduction

Protection of online privacy is lately attracting a lot of attention. Concerns about the ease at which excessive collection of personal data can take place online are reflected in research, legislation and public opinion. Within the new data protection directives, the European Commission has identified enhancing the control a user has over his personal data as a key objective [1]. Privacy breaches regularly appear in popular media along with suggestions for tools to protect users during their browsing [2]. On the other hand the data collected from thousands of customers represents a big economical asset for companies, one they would not easily give up [1].

Surveys show that also users are deeply concerned about privacy [3], and that they would be prone to pay some money to shop on websites with good privacy policies [3, 4]. However, there are some misconceptions about privacy policies, since users think that the sole presence of a privacy policy means the website will protect, and will not share, their personal data [5]. In reality, privacy policies often serve more as liability disclaimers for service providers than as assurances of privacy for end-users [6]. Moreover, since policies are often ignored by users, they fail in their goal of increasing privacy awareness.

---

[*] This work has been partially funded by the THeCS project in the Dutch National COMMIT program.

R. Di Pietro et al. (Eds.): DPM 2012 and SETOP 2012, LNCS 7731, pp. 146–159, 2013.
© Springer-Verlag Berlin Heidelberg 2013

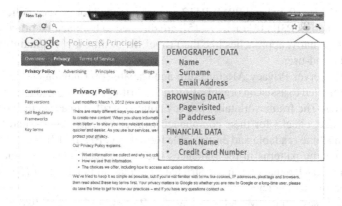

Fig. 1. An example of how the list of personal data collected can be presented to the user

In this paper we describe a solution, based on Information Extraction (IE) techniques, to extract the list of data collected by a website, according to what it is stated in its privacy policy. We believe that presenting such information to the user, for example using a browser extension as depicted in Figure 1, will increase his privacy awareness, and will help him to take more informed decisions. Without having to read the complete privacy policy, the user can see what data is collected, and can judge whether or not the information required is justified by the service offered (e.g. the Social Security Number is required by an e-commerce service). Moreover, solving the problem of automatically extracting useful information from privacy policy is a step towards being able to rate a website, based on the contents of its privacy policy.

The work described in this paper is, indeed, part of a larger framework which aims at automatic grading the privacy protection offered by a website. This grading is intended to be done by considering several aspects of privacy management, starting from the privacy policy [7]. In this paper we focus on analyzing the contents of a policy, namely the part regarding data collection. The same approach, once has been shown effective, can be applied to extract other information, such as the sharing practices or the security mechanisms applied, useful to verify how good a website protects the privacy of its users.

The rest of the paper is organized as following: we first discuss related work in Section 2, and employed extraction methods and tools in Section 3, before presenting the process followed to build our system in Section 4. The results are described in Section 5, while conclusion and further work are addressed in Section 6.

2 Related Work

Understanding privacy policies, often complex and ambiguous, is not an easy task for end-users [8, 9]. Privacy policies represent an important resource for privacy protection since they describe how personal data is managed. Several approaches, aiming at improving privacy protection by the means of privacy policies, exist. Some of them, such as SPARCLE [10, 11] and PPMLP [12, 13] are intended for privacy policy authors, while others, such as P3P [14] or UPP [15], are directed to both actors: privacy authors and end-users. Finally, approaches like the PrimeLife Dashboard [16] mainly focus on supporting the end-user.

SPARCLE (Server Privacy ARchitecture and CapabiLity Enablement) [10, 11] is a framework intended to assist an organization in the writing, auditing and enforcement of privacy policies. The framework takes privacy policies written in a specific constrained natural language, checks for their compliance with privacy principles, and translates them into a machine readable and enforceable format, e.g. EPAL [17] or XACML [18]. The use of specific patterns in the sentences and constrained natural language, i.e. a subset of a natural language with a restricted grammar and/or lexicon [19], makes it possible to parse such policies.

PPMLP (Privacy Policy Modeling Language Processor) [12, 13], like SPARCLE, aims at helping organizations in generating privacy policies compliant with privacy principles: authors specify a meta-privacy policy that will automatically be enriched with rules allowing such compliance. The meta-policy is then translated in EPAL rules, ready for the enforcement. The meta-policy is also translated in natural language (using static matching rules), for the presentation to the end-user. Within the system, a PPC (Privacy Policy Checker) is also present, to allow the users to verify whether a website enforces its privacy policy.

P3P (Platform for Privacy Preferences) [14] is the W3C's attempt to manage privacy policies, allowing the website to express them in a XML-based machine-readable format. The user is able to automatically check those policies against his preferences, by the means of P3P-enabled browsers [14]. Privacy Bird [20] and Privacy Finder [4] are examples of P3P user agents, able to compare P3P policies with users preferences, thus users do not need to read the privacy policies of every web site they visit [21].

UPP (User Privacy Policy) [15] is an approach similar to P3P, but mainly focused on social network websites. The mechanism allows a user to define policies to protect his resources (e.g. pictures or videos). Other users (his *friends*) can access such resources only if they guarantee the enforcement of the policies.

A limitation of the P3P approach, shared by SPARCLE, PPMLP and UPP, is that it needs server-side adoption, which is not easily obtained: according to [22] only 20% of the websites amongst the E-Commerce Top 300 is P3P enabled.

The PrimeLife Privacy Dashboard [16] is a recent browser extension aiming at helping the user to track what information is collected by the websites he visits. To this end, it collects information about the website the user is currently visiting, such as whether it has a P3P policy, whether it collects cookies, and whether it is certified by trust seals. The dashboard then provides a visual 'privacy quality' rating of a website: the presence of a P3P version of the privacy policy increases the rating, while the presence of external or flash cookies decreases it. The low adoption of P3P limits the effectiveness of this approach: a website may have a good privacy policy, but may be rated low because of the lack of a P3P version. Also, the content of the privacy policy, if it does exist, is not taken into account.

The solution presented in this paper, like the PrimeLife Dashboard, aims at letting the user know what personal data a website collects. However, it only requires the existence of a plain text privacy policy and no P3P version is needed. As such, it can easily be adopted by privacy-concerned end users, without requiring server-side adoption.

3   Methodologies and Tools

We use *Information Extraction* (IE) to extract the list of data collected by a website, by analyzing what is stated in its privacy policy. IE is a technique for analyzing natural language texts, to extract relevant pieces of information [23]. The analysis takes raw text as input and produces fixed-format, unambiguous data as output [24].

An IE system applies IE techniques to a specific scenario or domain. To build an IE system, an in-depth understanding of the contents of texts is needed [25]. IE systems have the advantage of accounting for the semantic contents of the text, rather than only for the presence/absence of given key words as it happens e.g. in Information Retrieval. Taking semantics into account gives the potential for systems that are accurate enough to really help people, reducing the time they need to spend reading texts [24].

Privacy policies, due to their legal nature, show strong formality and fixed patterns. Because of this, applying IE techniques to privacy policy text may lead to high accuracy, as confirmed by the results presented in Section 5. The fact that IE only extracts information on/in a-priori selected subjects/format fits well with our idea of showing to the user only specific information, i.e. the list of data collected.

The general architecture of an IE system may be defined as "*a cascade of transducers or modules that, at each step, add structure to the documents and, sometimes, filter relevant information, by means of applying rules*" [25, 26]. Figure 2 describes the architecture of our IE system, showing the cascade of modules we used. The raw privacy policy is given as input to the *Tokenizer* that splits the text into very simple tokens, to which a type (i.e. number, punctuation or word) is associated. The *Sentence Splitter* divides the text into sentences, while the *POS Tagger* annotates each word with the related part-of-speech (POS) tag. A POS tag specifies whether a word is a verb, a noun or another lexical category[1]. The *Named Entity (NE)* recognition module seeks the text for concepts of the application domain, while the *Annotation Patterns Engine* provides the means to define extraction rules, needed to detect the information wanted, according to specific syntactic-semantic patterns.

Note that, as described in Figure 2, at each stage a new *Annotation Set* is added to the document. *Annotations* can be seen as meta-data attached to part of the text giving specific information. For example POS tagger annotations can state that the word '*and*' is a *conjunction*. Every annotation has a type (e.g. *conjunction*) and a value (e.g. '*and*'), and belongs to an *Annotation Set* (e.g. POS Annotation Set) that groups together similar annotations. Annotations Sets that are output of earlier modules, can be used as input of later stages.

The structure shown in Figure 2 is a basic cascade of modules. Such a cascade can be extended by adding other modules for language processing. For example, co-reference and anaphora resolution [27] could be added to verify whether two noun phrases refer to the same entity [28], e.g. '*email address*' and '*it*' in the sentence "*We store your* **email**

---

[1] The complete list of POS tags we used is available at
http://gate.ac.uk/sale/tao/splitap7.html#x37-729000G

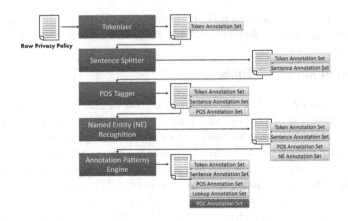

Fig. 2. The cascade of modules used in our IE system

address, it will be used to inform you that your order has been shipped". The use of ontologies, which associate a concept with the terms expressing it [23], may enrich the domain knowledge. Finally, syntactic parsing could help to find the main constituents of a sentence such as noun, verbs, and prepositional phrases. The decision of whether or not to add one or more of these modules is a trade off between the increased accuracy they can grant and the added computational costs they will bring. Since we aim at building a system with a good response time, we only use the modules presented in Figure 2 in this paper. The benefits and costs of adding other modules are discussed in Section 6, as part of our further works.

To develop our system we used the GATE (General Architecture for Text Engineering) framework [29, 30], and the ANNIE (A Nearly-New Information Extraction System) [31] suite. These tools, amongst other functionalities, make available multiple implementations of the modules depicted in Figure 2.

4   The Process

The process we followed to build and evaluate our IE system is described in Figure 3. In this section we give details for activities of this process such as the definition of Named Entity (Section 4.1), the selection, annotation and splitting of the Corpus (Section 4.2), and the creation of extraction rules (Section 4.3). The evaluation and the results are discussed in Section 5.

4.1   Named Entities

Information extraction uses Named Entities (NEs) to represent important concepts within a certain domain[2]. For example, in the domain of novels, the *author*, the *title*, and the *characters* are important concepts that can be modeled as NEs.

---

[2] A discussion about the difficulties of defining *Named Entity* is available at
http://webknox.com/blog/2010/09/named-entity-definition/

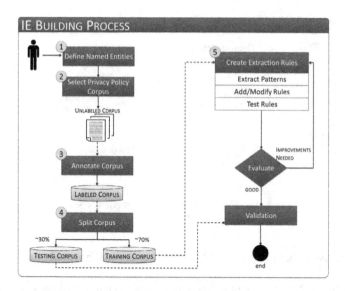

Fig. 3. IE building process

Defining NEs requires a deep knowledge of both the application domain and the type of information to be extracted. Since we aim at extracting the list of personal data collected by a website, we need entities modeling concepts of this scenario. To select our named entities we analyze several privacy policies. In this way, we discovered that the description of data collection practices is usually done in one of the following ways:

1. The policy states the website may require user's personal data for some purposes, e.g. registration or shipping;
2. The policy states the user may provide his personal data to the website, e.g. by filling in profile information;
3. The policy states the website may use automatic tools to get users' personal data, e.g. cookies to track user's on-line behavior.

This knowledge leads to choose the NEs presented in Figure 4 as part of our system. The **Data Provider** represents the data owner, generally the user, that provides his personal information; the **Data Collector** refers to the website (or the company behind it) that collects the personal information; while the **Collection Tools** is used to describe web technologies, such as cookies or web beacons, used to track users' online activities. The NE mentioned so far can be seen as *subjects* of the *actions* leading to data collection. The actions related are respectively modeled as **Provider Action**, including verbs such as *provide* or *supply*; **Collector Action**, with verbs such as *request, collect, use, store*; and **Tools Action** including verbs describing tracking activities, such as *track* or *monitor*. The core entity of our domain is the **Personal Data Collected** (or **PDC**), actually divided into two sub-entities: **Generic Data** to refer to general concepts of personal information such as *contacts information, personal identifiable information, browsing information*; and **Specific Data** to refer to personal data units such as *name, surname,*

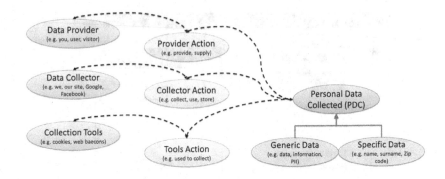

Fig. 4. The Named Entities (NEs) of our system

or *nationality*. Note that the list of PDC is the one that will be finally presented to the user.

Once the list of NEs has been defined, it is necessary to populate it by adding instances to the concepts, e.g. to list *name, surname* and *address* as instances of the entity *Specific Data*, and *you* and *user* as instances of *Data Provider*. The population process is performed by creating files listing instances for each NE (the so called gazetteer lists).

Note that, as suggested in [6, 32], while listing the instances of *Specific Data* we consider as PDC any data belonging to an individual, i.e. his PII (Personal Identifiable Information such as *name, surname* or *birthdate*), but also tracking data related to him such as the *current GPS location*, the *clickstream*, or the *friend list*.

4.2   Corpus

A corpus is a set of documents forming the core of an IE system. Its importance is twofold: its analysis drives the acquisition of knowledge necessary to extracting patterns and creating rules, and, once annotated, it is used to test the accuracy of the IE system. According to EU directives (e.g. EU 95/46/EC and the EU 2006/24/EC), privacy policies have to address specific topics of interest for the end user, such as what data they collect, how long they retain the data, whether they share it and so on. Each topic is usually discussed in specific paragraphs of the policy, leading to documents with fixed and similar structures.

In our system we use a corpus containing two types of document: **corpus A** is the part containing 128 paragraphs extracted from the *collection section* of different privacy policies; while **corpus B** is the part formed by 12 complete privacy policies. The use of corpus A helped us to focus on modeling recurrent patterns used to describe collection practices. On the other hand, the use of corpus B lets us test the feasibility of our approach in terms of satisfactory response time, and verify that the accuracy of the system does not decrease when it is applied to complete policies, i.e. extending the analysis to other sections of the policy does not introduce too many false positives.

The privacy policies of our corpus have been collected from websites of different application domains such as e-commerce (e.g. eBay, Paypal, Amazon), searching

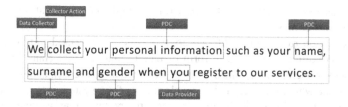

Fig. 5. Example of text annotation

(e.g. Google, DuckDuckGo), social networking (e.g. Facebook, LinkedIn), and news and communities (e.g. WordPress, FileTube, and TripAdvisor). Dealing with different application domains is especially useful to enrich the gazetteer lists. For example, by analyzing social network policies, new instances of *Specific Data*, such as *profile, friends list* or *profile picture*, can be detected.

Once the corpus has been selected, and named entities defined, the annotation task can take place. During the corpus annotation, a human annotator reads every document, and tags each occurrence of NE instances. For example, in a document with the sentence *"We collect your personal information such as your name, surname and gender when you register to our services"*, *'we'* will be annotated as Data Collector, *'collect'* as Collector Action, and so on, as described in Figure 5. It is important to note that instances of Specific Data (SP) and Generic Data(GD) are annotated as PDC only if the text makes clear that such data will be retained by the website. For example, in a sentence like *"If you do not want to receive e-mail from us, please adjust your preferences"*, the term *e-mail* will not be annotated as PDC.

In the following, we refer to the manual annotations as *Standard Gold Set*, and to the annotations resulting by running our IE system as *Response Set*. To evaluate the accuracy of the system, PDC annotations of the *Response Set* will be compared to PDC annotations of the *Standard Gold Set*. Intuitively, the more similar the two sets are, the better the accuracy of the system.

Once the annotation task is completed, each sub-corpus is divided into a training ($\sim$ 70% of the documents of the sub-corpus) and a testing (the remaining $\sim$ 30%) set. After the splitting, corpus A contains 87 paragraphs in the training set, and 34 in the testing set, while corpus B contains 9 complete policies in the training set, and 3 in the testing set. The training sets are used to develop the extraction rules, while the testing sets are kept apart until the very end, when they are used to measure the system's accuracy. The training set of B is especially useful to verify whether patterns extracted by analyzing A do not occurs in other sections of a complete policy as well.

4.3 Extraction Rules

Extraction rules are used to detect specific regularities and patterns in the text. To define such rules, specific declarative languages can be used [33–35]. To develop our IE system we used the Jape language [35]. Jape provides mechanisms to recognize regular expressions in annotations made over a document. For example, it allows to create rules that annotate as a *Person* a word that starts with a capital letter, and that is preceded by the word *Mr*, *Mrs* or *Miss*.

Jape's extraction rules consist of two components: a Left Hand Side (LHS), representing the condition, expressed in form of pattern, and a Right Hand Side (RHS), representing the conclusion, i.e. the action to take once the pattern matches.

Recall that the whole idea behind the development of our system is that privacy policies share a set of fixed patterns. Table 1 presents the patterns that we detected during our analysis. In the table, each pattern is expressed as a sequence of *NE annotations*, but also *Token* and *POS annotations* (like *MODAL, SUCH_AS, TO, INCLUDE*), created by earlier steps of the process (see Figure 2). Moreover, for each pattern, one or more matching sentences are presented. For example, the pattern n.1 of Table 1 will match every sentence where the website is asking the user to provide personal information.

Table 1. List of the *collection* patterns detected by analyzing our corpus

	Pattern
n.1	**DATA_COLLECTOR** *MODAL* **COLLECTOR_ACTION** **DATA_PROVIDER** *TO* **PROVIDER_ACTION** *your* **GENERIC_DATA** (*SUCH_AS*)? (**SPECIFIC_DATA**)*.
	We may ask you to provide your personal data such as name, surname, and gender.
	The website may request you to provide your financial information.
n.2	**DATA_COLLECTOR** *MODAL* **COLLECTOR_ACTION** *your* **GENERIC_DATA** (*SUCH_AS*)? (**SPECIFIC_DATA**)*.
	We may collect your personal data such as name, surname, and gender.
	Google may gather your contact information.
n.3	**DATA_PROVIDER** *MODAL* **PROVIDER_ACTION** *us* *with* *your* **GENERIC_DATA** (*SUCH_AS*)? (**SPECIFIC_DATA**)*.
	You must provide us with your personal data including your name, surname, and gender.
	The user should supply his personal information.
n.4	*The* **GENERIC_DATA** **DATA_COLLECTOR** **COLLECTOR_ACTION** *MODAL* *INCLUDE* *your* (**SPECIFIC_DATA**)*.
	The personal data we collect may include your name, surname, and gender.
n.5	**COLLECTION_TOOLS** *MODAL* *BE_USED* *TO* **TOOLS_ACTION** *your* **GENERIC_DATA** (*SUCH_AS*)? (**SPECIFIC_DATA**)*.
	Cookies may be used to track your browsing data such as your IP address, browser type and pages visited.
	Web beacons may be used to monitor your browsing activities.

?: zero or one repetition

*: zero or more repetition

italic: terms not relevant for the pattern

ITALIC: temporary annotations

BOLD: named entities

Underline: examples of matching sentences

Once patterns have been defined (LHS), it is necessary to create the output (RHS). Figure 6 describes how a pattern can be translated in a Jape rule, by referring to the first pattern of Table 1. The LHS describes the pattern, and when a match occurs, the RHS is called to annotate *specific* and *generic data* as PDC. Note that in Jape the symbols ?, * and + means respectively zero or one, zero or more, and one or more occurrences.

For each pattern of the table, one or more rules have been created. We created rules accounting for positive and negative ('*we collect*' versus '*we do not collect*'), and for active and passive ('*we collect your data*' versus '*your data are collected*') forms of the patterns. Of course a negative pattern indicates the specified personal data is not collected, so it is not added to the *Response Set*. Moreover, rules have been created in such a way that tokens not relevant for the pattern are ignored (e.g. in a sentences like '*we ask you to provide your personal data*', the presence of the token *your* does not stop the rule to match).

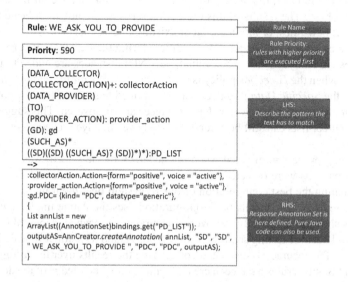

Fig. 6. An example of a JAPE extraction rule

5   Evaluation and Results

In this section we discuss the methodology used to evaluate the accuracy of the IE we developed, and the results we obtained. We evaluate our IE system by measuring the recall, the precision, and the F_1 score obtained by comparing the *Response Set* to the *Standard Gold Set*.

Recall and precision can be computed using *strict* or *lenient* measures. Such measures are different for the way they treat partial matches. A partial match is obtained when the result of the *Response Set* does not completely match the one of the *Standard Gold Set*, for example the manual annotation is "*e-mail addresses = PDC*" but the *Response Set* only recognizes "*e-mail address= PDC*". In this cases, *strict* measures would consider the result as a mistake, while *lenient* measures would treat it as a correct result. The observation of partial matches leads us to conclude that they are generally sufficient for our purposes to be considered correct, so we use lenient measures for evaluating the accuracy.

Table 2. Accuracy of the system over the training and the testing sets of corpus A and B

	Time(sec. per set)		Precision		Recall		F_1 score	
	A	B	A	B	A	B	A	B
Training Set	3.22	9.25	76%	75%	90%	83%	83%	79%
Testing Set	1.28	3.25	78%	80%	81%	87%	**80%**	**83%**

Since the process of creating the rules of an IE system is iterative, and it involves tests over the training set, the evaluation of the accuracy takes place during the whole development phase. The results of this evaluation serve as a guide to indicate whether the addition of new rules, or modification of existing ones, is needed.

Besides rules, gazetteer lists are also modified during the development process: privacy policies are analyzed and, when found, new NEs instances are added to the lists. For example, when the *Facebook* policy is analyzed, the terms *profile* and *profile picture* are added to the *Specific Data* gazetteer list. We noticed that, when the last policies of the corpus are reached, only few new NEs instances are discovered. This suggests that, although gazetteer lists can still be extended, they have already reached a good level of completeness.

The building process terminated when the accuracy of the system was satisfactory and no new patterns were detected. Table 2 shows precision, recall and F_1 score obtained by running the best configuration of our IE system over the training and testing sets of the corpus A and B. This best configuration uses the Annie implementation of the modules shown in Figure 2. The overall accuracy we reached, captured by the F_1 score obtained over the testing set, is 80% for corpus A, and 83% for corpus B. To avoid biased results, the accuracy is evaluated considering the results over the *testing* sets of corpus A and B, since rules have been created without any knowledge of the documents in such sets.

We believe that the obtained results are very promising, and that users could benefit from a system based on our approach. In fact, considering that average users do not read privacy policies, we increase their knowledge on data collection from 0 to 80%. Also, the results are obtained by using a very basic pipeline, and a limited set of rules. Therefore the accuracy could be improved by adding new modules (such as co-reference or ontologies) and enlarging the rule set. Finally, note that the results presented in Table 2 do not take repetition into consideration, i.e., if a personal data item (e.g. *name, e-mail*) appears in two sentences, but it is only detected once, we have one correct result and one wrong result, leading to an accuracy of 50%. In our settings, the fact that at least one occurrence of the same data item is correctly identified suffices to have 100% accuracy (for that specific item). Taking this into account, the accuracy can raise from 79% to 92%, if we consider the training set of corpus B.

The main bottleneck for our system is the accuracy of the POS tagger module. Most of the errors in the *Response Set* are due to erroneous results provided by this module in our experimental tests. The POS tagger is in charge of distinguishing whether a word represents a verb, a noun or another lexical category. That means it should be able to say that the word '*place*' represents a noun in the sentence "*we collect information about the place you took your photo*", while it represents a verb in the sentence "*we store your*

Table 3. Comparison of performances obtained by using different POS tagger over the **testing set** of the corpus A and B

POS Tagger	Time(sec)		Precision		Recall		F_1 score	
	A	B	A	B	A	B	A	B
OpenNLP	1.55	4.50	77%	70%	80%	83%	78%	77%
LingPipe	2.45	3.95	79%	75%	68%	84%	73%	79%
Annie	1.02	3.25	78%	80%	81%	87%	**80%**	**83%**

mail address when you place an order". Since our rules are based on the POS tagger annotations (e.g. *provide* is considered a **PROVIDER_ACTION** if and only if it has been annotated as a *verb* by the POS tagger), an error in the tagger's results leads to an error in our system's results.

Let us consider the following sentence: *"LinkedIn **requests** other information from you during the registration process, (e.g. gender, location, etc.)"*. If *'requests'* is not recognized as a verb by the POS tagger, no extraction rule will fire, and the words *gender* and *location* will not be annotated as PDC. That means the accuracy of our system strongly depends on the accuracy of the POS tagger, and that it can be improved by decreasing the tagger error rate.

Since multiple implementations of the POS tagger exist, we tested how the accuracy of the system changes according to the tagger used. The results of this comparison, running the system over the testing sets, are shown in Table 3. We used three different POS tagger implementation: the OpenNLP, the LingPipe[3], and the Annie POS tagger. As we can observe, the use of the LingPipe tagger leads to the worst performance over the corpus A, with a difference of 5% when compared with the best results, obtained by using Annie tagger. The results confirm that the choice of the POS tagger has a considerable impact on the performance of the system. Although Annie is the best performing tagger in our setting, it still shows several errors. A possible way to improve the POS performances, and with it our system's accuracy, is by training a POS tagger over the privacy policy domain.

Finally, note that our solution, which was not optimized for time performances, can be executed in near real-time. As reported in the *Time* column of Table 2, the system needs 9.25 seconds to process 9 complete privacy policies (training set of B), therefore the analysis of a single policy requires around one second. This means our approach is applicable to real scenarios, where providing real time responses to the user is an important requirement.

6   Conclusions and Further Work

In this paper we discuss the creation of an IE system, able to extract the list of personal data collected by a website by analyzing the content of its privacy policy. The system shows an accuracy around 80%. Although we believe this accuracy is reasonable and able to benefit the users, improvements can still be made. Adding co-reference

---

[3] For the LingPipe the *pos-en-general-brown model* was used.

and anaphora resolution modules can increase the accuracy by verifying that, for example, 'we' refers to the 'website' when annotating it as DATA_COLLECTOR (so far we assumed this is always true). Also, the accuracy can be improved by using ontologies and thesaurus, to enrich the gazetteer lists with synonyms and close lexical concepts. On the other hand, we believe the system would not benefit of the use of syntactic parsing, since its computational costs would not allow to provide real time responses to the users [4]. It is also important to verify that users find our system beneficial, for example by carrying on a user study. Since the manual creation of extraction rules is a complex and error prone task, the use of systems for the automatic creation of extraction rules, e.g. by applying machine learning techniques, can also be considered (see [36]). Finally, in regards to our more general goal of grading privacy policies, we wish to apply the approach presented in this paper to other sections of privacy policies, e.g. to analyse the *data sharing* practices, and to define a policy grading system based on the results of such analysis.

References

1. Kosta, E., Dumortier, J., Graux, H., Tirtea, R., Ikonomou, D.: Study on data collection and storage in the EU. Technical report, ENISA, European Network and Information Securiy Agency (2012)
2. Newman, J.: 8 Tools for the Online Privacy Paranoid (2012)
3. Spiekermann, S.: Engineering privacy. IEEE Software Engineering 35(1) (2009)
4. Tsai, J., Egelman, S., Cranor, L.: The effect of online privacy information on purchasing behavior: An experimental study. Information Systems Research 21 (2011)
5. Turow, J., Hoofnagle, C.J., Mulligan, D.K., Good, N., Grossklags, J.: The FTC and Consumer Privacy in the Coming Decade. Federal Trade Commission (2006)
6. Tene, O.: Privacy in the Age of Big Data: A Time for Big Decisions. Stanford Law Review Online (2012)
7. Costante, E., Sun, Y., Petkovic, M., den Hartog, J.: A machine learning solution to assess privacy policy completeness (short paper). In: WPES 2012, pp. 91–96 (2012)
8. Holtz, L.-E., Nocun, K., Hansen, M.: Towards Displaying Privacy Information with Icons. In: Fischer-Hübner, S., Duquenoy, P., Hansen, M., Leenes, R., Zhang, G. (eds.) Privacy and Identity Management for Life. IFIP AICT, vol. 352, pp. 338–348. Springer, Heidelberg (2011)
9. Anton, A.I., Earp, J.B., Qingfeng, H., Stufflebeam, W., Bolchini, D., Jensen, C.: Financial privacy policies and the need for standardization. IEEE Security and Privacy 2(2) (2004)
10. Brodie, C.A., Karat, C.M., Karat, J.: An empirical study of natural language parsing of privacy policy rules using the SPARCLE policy workbench. In: Proc. of SOUPS 2006. ACM (2006)
11. Brodie, C.A., Karat, C.M., Karat, J., Feng, J.: Usable security and privacy: a case study of developing privacy management tools. In: Proc. of SOUPS 2005. ACM (2005)
12. Yu, W.D., Doddapaneni, S., Murthy, S.: A Privacy Assessment Approach for Serviced Oriented Architecture Application. In: Proc. of SOSE 2006. IEEE (2006)
13. Yu, W.D., Murthy, S.: PPMLP: A Special Modeling Language Processor for Privacy Policies. In: Proc. of ISCC 2007. IEEE (2007)

---

[4] Preliminary tests show the Stanford Parser needs 123 seconds to process the Google privacy policy.

14. Cranor, L., Langheinrich, M., Marchiori, M., Presler-Marshall, M., Reagle, J.: The platform for privacy preferences 1.0 (P3P1. 0) specification. W3C (2002)
15. Aïmeur, E., Gambs, S., Ho, A.: UPP: User Privacy Policy for Social Networking Sites. In: Proc. of ICIW 2009. IEEE (2009)
16. W3C: Privacy Enhancing Browser Extensions. Technical report, W3C (2011)
17. Ashley, P., Hada, S., Karjoth, G., Powers, C., Schunter, M.: Enterprise privacy authorization language (EPAL). Technical report, IBM Research (2003)
18. OASIS: extensible access control markup language (xacml) version 2.0. Technical report, OASIS (2008)
19. Schwitter, R.: English as a Formal Specification Language. In: Proc. of DEXA 2002. IEEE Computer Society (2002)
20. Cranor, L., Arjula, M.: Use of a P3P user agent by early adopters. In: Poc. of WPES 2002 (2002)
21. Reagle, J., Cranor, L.: The platform for privacy preferences. Communications of the ACM 42(2) (1999)
22. Beatty, P., Reay, I., Dick, S., Miller, J.: P3P Adoption on E-Commerce Web sites: A Survey and Analysis. IEEE Internet Computing 11(2) (2007)
23. Nédellec, C., Nazarenko, A.: Ontologies and Information Extraction. CoRR abs/cs/060 (July 2006)
24. Cunningham, H.: Information extraction, automatic. In: Brown, K. (ed.) Encyclopedia of Language and Linguistics, vol. 5. Elsevier (2005)
25. Turmo, J., Ageno, A.: Adaptive information extraction. ACM Computing Surveys (CSUR) 38(2) (2006)
26. Hobbs, J.: The generic information extraction system. In: Proc. of MUC 1993 (1993)
27. Deemter, K., Kibble, R.: On coreferring: Coreference in MUC and related annotation schemes. Computational Linguistics (2000)
28. Hirschman, L., Robinson, P., Burger, J.D., Vilain, M.B.: Automating coreference: The role of annotated training data. CoRR cmp-lg/9803001 (1998)
29. Cunningham, H.: GATE, a General Architecture for Text Engineering. Computers and the Humanities 36(2) (2002)
30. Cunningham, H., Maynard, D., Bontcheva, K.: Text Processing with GATE (Version 6). GATE (2011)
31. Cunningham, H., Maynard, D., Bontcheva, K., Tablan, V.: GATE: A Framework and Graphical Development Environment for Robust NLP Tools and Applications. In: Proc. of ACL 2002 (2002)
32. Ohm, P.: Broken promises of privacy: Responding to the surprising failure of anonymization. UCLA Law Review 57 (2010)
33. Krishnamurthy, R., Li, Y., Raghavan, S., Reiss, F., Vaithyanathan, S., Zhu, H.: SystemT: a system for declarative information extraction. SIGMOD Rec. 37(4) (2009)
34. Ashish, N., Mehrotra, S., Pirzadeh, P.: Xar: An integrated framework for information extraction. In: WRI World Congress on Computer Science and Information Engineering (2009)
35. Cunningham, H., Maynard, D., Tablan, V.: Jape: a java annotation patterns engine (1999)
36. Xu, F.: Bootstrapping Relation Extraction from Semantic Seeds. PhD thesis, Saarland University (2008)

Automating Privacy Enforcement
in Cloud Platforms*

Peng Yu[1], Jakub Sendor[2], Gabriel Serme[2], and Anderson Santana de Oliveira[2]

[1] Université de Technologie de Compiègne, France
peng.yu@etu.utc.fr
[2] SAP Research, France
firstname.lastname@sap.com

Abstract. Privacy in cloud computing is a major concern for individuals, governments, service and platform providers. In this context, the compliance with regards to policies and regulations about personal data protection is essential, but hard to achieve, as the implementation of privacy controls is subject to diverse kinds of errors. In this paper we present how the enforcement of privacy policies can be facilitated by a Platform as a Service. Cloud applications developers can use non-obtrusive annotations in the code to indicate where personally identifiable information is being handled, leveraging the aspect-oriented programming (AOP) features. Subsequently the evaluation of user defined preferences is performed by trustful components provided by the platform, liberating developers from the burden of designing custom mechanisms for privacy enforcement in their software.

1 Introduction

In order to speed up the deployment of business applications, and to reduce overall IT capital expenditure, many cloud providers nowadays offer the Platform as a Service (PaaS) solutions as an alternative to leverage the advantages of cloud computing. We can mention for instance SAP NetWeaver Cloud, Google App Engine, or VMware Cloud Foundry, to cite a few. PaaS brings an additional level of abstraction to the cloud landscape, by emulating a virtual platform on top of the infrastructure, generally featuring a form of mediation to the underlying services akin to middleware in traditional communication stacks.

As the consequence of that shift we observe that more and more personally identifiable information (PII) is being collected and stored in cloud-based systems. This is becoming an extremely sensitive issue for citizens, governments, and companies, both using and offering cloud platforms. The existing regulations, which already established several data protection principles, are being extended to assign new responsibilities to cloud providers with respect to private data handling.

The provision of privacy preserving services and tools will be one of the arguments favoring the choice of one PaaS provider over the other when a company

* Supported by the French ANR, grant number 09-SEGI-002-01, CESSA Project.

R. Di Pietro et al. (Eds.): DPM 2012 and SETOP 2012, LNCS 7731, pp. 160–173, 2013.

is hesitating where to deploy new cloud application. The proposed reform of the European data protection regulation points out that privacy-aware applications must protect personal data by design and by default: "Article 22 takes account of the debate on a 'principle of accountability' and describes in detail the obligation of responsibility of the controller to comply with this Regulation and to demonstrate this compliance, including by way of adoption of internal policies and mechanisms for ensuring such compliance. Article 23 sets out the obligations of the controller arising from the principles of data protection by design and by default. Article 24 on joint controllers clarifies the responsibilities of joint controllers as regards their internal relationship and towards the data subject[1]."

The correct enforcement of privacy and data usage control policies has been recently subject of several incidents reported about faulty data handling, perhaps on purpose, see for instance the cases of Facebook[2].

Therefore, addressing compliance requirements at the application level is a competitive advantage for cloud platform providers. In the specific cases where the cloud platform provider is also considered a joint controller, a privacy-aware architecture will address the accountability requirement for the PaaS provider with regards to the next generation of regulations. Such architecture can enable compliance also for the Software as a Service delivery model, if we assume the software was built over a privacy-aware platform. On the other hand, this could be hardly achieved in the context of Infrastructures as a Service, since there would be no interoperability layer on which the privacy controls can rely on.

In order to achieve this, the PaaS must implement some prominent, possibly standardized, privacy policy framework (such as EPAL[2], P3P[7]), where privacy preferences can be declared in a machine-readable form, and later enforced automatically. In such a setting, the privacy enforcement controls could be easily incorporated into new deployment landscape accelerating the development process of compliant applications. Furthermore the cloud platform can offer the guaranties ensuring the correct implementation of the enforcement components. This could be offered either via a certification mechanism or an audit of an existing cloud landscape that would be executed by the governing entities.

In this paper we present work towards the implementation of privacy-aware services in a PaaS. We aim to empower the cloud platform with capabilities to automatically enforce the privacy policy that is result of the end-user consent over the application provider privacy policy. End-user policies and service provider terms of use are defined in a state of the art privacy and usage control language [3]. In order to leverage the provided implementation of privacy-aware services, cloud application developers need to introduce simple annotations to the code, prior to its deployment in the cloud. These indicate where PII is being handled, towards automating privacy enforcement and enabling compliance by design and by default. The idea is outlined in Figure 1, and consists of design-time steps (declaring policies, annotation of the code and deployment in the

---

[1] http://ec.europa.eu/justice/data-protection/document/review2012/
  com_2012_11_en.pdf
[2] http://mashable.com/2011/10/21/facebook-deleted-data-fine/

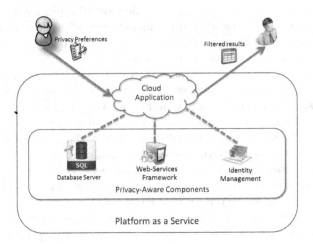

Fig. 1. Privacy aware PaaS components

cloud); and run-time steps (including policy matching, privacy control and obligation execution).

The enforcement mechanisms are provided by the platform with the help
of a new approach for aspect-oriented programming where aspects can be manipulated at the process and at the platform levels [8]. That approach gives a
possibility to maintain a more flexible configuration of the enforcement mechanisms. The mechanisms interpret end-user preferences regarding handling of
the PII, presented in form of opt-in or opt-out choices among available privacy
policies of a cloud application, and later perform the required actions (filtering,
blocking, deletion, etc). We experimented on a Java-based Platform as a Service,
SAP NetWeaver Cloud, to demonstrate how privacy preferences can be handled
automatically thanks to the use of simple Java annotation library provided in
our prototype. The platform provider can make in this way an important step
towards providing built-in compliance with the personal data protection regulations transparently, as we describe in the next sections.

The remainder of the paper is organized as follows: in Section 2 we present our
use case and we give a brief overview of the privacy policy language we adopt
in this work, in Section 3 we introduce the technical architecture allowing to
enforce privacy on multiple PaaS layers, Section 4 brings a discussion on related
works and Section 5 presents future perspectives and concludes the paper.

2   Privacy-Aware Applications in the Cloud

In this section we present our use case involving multiple stakeholders accessing
users' PII in the cloud, as well as some background on privacy policy language
that we used.

2.1   Use case

In our use case we consider a loyalty program offered by a supermarket chain, accessible via a mobile shopping application that communicates with back-end application deployed on the PaaS cloud offering. The supermarket's goal is to collect the information about consumers' shopping behavior that results in the creation of a consumer profile. This profile could then be used to provide consumers more precise offers and bargains. Supermarket's business partners may also want to access this information in order to propose personalized offers to the mobile shopping application users themselves.

The back-end application for the supermarket loyalty program is developed using Java programming language and uses the cloud persistency service to store application data. The interface to access the persistency service is based on Java Persistence API (JPA)[3], which is nowadays one of the most common ways of accessing a relational database from Java code.

The supermarket employees can access detailed results of database queries regarding the consumers' shopping history and also create personalized offers, via a web-based portal. Moreover, the cloud application exposes web services through which third parties interact with the back-end system to consume collected data: both for their own business analysis, but also to contact directly the consumers for marketing purposes.

The interface for the consumers makes it possible to indicate privacy preferences with respect to the category of products (health care, food, drinks, etc) that one wants to share his shopping habits about. The consumer can also indicate whether he permits the supermarket to share personally identifiable information with its business partners, among other usages. This choices are then reflected by the private data access control mechanism that we will describe in Section 3.

2.2   Background: Privacy Policy Language

The users of the mobile shopping application are asked to provide various kinds of personal information, starting from basic contact information (addresses, phone, email) to more complex data such as shopping history or lifestyle preferences. Service providers describe how users' data are handled using a privacy policy, which is explicitly presented to users during the data collection phase.

In this paper we adopt the PrimeLife[4] Policy Language (PPL) [3], which extends XACML with privacy-related constraints for access and data usage. PPL policy is then used by the application to record its privacy policy. It states how the collected data will be used, by whom, and how it could be shared. On the other hand, the end-user also selects among the possible choices as to the conditions of the data usages, that are derived from privacy policies specific to the application. This user opt-in/opt-out choice is managed by the application and as such is not part of the generic enforcement mechanism developed by us. Before

---

[3] http://docs.oracle.com/javaee/5/tutorial/doc/bnbpz.html
[4] www.primelife.eu

```
- <ppl:DataHandlingPreferences>
    - <ppl:AuthorizationsSet>
        - <ppl:AuthzUseForPurpose>
            <ppl:Purpose>http://www.w3.org/2002/01/P3Pv1/individual-analysis</ppl:Purpose>
            <ppl:Purpose>http://www.w3.org/2002/01/P3Pv1/admin</ppl:Purpose>
            <ppl:Purpose>http://www.w3.org/2002/01/P3Pv1/contact</ppl:Purpose>
        </ppl:AuthzUseForPurpose>
        <ppl:AuthzDownstreamUsage allowed="false"/>
    </ppl:AuthorizationsSet>
    + <ob:ObligationsSet>
</ppl:DataHandlingPreferences>
```

Fig. 2. Excerpt of a PPL policy rule

disclosing personal information, the user can match his preferences against the privacy policy of the service provider with the help of a policy matching engine. The result of the matching process is an agreed policy, which is then translated into the set of simple rules that are stored together with users' data inside the cloud platform's database servers.

In summary a PPL policy defines the following structures [3]:

- Access Control Elements: inherited from the XACML attribute-based access control mechanism to describe a shared resource (in our case PII) in general, as well as entities (subjects) that can obtain access to the data.
- Data Handling Preferences: expressing the purpose of data usage (for instance marketing, research, payment, delivery, etc.) but also downstream usage (understood here as sharing data with third parties, e.g. advertising companies), supporting a multi-level nested policy describing the data handling conditions that are applicable for any third party retrieving the data from a given service.
- Obligations: specify the actions that should be carried out with respect to the collected data, e.g. notification to the user whenever his data is shared with a third party, or deletion of the credit card number after the payment transaction is finished, etc. Obligations in PPL can be executed at any moment throughout whole lifetime of the collected data and can affect future data sharing transactions, e.g. with third parties.

An excerpt of a policy is shown in Figure 2. It shows part of a policy rule, stating the consent to use the data collected for three distinct purposes (described using P3P purpose ontology), but forbids downstream usage.

Consumer opt-in/opt-out choice is linked with PPL policy rule via XACML conditions that we adopted for this purpose. We have reused *EnvironmentAttributeDesignator* elements syntax to refer to the actual recorded consumer choice in the application data model, as shown in Figure 3. The location is provided as the *AttributeId* value and can be read as TABLE_NAME:COLUMN_NAME of the database table where this choice is stored (CONSUMER_CONSENT) as well as a foreign key to the product category table (CATEGORY_ID) that is used to join products table. This information is used when enforcement mechanism is put in place to take consumer consent into account whenever information about consumer's shopping history (for certain product categories) is requested. This

```
<xacml:Condition>
<xacml:Apply FunctionId="urn:oasis:names:tc:xacml:1.0:function:and">
    <xacml:Apply FunctionId="urn:oasis:names:tc:xacml:1.0:function:string-equal">
        <xacml:EnvironmentAttributeDesignator
                AttributeId="CONSUMER_CONSENT:CATEGORY_ID"
                DataType="http://www.w3.org/2001/XMLSchema#string" />
        <xacml:EnvironmentAttributeDesignator
                AttributeId="PRODUCT_CATEGORY:CATEGORY_ID"
                DataType="http://www.w3.org/2001/XMLSchema#string" />
    </xacml:Apply>
</xacml:Apply>
</xacml:Condition>
```

Fig. 3. Excerpt of a PPL policy condition

policy definition of how user consent is linked to the rest of the application data model is left in charge to the application developer as he is the one possessing full knowledge of the application domain.

3   Privacy Enhanced Application Programming

We have designed a framework able to modify, at the deployment time, the architectural elements (such as databases, web service frameworks, identity management, access control, etc) enriching it with the further components in order to enforce user privacy preferences. In this landscape the new applications deployed on the modified platform can benefit from privacy-aware data handling.

3.1   Programming Model

The privacy-aware components are integrated seamlessly with cloud application at the deployment time, so that the enforcement of privacy constraints is done afterwards automatically. They mediate access to the data sources, enforcing privacy constraints. In this case we are taking full benefit of the uniform database access in the PaaS landscape that is exposed via standard Java database interfaces such as JDBC (Java Database Connectivity) or JPA.

Usually the application code handling privacy related data is scattered and tangled over the application, being difficult to handle and to maintain if any changes in the privacy policy are introduced. As we observed in the existing applications the operations, which are performed on the private user data to ensure that privacy policies are enforced, are typically cross-cutting concerns in aspect-oriented programming paradigm. Inspired by this, we designed a process for the application developer that contributes to simplifying a way the data protection compliance could be achieved. It consists of adding meta-information to the application code via Java annotation mechanism in the JPA entity classes. Entity class in JPA terms is the one that is mapped into a database structure (usually a table, but also more complex type of mappings exist, e.g. to map object inheritance hierarchy) and enables the objects of that class to be persisted in a

```
1   @Entity
2   @PII
3   public class ShoppingHistory implements Serializable
4   { ... ... }
```

Fig. 4. JPA entity class annotation indicating persistency of private information

```
5    @PiiAccessClass
6    public final class ShoppingHistoryDAO extends DaoImpl<ShoppingHistory>
7    {
8       ...
9       @Info(purpose= "http://www.w3.org/2006/01/P3Pv11/marketing" )
10      public final List<ShopHistory> getHistories()
11      { ... }
12      ...
13   }
```

Fig. 5. Annotating private data usage class with PII meta-information

database. We provide also a second type of annotations, for the methods that make use of a private data, to indicate the purpose of the data usage.

The modifications to the code are non-intrusive, in the sense that the application business functions flow will stay exactly the same as before, except for the data set it will operate on, that will be obtained from database by adhering to the privacy policy. The changes are as transparent as possible from the application point-of-view as new platform components propose the same set of API as in the traditional platforms (in our case this API is JPA) and additional functionality is obtained via non-obtrusive code annotations that in principle could be easily removed in case described features are not required or not available.

This approach adds value with respect to legacy applications while allowing privacy management when needed. Another advantage is that the cloud service provider can easily move to another cloud platform without being locked into the certain vendor, apart from the fact that the guarantees given by the platform about private data handling could not be the same.

The platform we used to develop our prototype offers the enterprise level technologies available for Java in terms of web services and data persistency (JEE, JPA). In most of the examples we present along the paper we assume that the application developer will likely use a framework such as the JPA to abstract the database access layer.

In our approach developers are required to add annotations to certain constructs, such as *@PII* annotation in the JPA entity class (Figure 4). This annotation indicates that the class comprises one or more fields having private data (that usually are represented in database as columns) or that all fields are to be considered as PII (thus whole database table row needs to be either filtered or kept during the privacy enforcement, as JPA entity is by default mapped to a database row).

In the business code that is handling the private data we propose to use two other annotations to indicate class and method that processes PII sets.

An example of annotated code is shown in Figure 5. In this figure the method annotation holds the information that the shopping history list items will be processed for marketing purpose.

In summary our library provides three different annotations:

@PII: It is a flag to indicate personally identifiable information inside a JPA entity class definition. Such information is usually stored in a database as a table or a column. In Figure 4 this annotation involves the scope of the class declaration, see lines 2 and 3.

@PiiAccessClass: This annotation should be put in the class to indicate where it contains access methods to personal data (see line 5 in Figure 5). We assume that PII access method performs queries to the database that are requesting private user data.

@Info: This annotation is applied to PII access method, to describe the purpose or set of purposes of the query performed in that method (see lines 9 and 10 in Figure 5).

We expect the application developers to use this annotations to mark each usage of personal data as well as to indicate correct purposes. Ultimately they seek compliance to regulations, therefore we trust them to correctly indicate via the annotations the intended usage of the data. One can envisage that automated code scanners and manual reviews can take place during an audit procedure in order to check whether the annotations are rightfully used.

3.2   Implementation

In this section we detail the components of our prototype architecture. Technically our code components are packaged as several OSGi (Open Services Gateway initiative framework[5]) bundles. A bundle is a component which interacts with the applications running in the cloud platform. Some of them are to be directly deployed inside the PaaS cloud landscape and managed by the cloud provider while the other are part of the library to be used by the cloud application developers. Cloud providers can easily install or uninstall bundles using the OSGi framework without causing side effects to applications themselves (e.g. no application restart is required if some of the bundles are stopped). In the context of our scenario, we have three main bundles managed by the cloud provider (JDBC Wrapper, Annotation Detector and SQL Filter) and one additional bundle (Policy Handler) that is providing a translation from an application privacy policy file written in the PPL language into an internal representation stored in the Constraints Database. The diagram in Figure 6 presents the architecture of the system, which we are going to describe in more details in the following subsections.

---

[5] http://www.osgi.org

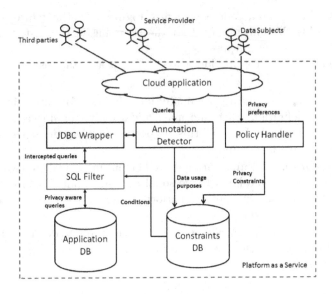

Fig. 6. Enforcement components

JDBC Wrapper. The Wrapper intercepts all queries issued by the cloud application directly or by the third parties which want to consume the collected data containing shopping history of the fidelity program participants. This component is provided on the platform as an alternative to the default JDBC driver in order to enforce consumers' privacy preferences. Actually the wrapper makes use of the default driver to eventually send the modified SQL calls to database.

JDBC Wrapper bundle implements the usual interfaces for the JDBC driver and overrides specific methods important to the Java Persistence API, necessary to track the itinerary of SQL queries. As a matter of fact, it is wrapping all JDBC methods that are querying the database, intercepting SQL statements and enriching them with proper conditions that adhere to privacy policy (e.g. by stating in the WHERE clause conditions that refer to the consumer consent table). In order to identify the purpose of each query, its recipient and the tables referred, we retrieve the call stack within the current thread thanks to the annotations described in the previous section. We look for the PII access class, then we look for the method that sends the request to get the further parameters that help properly enforce privacy control.

Annotation Detector. First task of this component is to scan Java classes at the deployment time and look for the JPA entities that are containing privacy-related annotation in its definition (@PII). List of such classes is then stored inside the server session context. Information about entities considered as PII is used to determine which database calls need to be modified in order to help preserve consumer privacy preferences.

In the second run the annotation detector scans the application bytecode in order to gather information concerning the operation that the application intends to perform on the data, annotated with `@PiiAccessClass` and `@Info` annotation. It is important to recall that the annotations are not a "programmatic" approach to indicate purpose, as they are independent from the code, which can evolve on its own. The assumption is that developers want to reach compliance, thus the purpose is correctly indicated, in contrast to [4], where it is assumed that end-users themselves indicate the purposes of the queries they perform. The cloud platform provider can instrument the annotation detector with a configuration file where the required annotations are declared. The detector can recognize custom annotations and stores information about related entity class in the runtime for future use.

SQL Filter. This component allows us to rewrite original queries issued to the database by replacing the requested data set with a projection of that data set that takes into account consumers' privacy choices. SQL Filter modifies only the `FROM` part of a query, implementing an adapted version of the algorithm for disclosure control described in [12], also similar to the approaches described in [1], [13], and [16].

The query transformation process makes the use of the pre-processed decisions generated by the Policy Handler that concerns each possible combination of the triple purpose, recipient and PII table.

The transformation of the SQL query happens at the runtime. Consumer's privacy preferences are enforced thanks to the additional join conditions in the query, relating data subject consent, product category and filtering rules. The output is a transformed SQL query that takes into account all stated privacy constraints and is still compatible with the originally issued SQL query (it means that the result set contains exactly the same type of data, e.g. number of columns and their types). From a business use-case perspective, it was always possible to visualize relevant data, e.g. shopping history information, etc, without disclosing personal data when user didn't give his consent. The process is illustrated in Figure 7. It depicts the process of query modification when application is accessing data from the **SHOPPING_HISTORY** table (top-left corner of this figure). Original query (bottom-left) is transformed so that it takes into account the information derived from privacy policy that was put by the Policy Handler in the **CONSUMER_CONSENT** table (top-center). This table stores the association between the consumers and the different product categories with which these consumers opt to reveal their shopping history. Modified query (bottom-right) yields the data set of the same structure as original query but without disclosing the information that consumers declined to share, as it can be seen in the **RESULT** table (top-right).

The negotiated privacy policies are stored under the form of constraints together with the data in the database component provided by the cloud infrastructure. Whenever a query is launched by the application, we use the information collected by the annotation detector in order to modify queries on the fly, thus using the constraints to filter out the data that is not allowed to appear in the query results.

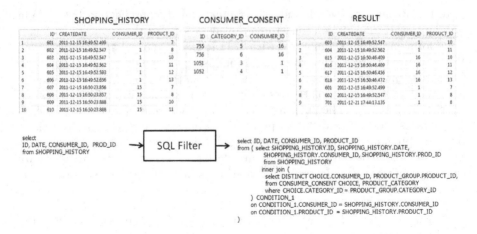

Fig. 7. SQL transformation example

This approach is interesting because the behavior of the application itself is not modified. The impact on the performance of the system is minor, as the policy enforcement is actually pushed into a database query and also the complexity of this query transformation algorithm is low, as shown in previous works [12]. The work in [1] brings some performance evaluation for the same kind of transformations. We advocate that the ability to implement privacy controls is more important than these performance questions when dealing with private data in cloud computing.

4   Related Works

There are many similarities between our approach and the work described in [13]. It proposes a holistic approach for systematic privacy enforcement for enterprises. First, we also build on the state of the art access control languages for privacy, but here with an up-to-date approach, adapted for the cloud. Second, we leverage on the latest frameworks for web application and service development to provide automated privacy enforcement relying on their underlying identity management solutions. We also have similarities on the way privacy is enforced, controlling access at the database level, which is also done in [1].

Although the query transformation algorithm is not the main focus of our work, the previous art on the topic [6,16,4] present advanced approaches for privacy preserving database query over which we can build the next versions of our algorithm. Here we implemented an efficient approach for practical access control purposes, but we envisage to enrich the approach with anonymization in the future.

On the other hand, we work in the context of the cloud, where a provider hosts applications developed by other parties, which can in their turn communicate with services hosted in other domains. This imposes constraints outside of the control of a single service provider. We went further in the automation, by providing a reliable framework to the application developer in order to transfer the complexity of dealing with privacy preferences to the platform provider. Our annotation mechanism provides ease of adoption without creating dependencies with respect to the deployment platform. More precisely, no lock in is introduced by our solution. However, changes in the database schema that involves PII data require an application to be redeployed in the plataform in order to process the eventually new annotations.

The work in [11] presents an approach based on privacy proxies to handle privacy relevant interactions between data subjects and data collectors. Proxies are implemented as SOAP based services, centralizing all PII. The solution is interesting, but it is not clear how to adapt the proxy to specific data models corresponding to particular applications in a straightforward way.

Our work is aligned with the principles defended in [15], in particular we facilitate many of the tasks the service designers must take into consideration when creating new cloud-based applications. In [14], a user-centric approach is taken to manage private data in the cloud. Control is split between client and server, which requires cooperation by the server, otherwise obfuscated data must be used by default. This is a different point of view from our work, where we embed the complexity of the privacy enforcement in the platform itself.

Automated security policy management for cloud platforms is discussed in [10]. Using a model driven approach, cloud applications would subscribe to a policy configuration service able to enforce policies at run-time, enabling compliance. The approach is sound but lacks of fine-grained management for privacy policies, as it is not clear how to deal with personal data collection and usage control.

In [9], cryptographic co-processors are employed to ensure confidentiality of private data protection. The solution is able to enforce rather low level policies using cryptography as an essential mechanism, without explicit support to design new privacy compliant applications. Several works exist on privacy protection in Web 2.0 and peer-to-peer environments, such as in [18], where an access control mechanism is adopted for social networks. Some of these ideas can be reused in the context of cloud applications, but our approach differentiates from this line of work in the sense we empower the cloud applications developers with ready to use mechanisms provided directly by the cloud platform.

In [5], aspect-oriented programming is used as well to enforce privacy mechanisms when performing access control in applications. The work adopts a similar approach to ours, but privacy mechanisms are created in a per-application basis. In our approach, by targeting the platform as a service directly, we are able to facilitate enforcement in multiple applications.

5   Conclusion and Future Works

We presented a solution to simplify the process of enabling personal data protection in Java web applications deployed on Platform as a Service solution.

We augment cloud applications with meta-data annotations and private data-handling policies which are enforced by the platform almost transparently from the developer perspective (the major overhead is only in placing the right annotations in the code).

The cloud consumer applications indicate how and where personally identifiable information is being handled. We adapt the platform components with privacy enforcement mechanisms able to correctly handle the data consumption, in accordance with an agreed privacy policy between the data subject and the cloud consumer.

The advantages of our approach can be summarized as follows: the implementation details of the privacy controls are hidden to the cloud application developer; compatibility with legacy applications, since the annotations do not interfere with the existing code; cloud applications can gracefully move to other platform providers that implement privacy-aware platforms in different ways. Sensible changes in the database schema, specifically those modifying PII, require the application to be redeployed in the cloud, possibly with new annotations.

Some future directions include the orchestration of other components such as event monitors, service buses, trusted platform modules, etc, in order to provide real-time information to users about the operations performed on their personal data. We plan to generalize our approach to enforce other kinds of policies, such as service level agreements, separation of duty, etc.

An important improvement of this work is the integration of advanced k-anonymization [17] process at the database access level. Such solution would be more adapted to business applications than access control, since the end-users could obtain more meaningful information, without fully disclosing the identities of the data subjects.

References

1. Agrawal, R., Kiernan, J., Srikant, R., Xu, Y.: Implementing p3p using database technology. In: Proceedings of the 19th International Conference on Data Engineering, pp. 595–606 (March 2003)
2. Ashley, P., Hada, S., Karjoth, G., Powers, C., Schunter, M.: Enterprise privacy authorization language (epal). Research report 3485 (2003)
3. Bussard, L., Neven, G., Preiss, F.S.: Matching privacy policies and preferences: Access control, obligatons, authorisations, and downstream usage. In: Camenisch, J., Fischer-Hübner, S., Rannenberg, K. (eds.) Privacy and Identity Management for Life, pp. 313–326. Springer, Heidelberg (2011)
4. Byun, J.W., Bertino, E., Li, N.: Purpose based access control of complex data for privacy protection. In: Proceedings of the Tenth ACM Symposium on Access Control Models and Technologies, SACMAT 2005, pp. 102–110. ACM, New York (2005)
5. Chen, K., Wang, D.W.: An aspect-oriented approach to privacy-aware access control. In: 2007 International Conference on Machine Learning and Cybernetics, vol. 5, pp. 3016–3021 (August 2007)

6. Cohen, S., Nutt, W., Serebrenik, A.: Rewriting aggregate queries using views. In: Proceedings of the Eighteenth ACM SIGMOD-SIGACT-SIGART Symposium on Principles of Database Systems, PODS 1999, pp. 155–166. ACM, New York (1999)

7. Cranor, L.: P3P: making privacy policies more useful. IEEE Security Privacy 1(6), 50–55 (2003)

8. Idrees, M.S., Serme, G., Roudier, Y., de Oliveira, A.S., Grall, H., Südholt, M.: Evolving Security Requirements in Multi-layered Service-Oriented-Architectures. In: Garcia-Alfaro, J., Navarro-Arribas, G., Cuppens-Boulahia, N., de Capitani di Vimercati, S. (eds.) DPM 2011 and SETOP 2011. LNCS, vol. 7122, pp. 190–205. Springer, Heidelberg (2012)

9. Itani, W., Kayssi, A.I., Chehab, A.: Privacy as a service: Privacy-aware data storage and processing in cloud computing architectures. In: DASC, pp. 711–716. IEEE (2009)

10. Lang, U.: Openpmf scaas: Authorization as a service for cloud & soa applications. In: CloudCom, pp. 634–643. IEEE (2010)

11. Langheinrich, M.: A Privacy Awareness System for Ubiquitous Computing Environments. In: Borriello, G., Holmquist, L.E. (eds.) UbiComp 2002. LNCS, vol. 2498, pp. 237–245. Springer, Heidelberg (2002)

12. LeFevre, K., Agrawal, R., Ercegovac, V., Ramakrishnan, R., Xu, Y., DeWitt, D.J.: Limiting disclosure in hippocratic databases. In: Nascimento, M.A., Özsu, M.T., Kossmann, D., Miller, R.J., Blakeley, J.A., Schiefer, K.B. (eds.) VLDB, pp. 108–119. Morgan Kaufmann (2004)

13. Mont, M.C., Thyne, R.: A Systemic Approach to Automate Privacy Policy Enforcement in Enterprises. In: Danezis, G., Golle, P. (eds.) PET 2006. LNCS, vol. 4258, pp. 118–134. Springer, Heidelberg (2006)

14. Mowbray, M., Pearson, S.: A client-based privacy manager for cloud computing. In: Bosch, J., Clarke, S. (eds.) COMSWARE, p. 5. ACM (2009)

15. Pearson, S., Charlesworth, A.: Accountability as a Way Forward for Privacy Protection in the Cloud. In: Jaatun, M.G., Zhao, G., Rong, C. (eds.) CloudCom 2009. LNCS, vol. 5931, pp. 131–144. Springer, Heidelberg (2009)

16. Rizvi, S., Mendelzon, A., Sudarshan, S., Roy, P.: Extending query rewriting techniques for fine-grained access control. In: Proceedings of the 2004 ACM SIGMOD International Conference on Management of Data, SIGMOD 2004, pp. 551–562. ACM, New York (2004)

17. Sweeney, L.: k-anonymity: A model for protecting privacy. International Journal on Uncertainty Fuzziness and Knowledge-based Systems 10(5), 557–570 (2002)

18. Tootoonchian, A., Saroiu, S., Ganjali, Y., Wolman, A.: Lockr: better privacy for social networks. In: Liebeherr, J., Ventre, G., Biersack, E.W., Keshav, S. (eds.) CoNEXT, pp. 169–180. ACM (2009)

Evaluation of Jif and Joana as Information Flow Analyzers in a Model-Driven Approach*

Kuzman Katkalov, Peter Fischer, Kurt Stenzel, Nina Moebius,
and Wolfgang Reif

Department of Software Engineering and Programming Languages,
University of Augsburg, Germany
{kuzman.katkalov,fischer,stenzel,moebius,
reif}@informatik.uni-augsburg.de

Abstract. Checking for information leaks in real-world applications is a difficult task. IFlow is a model-driven approach which allows to develop information flow-secure applications using intuitive modeling guidelines. It supports the automatic generation of partial Java code while also providing the developer with the ability to formally verify complex information flow properties. To simplify the formal verification, we integrate an automatic Java application information flow analyzer, allowing to check simple noninterference properties. In this paper, we evaluate both Jif and Joana as such analyzers to determine the best suiting information flow control tool in the context of, but not limited to the IFlow approach.

Keywords: information flow, IFC, Jif, Joana, IFlow, model-driven.

1   Introduction

Information leaks in real world applications are a serious threat to the privacy of their users. Today, many of such applications that handle confidential data are distributed between several agents like smartphone apps and web services, which makes information flow (IF) analysis even harder. However, with the rising popularity of such applications this task also becomes increasingly important.

Current security systems are based on access control, sandboxing and/or a coarse permission system, which is included in all major mobile platforms like iOS, Android and Windows Phone. Such mechanisms, however, are not enough to protect the user's private information stored on his device or in the cloud. Reports on applications leaking confidential data like address books, phone IDs and location data accidentally or on purpose to third parties such as numerous advertisement networks appear frequently in the media and academic papers (e.g. [3]). The main reasons for this is the open nature of the Android application marketplace, with anyone being able to submit his own application without prior security screening, as well as the rather coarse-grained, inflexible permission

---

* This work is sponsored by the Priority Programme 1496 "Reliably Secure Software Systems - RS³" of the Deutsche Forschungsgemeinschaft (DFG).

R. Di Pietro et al. (Eds.): DPM 2012 and SETOP 2012, LNCS 7731, pp. 174–186, 2013.

system [4]. A set of permissions defining whether the application is allowed to access the internet, device sensors etc. is determined by the developer and has to be approved by the user prior to the installation of the application. However, application permissions do not restrict which data can be sent over the internet, or how the application deals with the sensor readouts. An application requiring both internet access and access to the GPS sensor may use the location data to submit anonymized location statistics to the developer, or leak the location of the user to any third party. Besides, applications with seemingly harmless permissions can collaborate with each other in order to create covert information flows in order to exfiltrate confidential user information [8,12].

The current landscape of distributed data- and user-centric applications calls for better, more precise information flow-aware security systems. However, going beyond the theoretical foundations and implementing a working, useful approach to analyzing real applications proves to be a challenging task.

We develop an approach called IFlow, with the overall goal of a model-driven software engineering methodology to create systems with provably secure information flow properties beyond simple noninterference, focusing on mobile applications. This includes a methodology to model systems with UML, automatic transformation of this model into code and into a formal specification, and formal proofs for security properties. The approach also allows to check simple noninterference properties for the generated code automatically using an IFC tool. The results of this check will be used in a formal verification of the application.

MoDelSec[1] is a model-driven approach resemblant of IFlow that formally considers secure information flow in software development. However, it does not focus on the ultimate goal of a deployable application. To our knowledge, IFlow is the only model-driven approach that supports the developer with creating a real, deployable application and formally considering its information flow.

We are aware of two existing code analyzing tools w.r.t. IF. The first is Jif[2], a security-typed extension to Java which promises support for information flow control in real-world Java applications annotated with Jif security types. The second is Joana[3], an automatic information flow analysis tool for Java applications which does not require code annotations. Both tools offer the developer different functionality to achieve the same goal, namely a secure Java application w.r.t. information flow, and they both meet our requirements (see subsection 2.3). We evaluated those tools to be used in our model-driven approach. The results of this paper are not limited to the IFlow project; rather, any project or approach with a similar set of requirements as IFlow can benefit from this evaluation.

---

[1] Modular Modeling of Delegation Security in Software Development (MoDelSec), http://www-jj.cs.tu-dortmund.de/secse/pages/research/projects/MoDelSec/index_en.shtml

[2] Java + information flow (Jif), http://www.cs.cornell.edu/jif/

[3] Joana: IFC in Program Dependence Graphs, http://pp.info.uni-karlsruhe.de/project.php?id=30

Section 2 gives an overview over the IFlow approach, its goals as well as its requirements to an IFC tool. Section 3 evaluates Jif as a possible candidate for such an IFC tool, while section 4 examines Joana as a viable alternative. Section 5 concludes this paper by giving a brief overview over related work and summarizing the results of the evaluation.

2   The IFlow Approach

2.1   Overview

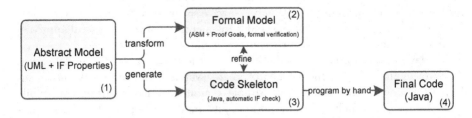

Fig. 1. IFlow model-driven approach

Fig. 1 illustrates the model-driven approach to develop IF-secure applications. The developer starts by modeling the system (1) using a subset of UML extended by a UML profile. The system's structure is modeled as well as its behavior. The latter is done with a focus on the communication between different participants of the system while local functionality is modeled as a black box. The modeling guidelines enable expressing security properties that have to be satisfied by this system of multiple stakeholders. These properties talk about confidentiality of data, i.e., where information may or may not flow under certain conditions. From the UML model, partial Java code is generated (3). To obtain the fully functional Java code (4), parts of the local functionality are then programmed manually. Of course, this must not introduce new information flows which is guaranteed by an information flow aware type check. It is the goal of this paper to determine a suitable information flow checker given the choice between Jif and Joana.

As we want to give security guarantees beyond plain noninterference, there is another branch in the model-driven approach where the UML model is transformed into a formal model (2) suitable for the theorem prover KIV [1]. Then it is possible to prove more specific information flow properties, e.g. that information can only flow after another action has occurred, or exactly what information flows through a declassification[4] channel. This is necessary since declassification essentially weakens an IF policy and is thus to be considered as particularly critical when verifying application specific information flow properties.

More information about the IFlow approach can be found in [9,5].

---

[4] Declassification: lowering the effective security level of a variable or a program statement; controlled release of information

2.2   Travel Planner: A Case Study

One of the IFlow case studies is *Travel Planner*, which is a travel booking system consisting of a *travel agency* service (TA) providing flight offers to the user of a mobile *travel planner* (TP) application, developed by the TA. The user is able to select a favored flight offer from a list of offers received from the TA and pay for the flight ticket directly at the *airline* service using the credit card data stored inside a *credit card center* application on his mobile device. The TA then receives a commission from the airline. Secure information flow within this system has to be ensured, e.g. to provide the user with the guarantee that his credit card data is only ever received by the intended airline, and only after his explicit confirmation.

The static part of an IFlow application consisting of agents and auxiliary classes is modeled with class diagrams (as shown in Figure 2), while the dynamic application components such as agent behavior and interaction is depicted using sequence diagrams. Classes, class attributes and sequence diagram messages can be annotated with security domains to express a noninterference property. Such annotations consist of a set of agents which are allowed to observe the value of the annotated class attribute (or, in case of an annotated class, the value of all its attributes); for annotated sequence messages, they restrict the security level of information allowed to be sent. Those annotations thus define the confidentiality of annotated data: the less confidential it is, the more agents are able to read it. The noninterference property then states that confidential information is only allowed to flow to equally or more confidential class attributes, or via equally or more confidential agent messages (e.g., any flight offer from the `flightOffers` list annotated with `{User,TravelAgency,Airline}` of the `Airline` class can theoretically be stored in `creditCardData` annotated with `{User}`).

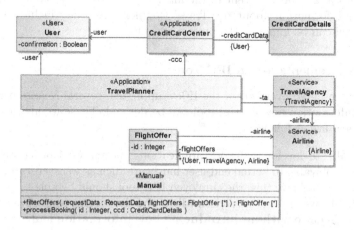

Fig. 2. Component diagram of the Travel Planner application

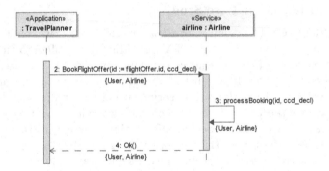

Fig. 3. Modeling the booking of a flight with IFlow

One of several sequence diagrams of the Travel Planner UML model is shown in Figure 3; it depicts an excerpt where `TravelPlanner` sends the message `BookFlightOffer` to the selected `Airline`. In a prior sequence, `TravelPlanner` has declassified the `creditCardData` attribute of the `CreditCardCenter` application (see Figure 2) and stored it in a local `ccd_decl` variable. Furthermore, the user has already selected a flight offer, which is stored in a local `flightOffer` variable of `TravelPlanner`.

The arguments of a message reference either attributes or local variables on the sender side. The assignment `id := flightOffer.id` is MEL syntax[5]. It means that the value `flightOffer.id` is stored in a local variable `id` on the receiving side. `processBooking` is a manually implemented method that is called with the values of `id` and `ccd_decl` as input. The `{User,Airline}`-annotation is employed to ensure that the credit card data (annotated with `{User}` in the class diagram) can only be sent to the airline after explicit declassification.

Further information about the Travel Planner case study including the full UML model can be found at the project website[6].

2.3 Requirements for an IFC Tool

From the presented overview of the IFlow approach, several requirements for a suitable information flow control tool can be derived. Those we identified to be most critical are as follows:

(a) To be able to develop real-world applications, the analyzed Java code must be made deployable to actual end user hardware such as webservers and smartphones. To achieve this, the employed IFC tool should be able to either analyze final Java application code or **allow the developer to derive final, deployable code without introducing new information leaks**. Optimally, it should be able to analyze Android and Java EE applications natively.

---

[5] MEL (Model Extension Language): simple language designed to denote message passing, method calls, variable initialization, assignments, object creation etc.

[6] http://www.informatik.uni-augsburg.de/lehrstuehle/swt/se/projects/iflow/

(b) Since in a model-driven approach the implementation of some application functionality is usually done manually by the developers, they should be able to do so effortlessly. The IFC tool must be **able to check final, manually extended code again**.

(c) The chosen IFC tool should also be able to analyze a distributed application consisting of several agents communicating e.g. over the internet; alternatively, it should be possible to **analyze a local, non-distributed application that can later be easily distributed**.

(d) Most importantly, the IFC tool must be able to **check the desired noninterference properties**. The IFlow approach focuses on the confidentiality aspects of information flow, and allows the developer to explicitly declassify individual pieces of information. This is a necessary prerequisite for IFC in real-world applications, as even a simple password check must reveal information about the confidential password by succeeding or failing. Integrity of information is not considered at the moment, as the presented case study has no integrity properties.

3   Jif: Java + Information Flow

3.1   Overview

Jif[10] is a security-typed extension of Java, providing support for language-based information flow control. It requires the developer to annotate Java applications with security labels, defining the security level of each variable and many program statements. The Jif compiler then performs a static check of the Jif application, while the Jif runtime enforces the IF policy established by the security labels dynamically. Jif is based on the Decentralized Label Model (DLM) theory, which was specifically designed to support applications in an environment of mutual distrust, with each participant being able to define his own security policy.

Jif policies are defined with labels of the form $\{o1 \rightarrow r1, r2; o2 \leftarrow w1, w2\}$. $o1$, $o2$, $r1$, $r2$, $w1$, $w2$ denote *principals* (authority entities), with $o1$ and $o2$ being the *owners* of the labeled data (the ownership concept is specific to Jif and DLM), $r1$ and $r2$ indicating the *readers*, $w1$ and $w2$ the *writers* of the labeled data. The owner of a policy is also included in the set of readers or writers respectively. Jif labels also form a lattice, with principle readers defining the confidentiality and writers the integrity of the annotated data type. Information is only allowed to flow to equally or more restrictively labeled program statements and variables, e.g. a variable labeled with $\{o \rightarrow r\}$ is allowed to be assigned to one labeled with $\{o \rightarrow\}$ but not vice versa.

Jif supports declassification by providing a built-in *declassify* function. Application agents implemented as Java classes can be assigned with the authority of several principles; they are able to declassify variables or statements using *declassify* if the policy owner of those variables matches their authority.

3.2   Compatibility with the Requirements from 2.3

Jif fulfills the requirements described in subsection 2.3 by enforcing information flow in a distributed system and allowing declassification.

Additionally, Jif offers the following functionality beyond statically type-checking the confidentiality of information in an application, which, however, is not part of the requirements listed in subsection 2.3.

- Jif policies incorporate the aspect of information integrity, which we do not adopt in our modeling.
- DLM dictates that every piece of information has an owner, as it considers IF from the point of view of each agent in an environment of mutual agent distrust separately.
- Jif is able to check IF dynamically during runtime, which, however, is only needed when the security level of some data is not known beforehand.

We applied Jif to our approach by treating security annotations in UML class and sequence diagrams as simplified Jif labels. Such simplified annotations contain a comma-separated set of reader principles. The owner of each label is assumed to be a default principle for which every agent class has the *authority*, so that any application agent is able to declassify any given piece of data (but not necessary able to read it). The set of writers is assumed to be empty. We manually implemented the appropriate Jif skeleton code for our case study (cf. Listing 1.1), and applied the annotations of UML sequence messages to method parameters and methods in the code by hand. Additionally, we added generic (e.g. least restrictive or easily inferred) Jif labels to other program elements.

Listing 1.1. Excerpt from Jif-code implementing the diagram shown in Figure 3

```
1   public OK{Default->User, Airline;*<-}
          bookFlightOffer{Default->User, Airline;*<-} (
3             BookFlightOffer[{Default->User, Airline;*<-}]{Default->User,
                  Airline;*<-} inmsg)
    {
5       try{
              int id = inmsg.id;
7             CreditCardData ccd_decl = inmsg.ccd;
              Manual.processBooking(id, ccd_decl);
9             return new OK();
        } catch(NullPointerException e){ return null; }
11  }
```

We treat each UML class depicting an agent as a Jif principle. Communication between agents is interpreted as method calls and returns; method arguments and return values correspond to instances of appropriate message classes (cf. sending BookFlightOffer-message in Fig. 3 is mapped to the method call bookFlightOffer of an instance of class Airline in List. 1.1). UML self-messages are translated to calls to manual functions, i.e. functions that can later be implemented manually by the developer in order to complete certain application functionality In both cases such methods and their return values are being assigned the Jif label corresponding to the message annotation in the abstract model. Declassification is modeled with a self-message `declassify`, annotated with source and target security levels of the result; this can be directly mapped to the Jif `declassify`-statement.

We were able to express the security property of our case study *"travel agency never learns the user's credit card data"* with Jif labels and code and successfully implemented Jif code skeletons by hand. A simplified excerpt of this code is shown in List. 1.1, which is part of the code skeleton for the agent application `Airline` of our case study. Here, previously declassified credit card details are being received and processed by the airline.

The Jif code for our case study passed the static Jif type check for the simple noninterference policy expressing the confidentiality property stated above and validated our expectations of the applicability of Jif (cf. subsection 2.3, requirement (d)). The developer of the application is able to implement manual methods using Jif without the `declassify` statement, so that his code can also be checked for illegal information flow (cf. subsection 2.3, requirement (b)). However, IF properties beyond simple noninterference still have to be formally verified, with (modeled) declassification statements carefully taken in consideration. Valid Java code can then be derived from Jif code by omitting Jif-specific language constructs.

Since the Jif runtime environment is not yet implemented for Android, it is not possible to execute Jif code on a smartphone. However, as Jif is just an extension of Java, it is possible to remove all Jif specific constructs and annotations and end up with executable Java code with the same functionality. We successfully tested this by manually stripping Jif labels from the Jif code of our case study application, which resulted in a valid Java application. We determined two possible ways to do so automatically. The Jif compiler is able to produce Java source code, which, however, contains references to the Jif runtime library. To be able to execute it on Android, one would need a full implementation of the Jif runtime library for Android, or a dummy implementation which ignores runtime IF checks (cf. subsection 2.3, requirement (a)). It is also possible to create an additional model transformation which disregards Jif annotations when generating code, thus producing Java code.

The Jif implementation of the case study is a monolithic application, which would have to be distributed in order to be deployed on different agents (cf. subsection 2.3, requirement (c)). This could be done by employing a Java wrapper library, which would implement the low-level agent communication or smartphone sensor access. The interface to this library would need to be annotated with Jif labels, so that the IF check can be executed for the entire application.

3.3 Results

Our experience with Jif matched those reported by other studies [6,11]. While Jif in theory satisfies all the requirements to some degree, the evaluation also revealed its several limitations. Firstly, Jif applications require very careful exception handling (note the necessary explicit `NullPointerException`-handling in Listing 1.1, absent from the model in Figure 3). Secondly, several additional annotations are needed compared to the abstact model of the application. This becomes apparent in Listing 1.1 (note the parameterizing of the BookFlightOffer-class with a Jif label in line 3, also absent from Figure 3). Additional declassify statements are also sometimes required, e.g. when handling a NullPointerException by aborting the application flow. This makes manual programming with Jif a painful experience; an experience an IFlow modeler and developer would have to live with when implementing manual methods. As we aim to automatically generate Jif skeleton code from the model, this also increases the complexity and maintenance efforts of model transformation scripts. More importantly, Jif offers little security label inference capability while enforcing IF very strictly, which also increases modeling efforts as most model elements like agent communication or object creation have to be explicitly and carefully annotated. The development of Jif seems to have stagnated, as there hasn't been a new release since early 2009.

4   Joana: Information Flow Control in Program Dependence Graphs

4.1   Overview

We evaluated the Joana tool as a possible alternative to Jif for information flow control in Java applications.

The ValSoft/Joana project and tool allows the automatic construction of program and system dependence graphs (PDGs and SDGs) for byte code of moderately complex Java (about 100kLOC [2]) applications. Program dependence graphs are used to model information flow within methods, while the interaction between methods is denoted with system dependence graphs. Each program statement denotes a node in a PDG, while edges between nodes imply data or control flow between statements. Joana strives to generate precise PDGs which can then be used to argue about possible information flow from and to any statement by computing a set of paths between corresponding PDG nodes. If no such path exists, there is no information flow; generated PDGs may contain too many edges due to analysis imprecisions but never too few. A connection between Goguen/Meseguer-style noninterference (similar to that used in the formal branch of the IFlow approach) and PDGs has been successfully established in [13] by showing that statement c interferes a iff there is a path from node c to a.

Joana allows PDG nodes to be marked with a security level from a lattice defined by the programmer. As the PDGs of an application already define its possible information flow, Joana is also able to infer security levels for other, unmarked nodes using security level propagation rules along PDG edges. Joana supports declassification from and to any security level by letting the programmer mark any PDG node as a declassification node. Any information with a specified security level passing through this node will then be declassified to a different specified level.

4.2   Compatibility with the Requirements from 2.3

Therefore, Joana is indeed an alternative to Jif, allowing us to only generate Java instead of both Java and Jif code and performing an automatic IF analysis on its byte code. Joana does not currently support the integrity aspect of noninterference, neither does it consider the ownership of information; however, both are not part of our proposed list of requirements (see subsection 2.3). [7,6] argue that IF analysis using PDGs instead of Jif-like language-based IFC is more precise and easier since the programmer only needs to mark the sources and sinks of information (e.g., classes, class attributes or method parameters) with a security level.

We applied Joana to our approach and tested those claims by using the security annotations from the application UML model as Joana security levels and providing a suitable security lattice, derived from the sets of agents. Using a similar model to code mapping as in subsection 3.2 (cf. Listing 1.2 for the resulting Java code for Figure 3) we implemented our case study in Java and annotated the PDGs created from the resulting bytecode by Joana with security labels for classes and class attributes from the UML model using Joana. Message labels, while necessary for both Jif and the formal model, proved redundant in order to check the noninterference property *"travel agency never learns the user's credit card data"* for our case study using Joana. They still can and will be used e.g. for IF properties that refer to specific service or application interfaces instead of agents as an entity. Declassification of data is done by labeling a dedicated method which simply returns its input as a declassification node in Joana.

Listing 1.2. Excerpt from Java-code implementing the sequence diagram shown in Figure 3

```
      public OK bookFlightOffer (BookFlightOffer inmsg)
2     {
          int id = inmsg.id;
4         CreditCardData ccd_decl = inmsg.ccd;

6         Manual.processBooking(id, ccd_decl);

8         return new OK();
      }
```

We successfully verified the security property, thus strengthening our assumptions of the applicability of Joana to check confidentiality properties for an application (cf. subsection 2.3, requirement (d)). Notably, we only needed five security level annotations as compared to about one hundred Jif labels in the original Jif implementation. The only IFC imprecision that we discovered while evaluating Joana was its inability to differentiate out of the box between the security levels of attributes of a class, if an instance of this class is passed to a method as an argument. This imprecision can be eliminated by tweaking the default configuration of Joana, however only at the expense of the tool performance.

To extend the partial Java code with the implementation of application functionality, the developer is free to edit manual method stubs in the static `Manual` class (cf. Listing 1.2, line 6). The final code can be checked again by Joana for newly introduced information leaks (cf. subsection 2.3, requirement (b)).

To distribute the final code and make it deployable on a smartphone or webservice, we implement a wrapper for platform specific functionality and communication. This wrapper has two interchangeable versions; a prototype version emulates this functionality and its information flow, and is used to check the application code with Joana. A deployment version implements this functionality using native platform APIs and is used to deploy a distributed version of the application on agent hardware (cf. subsection 2.3, requirement (c) and (a)). We noted that in unusual, special cases, the move to a distributed version of an application could result in additional IF undetected by Joana, e.g., due to the possibility of repeated queries of a service interface. The detection and handling of such cases will be the subject of future investigation.

4.3   Results

We found Joana to be a more suitable IFC tool than Jif w.r.t. the requirements outlined in subsection 2.3. Joana minimizes the modeling efforts by inferring most of the annotations needed for specifying IF security policies, simplifies code generation as only Java code needs to be generated and increases the accuracy of IF analysis. As in Joana only sources and sinks of information are explicitly annotated, the security levels of called methods and their return values are no longer defined prior to the type check as they were in Jif but inferred automatically. We therefore have to take precautions when generating stubs for manual methods by implementing explicit data dependencies between method input parameters and their return values; otherwise, Joana would detect that there is no information flow between inputs and outputs of manual methods in skeleton code, which will take place in implemented, final code. Unlike Jif, the IFC component of Joana is being actively maintained and worked on.

5   Conclusion and Related Work

Guaranteeing the privacy of user data in a real-world scenario is a challenging task. We tackle this challenge by developing a model-driven approach for creating smartphone and web service applications. This approach, called IFlow, utilizes automated information flow checking as well as interactive verification to guarantee the privacy of sensitive data. It does not rely on the flawed concept of application permissions to enforce secure information flow; it also eliminates the possibility of malicious collaboration between several apps as all agents are part of the abstract application model and their behavior is considered at the source code level.

We evaluated Jif and Joana as automatic information flow checkers given a list of requirements and found Jif to offer additional functionality compared to Joana. However, this additional functionality provided by Jif proved to be irrelevant if a distributed application is considered as an entity and data integrity is not an issue. In contrast, Joana offers a much more convenient and transparent mechanism to check an application for information leaks. This transparency and ease of use benefits the approach, as it simplifies the automatic model to code transformations. Another advantage is that the application developer is able to implement the application functionality in native Java instead of Jif.

During the course of this evaluation we determined a way to integrate Joana with a model-driven approach for developing distributed applications. To achieve this, we used clear separation between generated and manually implemented code and utilized a wrapper library allowing us to consider any resulting application as monolithic. There are ongoing efforts to allow Joana to analyze Android code natively[7]; we currently rely on the wrapper to provide and encapsulate platform-specific (Android and Java EE) functionality such as database or smartphone sensor access.

The evaluation result of this paper is in accord with other published work discussing Jif and Joana. [6] compares Joana to Jif favorably by examining an example application written in Jif and analyzing its Java equivalent with Joana. [11] evaluates Jif without considering Joana by implementing a electronic retailing case study, commenting on the complexity and expressing doubts about the practical suitability of Jif. We will continue investigating and integrating Joana into the IFlow approach, by extending the wrapper library and integrating the Joana check results into the interactive verification of an IFlow application.

References

1. Balser, M., Reif, W., Schellhorn, G., Stenzel, K., Thums, A.: Formal System Development with KIV. In: Maibaum, T. (ed.) FASE 2000. LNCS, vol. 1783, pp. 363–366. Springer, Heidelberg (2000)
2. Binkley, D., Harman, M., Krinke, J.: Empirical study of optimization techniques for massive slicing. ACM Trans. Program. Lang. Syst. 30 (November 2007)
3. Enck, W., Octeau, D., McDaniel, P., Chaudhuri, S.: A study of android application security. In: Proceedings of the 20th USENIX Conference on Security, SEC 2011, p. 21. USENIX Association, Berkeley (2011)
4. Felt, A.P., Chin, E., Hanna, S., Song, D., Wagner, D.: Android permissions demystified. In: Proceedings of the 18th ACM Conference on Computer and Communications Security, CCS 2011, pp. 627–638. ACM, New York (2011)
5. Fischer, P., Katkalov, K., Stenzel, K., Reif, W.: Formal Verification of Information Flow Secure Systems with IFlow. Technical Report 2012-05, Universität Augsburg (2012), http://www.informatik.uni-augsburg.de/lehrstuehle/swt/se/publications/
6. Hammer, C.: Experiences with PDG-Based IFC. In: Massacci, F., Wallach, D., Zannone, N. (eds.) ESSoS 2010. LNCS, vol. 5965, pp. 44–60. Springer, Heidelberg (2010)

---

[7] IFC for Mobile Components, http://pp.info.uni-karlsruhe.de/projects/rs3/rs3.php

7. Hammer, C., Snelting, G.: Flow-sensitive, context-sensitive, and object-sensitive information flow control based on program dependence graphs. International Journal of Information Security 8(6), 399–422 (2006); Supersedes ISSSE and ISoLA 2006
8. Hardy, N.: The confused deputy: (or why capabilities might have been invented). SIGOPS Oper. Syst. Rev. 22(4), 36–38 (1988)
9. Katkalov, K., Fischer, P., Stenzel, K., Reif, W.: Model-Driven Code Generation of Information Flow Secure Systems with IFlow. Technical Report 2012-04, Universität Augsburg (2012),
   http://www.informatik.uni-augsburg.de/lehrstuehle/swt/se/publications/
10. Myers, A.C., Liskov, B.: Protecting privacy using the decentralized label model. In: Foundations of Intrusion Tolerant Systems, 2003 [Organically Assured and Survivable Information Systems], pp. 89–116 (2003)
11. Preibusch, S.: Information flow control for static enforcement of user-defined privacy policies. In: 2011 IEEE International Symposium on Policies for Distributed Systems and Networks (POLICY), pp. 133–136 (June 2011)
12. Schlegel, R., Zhang, K., Yong Zhou, X., Intwala, M., Kapadia, A., Wang, X.: Soundcomber: A stealthy and context-aware sound trojan for smartphones. In: NDSS. The Internet Society (2011)
13. Snelting, G., Robschink, T., Krinke, J.: Efficient path conditions in dependence graphs for software safety analysis. ACM Transactions on Software Engineering and Methodology 15(4), 410–457 (2006)

Analyzing HTTP User Agent Anomalies
for Malware Detection

Nizar Kheir

Orange Labs
38-40 rue du Général Leclerc, 92794 Issy-Les-Moulineaux
nizar.kheir@orange.com

Abstract. This paper analyzes User Agent (UA) anomalies within malware HTTP traffic and extracts signatures for malware detection. We observe, within a large set of malware HTTP traffic provided by a local AV company, that almost one malware out of eight uses a suspicious UA header in at least one HTTP request. Such anomalies include typos, information leakage, outdated versions, and attack vectors such as XSS and SQL injection. Nowadays UA anomalies are still manually analyzed, whereas thousands of new malware samples are collected daily. On the other hand, just blacklisting unusual UA strings is not viable because malware developers may use random values or encode variable patterns. This paper automatically classifies UA anomalies and extracts signatures for malware detection. Our approach is implemented on top of network-based detection systems. We extracted signatures from an overall set of 100 thousand malware samples, and we tested these signatures on real-world malware traffic. Experimental results show that our solution detects unknown malware by the time of extracting our signatures.

1 Introduction

Malware constitutes by far the most prominent threat against ICT systems worldwide. According to a recent cyber intelligence report by Symantec; malware activity has witnessed a spectacular increase of 81% in 2011 [1]. The huge volume of personal data shared on the internet through social media networks represent valuable resources that attract cybercriminals. Besides, mobile services and access to business information everywhere on mobile devices add a plethora of possibilities to break into an information system. Targeted malware attacks have also increased recently, including examples like Stuxnet[2] and Flamer[3]. Securing ICT systems only by shielding their boundaries became totally outdated. Interests thus shifted towards observing network activity in order to identify and isolate malware intrusions in their early stages.

Malware developers currently implement several techniques to dissimulate their malicious activity within the huge volume of network traffic. Malware reports by AV companies only reveal the tip of the iceberg, the bulk of malware activity remains undetected. Unfortunately, system-level signatures provided by AV solutions usually fall short with polymorphism and malware obfuscation

R. Di Pietro et al. (Eds.): DPM 2012 and SETOP 2012, LNCS 7731, pp. 187–200, 2013.
© Springer-Verlag Berlin Heidelberg 2013

techniques [4]. On the other hand, network signatures are more attractive when compared to system-level signatures. These are easy to implement and require no access to the infected nodes. Furthermore, malware needs network connectivity in order to execute its malicious activities and communicate with its command servers. It is thus susceptible of being detected by identifying its network footprints. Nowadays the most common type of malware is *bots*. Compared to other malware families, bots have the ability to establish a command and control (C&C) channel that allows an attacker to update and execute commands on the infected nodes. Bot-infected nodes that are controlled by a single entity (known as botmaster) constitute a so-called botnet [5, 6].

The network behavior of malware often includes anomalies that can be accounted for during detection and diagnosis [7]. Crowd effects [8], unusual activity sequences [9] and mixture of both [10] are all signs of a malware activity. Other approaches analyze malware in isolated environments in order to extract behavior signatures [11, 12]. Such behaviors are still easily misled by malware developers with little noticeable effort. They use techniques like delays, padding and noise injection in order to hide malicious activities within the large set of legitimate traffic [13].

This paper focuses on bots that use the HTTP protocol to communicate with their control servers and to perpetrate malicious activities. As in [7], HTTP is the most prevalent protocol implemented by malware, with up to 60% of malware showing at least one outgoing HTTP connection. Our database also shows that up to 82% of collected malware generate some HTTP activity. Web-based malware control toolkits are also accessible for sale on the internet, which makes it easier using on-the-shelf components for malware development [11]. We observe that malware HTTP traffic often includes patterns and anomalies that can be used to define network footprints. Anomalies may include unusual content lengths (e.g. kelihos malware [14]), inconsistent accepted languages or non-matching encodings [15]. *We analyze in this paper the anomalies in the user agent field within malware HTTP traffic.* Note that our approach does not compete with the one presented by Perdisci et al. in [11]. Authors in [11] classify malware HTTP traffic based on URIs and extract network signatures, but they do not handle HTTP header anomalies.

The HTTP protocol does not designate an exact syntax for the user-agent header field [16]. It is usually set by the HTTP toolkit implemented within the malware source code. Certain malware families use static user agent strings, while others hijack the browser running on the infected node. We analyze in this paper the static user agent strings that include anomalies such as typos, unknown or outdated values [17]. This paper proposes an automated technique to extract user agent anomalies and infer signatures for malware detection. In fact, malware analysis reports often observe anomalies in the user agents implemented by malware, including the recently discovered Flamer malware [3]. Unfortunately, there is not yet a comprehensive approach to classify such anomalies and use these for malware detection. Current user agent signatures are manually extracted through manual analysis of malware HTTP headers. The increasing number of malware samples being discovered on a daily basis makes such a manual analysis infeasible. Besides, certain malware encodes information such as malware ID or public IP within the user agent header. Therefore, the manual analysis of user agent fields rapidly falls short with the volume of data to be processed, thus missing valuable detection signatures.

This paper presents a systemic approach that includes the following steps. Using a large set of malware HTTP traffic provided by a local AV company, we extract all user agent strings implemented by malware. We handle indifferently C&C and noise malware traffic as they may include, both, abnormal user agent strings. Note that we detect infected nodes within a network boundaries, but we do not identify C&C channels in a first place. Then we filter-out *benign* user agent strings by checking our list against a public user agent database[1]. These are user agent strings implemented by malware, but that match known benign agents. Malware that implements the same web toolkit and malware controlled by the same botmaster are likely to include common user agent patterns. These common patterns are likely to be described with the same set of signatures. We thus proceed through a clustering step that groups user-agent strings according to their syntactical similarities. User agent clustering is an unsupervised learning process where user agents are grouped together with no *a-priori* knowledge about the number of clusters and their structure. We further extract for each cluster the set of signatures that match all user agents using generalized suffix trees.

The remaining of this paper is structured as follows: Section 2 describes related work. Section 3 presents our clustering and signature extraction approach. Section 4 describes our experimentations. Section 5 discusses the limitations and future work, and section 6 concludes.

2   Related Work

Malware clustering and the extraction of signatures for malware detection has been extensively studied in the recent years. Techniques to classify malware activities apply either at the system-level [18, 19], the network-level [10–12] or mixture of both [20].

System-level malware clustering in [19] aims to regroup malware according to sequences of system calls that characterize a specific malware class. The use of network level information is limited to some high level features such as HTTP methods and downloaded files. Our approach is different than the one presented in [19]. In fact, we do not aim to classify malware behaviors, but only user agent anomalies that characterize a common malware family or a common web toolkit. Furthermore, we classify malware patterns in order to extract network signatures that directly apply to network traffic, as opposed to system-level signatures in [19].

Other techniques analyze bot traffic in order to extract useful patterns for malware detection. In [11], authors classify malware according to similarities in URLs extracted from malware HTTP requests. Due to the large amount of URLs

---

[1] http://www.user-agents.org/

in malware traffic, authors propose a two steps clustering process that includes coarse-grained and fine-grained clustering. Our approach is less vulnerable to noise injection because we consider only anomalous user agents, as opposed to [11] that uses all HTTP requests during the clustering process. In fact, authors in [11] extract all malware HTTP requests, including both command requests and other benign operations such as connectivity checks. Therefore, the approach in [11] is vulnerable to noise injection and malware obfuscation techniques. Another technique presented in [12] extracts statefull signatures by observing malware traffic during longer observation periods. It applies the change point detection algorithm on malware traffic in order to detect responses attributable to a command issued by the botmaster. It further analyzes the traffic snippet that just precedes the changing point in order to extract signatures of bot commands. As in [11], this approach is vulnerable to noise injection, where a malware hides its change points within the noise traffic so they cannot be identified. We also refer to several previous studies that extract network signatures, as in [21–23]. However, these studies mainly focus on worm fingerprinting, as opposed to our approach that analyzes malware communications.

Last of all, a recent study by [20] proposes a new approach to identify C&C channels within malware traffic. It offers a new solution against noise injection and malware obfuscation techniques. This approach uses a joint network and system level analysis of malware behavior. It generates system-level behavior graphs by executing a malware in a sandbox. It uses a supervised machine learning technique to identify subparts of these graphs that are associated with command and control communications. Network connections associated with these subgraphs are further identified as command and control channels. This approach identifies command and control servers so they can be blacklisted at system ingress points. Our approach is thus complementary to [20] because we detect infected nodes within a system boundaries so they can be neutralized.

3   HTTP User Agent Signatures

This section describes the malware clustering approach and its subsequent signature generation framework. The former, malware clustering, aims to regroup strings of user agents that have similar structures so they can be described using common patterns. The latter, signature generation, extracts HTTP-based signatures using the already identified malware clusters. Note that the clusters obtained using our approach cannot be compared against malware families provided by AV editors. In fact, user agents characterize only web toolkits implemented by malware, but not necessarily the way they communicate with their C&C servers.

We are interested in this study only with anomalous user agent strings. These are strings which cannot be verified against known user agent footprints. Anomalous user agents usually include inappropriate specifications for known web clients, or yet unknown and ambiguous user agents. A malware may also encode its class or ID in the user agent field. The table in Fig. 1 illustrates

User agent	Malware	Semantic
'Aldi Bot FTW! :D' 'MyLove'	Aldi Bot Aurora	Unknown string
'KUKU v5.05exp =27326558776' 'Agent614139'	W32.Sality W32.Agent	Bot ID
'gbot/R.2' 'imrabot'	backdoor.W32.gbot W32/imrabot	Bot family
WinXP Pro Service Pack 2mj_5_mn_1	Trojan Downloader	Information leak
Mozilla/4.0 (MSIE 6.0; Windoss NT)	Trojan Storm	Typo

Fig. 1. Encountered semantics for malware user agents

different user agent semantics from our malware database. Malware detection by only matching raw user agent strings yields a large set of signatures. These are also too specific when used against yet unknown variants of existing malware. Therefore, we first cluster user agent strings based on their structural similarities. Then we extract signatures that match values within the same cluster. By clustering user agents, we obtain generic enough signatures that match not only values in our learning set, but also unknown derivatives of those values.

3.1   Clustering of User Agents

We consider structural similarities between user agent (UA) strings during our clustering process. We aim to regroup, within clusters, values of UA strings that are similar enough so they can be described with a small set of signatures. Signatures should be specific enough to match only UA strings within a given cluster, but also generic enough to match slight variations of those strings. UA clustering requires first to implement a similarity function that evaluates the resemblance between two UA strings. It shall also define a process that finds similar UA strings and builds clusters with no *a-priory* knowledge about their numbers.

User Agents Distance: We observe that most anomalous UA strings include invariant sequences that usually characterize certain malware families. They also include variant sequences that characterize a given malware instance or identify a single bot machine. The distance function should thus assign a higher priority to potentially invariant characters, and a lower priority to other variant sequences. Priorities should not be obtrusive and do not prevent the clustering of user agents that are similar in their lower priority characters.

We rewrite twice every user agent (ua_{low} and ua_{high}), replacing either letters or numbers with the special character '#', as in the examples of Fig. 2. We consider letters as high priority patterns and numbers as low ones. This heuristic is motivated by our observations that a malware usually encodes within readable words its invariant UA parts, and uses numbers to encode its variant parts such as version, ID or public IP. Although this assumption cannot be generalized

User agent	Weighted variants
Agent614139	Agent###### #####614139
KUKU v5.05exp =27326558776	KUKU v#.##exp =########## ######5#05####27326558776
User-Agent: -Agent: Host:201.74.236.85	User-Agent: -Agent: Host:###.##.###.## ####################201#74#236#85

Fig. 2. Rewriting malware user agents

to all malware instances, it does not prevent the clustering of other types of malware. Those malware samples would have similar distances for their low and high priority patterns. The weighted mean of their high and low priority parts would thus slightly modify the values of these measures. We may also dispose off the *weighted* distance if we figure out new trends in malware UA patterns. We compute the Levenshtein distance between every pair of rewritten strings and combine both measures using a weighted mean.

$$Lev(ua_1, ua_2) = \frac{k_{low}.Lev(ua_{1_{low}}, ua_{2_{low}}) + k_{high}.Lev(ua_{1_{high}}, ua_{2_{high}})}{k_{low} + k_{high}}$$

We tested several values for the ratio $\frac{k_{low}}{k_{high}}$, each time obtaining a new clustering result. We thus experimentally set this ratio to $\frac{1}{3}$, which provides an optimal measure of the cluster cohesion index for the data set at our disposal, as further explained in section 4.2.

Incremental K-means Clustering. We implement the *incremental k-means* algorithm to cluster UA strings using our modified Levenshtein distance. Incremental k-means creates a new malware cluster when the distance of a UA string to all existing clusters exceeds a given threshold $th \in]0, 1[$. It provides a better solution because of the following reasons. First of all, it does not require specifying, a-priory, the number of malware clusters. These are incremented throughout the clustering process as we find new malware instances that do not fit with any previous malware in our dataset. Second, incremental k-means does not require keeping a distance matrix throughout the clustering process. Such matrix would rapidly explode in size as new malware feeds our signature generation module on a daily basis. Third, clustering new malware instances should not alter previous malware clusters, and only new malware instances should be processed. Using incremental k-means, we compute the distance of a new malware to all existing clusters. The malware belongs to the closest cluster, i.e. the cluster with the shortest distance. If no existing cluster satisfies a distance lower than th, a new cluster is created and assigned with the new malware instance. Note that a low value of th leads to small and homogeneous clusters while a high value leads to large and sparce clusters. We experimentally set a threshold of 55% resemblance between two UA strings within the same cluster, thus corresponding to a value of $th = 0.45$.

Incremental k-means usually applies to entries in $\mathcal{R}^n$. Distance to a cluster is evaluated as the distance between an entry and the cluster centroïd. The latter is shifted *inline* as new values are added to the cluster. The Levenshtein distance applies to UA strings, ruling out the possibility of building cluster centroïds. We thus consider the distance to a cluster as the mean distance to all UA strings in this cluster. This obviously increases complexity as we compute the distances to all UA strings in the database each time a new malware should be added. This is a common shortcoming to all string-based clustering methods, compared to other vector-based classifiers [24].

The output of our clustering approach is a variable set of clusters, depending on the initial learning set and the threshold th. As shown later in this paper, a population of 100 thousand malware samples randomly collected yields a set of 13,558 anomalous UA strings. Using the threshold value of $th = 0.45$, we obtained a total number of 2,799 UA clusters.

3.2   Common Tokens Extraction

We build signatures of user agents using the token-subsequence algorithm described in [23]. Token-subsequences can be easily translated into network-based signatures implemented using Snort or Bro. Tokens extraction is the process by which we identify common substrings that are shared between UA strings within the same cluster. This process is implemented in [23] by iteratively applying the best alignment to all UA strings in a given cluster. The best string alignment finds the Longest Common Substring (LCS) for all UA strings. Finding the LCS for a set of signatures is not a contribution for this paper; we refer readers to [23] for more insights on this approach. Nonetheless, our experience with UA strings shows that such an approach would provide poor signatures if implemented with no further refinements. We illustrate the problem using the anomalous user agent samples in Fig. 3.

As shown in Fig. 3, trying to match all UA strings in a given cluster during LCS extraction sometimes leads to poor tokens. In fact, UA strings within the same cluster could be distributed into subgroups with strong Intra-group resemblance and (relatively) poor inter-group resemblance. We propose to adapt the LCS algorithm by trying to match not all UA strings within a cluster, but optimal k out-of-m strings. We extract the LCS from a set of UA strings using Generalized Suffix Trees (GST) [25]. Extracting longest common substrings

Cluster	LCS	Optimal
'cpush_updater' 'cpush_dre' 'av_update' 'ppvaupdate'	'p'	'cpush_' 'update'
'bar-get' 'bart' 'iexp-get'	't'	'-get' 'bar'
'My Sesssion' 'Session' 'Sesssion' 'My Session'	'sion'	'Sesssion' 'Session'
'Roadie' 'Loading' 'Loaris'	'oa'	'oadi' 'Loaris'
'doublevaccine' 'plusvaccine' 'doublevaccine_agency'	'vaccine'	'doublevaccine' 'plusvaccine'
'ouctb' 'oucte' 'out'	'ou'	'ouct' 'out'

Fig. 3. Common token extraction examples

from k out-of-m strings requires slight modification to the GST algorithm. The output of this algorithm is an ordered list of tokens, each one being shared with at least k out-of-m UA strings that constitute a given cluster.

Algorithm 1: Token-subsequence extraction

Data: $\mathcal{L}$ is the list of User Agents
Result: $\mathcal{S}$ is the set of token-subsequences

```
1  begin
2  │   C ⟵ kmeans(L); %Compute UA clusters using the k-mean algorithm
3  │   S ⟵ ∅; %Start with an empty set of signatures
4  │   for cl ∈ C do
5  │   │   tks = GenSuffixTree(cl); %Build the list of common tokens
6  │   │   SortbyLgth(tks); %Sort the list by token length
7  │   │   for tk ∈ tks do
8  │   │   │   mUA = getMatchingUA(cl, tk); %Find UAs with the longest token
9  │   │   │   cl.pop(mUA); %Pop mathing UAs from the list of UAs to process
10 │   │   │   rewrite(mUA, tk); %Rewrite matching UAs as a sequence of tokens
11 │   │   │   S.add(bestAlign(mUA)); %Get token-subsequence by pairwise best align
12 │   │   │   if cl == ∅ then
13 │   │   │   │   break; %Skip if no longer UAs to process
```

For each cluster, we dynamically set k to the value $k_i = (1 - th) \times m_i$, where m_i is the number of elements in cluster i. In fact, the clustering process presented in the previous section tolerates a maximal dissimilarity ratio th. It clusters together strings as long as their normalized distance does not exceed the ratio th. We thus adapt our LCS algorithm by extracting the LCSs from at least k elements within a cluster, but not necessarily all elements. k is a proportion of user agent strings within a cluster that is attributable to the maximal dissimilarity ratio th. Note that the LCS can still be shared between more than k elements, depending on the cluster cohesion, as shown later in this paper.

The algorithm we implemented is shown, as pseudo code, in the listing of algorithm 1. It builds token-subsequences starting with the longest token in the ordered list of LCSs (lines 5-6). We extract all UA strings that contain this token (lines 8-9), and we rewrite those strings as sequences of tokens separated with the special character '#' (line 10). In fact, we rewrite UA strings to avoid reaching local minimums when applying the *greedy* best alignment algorithm [23], as in line 11 of algorithm 1.

3.3   HTTP Signature Generation

Incremental k-means clustering regroups user agents with shared pattern sequences into the same clusters. The token-subsequence algorithm further extracts these shared patterns and builds lists of dot-separated token sequences. These are translated into signatures that apply either at the network or application layer using web proxies.

Signatures extracted from our learning set cannot be used directly for malware detection in an operational environment. In fact, the learning set includes anomalies due to the inability to filter out all not suspicious user agents. For example, some malware used `Google Updater` or `Microsoft BITS` as fake user agent strings. These were not discarded from our learning set following the whitelist check, and thus we obtained signatures for these benign agents. Furthermore, certain malware designates user agent strings that are too short. They would *de-facto* generate poor signatures that suffer from a high false positives rate. We illustrate the following cluster example that we obtained after applying the incremental k-means on our learning set: [at_2, at_5, it_2, aq_4]. We implemented the LCS algorithm, obtaining the longest common subsequences for k out-of-m UA strings, with $k = 0.75 \times m$, that is $k = 3$. The output of the best alignment process includes the following token-subsequences: [#t_#, a#_#]. These subsequences should be discarded as they generate a large false positives rate. We overcome these challenges by pruning our set of signatures, testing these against a large set of benign user agents. We prune our set of signatures using a public list of most used user agent families[2]. We thus discard all signatures that match entries in this list, and keep the remaining signatures as output to our framework.

4   Experimentation

4.1   Experimental Setup and Data Processing

This section describes our malware data set and the experimental testbed that we used to test and validate our approach. Our learning set is provided by a local AV company. It corresponds to the traffic generated by up to 100,000 malware samples executed during ten minutes in a sandbox with open internet access. We implemented an automated script that executes a port-independent inspection of malware HTTP traffic, using tshark, in order to extract all HTTP user agents. We extracted up to 15,632 *distinct* user agents, including both benign and anomalous values.

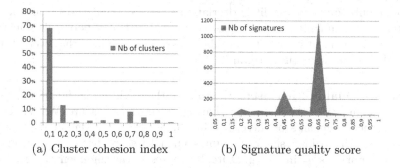

(a) Cluster cohesion index   (b) Signature quality score

Fig. 4. Cluster validity measures

---

[2] http://user-agent-string.info/top-ua-family

We first discard benign user agents by checking these against a database of known benign user agents. We use the public database accessible on the website `http://www.user-agents.org/`. It provides an XML implementation that includes a list of known user agents and their types. We discard all user agents that match with entries in this database, and keep remaining values as input to our signature extraction module. We obtained a set of 13,558 anomalous user agents that we use as a learning set for signature extraction, thus discarding 2,074 benign strings. The remaining 13,558 anomalous user agents were extracted from 13,247 distinct malware traffic traces, resulting in a ratio of one malware out of eight in our dataset that implements a suspicious user agent string.

We implement the incremental k-means clustering algorithm using our modified Levenshtein distance. We set the threshold th for the maximal accepted distance to a cluster to the value 0.45. We made our experiments using a dual core 2.66 GHz Intel Core-i6 machine with 2GB RAM. We obtained a resulting set of 2,799 clusters within 1h35min process time under 100% single CPU utilization. Our algorithm reached a maximal memory usage of 65%. We applied the token extraction algorithm based on Generalized Suffix trees, and we obtained an overall set of 3,700 signatures. Then we pruned our set of signatures as described in section 3.3. We thus discarded 242 signatures, and we kept the remaining 3,458 signatures as output to our framework.

4.2   Cluster Validity

Cluster Cohesion Index: We evaluate the cohesion of our clusters as a way to validate our clustering process. The cluster cohesion index is the ratio between the mean intra-cluster distance and the minimal inter-cluster distance. We set the inter-cluster distance to the threshold $th = 0.45$, which is the worst case inter-cluster distance. We measured the mean intra-cluster distance for every final cluster. Fig. 4(a) shows the cluster cohesion index computed for every cluster of user agents. It shows that 82% of user agent clusters have a cohesion index which is less than 0.2. In other terms, 82% of clusters satisfies a ratio of 1 to 5 between their mean intra-cluster distance and the minimum inter-cluster distance. Such high cluster cohesion yields higher quality signatures with longer common subsequences and little overlapping between signatures from different clusters. We manually checked those clusters that had a poor cohesion index (> 0.7). They mostly include too short user agent values that were further discarded by the signature pruning process.

Signature Quality Measure: We evaluate the quality of a signature by measuring the quality of the alignment that provided this signature. We use for this purpose the alignment score described in [23]. This score is computed as the sum of token lengths within a signature, minus a penalty score that is proportionate to the number of gaps '#' in the signature. We represent the alignment score for a signature f_{ij} extracted from cluster c_i as $Sc(f_{ij})$. Let c_{ij} be the subset of user agents within cluster c_i that match the signature f_{ij}, and n_{ij} the number of elements in c_{ij}. We use the following metric to evaluate the quality of a signature.

$$\mathcal{Q}_{ij} = \frac{n_{ij} \times Sc(\int_{ij})}{\sum_{ua \in c_{ij}} Length(ua)}$$

The $\mathcal{Q}_{ij}$ score is included in the $[0..1]$ interval, with values closer to 1 for high quality signatures. The quality score represents the quantity of information within each user agent string that is represented by a signature. High quality signatures would include longer tokens, thus reducing the probability to match non suspicious user agent strings. Meanwhile, signatures with very high quality scores (too close to 1), would be too specific, and therefore cannot be generalized.

Fig. 4(b) illustrates the quality measures for our set of signatures. Almost 70% of signatures have a quality score around 0.65, and another 20% of signatures have a quality score of 0.45. It means that, for 70% of signatures, only 35% of information in their originating user agent strings are not represented (i.e. a ratio of 1 to 3). This ratio, combined with the 1 to 5 dissimilarity ratio between clusters, is a good quality measure for our signatures. In other terms, the level of abstraction within each signature does not overshadow the level of dissimilarity between clusters.

4.3   Performance Analysis

This section evaluates the coverage of our signatures. It evaluates their ability to detect known malware samples, but also yet unknown malware by the time of generating these signatures. We extract a sample of 5,500 anomalous user agent strings from our initial learning set that includes 13,558 values. This sample includes the first 5,500 anomalous user agent strings that were collected during the first month of our malware collection process. In fact, our initial learning set includes malware samples collected during three months observation period, between January and March 2011. We split this set into three parts according to the month within which a malware was collected. We test our signatures against each of these parts in order to evaluate both their coverage and durability.

We apply our clustering mechanism to the set of malware collected in January 2011, and then we execute our signature extraction process. We filter out signatures that generate false positives by testing these against the public list of most implemented user agent strings. We obtained a resulting set of 1.683 signatures. Table 5 summarizes the detection rates that we obtained when testing our signatures against each subset of user agents. Our experiments show that the detection rate decreases as new malware samples are collected. However, our signatures still satisfy a 50% detection rate even after a three months period

	Jan11	Feb11	Mar11
nb of samples	5,500	3,978	4,080
nb of matches	4,703	2,373	2,015
detection rate	86%	59%	49%

Fig. 5. Malware detection rates

since these signatures have been extracted. These measures prove that our signatures are generic enough to match new variants of malware in our dataset. On the other hand, we couldn't reach a 100% detection rate for malware collected in January as some of these malware used too short user agent strings. Signatures created using those strings were discarded during our pruning mechanism as they were found to match benign user agents.

5   Limitations and Future Work

The approach presented in this paper observes malware traffic and extracts detection signatures. The coverage of this approach depends on the initial malware set, and more importantly on malware samples that generate suspicious activity during observation. This is a common shortcoming for all learning-based malware clustering techniques [11, 19]. A malware that does not generate any suspicious activity during observation time would not contribute to signature generation. We may refer to some existing studies, such in [26], in order to identify trigger-based events in malware and learn their behavior. However, these approaches usually apply at the system level, and they are out of scope in this study.

Our approach handles only user agent anomalies, whereas a significant proportion of malware shows no unusual signs or just leaves empty its user agent header. Therefore, this solution cannot be used in standalone as it only detects malware samples that implement abnormal user agent strings. One possibility to extend our approach is to consider behavioral user agent anomalies in addition to syntactical anomalies. While certain malware samples hijack the user agent on the infected node, others use empty or static but unexpected user agent strings. As an extension to this approach, we aim to observe sequences of user agent strings in malware traffic, and to build behavioral models that will be matched against HTTP traffic generated by a network node.

Our approach detects a malware by analyzing the content of its HTTP headers. It cannot detect a malware that uses secure HTTP connections where access to packet content is indeed impossible. One possibility to handle this problem is by implementing our signatures on top of a web proxy that intercepts HTTPS communications (e.g. [27]). It acts as a trusted man-in-the-middle, intercepting HTTPS connections and forwarding only trusted connections to their destinations.

Last of all, like any other malware traffic analysis approach, our technique may be vulnerable to evasion and noise injection attacks. In fact, it generates signatures for intentional or accidental (typos) anomalies left by malware developers. Malware that injects random user agent strings would exhaust resources during our clustering process. Furthermore, such malware does not specify the same user agent value for every malware instance, and so it would not be detected using our approach. These types of malware can be detected using a behavior based analysis of user agents, and that we aim to address as a future extension to this approach.

6   Conclusion

This paper presented a new technique to classify malware user agent anomalies. We observe that user agent anomalies are frequent in malware HTTP traffic. This is mainly because malware developers often use on-the-shelf web toolkits, and they would thus reproduce the same anomalies. Nonetheless, there is not yet a solution that classifies such anomalies and extracts useful signatures. We admit that our approach does not provide a comprehensive solution against HTTP-based malware as they do not always use malformed user agents. However, our experimental results show that this approach considerably increases the malware detection rate in a network. The battle against malware is still on a long run, but our solution adds a new level of defense. It constrains malware developers to hijack user agents on infected nodes, or to constantly update their user agent headers according to new user agent releases and to avoid obsolete ones. In consequence, using on-the-shelf web toolkits for malware development is not straightforward anymore. Our approach also requires no additional equipments. Our signatures can be directly configured within detection systems either at the network or the application layer using web proxies.

References

1. Symantec: Internet security threat report (istr) - 2011 trends (April 2012)
2. Falliere, N., Murchu, L.O., Chien, E.: W32.stuxnet dossier. Technical report, Symantec Response Team (2011)
3. sKyWIper Analysis Team: skywiper (a.k.a. flame a.k.a. flamer): A complex malware for targeted attacks. Technical report, Laboratory of Cryptography and System Security (CrySyS Lab) (May 2012)
4. Kane, P.O., Sezer, S., McLaughlin, K.: Obfuscation: The hidden malware. IEEE Security & Privacy 9, 41–47 (2011)
5. Dagon, D., Gu, G., Lee, C.P., Lee, W.: A taxonomy of botnet structures. In: Proceedings of the 23rd Annual Computer Security Applications Conference (2007)
6. Rajab, M.A., Zarfoss, J., Monrose, F., Terzis, A.: A multifaceted approach to understanding the botnet phenomenon. In: Proceedings of the 6th ACM SIGCOMM Conference on Internet Measurement (2006)
7. Rossow, C., Dietrich, C.J., Bos, H., Cavallaro, L., van Steen, M., Freiling, F.C., Pohlmann, N.: Sandnet: Network traffic analysis of malicious software. In: Workshop on Building Analysis Datasets and Gathering Experience Returns for Security, Salzburg (2011)
8. Gu, G., Zhang, J., Lee, W.: Botsniffer: Detecting botnet command and control channels in network traffic. In: Proceedings of the 15th Annual Network and Distributed System Security Symposium (2008)
9. Gu, G., Porras, P., Yegneswaran, V., Fong, M., Lee, W.: Bothunter: Detecting malware infection through ids-driven dialog correlation. In: Proceedings of the 16th USENIX Security Symposium (2007)
10. Gu, G., Perdisci, R., Zhang, J., Lee, W.: Botminer: Clustering analysis of network traffic for protocol- and structure-independent botnet detection. In: Proceedings of the 17th USENIX Security Symposium (2008)

11. Perdisci, R., Lee, W., Feamster, N.: Behavioral clustering of http-based malware and signature generation using malicious network traces. In: USENIX Symposium on Networked Systems Design and Implementation (2010)

12. Wurzinger, P., Bilge, L., Holz, T., Goebel, J., Kruegel, C., Kirda, E.: Automatically Generating Models for Botnet Detection. In: Backes, M., Ning, P. (eds.) ESORICS 2009. LNCS, vol. 5789, pp. 232–249. Springer, Heidelberg (2009)

13. Perdisci, R., Dagon, D., Lee, W., Fogla, P., Sharif, M.: Misleading worm signature generators using deliberate noise injection. In: Proceedings of the IEEE Symposium on Security and Privacy (SSP) (2006)

14. abuse.ch: Kelihos back in town using fast flux. Malware & Virus Analysing (March 2012)

15. Arbor Networks: Anatomy of a botnet - how the arbor security engineering & response team discovers, analyzes and mitigates ddos attacks. White paper

16. Fielding, R., Irvine, U., Gettys, J., Mogul, J., Frystyk, H., Masinter, L., Leach, P., Berners-Lee, T.: Hypertext transfer protocol. Request for Comments: 2616 (1999)

17. Manners, D.: The user agent field: Analyzing and detecting the abnormal or malicious in your organization. In: SANS Institute Reading Room Site (2012)

18. Bailey, M., Oberheide, J., Andersen, J., Mao, Z.M., Jahanian, F., Nazario, J.: Automated Classification and Analysis of Internet Malware. In: Kruegel, C., Lippmann, R., Clark, A. (eds.) RAID 2007. LNCS, vol. 4637, pp. 178–197. Springer, Heidelberg (2007)

19. Bayer, U., Comparetti, P.M., Hlauschek, C., Kruegel, C., Kirda, E.: Scalable, behavior-based malware clustering. In: Network and Distributed System System Security Symposium (2009)

20. Jacob, G., Hund, R., Kruegel, C., Holz, T.: Jackstraws: Picking command and control connections from bot traffic. In: 20th USENIX Security Symposium (2011)

21. Li, Z., Sanghi, M., Chen, Y., Yang Kao, M., Chavez, B.: Hamsa: fast signature generation for zero-day polymorphic worms with provable attack resilience. In: IEEE Symposium on Security and Privacy (2006)

22. Yegneswaran, V., Giffin, J.T., Barford, P., Jha, S.: An architecture for generating semantic-aware signatures. In: USENIX Security Symposium (2005)

23. Newsome, J., Karp, B., Song, D.: Polygraph: Automatically generating signatures for polymorphic worms. In: IEEE Symposium on Security and Privacy (2005)

24. Spillmann, B., Neuhaus, M., Bunke, H., Pękalska, E.Z., Duin, R.P.W.: Transforming Strings to Vector Spaces Using Prototype Selection. In: Yeung, D.-Y., Kwok, J.T., Fred, A., Roli, F., de Ridder, D. (eds.) SSPR&SPR 2006. LNCS, vol. 4109, pp. 287–296. Springer, Heidelberg (2006)

25. Bieganski, P., Ned, J., Cadis, J.V.: Generalized suffix trees for biological sequence data: applications and implementation. In: Proceedings of the Twenty-Seventh Hawaii International Conference on System Sciences, vol. 5, pp. 35–44 (1994)

26. Brumley, D., Hartwig, C., Liang, Z., Newsome, J., Song, D., Yin, H.: Automatically identifying trigger-based behavior in malware. In: Botnet Detection. Springer (2008)

27. Microsoft: Forefront threat management gateway, http://www.microsoft.com/en-us/server-cloud/forefront/threat-management-gateway.aspx

AS5: A Secure Searchable Secret Sharing Scheme for Privacy Preserving Database Outsourcing

Mohammad Ali Hadavi[1], Ernesto Damiani[2], Rasool Jalili[1], Stelvio Cimato[2], and Zeinab Ganjei[1]

[1] Data and Network Security Laboratory (DNSL), Department of Computer Engineering, Sharif University of Technology, Tehran, Iran
{mhadavi@ce.,jalili@,zganjei@ce.}sharif.edu
[2] SErvice-oriented Software Architecture Research (SESAR) Lab, Dipartimento di Tecnologie dell'Informazione, Università degli Studi di Milano, Crema, Italy
{ernesto.damiani,stelvio.cimato}@unimi.it

Abstract. Researchers have been studying security challenges of database outsourcing for almost a decade. Privacy of outsourced data is one of the main challenges when the *"Database As a Service"* model is adopted in the service oriented trend of the cloud computing paradigm. This is due to the insecurity of the network environment or even the untrustworthiness of the service providers. This paper proposes a method to preserve privacy of outsourced data based on Shamir's secret sharing scheme. We split attribute values into several parts and distribute them among untrusted servers. The problem of using secret sharing in data outsourcing scenario is how to search efficiently within the randomly generated pool of shares. In this paper, at first, we customize Shamir's scheme to have *A Searchable Secret Sharing Scheme* (AS4) that enables the efficient execution of different kinds of queries over distributed shares. Then, we extend our method for sharing values to *A Secure Searchable Secret Sharing Scheme* (AS5) to tolerate statistical attacks based on adversary's knowledge about outsourced data distribution. In AS5 data shares are generated uniformly across a domain to prevent information leakage about the outsourced data.

Keywords: Secure database outsourcing, data confidentiality, secret sharing, query processing.

1 Introduction

Nowadays cloud computing environments provide infrastructure as a service, software as a service, and even database as a service to reduce information technology related burden of organizations businesses. Rapid improvements in the area of network and software technology increase the motivation of companies to outsource their supplementary services, the supporting services of their core business, to third party service providers. Nevertheless, outsourcing data and its management raises security challenges regarding confidentiality of outsourced data due to the insecurity of network environment, or even to the untrustworthiness of service providers. Security challenges of database outsourcing are an obstacle to the success of *"Database As a Service"* model in operation compared to infrastructure or software as a service.

R. Di Pietro et al. (Eds.): DPM 2012 and SETOP 2012, LNCS 7731, pp. 201–216, 2013.

A naïve solution for confidentiality of outsourced data is to encrypt data before its outsourcing [1-5]. In encryption based solutions the service provider does not have the decryption key. It must be able to execute submitted queries without decryption. The vast majority of research on secure data outsourcing has focused on query execution over encrypted outsourced data. Generally, encryption based solutions suffer from key management overheads and either inefficiency or vulnerability to statistical inferences over encrypted values [6, 7].

Departing from encryption, fragmentation is another approach for outsourced data confidentiality. It tries to hide sensitive associations of values defined by a set of confidentiality constraints over attributes/tuples of a relation. The data owner partitions a relation, vertically [8, 9] or horizontally [10, 11], into several parts and outsources them to different servers. In this approach, query execution is generally more efficient compared to encryption based solutions. However, encryption is sometimes unavoidable because fragmentation cannot preserve confidentiality of a single sensitive attribute [12, 13]. The vulnerability to statistical database attacks in the case of collusion between servers, in which different partitions are hosted, as well as servers inferences on data updates are two major disadvantages of fragmentation-based solutions.

Agrawal *et al.* [14] use secret sharing to preserve outsourced data confidentiality. They utilize hash functions to reproduce distribution polynomials and data shares. While their solution efficiently supports different kinds of queries, it is susceptible to statistical inferences in the case that the untrusted servers have *a priori* knowledge of data distribution or frequency. Hadavi *et al.* [15, 16] use secret sharing as well to distribute data among untrusted servers. They use a B^+ index tree on order preserving encrypted values of attributes to be able to search within data shares.

Utilizing the secret sharing concept, in this paper we introduce a solution for confidentiality of outsourced data. We fragment a relation into several parts, neither vertically nor horizontally, by splitting attribute values into randomized shares, and distribute each share to a server. Observing data shares, the servers cannot improve their knowledge about outsourced data, even if they collude. The main problem of sharing attribute values among servers is how to efficiently search within the pool of randomly generated shares. Focusing on this problem, we propose *A Searchable Secret Sharing Scheme* (AS4) for data outsourcing that supports efficient query processing. Then, we extend it to *A Secure Searchable Secret Sharing Scheme* (AS5) to tolerate an intensified threat model in which servers have *a priori* knowledge about data distribution.

This paper is organized as follows. Section 2 contains background information on using secret sharing in data outsourcing scenario, our problem definition, and the threat model. Section 3 introduces AS4 as our basic scheme for efficient search on distributed shares. Then, in Section 4 we introduce a security extension to AS4, namely AS5, to make the secret sharing scheme secure under statistical analysis based on adversary's prior knowledge about data distribution. Section 5 includes query processing scenarios in our proposed approach. In Section 6 we discuss some security issues in AS5. Finally, Section 7 concludes the paper and expresses some directions of future work.

2   Secret Sharing in Outsourcing Scenario

A Secret sharing scheme is a method of sharing a secret s among a set of participants $U = \{u_1, u_2, ..., u_n\}$ such that only authorized subsets of U, called access structure, can reconstruct s. We use threshold (k, n) secret sharing scheme, proposed by Shamir [17], where the access structure is a subset A of 2^U such that $\forall~B \in A,~|B| \geq k$. That is, every k or more participants can reconstruct s while less than k participants cannot.

We follow a database outsourcing model in which an owner outsources his confidential data to honest but curious servers. Then, the owner and authorized users/clients, given required credentials, submit their queries to the servers.

Using threshold (k, n) secret sharing in data outsourcing scenario, the data owner becomes the distributor of shares among n servers, $S_1, S_2,..., S_n$, that are the participants. Each attribute value v is a secret that is split into n shares, $share_i(v)$ $(1 \leq i \leq n)$. To compute the share values of attribute value v, the data owner produces a polynomial of order $k\text{-}1$, $p(x) = a_{k\text{-}1}x^{k\text{-}1} + a_{k\text{-}2}x^{k\text{-}2} + ... + a_1x + a_0$, where $a_0 = v$ and other coefficients are chosen randomly from $GF(P)$. Having a secret vector X $(x_1, x_2, ..., x_n)$, x_i corresponds to S_i, the owner computes $share_i(v) = p(x_i)$ and stores it on S_i $(1 \leq i \leq n)$. In fact, for each attribute value, there are n points $(x_i, p(x_i))$ through which the polynomial $p(x)$ passes. k distinct points are enough to uniquely reconstruct a polynomial of order $k - 1$. Therefore, when a trusted party, who knows the distribution vector X, receives at least k shares of the secret v, the secret can be reconstructed. On the other hand, the servers infer nothing about v even if they collude and pool their shares because they do not have the distribution vector X.

Let us model a database table with m rows and l columns as a matrix $M_{m}x_l$. Fig. 1 shows outsourcing a relation, as an mxl matrix M to n servers, each of them is given an mxl matrix $Share_i(M)$, where v_{xy} as a cell of M, is mapped onto $share_i(v_{xy})$ of matrix $Share_i(M)$ $(1 \leq i \leq n)$.

2.1   Problem Definition

The theoretic security of Shamir's scheme guarantees outsourced data confidentiality, keeping in mind that the distribution vector X is hidden from the untrusted servers. This solution provides the highest level of data confidentiality because the data shares are produced using random coefficients and do not leak any information about the distribution or the frequency of original values. This is caused by generating random shares for values which results in different polynomials and consequently different shares for two equal values.

In outsourcing scenario, authorized users are supposed to query outsourced data and request the servers for retrieving the appropriate shares. While the owner or authorized users do not store the random coefficients, data retrieval becomes a problem. Obviously it is not efficient to send back all shares in response to a query, and execute the query over the reconstructed values at client side. For this purpose, a method is required to identify the shares, stored on the servers, that satisfy the query condition.

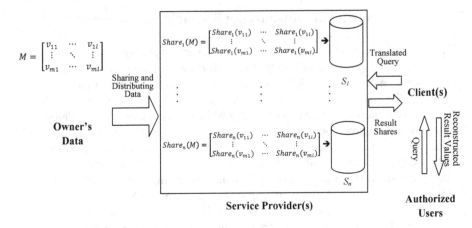

$$M = \begin{bmatrix} v_{11} & \cdots & v_{1l} \\ \vdots & \ddots & \vdots \\ v_{m1} & \cdots & v_{ml} \end{bmatrix}$$

$$Share_1(M) = \begin{bmatrix} Share_1(v_{11}) & \cdots & Share_1(v_{1l}) \\ \vdots & \ddots & \vdots \\ Share_1(v_{m1}) & \cdots & Share_1(v_{ml}) \end{bmatrix}$$

$$Share_n(M) = \begin{bmatrix} Share_n(v_{11}) & \cdots & Share_n(v_{1l}) \\ \vdots & \ddots & \vdots \\ Share_n(v_{m1}) & \cdots & Share_n(v_{ml}) \end{bmatrix}$$

Owner's Data

Sharing and Distributing Data

S_1

S_n

Translated Query

Client(s)

Result Shares

Query

Reconstructed Result Values

Service Provider(s)

Authorized Users

Fig. 1. Sharing a database relation, as a matrix, among n servers

To solve the above problem we propose a solution in which searching a subset of shares is possible, while the confidentiality of outsourced data is preserved. At first, we redefine Shamir's secret sharing scheme to preserve the order of values in their corresponding shares and at the same time to perturbate the distribution of values in their shares. The obtained scheme, AS4, is still vulnerable to statistical analysis since the order of attribute values is preserved in their shares. We extend AS4 in terms of security to AS5, a solution that tolerates statistical analysis on data shares based on adversary's prior knowledge about outsourced data. We also examine query processing support for different kinds of queries in our approach and discuss about security achievement considering possible attack scenarios on data confidentiality.

2.2   Threat Model

We have the following assumptions for our threat model:

- Service providers are honest but curious. They execute submitted queries honestly on outsourced data and send complete and authenticated results. They are curious and try to increase their knowledge about confidential data by observing data shares and submitted queries
- Service providers have *a priori* knowledge about outsourced data. For example, they might know the domain of values, the minimum or maximum values, or some information about the frequency of values.
- The servers can communicate and collude with each other to extract knowledge about outsourced data.
- An adversary who has compromised the servers can observe data shares and sub-mitted queries as well as the service providers.

Also we assume that clients, as users' machines that mediate user requests to service providers, are trusted. Moreover, users are given appropriate authorities and creden-tials to submit a query through a client and see the result.

3   A Searchable Secret Sharing Scheme (AS4)

To have a searchable secret sharing scheme with threshold (k, n) we define a scheme, called AS4, in which the order of attribute values is preserved in their corresponding shares but not the frequency of values. This scheme is required to satisfy two following properties:

1. Order preserving: Let V be the domain of attribute values. The order of values must be preserved in their corresponding shares. That is:
$$\forall \, v, v' \in V: \quad if \quad v < v' \Rightarrow share_i(v) < share_i(v') \quad (1 \le i \le n)$$

2. Distribution perturbation: The original data distribution must be perturbated by changing the frequency of attribute values in their corresponding shares. That is, two equal values have different shares with a high probability:
$$\forall \, v, v' \in V \quad (v \text{ and } v' \text{ are attribute values in different database tuples}):$$
$$if \quad v = v' \Rightarrow \Pr[share_i(v) = share_i(v')] < \varepsilon \quad (1 \le i \le n)$$

The first property is aimed at making query execution efficient. The second property indicates that the sharing is not deterministic. It is aimed at concealing the frequency of original values. This property improves the robustness against statistical analysis. In the above formula, ε is a small value, dependent on the domain size of shares.

Redefining the Shamir's threshold scheme, now we introduce AS4 as "a searchable secret sharing scheme" whose shares, while preserving the ordering of original values, substantially change the original data distribution.

Choosing values of k and n for a threshold secret sharing (k, n) has some influences on the availability and fault tolerance aspects of the system that are not the focus of this work. In our system, choosing large k increases the communication cost while it does not offer more security in terms of confidentiality. Therefore, in the remaining parts of this paper we assume a threshold $(2, 3)$ secret sharing scheme with the polynomial of the general form $p(x) = ax + v$ where "a" is a random coefficient of a specified domain. The domain of a searchable attribute in a relation is a set of values $V = \{v_1, v_2, ..., v_t\}$ where $v_1 < v_2 < ... < v_t$.

To obtain AS4 we follow two steps: first, we partition the coefficient domain, and second, we assign each attribute value to a partition from which the coefficient a is randomly chosen. Let us have a detailed view for these two steps.

1. **Partitioning the domain of the coefficient:** The first step is to partition the coefficient's domain D (of real numbers) considering the following definition for partitioning.

    Definition- *Partitioning* a domain D of values is defined as dividing D into t parts d_i $(1 \le i \le t)$ where

    1. $d_i \subseteq D \, (1 \le i \le t)$ is a range of values in D
    2. $\bigcup_{i=1}^{t} d_i = D$
    3. $\forall \, d_i, d_j \subseteq D \, (i \ne j): \quad d_i \cap d_j = \emptyset.$ ∎

A possible way of partitioning a domain D is to divide it into a sequence of an arbitrary number of equal partitions. With D as values in the range $[d_s .. d_e]$ being the coefficient's domain, we divide it into $t = |V|$ equal consecutive partitions including $[d_s \, .. \, d_s+\frac{|D|}{t})$, $[d_s+\frac{|D|}{t} \, .. \, d_s+2\frac{|D|}{t})$, $[d_s+2\frac{|D|}{t} \, .. \, d_s+3\frac{|D|}{t})$, ..., and $[d_s +(t-1)\frac{|D|}{t} \, .. \, d_e]$.

2. **Value-Partition Assignment.** The next step is to define a function to map a value $v \in V$ onto a partition $d \subseteq D$.

Definition- *Mapping function F is a function that maps a value $v \in V$ onto a partition $d \subseteq D$ where*
$$\forall \, v, v' \in V, F(v) = d, F(v') = d' \, (d, d' \subseteq D) : v \neq v' \Rightarrow d \cap d' = \emptyset$$
■

For AS4, we define F as a total order function such that maps $v \in V$ onto $d = [d_s+(v-v_1)\frac{|D|}{t} \, .. \, d_s+(v-v_1+1)\frac{|D|}{t})$. For sharing attribute value v among three servers, the owner choose a randomly from the above range and construct the polynomial $p(x_i) = ax_i + v$ to compute the data share of S_i ($1 \le i \le 3$).

Fig. 2 exemplifies sharing Age values (integer values of the range [1..100]) of Employee relation (Table 1) among three servers with a sample distribution vector $X = \{x_1=9, x_2=14, x_3=2\}$ and integer random coefficients of the range [1..1000]. For simplicity, in this example we only show sharing Age values. All searchable attributes should be distributed in an order preserving manner to be efficiently searchable in the future.

For query processing, when a user submits her query via a client, the client translates the query into a query over data shares and sends it to the servers. In our example of Employee relation (Table 1) and sharing Age values (Fig. 2), the query "SELECT Salary FROM Employee WHERE Age = 45" is translated into "SELECT Share₁(Salary) FROM Employee WHERE (9*441 + 45) ≤ Share₁(Age) ≤ (9*450 + 45)" and sent to S_1. The client does similar translations for S_2 and S_3 with respect to the distribution vector X and the mapping function F. It is worth mentioning that if the mapping function F is defined in such a way, the owner or users/clients do not need to store F to find the association of values to partitions for query translation. In Section 5 we elaborate more on the query processing scenario for different kinds of queries.

Now we verify the satisfaction of our two desired properties, i.e., order preserving and distribution perturbation, in two following lemmas.

Table 1. The Employee relation

ID	Age	Salary
1	45	100
2	84	200
3	78	150
4	46	350
5	45	200
6	80	210
7	45	175
8	57	200

Share$_1$(Age)	Share$_2$(Age)	Share$_3$(Age)
$9a_{45} + 45$ $441 \leq a_{45} \leq 450$	$14a_{45} + 45$ $441 \leq a_{45} \leq 450$	$2a_{45} + 45$ $441 \leq a_{45} \leq 450$
$9a_{84} + 84$ $831 \leq a_{84} \leq 840$	$14a_{84} + 84$ $831 \leq a_{84} \leq 840$	$2a_{84} + 84$ $831 \leq a_{84} \leq 840$
$9a_{78} + 78$ $771 \leq a_{78} \leq 780$	$14a_{78} + 78$ $771 \leq a_{78} \leq 780$	$2a_{78} + 78$ $771 \leq a_{78} \leq 780$
$9a_{46} + 46$ $451 \leq a_{46} \leq 460$	$14a_{46} + 46$ $451 \leq a_{46} \leq 460$	$2a_{46} + 46$ $451 \leq a_{46} \leq 460$
$9a_{45} + 45$ $441 \leq a_{45} \leq 450$	$14a_{45} + 45$ $441 \leq a_{45} \leq 450$	$2a_{45} + 45$ $441 \leq a_{45} \leq 450$
$9a_{80} + 80$ $791 \leq a_{80} \leq 800$	$14a_{80} + 80$ $791 \leq a_{80} \leq 800$	$2a_{80} + 80$ $791 \leq a_{80} \leq 800$
$9a_{45} + 45$ $441 \leq a_{45} \leq 450$	$14a_{45} + 45$ $441 \leq a_{45} \leq 450$	$2a_{45} + 45$ $441 \leq a_{45} \leq 450$
$9a_{57} + 57$ $561 \leq a_{57} \leq 570$	$14a_{57} + 57$ $561 \leq a_{57} \leq 570$	$2a_{57} + 57$ $561 \leq a_{57} \leq 570$
S_1	S_2	S_3

Fig. 2. Sharing Age values of Employee relation (Table 1) among three servers

Lemma 1- *AS4 preserves the order of attribute values in their corresponding shares.*

Proof: $\forall v, v' \in V: v < v' \Rightarrow$

$$a_v \in [d_s + (v - v_1)\frac{|D|}{t} \,..\, d_s + (v - v_1 + 1)\frac{|D|}{t}) < a_{v'} \in [d_s + (v' - v_1)\frac{|D|}{t} \,..\, d_s + (v' - v_1 + 1)\frac{|D|}{t}) \Rightarrow$$

$$a_v x_i + v < a_{v'} x_i + v' \quad \Rightarrow \quad share_i(v) < share_i(v') \qquad (1 \leq i \leq 3) \qquad \square$$

Lemma 2– *AS4 perturbates the distribution of attribute values in their corresponding shares.*

Proof: $\forall v, v' \in V$, $v = v'$ and v, v' are in different database tuples:

$$Pr[share_i(v) = share_i(v')] \;\; = Pr[a_v x_i + v = a_{v'} x_i + v'] \quad (1 \leq i \leq 3) \;\; \Rightarrow$$

$$Pr[share_i(v) = share_i(v')] = Pr[a_v = a_{v'}]$$

Considering that a_v and $a_{v'}$ are random numbers, independently chosen from the corresponding partition of v (or v'), $Pr[a_v = a_{v'}] < \varepsilon$ where $\varepsilon < 1$ and its value is affected by the size of the partition. $\square$

In the next Section, we extend our scheme in terms of security so that data shares reveal neither the order nor the frequency of outsourced data.

4 A Secure Searchable Secret Sharing Scheme (AS5)

Statistical inferences in our basic scheme (AS4) are possible since the order of attribute values is preserved in their shares. That is, observing data shares, the untrusted servers may statistically deduce some information about original values. Consider an outsourced relation of employees of an organization and assume that the adversary knows that the minimum and maximum ages of employment are 25 and 75, respectively. So, the maximum share value of Age for each server may correspond to the maximum possible Age value, which is 75 in our example. These kinds of information help the adversary to make inferences about original values that may result in revealing the mapping function or even the secret distribution vector X. Such inferences are originated by the two following characteristics in AS4:

1. having equal-length partitions of the coefficient's domain and
2. the definition of mapping function F in a way that preserves the order of values in their corresponding shares.

A generic countermeasure solution is to introduce a weighted partitioning as well as an order-obfuscated mapping function to break the two above characteristics of AS4. Therefore, the first line of AS4 extension focuses on the partitioning method of the coefficient domain. It is intuitively acceptable that when data shares are uniformly distributed across their domain they reveal as least information as possible for an adversary aimed at making inferences on outsourced data. So, the first goal in AS5 is to generate data shares, which have been distributed uniformly across their domain, while query processing is still efficient.

The second line of AS4 extension is related to the mapping function F (by which attribute values are mapped onto partitions) and tries to hide the ordering relation of values in their corresponding shares. Therefore, the goal is to define a mapping function so that the ordering relation between values is obfuscated in their corresponding shares.

Given an original data distribution for a searchable attribute, the owner follows four following steps to generate uniformly distributed - order obfuscated data shares:

1. partitioning the domain of shares
2. obfuscating the ordering relation between values and their corresponding shares
3. partitioning the domain of random coefficient in the distribution polynomial
4. sharing attribute values

Let us have a more detailed view to these steps.

1. **Partitioning the domain of shares**: The owner calculates the length of each partition based on the given data distribution. Let us model the data distribution (for a searchable attribute value) by pairs (v_i, f_i) where $v_i \in V$ is an attribute value and f_i is v_i's frequency in the relation. It is clear that $|V|$ is the required number of partitions and $N_{tuple} = \sum_{i=1}^{|V|} f_i$ is the number of database tuples. Each $v \in V$ is associated with $d \subseteq D$ where the length of d, denoted by $|d|$, is calculated by $|d| = \frac{|D| f_i}{N_{tuple}}$. We have a weighted partitioning based on the values' frequencies in the relation.

2. **Defining an order-obfuscated mapping function**: the owner defines the mapping function F such that the ordering relation between attribute values is not preserved in their corresponding partitions. To this end, a random permutation of d_is $(1 \leq i \leq |V|)$, among $|V|!$ possible permutations, is chosen by the owner. Fig. 3 illustrates partitioning a domain of shares based on values' frequencies and an order preserving (a) and an order-obfuscated (b) mapping function.

3. **Partitioning the domain of random coefficient**: Considering that the owner uses $Share_i(v) = ax_i + v$ to compute S_i's share of v, the next step is to partition the domain of coefficient a such that it generates a set of shares which have been distributed uniformly across their domain. It is simply done by putting minimum and maximum values of $Share_i(v)$ into $a = \frac{Share_i(v) - v}{x_i}$ to find the range boundaries of a partition in the coefficient domain corresponding to v.

4. **Sharing attribute values**: For the final step, the data owner uses the calculated ranges of the coefficient domain to compute data shares of each value. He chooses a randomly from the specified range (previous step) and put it into the equation $Share_i(v) = ax_i + v$. Then, the computed share $Share_i(v)$ is outsourced to S_i.

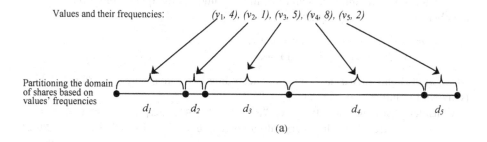

(a)

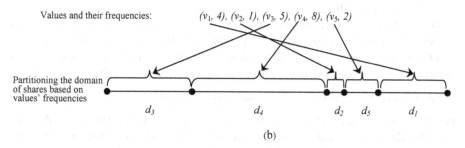

(b)

Fig. 3. An order preserving partition assignment (a), and an obfuscated partition assignment (b) of an attribute with a domain of five values.

Obviously, the mapping function F must be kept hidden from an adversary who may know some information about original data distribution. The owner informs authorized users/clients about the mapping function F for further use in query translation.

Compared to AS4, the extra imposed cost in AS5 is to store F at owner and client sides for query translation. To store F, the owner requires the storage cost of the order $O(|V|)$. This is reasonable for a database size of order $O(|N|)$ where N is the number of database tuples. For example, for the attribute Age with the domain size $|V| = 100$ and 4-Byte share values, the owner needs eight bytes to specify a partition. While the size of a database with one million 64-Byte tuples is almost 64MB, less than 1KB (800 Bytes) is enough to store the mapping function at owner and client sides.

5   Query Processing

In this section we examine the query execution scenario of typical equality, range, projection, join, aggregation, and update queries. The query processing scenarios in AS4 and AS5 are almost similar considering that in AS5 case, clients have the mapping function F to translate submitted queries into server side queries over shares. The only difference is that the execution of range queries in AS5 is less convenient than in AS4 because in AS5 the ordering relation is obfuscated in data shares.

Equality Queries. The condition "$att = v$", where att is a searchable attribute and v is a value, is translated by a client into "$min(Share_i(v)) \leq att \leq max(Share_i(v))$" and sent to S_i ($1 \leq i \leq 3$). The minimum and maximum values of the query condition predicate are obtained by following equations

$$min(Share_i(v)) = (min(a)).x_i + v \quad,$$
$$max(Share_i(v)) = (max(a)).x_i + v$$

where $min(a)$ and $max(a)$ are computed according to the mapping   function F, which is known for authorized users/clients.

Consider a simple equality query "SELECT * FROM Employee WHERE Age = 20". The client translates the query into a range query of the form "SELECT * FROM Employee WHERE $min(Share_i(20)) \leq$ Age $\leq max(Share_i(20))$", and submits it to S_i ($1 \leq i \leq 3$). Receiving shares of satisfying tuples from two servers, the client interpolate original values.

This method guarantees that all tuples with Age = 20 are returned exclusively as query results. Let $Res_i = \{Share_i(v) \mid min(Share_i(v)) \leq Share_i(v) \leq max(Share_i(v))\}$ be a set of satisfying shares in S_i ($1 \leq i \leq 3$) based on a query condition. The execution of equality queries in our scheme generates a *sound* and *complete* result set.

Lemma 3- *The returned result of an equality query is sound.*

Proof: The result set is not sound if there is a $share_i(v') \in Res_i$ where $v' \neq v$. According to the threat model that assumes honesty of servers, they send back all appropriate shares based on the selection predicate of a submitted query, whose condition predicate has been translated.

According to the definition of partitioning which states that partitions are disjoint and with respect to our mapping function in which each value v is mapped to a different partition we have:
$\forall v, v' \in V, v' \neq v :$
$[min(Share_i(v)) .. max(Share_i(v))] \cap [min(Share_i(v')) .. max(Share_i(v'))] = \emptyset \Rightarrow$
$Share_i(v') \notin [min(Share_i(v)) .. max(Share_i(v))] \Rightarrow share_i(v') \notin Res_i \quad (1 \leq i \leq 3) \square$

The Soundness of query result means that there is not any false hit in returned results of the servers, bringing less client side computation (for result pruning) as well as less communication cost.

Lemma 4- *The returned result of an equality query is complete.*

Proof: The result set is complete if $\forall\ v' \in V$, $v' = v$: $Share_i(v') \in Res_i$ $(1 \leq i \leq 3)$. Suppose that there is a $v' = v$ for which $Share_i(v') \notin Res_i$. Then we have:

$$\exists\ v, v' \in V, v = v', Share_i(v) \in Res_i, Share_i(v') \notin Res_i$$

$$Share_i(v') \notin Res_i \Rightarrow Share_i(v') \notin [min(Share_i(v)) .. max(Share_i(v))] \overset{(v=v')}{\Longrightarrow}$$
$$Share_i(v') \notin [min(Share_i(v')) .. max(Share_i(v'))]$$

which is a contradiction with respect to our secret sharing scheme.   □

Simply it is possible to have conjunctive or disjunctive conditions on searchable attributes. In such a case, the servers return a set of shares so that the whole condition, as the composition of conditions, is satisfied.

Range Queries. In AS4, range queries are processed similar to equality queries except the change in the range boundaries. That is, for the lower bound of the range the minimum possible value and for the upper bound of the range the maximum possible value are used. Consider a simple range query "SELECT * FROM Employee WHERE 50 ≤ Age ≤ 80". The submitted query to S_i $(1 \leq i \leq 3)$ is: "SELECT * FROM Employee WHERE $min(Share_i(50)) \leq$ Age $\leq max(Share_i(80))$".

In AS5 the translation of range queries is not as straightforward as in AS4 caused by the order-obfuscated mapping function in AS5. In AS5, a range of attribute values is usually mapped onto several ranges of shares. Consider the sample range query "SELECT Salary FROM Employee WHERE 50 < Age < 55". The query is translated into the following query and sent to S_i $(1 \leq i \leq 3)$:
"SELECT Salary FROM Employee WHERE

$$min(Share_i(51)) \leq Age \leq max(Share_i(51))\ \text{OR}$$
$$min(Share_i(52)) \leq Age \leq max(Share_i(52))\ \text{OR}$$
$$min(Share_i(53)) \leq Age \leq max(Share_i(53))\ \text{OR}$$
$$min(Share_i(54)) \leq Age \leq max(Share_i(54))"$$

Range queries generate a complete set of results without any false hits as well as equality queries.

Lemma 5- *The returned result of a range query is sound and complete.*
Proof: We can consider the result set of a range query as the union of the result sets of a sequence of equality queries. Each equality query, for which we have a sound and complete result set, is executed independently over a partition. Consequently, the result set of a range query is sound and complete regarding that each value is assigned a distinct partition and partitions are disjoint.   □

Projection Queries. Projection is supported in AS5 as well as AS4 without extra overheads, since the granularity of sharing is attribute value. For a query such as "SELECT Salary FROM Employee WHERE 20 ≤ Age ≤ 25", each S_i $(1 \leq i \leq 3)$ finds satisfying share values of Age and then, returns the corresponding Salary shares to the client. The client can interpolate original Salary values after receiving Salary shares of two servers.

Aggregate Queries. Queries with SUM aggregation function are supported in both AS4 and AS5 thanks to the additive homomorphism property of the secret sharing scheme. Consider a query with SUM aggregation function such as "SELECT SUM(Salary) FROM Employee WHERE 20 ≤ Age ≤ 25". The client translates it and sends the query "SELECT Salary FROM Employee WHERE $min(Share_i(20)) \le$ Age $\le max(Share_i(25))$" to S_i ($1 \le i \le 3$). Then, S_i locally calculates the summation of satisfying Salary values. Thanks to the additive homomorphism property of Shamir's scheme, the client can compute the total summation value when it receives two values from the servers.

Queries containing CONUT function such as "SELECT COUNT(Salary) FROM Employee WHERE Age = 20" are executed simply by reforming as "SELECT COUNT(Salary) FROM Employee WHERE $min(Share_i(20)) \le$ Age $\le max(Share_i(20))$" for S_i ($1 \le i \le 3$). Since the servers are honest but curious, COUNT queries of the above form can be sent to only one S_i instead of sending to all, incurring less communication overhead.

Executing MIN/MAX queries in both AS4 and AS5 is not as straightforward as COUNT and SUM queries and may need several rounds of client mediation to have the final result. Consider a sample MIN/MAX query such as "SELECT Salary FROM Employee WHERE Age = MIN(Age)". This query is translated into "SELECT $Share_i$(Salary) FROM Employee WHERE $min(Share_i(v_1)) \le$ Age $\le max(Share_i(v_1))$" and sent to S_i ($1 \le i \le 3$). v_1 is the minimum value of the Age domain. If the query returns no shares, the client continues with the next possible minimum, e.g. v_2, to reach the result finally. In our example, the client continues to query the servers until it sends "SELECT $Share_i$(Salary) FROM Employee WHERE $min(Share_i(45)) \le$ Age $\le max(Share_i(45))$" to S_i ($1 \le i \le 3$) and receives the result shares.

Some mechanisms such as client side storage of minimum and maximum values of a searchable attribute or using an auxiliary table to maintain the ordering of values [16] can also be used to tackle the problem of MIN/MAX queries in our approach.

For more complex queries with aggregation functions in their selection predicates such as "SELECT MIN(Salary) FROM Employee where Age = 50" or "SELECT MAX(Salary) FROM Employee WHERE Age = MIN(Age)" the final result is computed at client side after receiving the satisfying values from at least two servers.

Join Queries. Join queries are performed on two tables with an attribute in common. Consider two simple relations T_1(ID, Dep, Salary) and T_2(ID, Name, Age) and the sample join query "SELECT Salary FROM T1, T2 WHERE T1.ID = T2.ID". This query is rewritten as a parameterized query "SELECT Salary FROM T_1, T_2 WHERE $(min(share(v_i)) \le T_1.ID \le max(share(v_i)))$ AND $(min(share(v_i)) \le T_2.ID \le max(share(v_i)))$" for ($1 \le i \le t$) where t is the maximum value of the attribute domain. To have a complete result, the client submits |V| queries to the servers and performs a union operation on the received results.

Update Queries. While some existing solutions suffer from frequent updates in dynamic environment, our approach supports update queries. The execution of update queries including INSERT, DELETE, and UPDATE is straightforward in AS4. A typical deletion query such as "DELETE FROM Employee WHERE Age = 80" is translated into "DELETE FROM Employee WHERE $min(Share_i(80)) \leq Age \leq max(Share_i(80))$" and sent to $S_i (1 \leq i \leq 3)$. Since equality and range queries return a complete result set without false hits, S_i removes exclusively a complete set of satisfying tuples from the target relation. To insert a new tuple, shares of attribute values in the tuple are computed and inserted into S_i $(1 \leq i \leq 3)$. For an update query, satisfying tuples based on the condition predicate of the query are selected and sent to the owner. The owner constructs a new polynomial and computes the values in SET predicate of the update query to substitute new shares with the old ones.

One can say that database update is a challenge in AS5. Because update queries change the distribution of a searchable attribute and consequently, the uniform distribution of shares is disorganized. In such a case it is required to repartition, redefine the mapping function, and redistribute data which is considerably costly for outsourcing scenario. To let AS5 be adopted in dynamic environments, a practical suggestion is to use standard distributions of attribute values instead of real distributions. Using such standard distributions, data updates do not deteriorate the distribution of attribute values when sharing the values of a new tuple. In other words, we will have almost the same distribution in different snapshots of the system. From a practical point of view, it may be acceptable to refer to an expected distribution of Age values stored in an organizational database. We plan to quantify the possible performance degradation of AS5 due to using standard data distribution instead of real ones.

6   Security Discussion

In this section we discuss about the security of our approach, focusing on AS5 as it provides more security guarantees. As an obvious assumption, the distribution vector X must be kept hidden from the untrusted servers. Therefore, even if the servers collude with each other and pool their shares, they cannot reconstruct the original values. Attribute values can be reconstructed by the trusted parties who know the distribution vector X. Moreover, the mapping function F in AS5 must be kept secret from the untrusted parties to prevent them from inferring the ordering relation between values.

Arithmetic calculations for sharing and reconstructing secrets in Shamir's scheme in defined over $GF(P)$ where P is a prime number. In AS5, Instead of modular arithmetic calculations, we uniformly distribute share values across a domain using random coefficients that belong to partitions of a specified domain. Having a uniform distribution of shares minimizes the information leakage for the adversary who observes the outsourced data shares. The imposed overhead is to have the share size bigger than the secret size. Theoretically, we need the domain D of share values with the size of $|D| \geq N_{tuple}$ to uniformly distribute N_{tuple} distinct shares across D. N_{tuple} is the maximum number of tuples in the relation (total frequency of values). In practice, having 4-Byte shares provides the possibility of more than four billion distinct values for shares which is enough for many applications. If the server side storage is an important concern, choosing an appropriate domain size for data shares is a trade-off between security and storage cost of the scheme. We plan to investigate more on the size of domain to have a minimum storage cost in addition to achieve desired level of security.

Although the original data distribution is perturbated in AS4, it is vulnerable to statistical analysis as it preserves the ordering relation of attribute values in their corresponding shares. We proposed AS5 as a security extension to AS4 where we change any given distribution of original values to a uniform distribution of shares across a domain. From the information theory viewpoint, uniform distribution has the highest entropy and reveals at least information as possible for the untrusted servers. However, there is an inference possibility in AS5 for the untrusted servers while executing queries. They are able to make inferences about frequency of attribute values using the interval width of satisfying shares. In other words, a group of shares for which the query condition is satisfied, form a partition in the domain of shares that can be mapped onto an attribute value. The untrusted servers can gradually find out the partitions and use their knowledge about outsourced data to find the hidden mapping function. To prevent this kind of inference, the client must frequently submit fake queries without taking care of their results. These queries target invalid intervals of shares (with respect to the mapping function) to mislead the servers of making valid inferences about associating requested partitions of shares to original values. Submitting fake queries together with the order obfuscated mapping function is a countermeasure against share alignment, which is an attack described in [18] as a security limitation of using secret sharing for outsourcing scenario.

There is another attack scenario considering the knowledge of system's query workload. While AS5 defends the confidentiality of outsourced data against adversaries powered by *a priori* knowledge of data distribution, it is susceptible to statistical inferences if we assume that adversaries are powered by *a priori* knowledge of system's query workload. Although the aforementioned fake queries can be considered as a countermeasure for this attack, it requires more investigation on the way of generating queries and their submission frequencies. To have a secure solution under the assumption of adversaries with prior knowledge about submitted queries, we should extend our approach to a solution with private information retrieval in which access confidentiality is preserved.

7   Conclusion

In this paper we proposed an approach for outsourcing confidential data to honest but curious servers. We used the idea of secret sharing to split a database relation into several parts, in the granularity of attribute values, and outsource each part to an honest but curious server.

We proposed a searchable secret sharing scheme in which the ordering relation between values is preserved in their corresponding shares, while the distribution of shares is different from the original data distribution. However, the order preserving property makes the scheme vulnerable to statistical analysis. We extended our searchable secret sharing scheme to be secure against adversaries powered by *a priori* knowledge of outsourced data to tolerate statistical analysis on data shares.

Our approach is promising in terms of provided security, as it uses secret sharing with strong theoretic background, and supporting different kinds of queries. Less computation time of secret sharing and reconstruction compared to encryption and decryption operations in encryption-based approaches, the additive homomorphism property of Shamir secret sharing scheme, and not to having false hits in returned results of the servers are of the main reasons for its efficient query processing support. Nevertheless, we should extend our solution to support character data considering pattern matching queries over string attributes.

While our approach targets data confidentiality with honest but curious servers, dealing with the correctness of query results is another issue for active adversaries who can manipulate outsourced data shares. We plan to investigate on share integrity and query result correctness using redundant shares in our threshold scheme for data outsourcing scenario.

References

[1] Hacigümüş, H., Iyer, B., Li, C., Mehrotra, S.: Executing SQL over Encrypted Data in the Database-Service-Provider Model. In: ACM SIGMOD International Conference on Management of Data, SIGMOD 2002, New York, USA, pp. 216–227 (2002)

[2] Agrawal, R., Kiernan, G.G.: System and method for fast querying of encrypted databases. US Patent 7,395,437: Google Patents (2008)

[3] Canim, M., Kantarcioglu, M.: Design and analysis of querying encrypted data in relational databases. In: The 21st Annual IFIP WG 11.3 working Conference on Data and Applications Security, pp. 177–194 (2007)

[4] Zhang, Y., Li, W.-X., Niu, X.-M.: Secure cipher index over encrypted character data in database. In: 2008 International Conference on Machine Learning and Cybernetics, pp. 1111–1116 (2008)

[5] Zhu, H., Cheng, J., Jin, R., Lu, K.: Executing Query over Encrypted Character Strings in Databases. In: 2007 Japan-China Joint Workshop on Frontier of Computer Science and Technology (FCST 2007), pp. 90–97 (2007)

[6] Damiani, E., Vimercati, S.D.C., Jajodia, S., Paraboschi, S., Samarati, P.: Balancing Confidentiality and Efficiency in Untrusted Relational DBMSs. In: Proceedings of the 10th ACM Conference on Computer and Communication Security, CCS 2003, New York, USA, pp. 93–102 (2003)

[7] Li, J., Omiecinski, E.R.: Efficiency and security trade-off in supporting range queries on encrypted databases. In: 19th Annual IFIP WG 11.3 Working Conference on Database and Applications Security, pp. 69–83 (2005)

[8] Aggarwal, G., Bawa, M., Ganesan, P., Garcia-Molina, H., Kenthapadi, K., Motwani, R., Srivastava, U., Thomas, D., Xu, Y.: Two Can Keep a Secret: A Distributed Architecture for Secure Database Services. In: 2nd Biennial Conference on Innovative Data Systems Research (2005)

[9] Samarati, P., Ciriani, V., Foresti, S.: Keep a Few: Outsourcing Data While Maintaining Confidentiality. In: 14th European Conference on Research in Computer Security, pp. 440–455 (2009)

[10] Wiese, L.: Horizontal Fragmentation for Data Outsourcing with Formula-Based Confidentiality Constraints. In: Echizen, I., Kunihiro, N., Sasaki, R. (eds.) IWSEC 2010. LNCS, vol. 6434, pp. 101–116. Springer, Heidelberg (2010)

[11] Soodejani, A.T., Hadavi, M.A., Jalili, R.: k-Anonymity-Based Horizontal Fragmentation to Preserve Privacy in Data Outsourcing. In: Cuppens-Boulahia, N., Cuppens, F., Garcia-Alfaro, J. (eds.) DBSec 2012. LNCS, vol. 7371, pp. 263–273. Springer, Heidelberg (2012)

[12] Ciriani, V., Vimercati, S.D., Foresti, S., Jajodia, S.: Combining Fragmentation and Encryption to Protect Privacy in Data Storage. ACM Transactions on Information and System Security (TISSEC) 13, 1094–9224 (2010)

[13] Ciriani, V., Vimercati, S.D.C.D., Foresti, S., Jajodia, S., Paraboschi, S., Samarati, P.: Fragmentation and Encryption to Enforce Privacy in Data Storage. In: 12th European Symposium on Research in Computer Security, pp. 171–186 (2007)

[14] Agrawal, D., Abbadi, A.E., Emekci, F., Metwally, A.: Database Management as a Service: Challenges and Opportunities. In: 2009 IEEE 25th International Conference on Data Engineering, pp. 1709–1716 (2009)

[15] Hadavi, M.A., Jalili, R.: Secure Data Outsourcing Based on Threshold Secret Sharing: Towards a More Practical Solution. In: VLDB 2010 PhD Workshop, Singapore, pp. 54–59 (2010)

[16] Hadavi, M.A., Noferesti, M., Jalili, R., Damiani, E.: Database as a Service: Towards a Unified Solution for Security Requirements. In: 36th International Conference on Computer Software and Applications, The 4th IEEE International Workshop on Security Aspects in Processes and Services Engineering, Izmir, Turkey, pp. 415–420 (2012)

[17] Shamir, A.: How to Share a Secret. Communications of the ACM 22, 612–613 (1979)

[18] Dautrich, J.L., Ravishankar, C.V.: Security Limitations of Using Secret Sharing for Data Outsourcing. In: Cuppens-Boulahia, N., Cuppens, F., Garcia-Alfaro, J. (eds.) DBSec 2012. LNCS, vol. 7371, pp. 145–160. Springer, Heidelberg (2012)

Configuration Assessment as a Service*

Matteo Maria Casalino, Henrik Plate, and Serena Elisa Ponta

SAP Research Sophia-Antipolis, 805 Avenue Dr M. Donat, 06250 Mougins, France
{matteo.maria.casalino,henrik.plate,serena.ponta}@sap.com

Abstract. Security of systems is most often compromised by misconfiguration rather than a lack of security mechanisms. As a result, configuration validation is of utmost importance within organizations. However, security policies, best-practices, and documentation of vulnerabilities are usually available in natual language and thus configuration validation is usually a manual and error-prone activity. Initiatives such as the Security Content Automation Protocol foster the automation of configuration validation and the exchange of configuration information by providing a standard language. However they only focus on single systems and are not flexible with respect to the creation of new security content. This paper proposes a tool for configuration validation as a service able to assess check and checklists defined over configurations of both generic and specific distributed systems.

1 Introduction

Configuration validation is a common denominator of several critical tasks organizations have to face, such as ensuring compliance with regulatory policies, fulfilling service level agreements, or protecting internal assets from possible attacks. As a consequence, different stakeholders within an organization share the need of checking software's configuration. At the same time this is difficult to achieve as shown by data breach reports such as [1], [2] and projects such as the OWASP Top 10 [3]. Public databases of vulnerabilities, such as NVD [4], and initiatives like the Security Content Automation Protocol (SCAP) [5] already aim at standardizing and automating the configuration validation process, by defining *(i)* languages to describe configuration checks and to-be-checked systems, *(ii)* algorithms to execute the checks and *(iii)* means to share and re-use them across organizations. However, the existing standards and tools lack flexibility. In particular, SCAP and other proprietary solutions focus on the granularity of hosts and operating systems, and as such cannot be easily applied to fine-granular and distributed systems independent from their environment, e.g., Java Web Applications. Furthermore, SCAP does not leverage standards and technologies in the area of system and configuration management, in order to separate check logic and information about configuration retrieval and reducing

---

* This work was partially supported by the FP7-ICT-2009.1.4 Project PoSecCo (no. 257129, www.posecco.eu).

R. Di Pietro et al. (Eds.): DPM 2012 and SETOP 2012, LNCS 7731, pp. 217–226, 2013.

the impact on the performances of productive systems. Such limitations hinder their implementation in many interesting practical use cases.

In this paper we propose a tool for performing configuration validation: *(i)* implementing a SCAP-based language (proposed in [6]), *(ii)* able to check configuration settings of distributed systems, *(iii)* able to execute checks and checklists assessing the status of an IT landscape, *(iv)* available as a service to be invoked manually, periodically or at run-time.

This paper is structured as follows. Section 2 overviews the SCAP languages used within the tool we propose, Section 3 introduces scenarios of practical interest and identifies the challenges for the implementation of a configuration validation service. Section 4 and 5 describe the solution we propose and its evaluation respectively. We conclude in Section 6 with some final remarks.

2   Security Content Automation Protocol

The Security Content Automation Protocol (SCAP) is a suite of specifications that support automated configuration, vulnerability and patch checking, as well as security measurement. SCAP is provided by the National Institute of Standards and Technologies [7], [5]. Among other specifications, SCAP comprises a language for the definition of checklists (XCCDF), a language that allows the specification of security checks to detect misconfiguration (OVAL), and a language for defining classes of platforms (CPE).

The Extensible Configuration Checklist Description Format (XCCDF) is an XML-based language to represent a structured collection of checks. An XCCDF document consists of Rules, each of which corresponds to a recommendation in a piece of guidance. The other structures in XCCDF, e.g., Groups, organize and refine Rules. In addition to supporting the structuring of guidance, XCCDF Rules also contain a check supporting automated processing, e.g., referencing an OVAL definition. An XCCDF interpreter is expected to read the checks and call some external tool that performs the automated check and returns a result value. XCCDF returns *Pass* if the recommendation has been followed and *Fail* if it has not. Thus, XCCDF serves not only as a source for document generation (using XML style-sheets or other tools) but can control a checking tool in evaluating a system against some piece of security guidance.

The Open Vulnerability Assessment Language (OVAL) is an XML-based community standard to promote open and publicly available security content. OVAL checks for the presence of vulnerabilities or desired configuration on a computer system. It provides three XML schemas for *(i)* representing configuration information of systems for testing; *(ii)* analyzing the system for the presence of the specified machine state (vulnerability, configuration, patch state, etc.); and *(iii)* reporting the results of the assessment. OVAL allows to define how to check for configurations by means of: definitions, tests, objects, and states. Each definition defines a boolean combination of tests. Each test defines an evaluation over an object and (optionally) a state. The object represents the configuration information that has to be collected from a system and then evaluated against the expected values defined within the state. The OVAL test can require to assess if the object exists in the system under analysis and/or how many of the collected objects satisfy the state.

The Common Platform Enumeration (CPE) is an XML-based standard to define names representing classes of platforms that can be compared in order to establish if two names are equal, if one of the names represents a subset of the systems represented by the other, or if the names represent disjoint sets of systems. Moreover a CPE Dictionary associates checks, e.g., OVAL definitions, to CPE Names. By running such checks on a system it is thus possible to establish if the system is part of the class represented by the corresponding CPE Name. Finally a CPE language allows to define more complex platforms as logical combinations of CPE Names.

3 Challenges

In this section, we describe two examples of such scenarios that pose challenges to the automatic validation of configurations in distributed environments. We then drive requirements for implementing a configuration validation tool.

Reporting on Holistic Systems Security (S1). This scenario captures the problem of assessing if a particular, possibly distributed, system environment is subject to vulnerabilities and is compliant with respect to policies or best practices.

Upon disclosure of a new security vulnerability, the susceptibility of systems has to be investigated. The conditions for a successful exploitation often concern specific configuration settings of the affected software, as well as the specific usage context and system environment. The formalization of both these aspects within machine-readable *vulnerability checks* would decrease time and effort required to discover a system vulnerability, and at the same time increase the accuracy with which the presence of vulnerabilities can be detected. It is important to check whether system configurations follow best-practices. Today, these are often described in prose and evolve over time, thus requiring continuous human intervention. Examples are the Tomcat security guide from OWASP [8], the SANS recommendations for securing Java deployment descriptors [9], and the United States Government Configuration Baseline (USGCB) for IT products. To foster the re-use of security knowledge, such *best-practice checks* as well as the aforementioned *vulnerability checks* should be specifiable in a generic standardized fashion and should support the flexible adoption to a specific environment. This means that the conditions for checks to be applicable to certain generic classes of software components need to come along with the checks.

Another case where compliance needs to be checked, is when configurations enforce a given security policy. In fact, in many cases, the security policies of an organization are enforced by the means of specific software configuration. The latter specifies a set of mandated settings that an organization expects to be active in its system. For instance an access control list is a piece of configuration which implements a designed access control policy. Any deviation from the mandated settings may reflect a violation of the policies, hence it must be detected. As such, *policy compliance checks* strongly reflect a particular system and environment and are therefore authored by the end-user organization rather than by externals. Clearly, they have to be executed on specific target instances and not on a class of targets which satisfy a common selection condition. As a consequence, in this case the information of the actual system where the check have to be applied (i.e. the set of instantiated targets), has to be provided with the check.

Described categories of checks are likely to be combined to form checklists, which produce reports on the security status of an entire IT infrastructure. Checklists are mainly useful to help humans understand, score and prioritize checks results. Such checklists can be executed either manually by system administrators or as part of the automated provisioning lifecycle of the software components managed by a Configuration Management Systems (CMS).

Runtime Configuration Validation (S2). This scenario consider the need of applications to automatically check configurations at runtime. Applications involved in the delivery of business services may leverage configuration validation as a preventive security control, whereby the detection of insecure or non-compliant system states is linked to the applications' runtime. By using any of the above-discussed configuration checks, it is possible to check if the entire system and application stack comply with an expected state before allowing the execution. In case misconfigurations are present, this information can be used to evaluate the risks of providing or denying the service. A service provider of web services may decide, for instance, to forbid at runtime the execution of a secure-sensitive web application, in case its container's configuration does not comply with the company security standards. In this case, differently from (S1), the applications need to execute single configuration checks rather than structured checklists.

The SCAP standards, and OVAL in particular, are not sufficient to cope with the aforementioned scenarios as, e.g., they limit configuration validation to the scope of a single system. The limitations of SCAP languages and proprietary languages and tools, e.g., Nessus, are extensively discussed in [6], where a SCAP-based configuration validation language supporting the mentioned types of checks is defined. However, an actual implementation of an interpreter for such an extended language has yet several challenges to face. First, generic targets that scope given checks must be instantiated by the interpreter, i.e. the actual systems to be checked are to be identified (cf. *vulnerability* and *best-practice checks*). In other cases already instantiated targets have to be provided (cf. *policy compliance checks*). Second, configurations must be collected from such potentially distributed targets, but flexibility is needed to directly provide the tool with the configuration settings to be checked either. In the following, we list requirements that a tool implementing the language presented in [6] has to deal with. Notice that all requirements but partly (C5) focus on aspects which are not supported by SCAP-enabled tools.

(C1) The tool must identify instances of generic targets within an IT infrastructure.

(C2) The tool must be able to collect configuration settings from distributed
systems.

(C3) The tool must be able to collect configuration settings in alternative ways,
herewith reusing existing system management procedures and technologies,
e.g., WS-Management and Java Management eXtensions (JMX), as well as
from systems hosting replicated configuration settings, e.g., a Configuration
Management Databases defined by the IT Infrastructure Library.

(C4) The actual source of configuration information must be customizable for
the administrator of a given domain.

(C5) Given the configuration settings of possibly distributed software components, the tool shall be able to compute check results according to conditions
formulated over such configuration settings.

(C6) The tool must be able to perform periodic or on-demand automated configuration validation, as well as allow different stakeholders to submit checks
to be performed.

4 Configuration Validation as a Service

COAS (Configuration Assessment as a Service) is a prototype for the automated
validation of configuration settings. The tool assesses if discrepancies between
predefined and actual configuration values exist over systems within a landscape.
This is done by relying on the language and approach defined in [6].

The Configuration Validation Language (CVL) proposed therein allows for the
specification of *check definitions* which combine OVAL definitions with information about the software component they apply to, i.e., the *target definition*. A
target definition is a generalization of CPE Names as it may use additional properties than the fields composing a CPE Name and can express relations among
distributed software components. Sets of check definitions can be processed by
a component (**TD Evaluator**) able to identify instances of the software components to which they apply by querying a data source containing information
about the IT infrastructure. The resulting artifacts are *system tests* defining
where each OVAL test have to be performed. System tests can also be provided
in input if the instantiated check targets are known. Then, an OVAL processor
collects configuration settings, evaluates the tests and provides *check results*.

In this paper we further enrich the configuration validation language of [6]
with the concept of checklist. A *checklist* defines the set of check definitions to
be executed and allows to organize them in groups. As groups can be included
in groups themselves, a checklist allows to define an arbitrary complex hierarchy of check definitions. This feature is supported by the XCCDF standard
(cf. Section 2). The CVL supports the vulnerability, best-practice, and policy
compliance checks described in Section 3 as it allows to define check definitions
for generic classes of software components, as well to bind a check to specific
software instances, both for single and distributed systems.

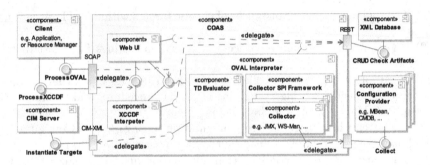

Fig. 1. COAS Component Diagram

A component diagram of COAS is shown in Figure 1. The COAS tool can be consumed as a Web Service or through the COAS Web User Interface (`Client` and `WebUI` components, resp.). As such configuration validation can be automatically triggered, e.g., periodically or upon activity, or manually executed. In this way COAS copes with the challenge (C6) described in Section 3. The fact that the tool is available as a service is a key feature as it allows the validation of configurations of distributed systems within a single check or checklist. Moreover, being application independent, it provides a unique approach for configuration validation that can be integrated into legacy tools, hereby establishing consistency among tools that are run by different people and at different application lifecycle phases within an organization.

Both in case of automatic and manual invocation, it is possible to execute a set of OVAL-based check definitions or an XCCDF checklist. OVAL-based check definitions specify the logic for assessing whether a configuration in place is compliant to best practices and application-specific policy requirements, and subject to known vulnerabilities. XCCDF checklists define a structured collection of check definitions. In the following we refer to check definitions as checks. The checks or checklist may be complemented by a set of system tests to univocally identify which systems to test, and the configuration files containing the settings to be tested. If the former is not provided, the information is retrieved by querying the `CIM Server` component. The latter can be obtained through the `Collector` components interfacing the `Configuration Providers`.

The flow diagrams of COAS in different scenarios are shown in Figure 2. The flow in Figure 2a shows how COAS addresses the scenario (S1) of Section 3. In this scenario COAS received the request to process an XCCDF checklist either from the WebUI or a client resource manager, e.g., a CMS. The result of the interpretation are checks which are then passed to the OVAL interpreter. Once the results are available, a report is shown. The flow in Figure 2b shows the usage of COAS for (S2). In this case COAS is used to test a set of checks and thus the OVAL interpreter is invoked directly by an application. According to the results, the execution of the application may be aborted. In both cases, the flow diagram of the OVAL interpreter is the same and the flow depends on which artifacts were submitted. First the OVAL interpreter establishes if system tests are provided. This is the case for checking policy compliance checks where the target

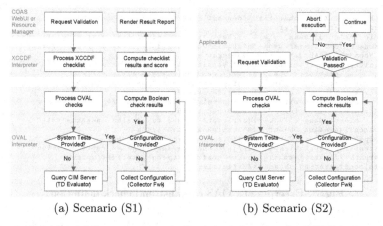

(a) Scenario (S1)   (b) Scenario (S2)

Fig. 2. COAS workflow per scenario (invariant flow for the OVAL interpreter)

system is known. If they are not available, COAS retrieves the information of which systems have to be validated (cf. vulnerability and best-practice checks). This is done by querying a CIM Server, e.g., OpenPegasus [10], which maintains a model — according to the Common Information Model [11] — of the managed IT infrastructure under analysis. The CIM Server is a possible implementation of the Data Source described in [6]. In particular we assume that each system in the CIM Server has information equivalent to what is contained in a CPE Name. Thus COAS retrieves the systems to be validated by matching the CPE Name defined within the OVAL definition with the CPE Name of each system of the landscape (cf. challenge (C1)). This is a simplification w.r.t. [6] carried out to make the adoption of COAS within industrial environments smoother before implementing the full functionalities. Once the systems are retrieved, COAS determines if the configuration settings were already provided. If this is not the case, a collector is used to retrieve configuration settings through a configuration provider. The latter can, for instance, access the file system to retrieve a configuration file, call an application management API implemented by the system, e.g., JMX, or use centralized management systems, e.g., a Configuration Management Database. By providing several collectors able to collect from different systems, COAS addresses the challenge (C2). Moreover (C3) is also fulfilled as a collector can rely on management software as well as retrieve from systems hosting replicated configurations. Which collector to use is defined through a configuration file listing all the available collectors, the OVAL objects they can collect, and the parameters they require (e.g., the targets' IP addresses). This can be customized by the system administrator as required by (C4). Parameters ideally are retrieved from the CIM Server, when targets are instantiated. In case a parameter is missing, a system administrator has to insert it manually. Upon collection, the OVAL interpreter computes the OVAL results by comparing collected objects and OVAL states according to the standard specification (cf. challenge (C5)). The result is a boolean value assessing if best practices and specific configuration are in place and if vulnerabilities are present.

```
1   <!-- From the XCCDF checklist document -->
2   <Group id="xccdf_sans_group_2">
3     <Rule id="xccdf_sans_rule_2"><check system="http://oval.mitre.org/XMLSchema/oval">
4       <check-content-ref name="oval:sans.sec:def:3" /></check></Rule></Group> ...
5   <!-- From the OVAL definition document -->
6   <definition class="vulnerability" version="1" id="oval:sans.sec:def:3"
7                platform="cpe:2.3:jsr77_webmodule:*:*:*:*:*:*:*:*:*">
8     <criteria comment="Session configuration tests" operator="OR">
9       <criterion test_ref="oval:sans.sec:tst:7"
10         comment="Transmit cookies securely" negate="true" />
11      <criterion test_ref="oval:sans.sec:tst:8"
12         comment="Deny client-side scripts access to cookies" negate="true" /> ...
13     <xmlconfiguration_object id="oval:sans.sec:obj:8">
14       <cpe>cpe:2.3:jsr77_webmodule:*:*:*:*:*:*:*:*:*</cpe>
15       <conf:representation>http://java.sun.com/xml/ns/j2ee</representation>
16       <xpath>//session-config/cookie-config/http-only/text()</xpath>
17     </xmlconfiguration_object></definition>
```

Fig. 3. Excerpts of COAS checklist and check definition

5   Evaluation

The main contribution of our work lays in the extension of several SCAP languages and a prototypical implementation to support configuration checks in distributed systems, and to strictly separate check logic and configuration collection in order to leverage existing IT service management tools and APIs. The COAS evaluation is therefore done by comparing the artifacts and efforts related to performing a given evaluation scenario with COAS or the current version of the SCAP languages and tools, e.g. openSCAP (http://open-scap.org).

To evaluate COAS, we have created one XCCDF checklist comprising two groups, the first containing three rules pointing to OVAL definitions representing the OWASP recommendations, the second containing four rules for the SANS best practices. Each OVAL definition referenced by the XCCDF checklist covers a set of guidelines for one or several configuration files, e.g., the *server.xml* configuration file for Apache Tomcat, or the *web.xml* deployment descriptor for Java Web applications. As an example, Figure 3 shows an excerpt of both the XCCDF checklist and the OVAL definition checking for session-related parameters. The OVAL definition combines several tests, whereby `oval:sans.sec:tst:8`, for instance, looks at the HTTP-ONLY flag to prevent access to cookies via client-side JavaScript. The corresponding OVAL object of type `xmlconfiguration_object` retrieves the actual configuration value with help of XPath. Lines 7 and 16 contain a `platform` attribute to indicate that OVAL definition and object apply to any Web module according to JSR77 (hereby extending CPE Naming, which only distinguish 3 coarse-granular kinds of platforms). Note that both documents do not comprise details concerning the target environment. Hence, they can be very well shared among security practitioners and organizations to be executed in arbitrary environments. When executing this checklist through COAS' WebUI, the OVAL interpreter sends CIM-XML queries to a CIM Server to identify all systems that match the given CPE name (cf. Figure 2). In the above case, the CIM Server returns all JSR77 Web modules, independent from the server they are deployed in. Then, a JMX collector is used to retrieve their deployment descriptors through MBean calls, leveraging the fact that J2EE compliant

```
1    <!-- From the XCCDF checklist document -->
2    <Group id="xccdf_sans_group_2">
3      <Rule id="xccdf_sans_rule_2"><check system="http://oval.mitre.org/XMLSchema/oval">
4        <check-export export-name="oval:sans.sec:var:1" value-id="path1"/>
5        <check-content-ref name="oval:sans.sec:def:3" /></check></Rule>
6      <Value id="path1" operator="equals" type="string">
7          <value>/usr/local/tomcat/webapps/srm/WEB-INF</value></Value></Group>...
8    <!-- From the OVAL definition document -->
9    <definition class="vulnerability" version="1" id="oval:sans.sec:def:3">
10     <external_variable datatype="string" id="oval:sans.sec:var:1" version="1"/>
11     <xmlfilecontent_object id="oval:sans.sec:obj:8">
12       <filepath var_ref="oval:sans.sec:var:1" />
13       <xpath>//session-config/cookie-config/http-only/text()</xpath>
14     </xmlconfiguration_object></definition>
```

Fig. 4. Excerpts of standard SCAP checklist and check definition

application servers offer JMX support, and avoiding the installation of dedicated collector software on target hosts.

Considering the current version of the SCAP languages and tools, the evaluation scenario can be realized by writing a generic OVAL definition using the xmlfilecontent_object, where the path to a Web application's deployment descriptor is determined by an external variable. Variable values are specified at the level of XCCDF rules, and passed as input to the OVAL processor (Figure 4 exemplifies XCCDF and OVAL content comparable to the excerpts presented in Figure 3). Since SCAP focuses on single hosts, a XCCDF checklist must be produced for every host of Web applications, even if such hosts logically belong together, e.g., in the context of clustering. Their production can be achieved by writing a custom CIM Server client that groups Web applications correspondingly. Moreover, the fact that such checklists are environment-specific hamper the sharing of checklists across organizations. The execution of several checklists and checks on the basis of file system paths requires a dedicated infrastructure to collect the actual configuration files on each host. Other collection methods are not considered by the respective OVAL object. Last, the creation of an overall compliance report requires to merge the individual checklist results, including the computation of respective compliance scores.

The comparison shows that COAS artifacts are environment-independent, herewith supporting the exchange and reuse of security knowledge across specific environments. The current version of SCAP requires environment-specific checklists to realize the presented evaluation scenario. Furthermore, while COAS is flexible with regard to the collection of configuration data, standard SCAP objects prescribe the collection method. This inflexibility, which results from SCAP's focus on single hosts, hinders the use of existing tools for application management but requires the installation of a dedicated collection infrastructure on target hosts. Moreover, the prescribed access method may not always work, in particular for fine-granular and container-managed objects such as Web applications, which do not necessarily reside in the file system. Also, COAS allows the assessment of overall-compliance with a given best-practice, while SCAP only supports the assessment per single host, one after the other.

6   Conclusion and Future Work

Configuration validation constitutes an important task for organizations to improve the security of their systems. This paper introduces practical scenarios where this is exemplified and identifies corresponding challenges that a tool for configuration validation should cope with, particularly in the scope of distributed system architectures. A discussion follows on the reasons why state-of-the-art tools do not suffice to this purpose and motivates the design and implementation of a novel architecture for Configuration Assessment as a Service (COAS). A preliminary evaluation of the proposed approach shows that it fulfills the envisaged requirements and can effectively improve the current practice.

Future work includes improving our evaluation methodology, e.g., by comparing the execution time of COAS with the quality of work and time required when a skilled security administrator in possession of the prose guidelines performs the same checks. Furthermore, we plan to support more complex conditions for the applicability of checks on targets, e.g., expressing relations over distributed targets, which is not possible with standard CPE Names.

References

1. 7Safe, the University of Bedfordshire: Uk security breach investigations report 2010 (2010), http://www.7safe.com/breach_report/Breach_report_2010.pdf
2. Verizon: 2009 data breach investigations report. Verizon (2009), http://www.7safe.com/breach_report/Breach_report_2010.pdf
3. Williams, J., Wichers, D.: Top 10 most critical web application security risks. OWASP (2010), https://www.owasp.org/index.php/Top_10_2010-A6
4. NIST: (National vulnerability databases), http://nvd.nist.gov
5. NIST: (Security content automation protocols), http://scap.nist.gov
6. Casalino, M.M., Mangili, M., Plate, H., Ponta, S.E.: Detection of configuration vulnerabilities in distributed (web) environments. In: Proceedings of Security and Privacy in Communication Networks, SecureComm (to appear, 2012)
7. Waltermire, D., Quinn, S., Scarfone, K.: The technical specification for the security content automation protocol (scap): Scap version 1.2. NIST (2011), http://csrc.nist.gov/publications/nistpubs/800-126-rev2/SP800-126r2.pdf
8. OWASP: (Securing Tomcat), https://www.owasp.org/index.php/Securing_tomcat
9. SANS Security: (Seven security (mis)configurations in java web.xml files), http://software-security.sans.org/blog/2010/08/11/security-misconfigurations-java-webxml-files
10. Opengroup: (OpenPegasus), https://collaboration.opengroup.org/pegasus/?gpid=18
11. Distributed Management Task Force: Common information model (CIM) core model. White Paper DSP0111, DMTF (2000)

Automated Smartphone Security Configuration

William M. Fitzgerald, Ultan Neville, and Simon N. Foley

Cork Constraint Computation Centre, University College Cork, Ireland
{wfitzgerald,u.neville}@4c.ucc.ie, s.foley@cs.ucc.ie

Abstract. Smartphones host operating systems that are on a par with modern desktop environments. For example, Google *Android* is a mobile operating system that is based upon a modified version of the Linux OS. Notwithstanding traditional threats to mobile phones, threats to desktop environments are also applicable to smartphones. Management of security configurations for the end-user has, to date, been complex and error-prone. As a consequence, misconfiguration of and/or a poor understanding of a security configuration may unnecessarily expose a smartphone to known threats. In this paper, a threat-based model for smartphone security configuration is presented. To evaluate the approach, a prototype smartphone security agent that automatically manages security configurations on behalf of the end-user is developed. A case study based on firewall access control demonstrates how automated security configuration recommendations can be made based on catalogues of countermeasures. These countermeasures are drawn from best-practice standards such as NIST 800-124, a guideline on cell phone and PDA security and NIST 800-41-rev1, a guideline on firewall security configuration.

1 Introduction

Modern smartphones with their processing power, operating systems and the wide variety of applications (apps for short) are on a par with modern desktop environments [25]. This has resulted in smartphones being used in a variety of domains from a personal device (such as for voice, Web browsing, Email and social media) to enterprise, medical and military domains [31]. The technological advances and the usage of smartphones in a variety of domains is not without its security implications. In addition to traditional mobile phone threats, threats to desktop environments are also applicable to smartphones [10,17,25]. For example, Malware threats such as DroidDream [8], a Android Market trojan app used to maliciously root Android smartphones, are on the increase [25].

Smartphones may host a variety of security mechanisms such as anti-virus, app monitoring and firewalls. In practice, security mechanisms are either disabled or configured with an open access policy [20]. Configuration of smartphone security mechanisms, for example a firewall, is typically performed by non-technical end-users. As a consequence, an effective security configuration may be hampered by a poor understanding and/or management of smartphone application requirements. Mis-configuration, may result in the failure to adequately provide

R. Di Pietro et al. (Eds.): DPM 2012 and SETOP 2012, LNCS 7731, pp. 227–242, 2013.

smartphone app services. For example, an overly-restrictive firewall configuration may prevent normal interaction of network-based apps. An overly-permissive firewall configuration, while permitting normal operation of the app, may leave the smartphone vulnerable to attack, for example, across open ports or malicious payloads.

Smartphones operate in mobile network environments and deploying security configuration for a global set of threats is not practical. For example, a smartphone may in one scenario be connected to an enterprise WiFi network, an open access WiFi network or a 3g operator network. Thus, the deployment of smartphone security configurations must be dynamic in order mitigate the relevant threats within a given scenario. That is, what may be considered a threat in one scenario may not be a threat in another. Consider the scenario where a security configuration that permits a set of apps (such as gaming and social media apps) within a home network environment may not longer be permitted within an enterprise or teleworking environment. For example, in a teleworking scenario it is considered best practice to permit the use of "*a different brand of Web browser for telework*" and prohibit the use of the everyday Web browser [23].

The contribution of this paper is as follows. A threat-based model for smartphone security configuration is presented. Catalogues of best practice standards for smartphones are encoded within this model. A case study for smartphone firewall configuration management is considered. This research extends the work in [13] by specialising the firewall catalogues of best practice for smartphones and new catalogues of best practice for example NIST 800-114 [23] are developed. A prototype firewall app agent is developed for the Android platform [1] to automatically manage firewall configurations on behalf of the non-expert end-user.

This paper is organised as follows. Section 2 provides an introduction to Linux iptables, the stock Android platform firewall. A threat-based security model for smartphones is presented in Section 3. Section 4 outlines a set of best practice standards that are encoded within the security model. The implementation of the smartphone best practice catalogue is discussed in Section 5. A prototype automated firewall app for the Android platform is discussed in Section 6. Related research is outlined in Section 7 and Section 8 concludes the paper.

2   Background

The Android platform is a software framework for mobile devices such as smartphones and tablet PC's, and is based upon a modified version of the Linux OS. This section provides an overview of the Linux iptables firewall.

2.1   Linux Iptables

Netfilter [14] is a framework that enables packet filtering, Network Address Translation (NAT) and packet mangling for Linux. A front-end called *iptables* is used to construct firewall rules that instruct Netfilter how to interpret packets.

As a firewall, iptables has stateless, stateful and application-layer packet filtering capabilities.

An iptables (firewall, NAT or mangle) rule requires the specification of a *table*, a *chain*, the accompanying *filter conditions* on packet fields that must be matched and an associated *action* outcome. With iptables, there are four tables: `filter`, `nat`, `mangle` and `raw`. A table is a set of chains and it defines the global context for common packet handling functionality. For example, the `filter` table defines the set for firewall rules, while the `nat` table defines the set of rules concerned with Network Address Translation. A chain is a set of rules that define the local context within a table. Rules within a chain are applied to the context defined both by the chain itself and the particular table. This paper focuses on the firewalling aspects of iptables, that is, the `filter` table. There are three built-in chains defined within the `filter` table that govern traffic being routed to (INPUT chain), from (OUTPUT chain) and beyond the firewall itself (FORWARD chain). Figure 1 illustrates the iptables packet traversal according to its associated chain. The reader is referred to [14,29] for further information.

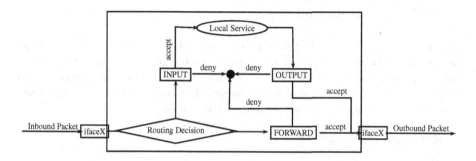

Fig. 1. Linux iptables Filter Table Chain Packet Traversal

Example iptables rule syntax. The following (whitelist) iptables access-control rule states that outbound (`OUTPUT -o wifi`) TCP packets (`-p tcp`) that have originated from the Firefox Web browser (`-m owner --uid-owner 10101`) executing on the smartphone destined to any external Web server (`-d 0.0.0.0/0 --dport 80`) will be permitted (`-j ACCEPT`).

```
iptables -A OUTPUT -o wifi -p tcp -d 0.0.0.0/0 --dport 80 -m
owner --uid-owner 10101 -j ACCEPT
```

3   Security Threat Model

The security *State* of a smartphone represents attributes of a phone in use that may introduce vulnerabilities and/or influence how threats are mitigated. These attributes may correspond to, for example, user-preferences (indicating for instance, security risk appetite), or how the smartphone is currently used (for instance, a WiFi or 3g Internet connection). While there is potentially a large number of such attributes, for this research we focussed on five which, in-part based on best practice recommendations, have a direct impact on Network Access Controls on smartphones.

Network Interface Attribute A smartphone may be configured to communicate over WiFi and/or 3g networks. Note that a network interface configuration of WiFi and 3g, combined, corresponds to a tethering state. Let *Iface* define the set ($\mathbb{P}\, X$ denotes powerset of X) of possible network interface configurations as

$$Iface \mathbin{\widehat{=}} \mathbb{P}\{\mathsf{wifi}, \mathsf{3g}\}$$

Network Connection Attribute Different network connections may be trusted in different ways. For example, a WiFi connection providing WPA2-Enterprise security may be considered trusted, while an open WiFi connection in a default configuration may be considered untrusted. Let *NetConn* define the possible network connection attribute states.

$$NetConn \mathbin{\widehat{=}} \{\mathsf{trusted}, \mathsf{untrusted}\}$$

Risk Appetite Attribute This user-selected attribute reflects the level of risk that the user is willing to accept [5]. An appetite of hungry means that the user is willing to take risks and is satisfied with minimal countermeasures necessary to mitigate threats. An appetite of averse means that the user wishes for the most extensive countermeasures, for example, defense in depth.

$$RiskAppetite \mathbin{\widehat{=}} \{\mathsf{averse}, \mathsf{hungry}\}$$

Note, future research may consider additional risk appetite granularity and include minimalist, cautious and open attributes [5].

Teleworking Attribute This attribute indicates whether the smartphone is used in teleworking, or non-teleworking mode. We define:

$$Telework \mathbin{\widehat{=}} \{\mathsf{true}, \mathsf{false}\}$$

Battery Level Attribute The experimental results outlined in Section 6.1 found that the number of firewall rules can have an impact on battery consumption. Therefore, when battery power is low, a user with a low risk appetite may wish to reduce the number of rules in the firewall. Thus, we include the current battery level in the state of the smartphone.

$$Battery \mathbin{\widehat{=}} \{\mathsf{lo}, \mathsf{hi}\}$$

Security State The set of all possible states of the smartphone is defined as:

$$State \mathbin{\widehat{=}} Iface \times NetConn \times RiskAppetite \times Telework \times Battery$$

Threats Let the set *Threat* define the set of all known threats (of interest). A threat is a potential for violation of security [27] and in this paper we are interested in network-based threats that can be mitigated using a firewall. For example, xmas $\in$ *Threat* represents the threat of a TCP half scan [18]. Let *threatens* define the relationship between threats and states.

$$threatens : Threat \leftrightarrow State$$

where, $threatens(t, s)$ indicates that threat t is considered to threaten a smartphone in state s. For example, we would expect a smartphone in a state with the WiFi interface enabled and an open WiFi connection to be threatened by xmas.

Countermeasures Let the set *Countermeasure* define the set of known countermeasures. For example, given firewall access-control rule:

$$f_1 = \langle \texttt{iptables -A INPUT -p tcp --tcp-flags ALL NONE -j DROP} \rangle$$

then $f_1 \in$ *Countermeasure*. In this paper, we are interested in iptables-based countermeasures, and therefore, members of this set are described in terms of iptables command syntax. This could be generalized to the threat ontology described in [13] in order to extend to other kinds of countermeasures. Let relation *mitigates* define the threats mitigated by a countermeasure:

$$mitigates : Countermeasure \leftrightarrow Threat$$

where $mitigates(c, t)$ indicates that countermeasure c mitigates threat t. For example, the firewall rule f_1 above mitigates the threat of a TCP half scan, that is, $mitigates(f_1, \text{xmas})$.

Blacklists and Whitelists as threats A blacklist is used to prevent the smartphone from initiating (outgoing) connections to known malicious hosts. Thus, a blacklisted host with IP address A is represented as a threat, denoted $\text{blist}_o(A)$, within our model. This threat is mitigated by blocking outgoing packets to A at the smartphone firewall, that is,

$$mitigates(\langle \texttt{iptables -A OUTPUT, ... ,-d } A, \texttt{ DROP} \rangle, \text{blist}_o(A))$$

A similar interpretation is used for blacklisting inbound (INPUT and FORWARD chains) connections.

A networked Android app has associated port(s), and whitelists are used to define the apps that are permitted to engage in network connections. Whitelists are modelled in terms of threats, whereby a firewall that does not permit a whitelisted app to access the network is treated as a threat and the countermeasure is a corresponding 'ACCEPT' iptables rule. For example, a whitelisted app that is permitted to initiate outgoing connections on port P is vulnerable to threat denoted $\text{wlist}_o(P)$, and we have countermeasure:

$$mitigates(\langle \texttt{iptables -A OUTPUT, ... ,--sport } P, \texttt{ ACCEPT} \rangle, \text{wlist}_o(P))$$

A similar interpretation is used for whitelisting inbound IP addresses and ports.

Countermeasure Deployment The countermeasures deployed on a smartphone should mitigate all threats for its current state. We define a deployment operation

$$deploy : State \rightarrow \mathbb{P} \; Countermeasure$$

which selects a suitable set of countermeasures $deploy(s)$ for the state s. The next section describes our current implementation for this operation, however, in general, it should uphold the following property.

$$\forall s : State; \; t : Threats \mid threatens(t, s)$$
$$\Rightarrow \exists c : Countermeasure \mid c \in deploy(s) \wedge mitigates(c, t)$$

In this paper, the implementation of $deploy(s)$ assumes the correct sequencing of the firewall rules. Future research will consider *structural analysis* techniques (for example [11] when automatically generating an anomaly-free firewall configuration. For example, the removal of redundant access-control rules.

4   Catalogues of Best Practice

A best practice standard is a high-level document that defines a set of recommended best practices (countermeasures) to protect sensitive and critical system resources. The following best practice standards NIST 800-41 [30], NIST 800-41rev1 [22], NIST 800-124 [16], NIST 800-114 [23] and NIST 800-153 [28] for firewall access control have been encoded within our model. For example, Table 1 and Table 2 illustrate excerpts of recommended best practice for general firewall configuration [30] and firewall configuration whilst teleworking [23] respectively. Note, the reader is referred to [13] for the systematic approach used to identify and categorise recommended firewall best practice in terms of detailed threats and mitigating countermeasures (iptables rules). Detailed threats identified are an interpretation of the recommendation descriptions.

The advantage of developing catalogues from best practice standards is two fold. Firstly, it provides a basis to automatically generate compliance-driven firewall configurations. Secondly, it provides a basis with which to consider real-world firewall access-control rules. For example, NIST 800-41rev1 recommendation FBPr1-2 in Table 1 recommends that (spoofed) packets arriving on an external interface claiming to have originated from either of the three RFC1918 reserved internal IP address ranges should be dropped. Such traffic indicates a denial of service attack typically involving the TCP syn flag. NIST 800-114 recommendation TBP-1 in Table 2 recommends that in a teleworking scenario a firewall should be configured with a whitelist of trusted network-based apps.

Catalogues developed as part of this work extends the catalogues in [13] specialised for mobile devices. New best practice catalogues, namely NIST 800-124 [16], NIST 800-114 [23] and NIST 800-153 [28] have also been developed.

The catalogue of firewall best practice for smartphones developed as part of this research consists of one hundred and thirty five distinct threat and counter-measure pairs. Future research will extend this catalogue to include knowledge about other best practice standards. Note, the majority of the catalogue countermeasures are templates. For example, the following firewall access-control rule outlined in NIST 800-114 recommendation TBP-2 (Table 2)

```
iptables -A OUTPUT -m owner --uid-owner $appUID state --state
NEW,ESTABLISHED,RELATED -j ACCEPT
```

is a template countermeasure that has an UID variable $appUID which is modified each time an access-control rule is applied to a locally executing network-based smartphone app.

Table 1. Extract of NIST-800-41-Rev1: Guidelines on Firewalls & Firewall Policy

ID	Recommendation Description	
FBPr1-1	*"deny by default policies should be used for incoming TCP and UDP traffic."* [23].	
	Threat	**Countermeasure**
	No inbound default deny policy	iptables -P INPUT DROP
	No outbound default deny policy	iptables -P OUTPUT DROP
	No forward default deny policy	iptables -P FORWARD DROP
ID	**Recommendation Description**	
FBPr1-2	*"...an invalid source address for incoming traffic or destination address for outgoing traffic ...should be blocked"* that is *"An IPv4 address within the ranges in RFC 1918"* and *"An address that is not in an ...IANA ...range"* [22]	
	Threat	**Countermeasure**
	Inbound local 192.168.0.0/16 Src IP Pkt	iptables -A INPUT -s 192.168.0.0/16 -j DROP
	Outbound local 192.168.0.0/16 Dst IP Pkt	iptables -A OUTPUT -d 192.168.0.0/16 -j DROP
	Inbound forward 192.168.0.0/16 Src IP Pkt	iptables -A FORWARD -i $iface -s 192.168.0.0/16 -j DROP
	Outbound forward 192.168.0.0/16 DstIP Pkt	iptables -A FORWARD -o $iface -d 192.168.0.0/16 -j DROP
	Inbound local 10.0.0.0/8 Src IP Pkt	iptables -A INPUT -s 10.0.0.0/8 -j DROP
	Outbound local 10.0.0.0/8 Dst IP Pkt	iptables -A OUTPUT -d 10.0.0.0/8 -j DROP
	Inbound forward 10.0.0.0/8 Src IP Pkt	iptables -A FORWARD -i $iface -s 10.0.0.0/8 -j DROP
	Outbound forward 10.0.0.0/8 DstIP Pkt	iptables -A FORWARD -o $iface -d 10.0.0.0/8 -j DROP
	Inbound local 172.16.0.0/12 Src IP Pkt	iptables -A INPUT -s 172.16.0.0/12 -j DROP
	Outbound local 172.16.0.0/12 Dst IP Pkt	iptables -A OUTPUT -d 172.16.0.0/12 -j DROP
	Inbound forward 172.16.0.0/12 Src IP Pkt	iptables -A FORWARD -i $iface -s 172.16.0.0/12 -j DROP
	Outbound forward 172.16.0.0/12 Dst IP Pkt	iptables -A FORWARD -o $iface -d 172.16.0.0/12 -j DROP
ID	**Recommendation Description**	
FBPr1-3	*"Organizations should also block ...IP source routing information"* [22]	
	Threat	**Countermeasure**
	SSRR firewall bypass.	iptables -A FORWARD -m ipv4options --ssrr -j DROP
	LSRR firewall bypass.	iptables -A FORWARD -m ipv4options --lsrr -j DROP
ID	**Recommendation Description**	
FBPr1-4	*"Organizations should also block ...directed broadcast addresses"* [22]	
	Threat	**Countermeasure**
	Inbound Local directed broadcast	iptables -A INPUT -d x.x.x.255 -j DROP
	Outbound Local directed broadcast	iptables -A OUTPUT -d x.x.x.255 -j DROP
	Inbound forward directed broadcast	iptables -A FORWARD -i $iface -d x.x.x.255 -j DROP
	Outbound forward directed broadcast	iptables -A FORWARD -o $iface -d x.x.x.255 -j DROP
ID	**Recommendation Description**	
FBPr1-5	To limit Denial of Service *"a firewall might redirect the connections made to a particular inside address to a slower route if the rate of connections is above a certain threshold."* [22]	
	Threat	**Countermeasure**
	Inbound forward DoS to tethered device	iptables -A FORWARD -i $iface -d $lanIP -m limit --limit $x/s --limit-burst $y -j ACCEPT

Table 2. Extract of NIST-800-114: User's Guide to Securing External Devices for Telework and Remote Access

ID	Recommendation Description	
TBP-1	Construct an access control whitelist of locally hosted applications trusted for telework network access: *"tele-workers should install and use only trusted software"* [23].	
	Threat	**Countermeasure**
	Inbound local application whitelist traffic not permitted	`iptables -A INPUT -m state --state ESTABLISHED,RELATED -j ACCEPT`
	Outbound local application whitelist traffic not permitted	`iptables -A OUTPUT -m owner --uid-owner $appUID state --state NEW,ESTABLISHED,RELATED -j ACCEPT`
ID	**Recommendation Description**	
TBP-2	...*"silently ignore unsolicited requests sent to it, which essentially hides the device from malicious parties."* [23].	
	Threat	**Countermeasure**
	ICMP ping network scan	`iptables -A INPUT -p icmp -j DROP`
	TCP XMAS network scan	`iptables -A INPUT -p tcp --tcp-flags ALL ALL -j DROP`
	TCP Null network scan	`iptables -A INPUT -p tcp --tcp-flags ALL NONE -j DROP`
	TCP Syn Fin network scan	`iptables -A INPUT -p tcp --tcp-flags SYN,FIN SYN,FIN -j DROP`
	TCP Rst Fin network scan	`iptables -A INPUT -p tcp --tcp-flags FIN,RST FIN,RST -j DROP`
	TCP Port 0 network scan	`iptables -A INPUT -p tcp --dport 0 -j DROP`
		`iptables -A INPUT -p tcp --sport 0 -j DROP`
ID	**Recommendation Description**	
TBP-3	*"Use a different brand of Web browser for telework"* [23].	
	Threat	**Countermeasure**
	Regular Web browser usage	`iptables -A OUTPUT -p tcp --dport 80 -m owner --uid-owner $untrustedHTTPUID -j DROP`
	Intended telework Web browser usage not permitted	`iptables -A OUTPUT -p tcp --dport 80 -m owner --uid-owner $trustedHTTPUID state --state NEW,ESTABLISHED -j ACCEPT`
ID	**Recommendation Description**	
TBP-4	*"Configuring primary applications to filter content and stop other activity that is likely to be malicious"* [23]	
	Threat	**Countermeasure**
	Outbound local unfiltered traffic	`iptables -A OUTPUT -m -string --algo bm --string '$filterString' -j DROP`
ID	**Recommendation Description**	
TBP-5	*"Personal firewalls should be configured to log significant events, such as blocked and allowed activity"* [23]	
	Threat	**Countermeasure**
	No inbound local audit control	`iptables -A INPUT -j LOG --log-level 7`
	No inbound forward audit control	`iptables -A FORWARD -i $iface -j LOG --log-level 7`

5   Firewall Catalogue Implementation and Deployment

In the smartphone implementation of the catalogue for firewall best practice, we have:

$$isMemberOfCategory : Threat \leftrightarrow Category$$

where $isMemberOfCategory(t, c)$ indicates that threat category c includes threat t. Table 3 illustrates a fragment of the threat classification developed. The relationship between security states and threats is implemented as:

$$threatenState : Category \leftrightarrow State$$

where $threatenState(c, s)$ indicates the set of threats categorised within category c threaten the smartphone in state s. The implementation of the *threatens* relation from the model defined in Section 3 is given by the relational composition $isMemberOfCategory \, \S \, threatenState$.

Table 3. Extract of Threat Catalogue

Detailed Threats	Threat Category
FBPr1-2 Threats	*Spoofing*
FBPr1-2 Threats	*DoS*
FBPr1-4 Threats	
FBPr1-5 Threats	
TBP-2 Threats	*Scanning*
FBPr1-3 Threats	*Source Routing*
TBP-4 Threats	*Malicious Content*
FBPr1-1 Threats	*Promiscuity Level*
TBP-1 Threats	
TBP-3 Threats	
TBP-5 Threats	*Non-Audit*

5.1 Threat Taxonomy

Having analysed the best practice standards outlined previously, threats where categorised in the following way: *Spoofing, Denial of Service, Scanning, Source Routing, Malicious Content, Promiscuity Level* and *Non-Audit*. Note, other threat categories could be chosen, for example Microsoft's STRIDE classification [15].

Threats classified as *Spoofing* are those that refer to IP address spoofing. For example, threats described by the FBPr1-2 recommendation in Table 1 are considered spoofing threats.

Denial of Service threats are those that have the capability of flooding network resources. For example, in Table 1 FBPr1-4 recommends IP address broadcast mitigation and FBPr1-5 recommends threshold-limiting to mitigate connection-based denial of service threats. Note, recommendation FBPr1-4 currently considers the more common /24 network broadcast range only and does not consider additional network broadcast ranges for example /25 or /26.

Network information disclosure threats, for example those outlined by NIST 800-114 recommendation TBP-2 in Table 2, are classified as *Scanning* threats.

Source Routing, for example NIST 800-41rev1 recommendation FBPr1-3 in Table 1, is a threat classification where an attacker may specify the route the packet takes through the network and has the potential to bypass firewalls.

From a firewall configuration perspective, *Malicious Content* threats are those that contain malformed application payloads such as URL parameters, form elements and SQL queries. Malicious Content may be mitigated in a variety of ways for example blacklisting known TCP/UDP ports or performing Deep Packet Inspection (DPI) on known malicious signatures. Recommendation TBP-4 in Table 2 illustrates a template DPI firewall rule that mitigates outbound Malicious Content threat communication.

Threats that are categorised as *Promiscuity Level* are those that refer to IP address (and/or port) reachability in terms of unintended whitelisting or backlisting. That is, an overly-promiscuous firewall configuration (unintended whitelisting), while permitting normal operation of the smartphone app, may expose other apps to unintended threats. Whilst, an overly-restrictive firewall configuration (unintended blacklisting) may prevent normal interoperation of services with the resulting failure of the smartphone app. An example of this is outlined by NIST 800-114 recommendation TBP-1 Table 2.

Non-Audit threats are those that do not log relevant traffic communications. From a compliance perspective, it is considered best practice to log traffic for auditing purposes. For example, NIST 800-114 recommendation TBP-5 in Table 2 outlines teleworking auditing threats and their corresponding firewall mitigation.

5.2   Security States

The (5-tuple) security *State* space defined in Section 3 provides a total of sixty-four states in which a smartphone may operate. However, we argue that certain attribute combinations are not valid and therefore the security state space may be reduced to twenty-eight. Table 4 illustrates the valid security state matrix.

In this paper, we assume that firewalls under the control of trusted network providers such as a 3g operator are compliant with best practice standards such as [22, 30]. A user with a risk appetite of hungry, for example state-7 in Table 4, may therefore not be concerned about threats of IP spoofing, denial of service, port scanning and/or source routing where it is assumed the upstream trusted network provider firewalls are mitigating these kinds of threats.

While the trusted network providers provide firewall mitigation against threats of IP spoofing, denial of service, port scanning and source routing, it is considered best practice to also restrict access at the smartphone firewall as part of a defense in depth strategy [22]. As a consequence, security states where the user has risk appetite of averse such as state-1, state-3, and state-25 are said to be also threatened by those threats (Table 4).

The number of firewall access-control rules can have an impact on battery consumption (Section 6.1). Therefore, when battery power is lo, despite a user having specified a risk appetite of averse, the number of access-control rules will be reduced. Security state state-4 is an example, where there is a trade-off of security in depth such as IP spoofing to conserve battery power. Effectively a smartphone with a lo battery where a user has specified a risk appetite of averse will default to a state where the user is not concerned as much about his/her smartphone's security configuration (risk appetite of hungry). For example security states state-15 and state-16.

In contrast, if the smartphone is operating in a state that involves teleworking, for example security states state-1, state-5 and state-10, then a defense in depth strategy will be applied to mitigate all threat categories regardless of the network connection, the risk appetite or the battery level. This is in keeping with NIST 800-114 [23] best practice recommendations.

5.3   Automatic Generation of Firewall Configurations

Suitable firewall configurations are automatically generated for each smartphone security state using the information contained in Table 4 and the threat catalogues (for example Table 2). Consider security states state-1 and state-3 where teleworking and non-teleworking occurs. The firewall configuration generated for

Table 4. Matrix of valid Security States

State	Interface	Network Connection	Risk Appetite	Teleworking	Battery	Spoofing	DoS	Scanning	Source Routing	Malicious Content	Promiscuity Level	Non-Audit
state-1	wifi	trusted	averse	true	hi	x	x	x		x	x	x
state-2	wifi	trusted	averse	true	lo	x	x	x		x	x	x
state-3	wifi	trusted	averse	false	hi	x	x	x		x	x	
state-4	wifi	trusted	averse	false	lo						x	
state-5	wifi	trusted	hungry	true	hi	x	x	x		x	x	x
state-6	wifi	trusted	hungry	true	lo	x	x	x		x	x	x
state-7	wifi	trusted	hungry	false	hi						x	
state-8	wifi	trusted	hungry	false	lo						x	
state-9	wifi	untrusted	averse	true	hi	x	x	x		x	x	x
state-10	wifi	untrusted	averse	true	lo	x	x	x		x	x	x
state-11	wifi	untrusted	averse	false	hi	x	x	x		x	x	x
state-12	wifi	untrusted	averse	false	lo	x	x	x		x	x	
state-13	wifi	untrusted	hungry	true	hi	x	x	x		x	x	x
state-14	wifi	untrusted	hungry	true	lo	x	x	x		x	x	x
state-15	wifi	untrusted	hungry	false	hi						x	
state-16	wifi	untrusted	hungry	false	lo						x	
state-17	3g	trusted	averse	true	hi	x	x	x		x	x	x
state-18	3g	trusted	averse	true	lo	x	x	x		x	x	x
state-19	3g	trusted	averse	false	hi	x	x	x		x	x	
state-20	3g	trusted	averse	false	lo						x	
state-21	3g	trusted	hungry	true	hi	x	x	x		x	x	x
state-22	3g	trusted	hungry	true	lo	x	x	x		x	x	x
state-23	3g	trusted	hungry	false	hi						x	
state-24	3g	trusted	hungry	false	lo						x	
state-25	3g,wifi	trusted	averse	false	hi	x	x	x	x	x	x	
state-26	3g,wifi	trusted	averse	false	lo					x	x	
state-27	3g,wifi	trusted	hungry	false	hi						x	
state-28	3g,wifi	trusted	hungry	false	lo						x	

security state state-1 will in addition to mitigating threat categories that similarly threaten security state state-3, include audit-based access-control rules in compliance with NIST 800-114 recommendation TBP-5 in Table 2.

While various security states may have been related to the same threat categories, the firewall configuration generated for each security state may be different. Consider security states state-3 and state-25 in Table 4. Both security states are threatened by threats within the category IP spoofing. However, the specific/individual IP spoofing threats such as those described by NIST 800-41rev1 recommendation FBPr1-2 in Table 1 will differ for both security states. Because security state state-25 is concerned with tethering, it must consider additional firewall access-control rules that mitigate IP spoofing threats along its iptables FORWARD chain to protect smartphone tethered devices [16]. Note, in a tethering scenario, the smartphone is an internet gateway for tethered devices.

There are also scenarios where permitted (trusted) network apps in one security state may no longer be permitted in another security state. For example, trusted networked apps such as telnet, FTP or games for example in security state-3 may alternate between whitelists and blacklists in a security state that involves teleworking, for example security state-1. This is ensures compliance with NIST 800-114 recommendation TPB-1 in Table 2. That is, only trusted apps defined in accordance with the enterprise-level teleworking security policy may be permitted. Note, while it may be advantageous to deny access to telnet in an enterprise network for a risk appetite of averse (for example state-3), it may also be acceptable to restrict access to telnet for trusted clients (IP address whitelist) while in a home network environment.

In a teleworking scenario, access control is not just defined at the level of IP addresses or TCP/UDP ports, for example prohibiting port 23 (Telnet) or port 80 (HTTP). Access control is also applied at the application level such as UID and Layer-7 filtering. For example, NIST 800-114 recommendation TBP-3 in Table 2 recommends that different Web browsers such Firefox and Google Chrome, should be used in teleworking and non-teleworking scenario. This is to minimise the Web browser used for for general use, which may have become compromised with malicious plugins, from communicating in a teleworking scenario. A set of suitable iptables countermeasures that filter using the owner-match extensionare defined.

6   Prototype Android Firewall Agent App

A prototype automated agent app is developed that manages the smartphone firewall configuration on behalf of the non-expert end-user. The test-bed used for the prototype was an *Android 2.1, Revision 1* platform on a HTC hero smartphone with an ARMv6 528MHz processor and a lithium-ion battery with a capacity of 1350 mAh. Note, a rooted and customised Android ROM image that includes additional iptables extensions such as *string match* and *recent match*. Figure 2 illustrates examples of the Graphical User Interface developed as part of the prototype. The user settings interface is illustrated in Figure 2a where a user may specify his/her risk appetite and whether or not the smartphone will

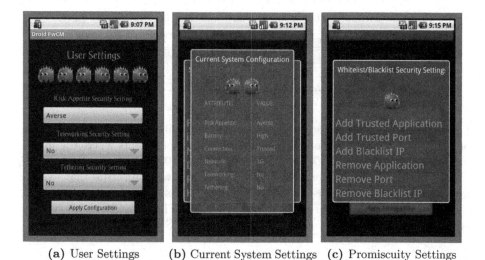

(a) User Settings   (b) Current System Settings   (c) Promiscuity Settings

Fig. 2. Example Screenshots of Firewall Agent App Graphical User Interface

operate as a tether or in telework environment. Figure 2b, illustrates an example of the current security state. The interface with which a user may define his/her whitelist and blacklist for (un-) trusted apps is illustrated in Figure 2c.

6.1   Firewall Configuration and Battery Consumption Correlation

A number of preliminary experiments where carried out to evaluate the impact of firewall configuration size with respect to battery consumption. The experimental set-up was as follows. Firewall configurations of 0, 500 and 1000 access-control rules where deployed on the smartphone for each of the three experiments. The battery capacity for each experiment was 100% (fully charged). A 2GB TCP data-stream was transmitted to the smartphone (from an external machine) where packets are not matched until the last access-control rule in the firewall configuration. Each experiment was repeated 5 times to get the average battery depletion rate. Table 5 illustrates the preliminary findings. The first column reflects the firewall configuration size. The second column reflects the remaining (average) battery level after each experiment. The results indicate that during periods of network communication, the firewall configuration size does have an impact on battery consumption. For example, to filter a 2GB data-stream, a firewall with a 1000 access-control rules consumed 36% more battery charge than a firewall with 0 access-control rules.

While in practice, smartphones do not tend to process large data-streams and/or be configured with a large number of access-control rules, these experiments were intended to stress test the smartphone. Note, in future work, an additional set of experiments that may reflect a more real world scenario will be considered. For example, a 20MB-90MB data-stream range (from Web

Table 5. Correlation between Firewall Configuration and Battery Level

# of Access-Control Rules	Battery Level
0	88%
500	70%
1000	52%

browsing to video streaming [2]) tested against firewall configurations consisting of 0, 100 and 250 access-control rules. In addition, experiments where the initial battery capacity is set to 50% and 25% rather than 100% should be considered. As the battery nears a capacity of minimal charge, we conjecture that even a modest sized rule-set consisting a few hundred access-control rules will have a significant impact on battery consumption [7,9,21]. Therefore, the battery level is considered within the security model presented in Section 3.

7 Related Research

There are a number of existing techniques for smartphone Malware and intrusion detection [25]. For example, the authors in [24] adopt a static analysis approach to detect Malware. A machine learning approach is taken in [26] to detect application anomalies. There are a number of Android apps for firewall configuration management, for example DroidWall [3] and WhipserMonitor [4]. However, the level of access control granularity provided is limited. For example, only egress access control (iptables OUTPUT chain) to whitelist or blacklist apps is considered. The model presented in this paper considers fine-grained ingress (iptables INPUT and FORWARD chains) and egress (iptables OUTPUT and FORWARD chains) access control. In existing works, Android firewall configuration is performed on an ad-hoc basis. For example, there are no recommended guidelines for whitelisting or blacklisting apps in a given security context. In contrast, the automatic generation of smartphone firewall configurations in this research is guided by best practice recommendations.

There are a number of existing techniques that can be used by enterprise security administrators to generate [12,13], query [13,19] and perform structural analysis [6,11] on network access control configurations. In this research, we do not consider these approaches and assume that smartphone firewall configurations are conflict free. Future research will explore the effectiveness of the approach for firewall configuration management outlined in [13] with respect to the Android platform.

8 Conclusion

This paper presented a formal model for smartphone security configuration. Catalogues developed as part of this work extends the catalogues in [13] specialised for mobile devices and provided a basis with which to evaluate the security model. The prototype firewall app agent may be used by non-expert end-users to automatically generate suitable firewall configurations that are compliant with best practice.

Future research will extend the current modelled smartphone firewall catalogues and consider for example catalogues related to smartphone Malware and intrusion detection mitigation. In addition, a future iteration of our (preliminary) security model may consider additional attributes. For example, the physical location of a smartphone where it may be advantageous to prevent a smartphone operating in a teleworking scenario for example when it is located in a certain (untrusted) country or region of the world.

Acknowledgement. The authors would like to thank the anonymous reviewers for their valuable feedback. This research has been supported in part by Science Foundation Ireland grant 08/SRC/11403.

References

1. http://www.android.com/
2. http://www.vodafone.ie/internet-broadband/internet-on-your-mobile/usage/
3. http://code.google.com/p/droidwall/
4. http://www.whispersys.com/
5. Thinking about risk - managing your risk appetite: A practitioner's guide. HM Treasury on behalf of the Controller of Her Majesty's Stationery Office (HMSO) (November 2006)
6. Al-Shaer, E.S., Hamed, H.H., Boutaba, R., Hasan, M.: Conflict Classification and Analysis of Distributed Firewall Policies. IEEE Journal on Selected Areas in Communications 23(10), 2069–2084 (2005)
7. Balanza, M., Abendan, O., Alintanahin, K., Dizon, J., Caraig, B.: Battery Discharge Characteristics of Wireless Sensor Nodes: An Experimental Analysis. In: 2nd Conference on In Sensor and Ad Hoc Communications and Networks. IEEE (September 2005)
8. Balanza, M., Abendan, O., Alintanahin, K., Dizon, J., Caraig, B.: DroidDreamLight Lurks Behind Legitimate Android Apps. In: 6th International Conference on Malicious and Unwanted Software (MALWARE) (April 2011)
9. Buennemeyer, T.K., Gora, M., Marchany, R.C., Tront, J.G.: Battery Exhaustion Attack Detection with Small Handheld Mobile Computers. In: IEEE International Conference on In Portable Information Devices (PORTABLE) (May 2007)
10. Chin, E., Felt, A.P., Greenwood, K., Wagner, D.: Analyzing inter-application communication in android. In: 9th International Conference on Mobile Systems, Applications, and Services (MobiSys), ACM, USA (2011)
11. Cuppens, F., Cuppens-Boulahia, N., García-Alfaro, J.: Detection and Removal of Firewall Misconfiguration. In: IASTED International Conference on Communication, Network and Information Security (CNIS) (November 2005)
12. Cuppens, F., Cuppens-Boulahia, N., Sans, T., Miège, A.: A Formal Approach to Specify and Deploy a Network Security Policy. In: 2nd Workshop on Formal Aspects in Security and Trust (FAST) (August 2004)

13. Foley, S.N., Fitzgerald, W.M.: Management of Security Policy Configuration using a Semantic Threat Graph Approach. Journal of Computer Security (JCS) 19(3) (2011)
14. Gheorghe, L.: Designing and Implementing Linux Firewalls with QoS using netfilter, iproute2, NAT and l7-filter. PACKT Publishing (October 2006)
15. Hernan, S., Lambert, S., Ostwald, T., Shostack, A.: Uncover Security Design Flaws Using The STRIDE Approach, http://microsoft.com/
16. Jansen, W., Scarfone, K.: Guidelines on Cell Phone and PDA Security: Recommendations of the National Institute of Standards and Technology. NIST-800-124 (2008)
17. Khadem, S.: Security issues in smartphones and their effects on the telecom networks. MSc Dissertation, Chalmers University of Technology, University of Gothenburg, Sweden (August 2010)
18. Lyon, G.: NMAP Network Scanning: Official Nmap Project Guide to Network Discovery and Security Scanning. Insecure LLC, CA, United States (2008)
19. Marmorstein, R., Kearns, P.: A Tool for Automated iptables Firewall Analysis. In: USENIX Annual Technical Conference, Freenix Track, pp. 71–81 (April 2005)
20. Ruggiero, P., Foote, J.: Cyber threats to mobile phones. TIP-10-105-01, United States Computer Emergency Readiness Team (US-CERT) (April 2010)
21. Saha, B., Goebel, K.: Modeling Li-ion Battery Capacity Depletion in a Particle Filtering Framework. In: Annual Conference of the Prognostics and Health Management Society, San Diego, CA, USA (September 2009)
22. Scarfone, K., Hoffman, P.: Guidelines on Firewalls and Firewall Policy: Recommendations of the National Institute of Standards and Technology. NIST Special Publication 800-41, Revision 1 (September 2009)
23. Scarfone, K., Souppaya, M.: User's Guide to Securing External Devices for Telework and Remote Access: Recommendations of the National Institute of Standards and Technology. NIST-800-114 (2007)
24. Schmidt, A.D., Bye, R., Schmidt, H.G., Clausen, J., Kiraz, O., Yüksel, K.A., Camtepe, S.A., Albayrak, S.: Static analysis of executables for collaborative malware detection on android. In: Proceedings of the 2009 IEEE International Conference on Communications, ICC 2009. IEEE Press, Piscataway (2009)
25. Shabtai, A., Fledel, Y., Kanonov, U., Elovici, Y., Dolev, S., Glezer, C.: Google android: A comprehensive security assessment. In: Security and Privacy, vol. 8(2). IEEE Computer Society (March 2010)
26. Shabtai, A., Kanonov, U., Elovici, Y., Glezer, C., Weiss, Y.: "andromaly": a behavioral malware detection framework for android devices. J. Intell. Inf. Syst. 38(1) (February 2012)
27. Shirey, R.: RFC 2828: Internet Security Glossary (May 2000), http://ietf.org
28. Souppaya, M., Scarfone, K.: Guidelines for Securing Wireless Local Area Networks (WLANs): Recommendations of the National Institute of Standards and Technology. NIST-800-153 (2012)
29. Suehring, S., Ziegler, R.L.: Linux Firewalls, 3rd edn. Novell Publishing (2006)
30. Wack, J., Cutler, K., Pole, J.: Guidelines on Firewalls and Firewall Policy: Recommendations of the National Institute of Standards and Technology. NIST-800-41 (2002)
31. Wei, X., Gomez, L., Neamtiu, I., Faloutsos, M.: Malicious Android Applications in the Enterprise: What Do They Do and How Do We Fix It? In: Workshop on Secure Data Management on Smartphones and Mobiles, Washington D.C (April 2012)

On the Detectability of Weak DoS Attacks in Wireless Sensor Networks

Denise Dudek

Institute of Telematics,
Karlsruhe Institute of Technology, Karlsruhe, Germany
denise.dudek@kit.edu

Abstract. Anomaly detection can be used to detect malicious attacks in wireless sensor networks. Because of the autonomous nature of many sensor network scenarios, it is desirable to use an auto-configuring anomaly detector. To accomodate the indeterministic wireless environment, the anomaly detection must also be able to adapt to changing conditions. This work presents a dynamic learning extension for a pre-exisiting, auto-configuring anomaly detection system for WSNs. Adaptability always results in possibilities for an attacker to exploit the adapting system; however, no quantitative analysis of this has been yet performed in a WSN scenario. This paper explores the trade-off between adaptability and exploitability of the system. The paper also shows that adaptability does not guarantee better false positive error rates for all attacks.

Keywords: wireless sensor networks, traffic anomaly detection, Markov chains.

1 Introduction

Wireless sensor networks (WSNs) are prone to fall victim to malicious attacks for several reasons: first, the communication medium can be easily accessed even by an external attacker with no need to access or compromise the sensor nodes themselves. Second, the resource constraints typical for WSNs leave them particularly vulnerable to brute force attacks, the most prominent of which are Denial of Service (DoS) attacks. While many attacks can be thwarted by cryptographically protecting the network's communication, DoS attacks cannot be prevented by such means; however, detecting Denial of Service attacks while they are occurring can provide valuable information to the network operator. For this reason, the problem of detecting malicious attacks in wireless sensor networks has been studied in a number of works up to date.

Out of the two principal categories of attack detection systems – i.e., *signature based* and *anomaly based* systems – anomaly based detection is the viable option in sensor networks. This is due to the fact that signature based systems require heavy maintenance in terms of signature databases, which a WSN might not be able to provide; more importantly, however, signature based systems are not capable of detecting previously unknown attacks. Many attacks, and DoS

R. Di Pietro et al. (Eds.): DPM 2012 and SETOP 2012, LNCS 7731, pp. 243–257, 2013.

attacks in particular, do not by definition contain strings that can be used as signatures. If such signatures occur, they are a by-product of wide-spread attack tools; to date, there are no such tools specifically designed for sensor networks. In contrast to signature systems, anomaly based systems define normal communication traffic by means of a traffic model; deviations from that norm are then identified as traffic *anomalies*. DoS attacks are accompanied by traffic anomalies. The choice of traffic modeling defines what anomalies can be detected, and consequently how well an attack detection system performs.

One major issue in anomaly based attack detection is trading off *adaptability* and *exploitability*. Adaptability is defined as the capability of the system to adapt the traffic model to changes in the observed communication traffic. In general, adaptability enables an attack detection system to autonomously improve its configuration during runtime. In the case of WSNs, adaptability is especially desirable due to the indeterministic properties of the communication medium. Exploitability, on the other hand, describes to what degree an attacker in possession of knowledge of the detection system can use its functionality in order to launch undetectable attacks. Adaptability *always* introduces exploitability, since by definition it does not exclude changes in the communication traffic that accompany attacks. A subtle enough attack can always go "under the radar" of an adaptable anomaly based attack detection system.

To the best of the author's knowledge, a quantitative analysis of adaptability versus exploitability has not been performed in a WSN scenario yet. This paper provides such an analysis. For this purpose, the lightweight Markov chain based attack detection scheme presented in [1,2] is extended by a dynamic learning subsystem that enables adaptability.

The remainder of this paper is organised as follows: in section 2 the basic attack detection system is introduced and briefly compared to existing work. Section 3 explains the dynamic learning extension to the original system and introduces the relevant parameters. Section 4 describes the scenario setup and attacker model used to evaluate the system. Evaluation results are presented in section 5. A conclusion is given in section 6.

2   Markov Chain Based Anomaly Detection

This section describes the Markov chain anomaly detection system. It gives an overview of its basic structure and principles as well as briefly compares this anomaly detection approach with existing schemes.

2.1   Principles of Functionality

A Markov chain C can be described as $C = \{I, P\}$, where I is a set of k states and P is a k-dimensional stochastical transition matrix, i.e., all its coefficients p_{ij} are non-negative and $\sum_{j=1}^{k} p_{ij} = 1$, for all i. A Markov chain describes a time-discrete process that transitions between states at every $t \in \mathbb{N}_0$.

For anomaly detection, time is divided into equal-length observation intervals, and communication traffic is perceived as a sequence of states. Each observed state is an abstract description of the traffic at time t of its observation. One way to describe traffic is by measuring a certain set of *traffic features* as a time series X. The feature space is potentially multi-dimensional. In the following, d denotes the dimensionality of the feature space, that is, each $x \in X$ is a d-dimensional vector of observed feature values. Examples for features describing traffic include the number of messages received during an interval at various layers of the communication stack, messages sent, number of clear channel assessments, etc.

As described in [2], a state in the Markov chain is defined as a set of similar observations. To determine states, the nodes observe the traffic features during a *learning phase*. It is assumed that during the learning phase, no attack occurs, and that therefore the learning phase is representative of the normal traffic that can be expected from the WSN application. At the end of the learning phase, each node possesses a time series X of such observations. This time series is then partitioned into k *clusters* that each correspond to a state of the Markov chain. In order to avoid state space explosion and in order to ensure a certain accuracy of the transition matrix, k should be configured depending on the length of the learning phase n in such a way that it scales in $O(\sqrt{n})$ only.

Once the states are defined, the observations in X can be classified as belonging to some state in I. The classification results, combined with the chronological ordering of X can be used to determine the transition matrix P of the Markov chain. The calculation of the transition matrix concludes the creation of the traffic profile describing the normal traffic.

To account for observations far outside the normal range, the traffic profile is extended by so-called *bolster states*. Bolster states are states that are assumed whenever an observation cannot reasonably be classified as belonging to one of the states in I. To determine this, each state in I needs to define *state boundaries*. Out of several options of doing so, this proposal defines the state boundary as a spheroid around the state *centroid* – i.e., around the average value of the observations in the according cluster. The spheroid's radius r is determined by the average distance ς of those observations from the centroid as $r = 3\varsigma$. The rationale behind this is that if the distance is normally distributed around 0, then over 99% of the observations belonging to the cluster fall into this spheroid. With that in mind, if an observation is made that does not lie within the boundaries of any state in I, it is assigned to a bolster state.

The transition matrix is modified to account for bolster states such that the probability p_{bolster} of transitioning into a bolster state from any given regular state satisfies $p_{\text{bolster}} << \min (p_{ij}), i, j \leq k$. This way the distortion introduced to the traffic profile by including bolster states is small. It is also ensured that the transition probability is comparably low, which is important for the following reason:

Let W be a time window of w consecutively observed states. That is, w defines a sequence of transition probabilities. The more likely the state sequence in W is, the less unlikely transitions occurred during W. This property can be exploited for anomaly detection: any two consecutive states i, j define a transition probability p_{ij}. Let score_t at time t be defined as

$$\text{score}_t = \Pi_{k=t-w}^{t} p_{ij}. \tag{1}$$

It is evident that the more unlikely transitions occur, the smaller the score value becomes. The time windows of length W during the learning phase provide an idea of what score values can be *expected* in the application scenario. They can thus be used to define a threshold value, below which a score will be considered anomalous. This way, it is possible to detect anomalies in communication traffic after the learning phase: the system detects an anomaly if unlikely transitions in the Markov chain amass within a time window of specifyable length w. The system has been evaluated with regard to false positive and false negative error rates with very good results (c.f. [2]).

2.2   Complexity of the Basic System

This section contains observations on the complexity of the basic Markov chain anomaly detection system as described in the previous section.

The *memory* complexity of the system is as follows. An observation must be stored for each interval of the learning phase. Thus, the memory consumption for observations is in $O(n \cdot d)$, where n is the number of learning phase intervals, and d is the dimensionality of the feature space. Each observation can be represented in $O(d)$ double values. After the learning phase, only the last two observations are stored. For the Markov chain, storing the states themselves requires memory in $O(k \cdot d)$; k is the number of states and is itself in $O(\sqrt{n})$. The matrix itself is in $O(k^2)$, i.e., in $O(n)$. As far as memory consumption is concerned, the learning phase is the bottleneck of the system. Hence, it is especially useful to examine scenarios with short learning phases to accomodate mote-class devices and their memory constraints.

Computational complexity of the anomaly detection varies from phase to phase. During the learning phase, each observation is simply stored; thus, the learning phase is in $O(1)$ computational complexity. At the end of the learning phase, however, the traffic profile is created. The computational complexity of that is in $O((n \cdot d)^3)$. Note that this is a *one-time* effort that does not need to be repeated. The most important aspect of computational complexity concerns the runtime, since this is when the system must be able to operate despite an ongoing attack. The runtime complexity itself is in $O(k \cdot d)$; it is caused by the classification of the current observation to one of the k states. The complexity itself does *not* depend on the actions of an attacker, hence cannot be influenced by an attacker in any way. Computing anomaly scores is done in $O(1)$. This means that overall runtime complexity amounts to $O(\sqrt{n} \cdot d)$.

2.3   Related Work

An often-made mistake when designing anomaly detection in wireless sensor networks is tailoring the anomaly detector to match *exactly* the traffic it is supposed to monitor. WSN scenarios invite this inefficient behaviour because they are usually designed to serve exactly one purpose, thus defining the "shape" of normal traffic much more succintly than other networks. For example, Internet traffic consists of millions of flows among millions of heterogeneous hosts; any description of normal traffic on the Internet must therefore be generic enough to account for this. In WSNs, there is less need for a generic traffic description. However, for all that an anomaly detector in a WSN *can* be highly specialised does not mean that it *ought* to be: it is not a trivial task to find a meaningful configuration for an anomaly detector according to a given WSN application, especially because WSN traffic tends to be strongly affected by indeterministic and unpredictable environmental influences. Rule-based frameworks like [3] do offer generic and potentially rich engines for anomaly detection; however, the rules that make up the traffic model are strongly application-dependent. The authors in [3] state that manually finding a set of rules is hard; they rely on simulation results to specify rule parameters, e.g., threshold values.

Another reason to avoid too specialised anomaly detectors is the effort it takes to adapt an anomaly detection system to different scenarios once an application or another aspect of a scenario changes. For instance, the scheme proposed in [4] depends on a cluster-based topology of the network. It is unclear whether the system can be used in other environments, but surveillance scenarios like [5], e.g., often use a flat grid topology. Other approaches to anomaly detection are based on assumptions as to the protocols used on the lower layers of the communication stack, the hardware, etc. For instance, [6] relies critically on the capability of the network to apply asymmetric cryptography.

Markov chains provide a lightweight means to detect anomalous events in a generic way that allows for use in many application scenarios without making such assumptions. Unlike in [3], there is no need to devise a complex set of rules, since anomalies are captured in terms of stochastic likelihood. The system also does not depend on specifics as to the hardware or topology. However, if hardware-dependent information is available, it is easy to extend the feature space accordingly.

Markov chains have been proposed as a means of anomaly detection in computer networks more than a decade ago. However, these early systems were explicitly designed to detect anomalies on Internet hosts. Consequently, a salient feature of those systems is a large state space, for instance [7]. Wireless sensor nodes however cannot provide the same performance due to their scarce resources, and especially their memory constraints. Therefore, it is necessary to impose boundaries on the state space when attempting to detect anomalies using Markov chains in WSN scenarios.

Both [8] and [9] use Markov chains to detect anomalous events in a WSN scenario. While acknowledging the need for a lightweight solution, they do not impose a strict limitation on the state space size. In [8], state space size depends on the application itself. Thus, applicability of the model depends on (implicit) assumptions the authors make about the application. The work proposed in this paper not only imposes a strict limit on the state space by specifying k explicitly, but it is is also fully independent of the application with regard to state space size.

3 Dynamic Learning

Dynamic learning is a means to improve the configuration of an anomaly detector during the runtime, i.e., after the learning phase is over. In particular, it can be used to improve false positive error rates in scenarios where no attack occurs. Note that this is not always true in scenarios with attacks – as is shown in the evaluation section of this paper.

For an attacker to exploit an adapting system, it must be predictable whether the change in communication traffic caused by an attack will be accepted as legitimate. In case of the anomaly detection described in the previous section, the traffic profile is based on observations. Therefore, the attacker must be able to estimate whether a particular observation will be drawn on to adapt the traffic profile. Their goal will be to cause as many anomalous observations as possible to be accepted. In contrast to this, the anomaly detection system must counteract predictability.

The Dynamic Learning module extends the anomaly detection system as described above by round-based adaptation functionality. It is round-based in that each observation interval is regarded as a "learning round", where the following steps are taken:

1. **Indeterministic initialisation**: according to a random parameter, each node decides whether to consider its current observation for adaptation of the model. If not, the round ends.
2. **Observation-dependent model adaptation**: depending on where – with respect to the regular states – the current observation lies, parameters for the adaptation process are set. Adaptation itself consists of the following parts:
   (a) Adjustment of the state centroids and boundaries
   (b) Adjustment of the transition matrix

3.1 State Centroids and Boundaries

The state centroids are defined as the average of all observations in the according cluster. This means that adapting the centroids is equivalent to re-calculating the average of the original observation set expanded by the current observation o. This is best achieved by estimating the true average via calculation of an exponentially weighted moving average (EWMA). To this purpose, the ith coefficient c_{t_i} of a centroid c_t at time t is adjusted by applying

$$c_{t_i} = \alpha \cdot o_i + (1 - \alpha) \cdot c_{t-1_i}, \qquad (2)$$

where α is a configurable parameter and o_i is the ith coefficient of the current observation o.

Similarly, the state boundaries are adjusted by estimating the average distance ς_t at time t of an observation in the cluster from its centroid as

$$\varsigma_t = \beta \cdot |c_t - o| + (1 - \beta) \cdot \varsigma_{t-1}, \qquad (3)$$

where $|\cdots|$ denotes a metric. The adjsted boundary is then defined as a spheroid around c_t with radius $3 \cdot \varsigma_t$, as indicated in section 2.

Both EWMA parameters α and β are set depending on the relative position of the current observation with regard to the traffic profile state being adapted. The greater α and β, the stronger the influence of the current observation on the whole state. The Dynamic Learning module handles the parameters as follows: if the current observation lies within the $3 \cdot \varsigma$ boundary of the according state, pre-configured default values for α and β are applied. If the current observation is between the $3 \cdot \varsigma$ and $4 \cdot \varsigma$ spheroids of the state, the EWMA parameters are reduced by half their current value. If the current observation is *not* within $4 \cdot \varsigma$, the EWMA parameters are reduced as before, and the observation is discarded. No profile adaptation takes place in the according round.

3.2 Transition Matrix

The transition matrix of the traffic profile is adapted without estimating its coefficients. This is mainly for the reason that estimation would lead to violation of the stochastic matrix property, i.e., $\sum_{j=1}^{k} p_{ij} = 1$ could not be guaranteed for all i. Exact calculation of the transition matrix on the other hand allows to preserve the Markov property of the traffic profile.

To this purpose, each learning round, the last transition is used for matrix adjustment. This is achieved by considering the predecessor state to the current, and then adapting the according row in the transition matrix. To be able to do so, information must be carried along about how often each state has been assumed. Let occ_i be the number of times state i has occurred in total. Let the current state be k, and its predecessor l. Then, at time t the lth row of the matrix is adjusted applying

$$p_{lj_t} = \begin{cases} p_{lj_{t-1}} \cdot \frac{occ_l}{occ_l+1} & \text{where } j \neq k \\ \frac{(p_{lj_{t-1}} \cdot occ_l + 1)}{occ_l + 1} & \text{otherwise.} \end{cases} \qquad (4)$$

Note that because adaptation is done indeterministically, occ_i contains only a random sample of state occurrences. Note further that some additional complexity ensues since it must be made sure that each state is only accounted for once.

After the adjustment of the traffic profile, the likelihood of transitioning into a bolster state p_{bolster} must be re-defined in order to guarantee that $p_{\text{bolster}} \ll \min(p_{ij})$.

3.3 Discussion

It is notable that the Dynamic Learning subsystem does *not* support creation of new states or merging of existing states. Once the basic Markov chain has been determined at the end of the learning phase, the state set I will remain fixed. The reason for this is that varying I can be exploited by an attacker to increase the memory consumption of the system – in the case of adding states –, or to reduce the system's granularity – in the case of merging states. Varying the state set therefore would constitute a DoS vulnerability in itself, which is to be avoided.

The required additional effort for state adjustment in terms of memory and cpu time consumption is nominal, i.e., in $O(d)$, where d is the dimensionality of the feature space. In particular, adaptation of the states does *not* depend on the number of states k, since only one state is adjusted per learning round. Selection of the state to adjust is a matter of classifying the current observation, which must be done irrespective of whether or not the system is adaptable. The additional overhead for adaptation of the transition matrix is in $O(k)$ since the system must count each state's occurrences. However, since the number of states k is small, this is not a major issue. Neither state adaptation nor matrix adaptation change the runtime complexity class.

The indeterministic initialisation of each learning round makes it harder for the attacker to predict whether or not attack traffic will be accepted as legitimate (and if so, by which of the nodes); however, it also slows down the adaptation process itself. This means that scenarios with strong trends in the application traffic itself might cause the system to raise false alarms. This topic is not the focus of this paper and will be explored in future work.

4   Scenario Setup

The anomaly detection system was implemented and tested using the discrete event simulation environment OMNeT++ and the MiXiM framework in order to support the simulation of wireless communication. The following section 4.1 describes the attacker model that was used to simulate attacks. The network and application are described in section 4.2. Section 4.3 explains the relevant simulation parameters.

4.1   Attacker

The attacker uses nodes within the network to launch attacks. They obtain control over those nodes by compromising them. It is a well-established assumption in WSN scenarios that an attacker is able to gain physical access to some percentage of the nodes and to compromise those nodes. The node compromise, among others, comprises reprogramming as well as acquiring all knowledge of that node, including internal states, cryptographic keys, etc.

The attacks themselves are simple: an attack consists of periodically broadcasting messages in a 1-hop environment of the attacking node. More complex attacks are viable, of course, but for the purpose of this evaluation, periodic broadcast is sufficient. Note that for the considered attacks, compromise is not necessary if the attacker can plant their own nodes inside the network or gain access to the channel via other means.

This paper focuses on the limits of detectability and therefore examines particularly *weak* attacks. None of the attacks herein actually exhaust the communication medium. Rather, they are just sufficiently strong to cause a strain on the sensor nodes *energy resources*. While this does not constitute a Denial of Service attack in classical networks, in sensor networks, such an attack might make a significant difference in network lifetime. If energy harvesting is applied, the attacks discussed herein might tip the energy balance so that the network no longer operates in a sustainable state, i.e., it uses more energy than it can harvest. For this reason, weak DoS attacks must be considered important in WSN scenarios.

The aspect of the attacker capturing cryptographic material and thus being able to authenticate as a legitimate node in the network has no bearing on the evaluation and is therefore out of scope of this paper.

4.2   Network

Each sensor node implements the IEEE 802.15.4 Narrowband MAC layer. On the network layer, multihop communication is achieved by probabilistic flooding.

A 2-dimensional feature space was used for anomaly detection. As traffic features, the number of messages received per observation interval by the *application layer* and the *network layer* respectively were chosen. The traffic features were chosen because they are expected to correlate with the presence or absence of a Denial of Service attack. That they are also correlated to one another is a by-product and has no bearing on the detection itself.

A protocol suite designed for a secure area surveillance scenario [5] was used for evaluation. It consisted – among others – of a time synchronisation protocol, a protocol to detect node failure and one for network partition detection. The protocols generate traffic simultaneously, overlaying each other's traffic patterns.

4.3   Simulation Parameters

This section describes the parameters used to evaluate the system proposed in sections 2 and 3 of this paper.

The evaluation goal is to measure up adaptability against exploitability. For this purpose, attacks of varying strength are examined. This is achieved by varying the *sending rate* of the attacker, ranging between 0.5 msgs/s and 4 msgs/s. Note that none of these attacks are strong attacks: none of them are sufficient to exhaust the communication channel. Their main benefit is that legitimate sensor nodes are kept busy receiving messages, thus wasting energy.

The Dynamic Learning subsystem of the anomaly detection is governed by three principal parameters: First, the *adaptivity* parameter defines with what probability an observation is taken into account for adaptation of the traffic profile. Accordingly, it ranges between 0 (no adaptation) and 1 (every interval). Adaptation itself, apart from these two cases, is not done in regular intervals but randomly in order to preclude the attacker knowing beforehand when (and which) nodes accept changes in traffic as normal. Second, the estimation parameters α and β for the adjustment of the state centroids and boundaries define how quickly a state is allowed to change, once the node has decided to adapt at all. Table 1 lists the scenario parameters.

Table 1. Scenario Parameters

Parameter	Value(s)
#nodes	16
Topology	regular grid, 10m distance
Observation interval [s]	5
Learning phase [intervals]([s])	120 (600)
Runtime [intervals] ([s])	240 (1200)
Attack duration [intervals] ([s])	120 (600)
Attack strength [msg/s]	0.5, 1, 1.2, 1.4, 1.6, 1.8, 2, 3, 4
Adaptivity parameter	0, .1, .2, .3, .4, .5, .6, .7, .8, .9, 1.0
EWMA β default	0.2, 0.05
EWMA α default	0.1

The table shows that most of the experimentation was done concerning the attack strength and the Dynamic Learning subsystem. Regarding the latter, a default α value of 0.1 was chosen. The values for β were chosen to represent a case where $\beta < \alpha$, and a case where $\alpha < \beta$. The *adaptivity* was varied within all its possible range.

Regarding the attacker, special focus was put on attacks between 1 and 2 messages per second, because it was found that the anomaly detection behaviour varies most with adaptivity in this region of attack strength.

As far as network size is concerned, the scenario analysed herein is a small multihop scenario with only a limited number of nodes to avoid unnecessary complexity; however, both [1] and [2] have shown that the anomaly detection scales very well with network size. Increasing the network size primarily leads to ambiguity in ground truth: as the attacker's influence is limited, a bigger network will contain nodes that are not, or only very weakly, influenced by the attacker. This makes evaluation very complex.

Attacking nodes were placed deliberately in such a way that all other nodes were affected by the attack. This was to ensure that all nodes can be evaluated with the same underlying *ground truth*. As for evaluation metric, the system was examined with regard to false negative and false positive error rates. Each configuration – consisting of an *attack strength* value, an *adaptivity* value and a value for the EWMA parameter β was run with 20 different random seeds to allow for some measure of statistical relevance.

5 Results

The results with regard to the false negative error rate are shown in fig. 1 and 2 for an EWMA β parameter of 0.2 and 0.05 respectively. Attack strengths are indicated above the plots; the plotted lines represent the error rates.

The figures show a tendency towards higher false negative rates with increasing adaptivity. One of the more interesting results of this experiment is the fact

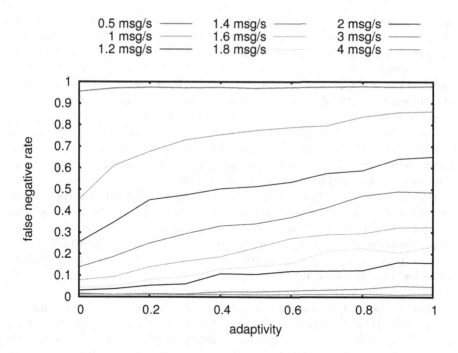

Fig. 1. False negative rate under varying attack strength, $\beta = 0.2$

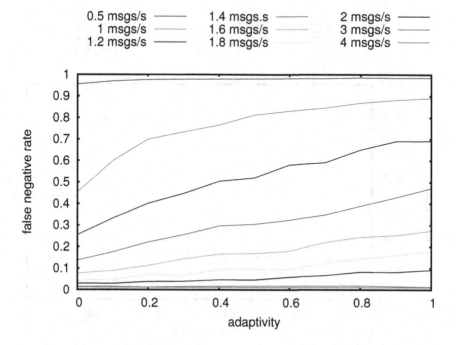

Fig. 2. False negative rate under varying attack strength, $\beta = 0.05$

that an attack with a sending rate of only 0.5 msgs/s is virtually undetectable, with a false negative rate near 100% regardless of adaptivity and EWMA β parameter. With increasing attack strength, adaptivity shows an impact on the false negative error rate. The impact is more evident in weaker attacks – e.g., with EWMA $\beta = 0.2$, false negative rates range from approx. 46% to near 90% with attack strength of 1 msg/s, but only between 2% and 5% for an attack strength of 3 msg/s. The same tendency can be observed for $\beta = 0.05$.

The varying impact of the adaptivity parameter is explained as follows: for weaker attacks, the observations range more closely to what is normal according to the traffic profile. Therefore, attack-influenced observations are generally more easily accepted. The extent to which this happens is governed by the adaptivity parameter. In contrast, stronger attacks cause traffic patterns that do not resemble the traffic profile at all. In this case, whether or not the system adapts is widely determined by the outlier observation position; thus, the value of the adaptivity parameter is less important in scenarios with stronger attacks.

Overall, the false negative rates are comparable for both β settings, if slightly better for $\beta = 0.05$ regarding the stronger attacks.

The according false positive error rates are illustrated in fig. 3 and 4.

The existence of three classes of attacks in the experiment sets was confirmed by the evaluation with regard to false positive error rates. The plot shows that the weak attack (0.5 msgs/s) stays firmly "below the radar" of the system, both scenarios showing no more than 1% false positive errors, regardless of EWMA setting. At the other end of the scale, the scenarios with the strongest attacks

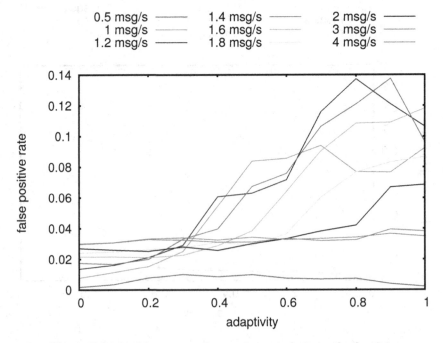

Fig. 3. False positive rate under varying attack strength, $\beta = 0.2$

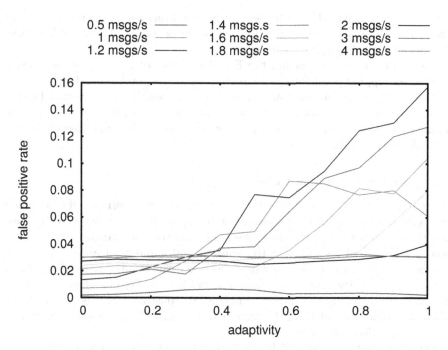

Fig. 4. False positive rate under varying attack strength, $\beta = 0.05$

show next to no variation in false positive rate, averaging at about 3% to less than 4%. It is noteworthy that the error rate is foremost the result of false positive errors occurring *directly after* an attack has ended. At that time, the anomaly score is not yet again in the normal range, as defined by the score threshold, c.f. section 2; however, since ground truth has it that no attack is currently taking place, the system's output is evaluated to false positive. The error rates for the strong attacks can be taken as a *base line* false positive error rate in scenarios with an attack. It stands to reason that it is not entirely necessary to know the *exact* point in time when the attack ends.

The weaker, yet still detecable attacks show the most surprising behaviour. Up to a certain adaptivity value between 0.3 and 0.6, these scenarios are comparable to the base line. However, for greater adaptivity values, false positive error rates increase rapidly. The explanation of this behaviour is as follows: during the attack, the nodes start adapting to the traffic, including attack traffic. As already stated in the discussion of the false negative rates, this happens the more easily the weaker the attack is. Additionally, it is likely – due to the various indeterministic influences of the wireless environment – that a node does not *see* the full extent of the attack at first, adapting to it in several dynamic learning rounds. Thus, the longer the attack lasts, the more the traffic profile adapts to it. Once the attack ends, the part of the traffic caused by the attack ceases to exist; this is an *abrupt* change of the traffic pattern. The nodes recognise it as anomalous, hence causing false positive errors – note that the ground truth is *no attack*! A re-run of the experiment with a smoother ramp-down behaviour at the end of the attack resulted in false positive rates comparable to the base line, thus confirming the explanation.

The figures show that again, the EWMA setting of $\beta = 0.05$ yields better results: the tipping point for the adaptivity – i.e., the maximum adaptivity that still produces a reasonably low amount of false positives – is higher for the smaller β value. This means that with a smaller β value, it is possible for the anomaly detection to run at higher adaptivity while still being able to do well in terms of error rates.

5.1   Interpretation of Results

Detection of an *attack* (as opposed to an *anomaly*) can be formalised by defining the percentage of all affected observation intervals that must be correctly classified as anomalous. For instance, one might say that an attack is successfully detected if 50% of its duration the affected nodes claim an anomaly. This is not unreasonable, since to an outside observer – such as the network operator – it is not necessary that every single interval is correctly classified. Note with regard to this that the base line as concerns false positive errors is less than 1%; a scenario that causes half of the records to be recognised as anomalous can be easily distinguished from this.

Let the *detection threshold* be 50% as indicated above, and the EWMA β parameter set to 0.2. In this case, the network operator can judge from the results presented in Fig. 1 that an *adaptivity* value of 0.3 results in attacks weaker than 1.2 msgs/s will go undetected by the system, whereas attacks with 1.2 msgs/s and more will be detected. Furthermore, the operator can conclude from Fig. 3 that the false positive error rates will be relatively low – at around or less than 3% – for any attack.

The choice of an *adaptivity* parameter of 0.5 in the same scenario will still let an operator detect a 1.2 msgs/s attack, since the according false negative error rate is still only around 50%; however, where false positive error rates are concerned, Fig. 3 shows that some of the weaker attacks will cause false positive errors after they end. For instance, an 1 msgs/s attack will result in 8% false positive errors *after* its end.

Interestingly, this information may still be used in a post mortem analysis. However, it is unclear whether it is possible to distinguish between the system behaviour correctly classifying 8% of a weak attack *during* the attack, and falsely classifying them *afterwards*. This is topic of current research and out of the scope of this paper.

6   Concluding Remarks

This paper has presented an auto-configuring Markov chain based approach to anomaly detection in wireless sensor networks. The approach is lightweight and avoids specialisation of the anomaly detector to exactly one application scenario, while still being application-aware and thus applicable in many scenarios.

Furthermore, the system was extended to be adaptable in terms of the traffic model; this is a very useful property in indeterministic wireless environments where outside conditions may change on the long term. The adaptivity itself is indeterministic and avoids DoS vulnerabilities regarding memory consumption.

Perhaps the most surprising result of the experiments conducted herein is the fact that greater adaptability of an anomaly detector does not guarantee less false positive errors. Further research will include a more thorough exploration of the parameter space of the adaptation module, as well as more complex attacks and adaptivity behaviour in scenarios without attacks.

References

1. Dudek, D.: DoS detection with markov chains. In: 9th European Conference on Wireless Sensor Networks (EWSN), Poster and Demo Proceedings (2012)
2. Dudek, D.: Collaborative detection of traffic anomalies using first order markov chains. In: 2012 Ninth International Conference on Networked Sensing Systems (INSS), pp. 1–4 (June 2012)
3. Krontiris, I., Giannetsos, T., Dimitriou, T.: Lidea: a distributed lightweight intrusion detection architecture for sensor networks. In: Proceedings of the 4th Int. Conf. on Security and Privacy in Communication Netowrks, SecureComm 2008, 20:1–20:10. ACM, New York (2008)
4. Su, W.T., Chang, K.M., Kuo, Y.H.: ehip: An energy-efficient hybrid intrusion prohibition system for cluster-based wireless sensor networks. Computer Networks 51(4), 1151–1168 (2007)
5. Dudek, D., Haas, C., Kuntz, A., Zitterbart, M., Krüger, D., Rothenpieler, P., Pfisterer, D., Fischer, S.: A wireless sensor network for border surveillance. In: Proceedings of the 7th ACM Conference on Embedded Networked Sensor Systems, SenSys 2009, pp. 303–304. ACM, New York (2009)
6. Wang, R., Du, W., Ning, P.: Containing denial-of-service attacks in broadcast authentication in sensor networks. In: Proceedings of the 8th ACM Int. Symposium on Mobile Ad Hoc Networking and Computing, MobiHoc 2007, pp. 71–79. ACM, New York (2007)
7. Ye, N., Zhang, Y., Borror, C.: Robustness of the markov-chain model for cyber-attack detection. IEEE Transactions on Reliability 53(1), 116–123 (2004)
8. Paschalidis, I.C., Chen, Y.: Statistical anomaly detection with sensor networks. ACM Trans. Sen. Netw. 7, 17:1–17:23 (2010)
9. Gao, Y., Chen, C., Bu, J., Dong, W., He, D.: Icad: Indirect correlation based anomaly detection in dynamic wsns. In: Proceedings of the Wireless Communications and Networking Conference (IEEE WCNC 2011), pp. 647–652 (March 2011)

μSec: A Security Protocol for Unicast Communication in Wireless Sensor Networks

Amrita Ghosal, Sanjib Sur, and Sipra DasBit

Department of Computer Science and Technology
Bengal Engineering and Science University, Shibpur, Howrah-711103, India
ghosal_amrita@yahoo.com, as-sanjib.sur11@gmail.com
siprad@hotmail.com

Abstract. Secure communication in wireless sensor networks (WSNs) not only needs to provide the basic security but also to defend various attacks. The challenge in providing security in this network is that the securing mechanism must be lightweight to make it implementable in resource-constrained nodes. In this paper we have devised a link layer protocol for securing unicast communication in wireless sensor network (WSN). The protocol (μSec) is developed in TinyOS platform which is an event-driven operating system used in WSN for networked applications. Our protocol supports the basic security features such as confidentiality, authentication and integrity along with defense against replay attacks. We have modified an existing cryptographic algorithm with a target to minimize computational overhead to make it implementable in WSN. A simple, counter based defense mechanism is proposed to thwart replay attack. Both qualitative and quantitative analyses are performed to measure the efficacy of the protocol. The protocol is compared with some of important security protocols developed around TinyOS. We claim that that μSec, in addition to basic security, thwarts replay attack with same overhead as in other protocols which have considered basic securities only. We further claim that the μSec requires 10% (avg.) less overhead compared to its competitor which also defends replay attack.

Keywords: Wireless sensor networks, Sensor Network Security, Authentication, Encryption, Unicast communication.

1   Introduction

The advent of efficient short range radio communication and advances in miniaturization of computing devices have made possible the development of wireless sensor networks (WSNs). The WSNs have gained popularity due to the fact that they are potentially low-cost solutions to a variety of real-world challenges. This network consists of a large number of small, battery-powered wireless sensor nodes where the nodes are usually equipped with hardware components such as sensing unit, processing unit with small memory, transceiver unit, power unit and a small piece of software e.g. TinyOS [1]. The TinyOS is an event-driven operating system for networked applications in wireless embedded systems. The WSN also has a base station

R. Di Pietro et al. (Eds.): DPM 2012 and SETOP 2012, LNCS 7731, pp. 258–273, 2013.

which is a high-end node compared to sensor nodes and acts as the network's interface with the outside world. The sensor nodes are responsible for gathering data from the environment and send data to the base station. The base station further processes the data before transmitting to the outside world.

WSNs are vulnerable to attacks that are more difficult from being launched in wired networks [2]. So, the need of ensuring security while communicating in presence of such attack is of utmost importance. An attack is defined as an attempt to gain unauthorized access to a service, resource, or information to compromise integrity, availability, or confidentiality. Replay attack is one such attack where packets are captured and replayed into the network by an adversary [3]. Further, one important difference of WSNs from other conventional wireless networks is dealing with extreme constrained resources in terms of battery power, bandwidth, processing capability and storage. Therefore, in order to consider such resource constraints it is desirable for providing reasonable security strength while limiting overhead. Traditional security protocols are difficult for implementation in sensor networks as they require more powerful resources which a WSN cannot provide.

Many works have been reported so far that have contributed towards securing communication of WSN. A few of them, however, has been developed [4-8] on TinyOS platform where the security features are added to TinyOS. Authors in [4] proposed TinySec, the first link layer security protocol which actually adds security feature to the TinyOS environment that lacked the inherent security properties. It covers the basic security needs such as message authenticity, integrity, and confidentiality. TinySec supports two different security options: authenticated encryption (TinySec-AE) and authentication only (TinySec-Auth). With authenticated encryption, TinySec encrypts the data and authenticates the packet with a MAC. The MAC is computed over the encrypted payload and the packet header. In authentication only mode, it authenticates the entire packet with a MAC, but the data is not encrypted. Here encryption is done using CBC mode for encryption. TinySec has been implemented in testbed using Berkeley sensor nodes and also has been simulated in TOSSIM simulator. But the drawback of the security feature of TinySec is that it is not strong enough as it employs a single network-wide key for all the nodes, such that every node in the network can impersonate as any other node. Also TinySec does not address any explicit attack e.g. replay attack.

In [5] the authors have developed a security protocol SNEP (Sensor Network Encryption Protocol) that provides basic security features such as data confidentiality, two-party data authentication, integrity and data freshness. Encryption is done using the counter mode (CTR) encryption algorithm. SNEP uses CBC-MAC algorithm over the ciphered data for data authentication. It also introduces a shared counter between the sender and the receiver which is used as an initialization vector (IV) for the block cipher. The receiver and sender updates the shared counter once they have received/sent a cipher block. However, since the counter value is not being sent with the packet, there might be synchronization problems caused by dropped packets. So a re-synchronization protocol may be needed to overcome this problem.

Authors in [6] have proposed a link layer security framework known as SenSec designed for sensor networks that work on Mica2 motes. It uses a hierarchical architecture where nodes are arranged in clusters at each level with the base station at the top of the hierarchy. It provides a resilient keying mechanism using three different keys such as global key (GK), cluster key (CK) and sensor key (SK) for combating node capture attack. Global key is generated by the base station and is present with each sensor node. Cluster key is generated by the cluster head that is assigned after the cluster formation and is used by the nodes for communication within the cluster. Every node shares the sensor key with the base station that is generated by the base station based on the id of individual sensor nodes. Although the authors have claimed that their scheme is capable of defending node capture attacks but they have not provided any explanation regarding how the different keys are being used in the various network levels for thwarting node capture attacks. Encryption has been done using a variant of Skipjack as the block cipher, called Skipjack-X. But using Skipjack-X incurs large memory usage, which is undesirable for sensor networks.

In [7] authors have proposed another link layer security solution named as Secure-Sense. This protocol provides security services dynamically based on runtime decisions that depend on observed external environments, internal constraints and application requirements. SecureSense is able to allocate resources optimally as it takes this decision during runtime. This decision is taken by a component known as the security broker which is inserted between the packet and radio modules. The task of the broker is to intercept the packets arriving from the radio level before passing them to the packet level and packets arriving from the packet level before passing them to the radio level. The service library invokes further cryptographic measures for fulfilling the required operations. For providing authentication SecureSense uses RC5 as the block cipher cryptographic algorithm. Though the authors have claimed that their scheme can significantly prolong network lifetime with respect to a static security model they have not dealt with any attacks that are prevalent in sensor networks.

Authors in [8] have introduced a new protocol named as MiniSec that provides security in the network layer for wireless sensor networks. The objective of MiniSec is providing confidentiality, data authentication, replay protection and data freshness. Confidentiality and data authentication in MiniSec is accomplished by applying OCB encryption [9]. Replay protection is done using a counter where the counter value is stored both at the sender and receiver ends. The sender sends few bits of the counter value with the packet. If the counter value in the packet is greater than the counter value stored by the receiver, the receiver accepts the packet else it rejects the same. MiniSec works in two modes- MiniSec-U and MiniSec-B. MiniSec-U is used in unicast communication while MiniSec-B for broadcast communication. Though MiniSec tries to minimize the energy overhead but it introduces high memory requirements in the nodes as it employs Skipjack, which requires large memory usage and also greater computation time for encryption and decryption.

In this paper an attempt has been made to design a secure link layer protocol µSec (MicroSec) for WSN, with relatively lower overhead compared to its competitors [4-8]. We have considered providing the basic security features such as confidentiality, integrity and authentication using µSec -Unicast protocol (µSec-U) as well as tried to achieve low energy consumptions keeping in mind the resource constraints of sensor nodes. The µSec-U has been developed for mica2 motes.

The rest of the paper is organized as follows. In section 2 the problem definition including the system model and the security properties considered here are described. The proposed securing scheme including its design and supporting algorithms is presented in section 3. Performance of the scheme is reported based on comparative qualitative analysis and simulation results. Concluding remarks and future scope are stated in section 5.

2   Problem Definition

2.1   System Model

The system model in the present work considers flat architecture. In this architecture the mode of communication between the nodes is unicast. We have considered mote class attackers where the adversaries are assumed to own same resources as ordinary sensor nodes. Further, we have not considered providing security services to the base station as it is highly powerful and have large amount of resources.

All the nodes are pre-deployed with a 128 bit key and a counter which is initialized to zero. Symmetric key cryptography is employed between the two nodes that communicate between themselves. The 128 bit key is used for encrypting/decrypting the message at the sender/receiver end while the counter value is used to detect the presence of replay attack.

2.2   Desired Security Properties

2.2.1   Confidentiality

Confidentiality [10] is defined as the property where the transmitted message must make sense only to the intended receiver. To all others, the message is to be considered as garbage and that will prevent other parties from discovering the plaintext. Confidentiality is typically achieved by encrypting the plaintext and sending the cipher text to the receiver.

TinySec uses CBC-encryption [11], while SNEP employs counter with CBC-MAC (CCM) encryption algorithm [12]. MiniSec provides confidentiality using OCB-encryption [9] with a non-repeating counter. We have compared several competing encryption schemes and selected the "Tiny Encryption Algorithm" (TEA) for optimum memory and CPU cycle count requirements. The justification of selecting TEA as encryption algorithm is established in section 4.1 through analysis and comparison of the other competing schemes.

2.2.2   Integrity and Authentication

Message integrity [13] means that data must arrive at the receiver exactly as they were sent. There must not be any change during the transmission, neither accidentally or maliciously. However, if such change has been found then the packet must be rejected by the receiver.

Authentication is a service beyond message integrity. Here the receiver needs to be sure of the sender's identity and that an imposter has not sent the message. So it empowers legitimate nodes for verifying whether a message indeed originated from another legitimate node (i.e., a node with which it shares a secret key) and was unchanged during transmission. As a result, illegitimate nodes should not be able to participate in the network, either by injecting their own messages or by modifying legitimate messages.

Typically, authentication and integrity are achieved by computing a message-authentication code (MAC). The MAC is generated by applying hash function over the payload and it is sent as part of the packet. Upon reception, the packet is considered as valid if the receiver once again computes the MAC and it matches with the received MAC.

2.2.3 Replay Protection

It is an attack in which a valid data transmission is maliciously or fraudulently repeated [14]. TinySec is not resilient to such an attack. Minisec provides a counter based approach to prevent this attack. Our scheme improvises on a similar approach but it takes less memory and time requirement than that of Minisec.

3   Proposed Securing Scheme (μSec-U)

TinyOS [1] is an event driven operating system running on Mica2 motes. It does not provide any security primitives. We have developed μSec (Microsec), a protocol which not only gives basic security solutions but also prevents replay attack and enables secure, unicast communication.

3.1   μSec-U Design

In this section we describe the mechanism of securing unicast communication of the proposed scheme. Before describing the communication mechanism we present the protocol stack and packet format used for the scheme.

3.1.1 Protocol Stack

Figure 1 shows the mapping of OSI layer protocol stack with the protocol stack of TinyOS. The functionalities [6] provided by the physical layer of the OSI model are done by the Radio layer in TinyOS. The data link layer of OSI is the packet and messaging layers in TinyOS. Similarly the middleware layer in TinyOS constitutes the network and transport layers in OSI. The work done by the session, presentation and application layers of OSI is done by the application layer in TinyOS. Generic communication interfaces is provided to the upper AM layer by TinyOS and it also uses the radio interfaces. We propose μSec-U to work in between packet and messaging layers of the TinyOS protocol stack. To be more specific μSec-U takes input from messaging layer, applies security measures and sends it for packet layer. Security services are provided in parallel to radio communication so that no additional delay is incurred.

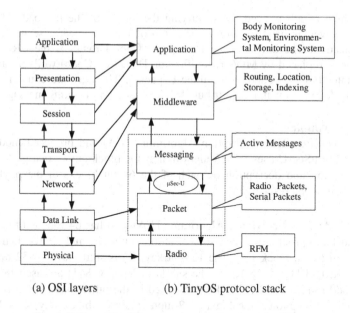

(a) OSI layers   (b) TinyOS protocol stack

Fig. 1. OSI vs. TinyOS protocol stack showing μSec-U

3.1.2 Packet Format

The packet format for TinyOS, TinySec, MiniSec and μSec-U are shown in Figure 2. The size of each attribute is denoted in bytes. The μSec-U packet is built upon the TinyOS packet with some modifications. The attributes in packet format that are shared by μSec-U with TinyOS are: Destination address, type and length.

TinyOS:

2	1	1	1	0...28	2
Destination Address	Type	Group	Length	Payload	CRC

TinySec:

2	1	1	1	2	0...28	4
Destination Address	Type	Length	Initialization Vector	Source Address	Encrypted Payload	MAC

MiniSec:

2	1	1	1	2	0...28	4	2	2
Destination Address	Type	Length	Initialization Vector	Source Address	Encrypted Payload	MAC	FCF	DstPAN

μSec-U:

2	1	1	2	0...28	1	4
Destination Address	Type	Length	Source Address	Encrypted Payload	Counter	MDC

Fig. 2. Packet formats

The attribute length is used for specifying the length of the payload. The attribute 'type', however, is used for future extension of our scheme for securing broadcast communication. The attribute that is changed from TinyOS is the CRC field. The CRC field is replaced by MDC (Modification Detection Code) while an additional 1 byte counter field is added to the μSec-U packet. The attribute counter is used for replay attack detection and the attribute MDC is used for checking message integrity.

3.1.3 Encryption

We have modified Tiny Encryption Algorithm (TEA) and proposed modified TEA (mTEA). The μSec-U uses mTEA algorithm as the block cipher that performs necessary encryption and decryption on each of the 64 bit blocks of the payload at the sender/receiver end respectively.

Brief on TEA: Tiny Encryption Algorithm (TEA) [15] has 64 rounds of simple arithmetic and logic processes comprising of shifts, additions and XORs. It uses 128-bit key (K) and 64-bit block size. The 128-bit key (K) is split into four 32-bit blocks or sub-keys K[0], K[1], K[2], K[3]. The sub-keys K[0] & K[1] are used in one of the rounds (odd round) and K[2] & K[3] are used in the other round (even round). The inputs to the encryption algorithm are a 2-tuple (plaintext block, key) data. Each block of data is divided into two halves. Encryption is performed on these two halves of each data block for 64 rounds by both left and right shifting of bits causing all bits of data as well as key to be mixed repeatedly. After the completion of 64 rounds, the encrypted cipher text is generated and is sent to the receiver. Similarly at the receiver end, decryption is performed that involves the same procedure as in encryption with the difference being only in the use of the sub-keys in reverse order.

The function part of TEA algorithm that comprises of shifting, addition and xoring operations is denoted as-

$$f(M, K[j, k], \partial[i])=((M<<4)+K[j]) \oplus (M+\partial[i]) \oplus ((M>>5)+K[k])$$

where M is the message, K[j, k] denotes the jth and k^{th} sub-keys, i is the round number and δ is the golden number [14] defined as- $(\sqrt{5}-1)2^{31}$.

Proposed modification of TEA (mTEA): The modification of the TEA algorithm has been done in the function part by including number of rounds (N) as part of the function. Further, 64 rounds involve enormous computations that are neither desirable for resource constrained sensor nodes nor essential for most of the WSN applications that require short lifetime. So security level has been made adaptable by changing N as per the need. The function part of mTEA is denoted as-

$$f(M, K[j, k], \partial[i])=((M<<4)+K[j]) \oplus (M+\partial[i]) \oplus ((M>>5)+K[k])<<N$$

3.1.4 Hashing

Hashing has been done for providing authentication and integrity to the message being sent from the sender to the receiver. The process of hashing has been implemented in μSec-U in two steps:

- Use compression function to produce fixed length compressed outputs
- Generate Modification Detection Code (MDC) or unkeyed hash function from Substitution box (S-box)

Table 1. Substitution box

I/P Range of Compression Function	Hash Value
Value : 0x00 – 0x1f	Value I Value I Value I Value
Value : 0x20 – 0x3f	Value I ~Value I Value I ~Value
Value : 0x40 – 0x5f	~Value I Value I ~Value I Value
Value : 0x60 – 0x7f	Value I Value I ~Value I ~Value
Value : 0x80 – 0x9f	~Value I ~Value I Value I Value
Value : 0xa0 – 0xbf	Value I Value I Value I ~Value
Value : 0xc0 – 0xdf	~Value I Value I Value I Value
Value : 0xe0 – 0xff	~Value I ~Value I ~Value I ~Value

The first step of hashing involves the compression operation where the inputs are the least significant 8 bits of the encrypted output from each block. Each of the inputs is compressed to produce 2 bits as output and stored in a temporary buffer. The compression is done using modulo 4 operation. After all the blocks undergo compression operation, the results are appended to form the output comprising of 2t bits considering t data blocks. Once the compression is done, in the next step, MDC (Fig 4: µSec-U packet format) is generated and is transmitted along with the encrypted payload. To generate MDC, concept of S-box [16] has been used as it obscures the relationship between the key and the ciphertext. The output of 2t bits obtained after compression is considered as inputs to the S-box (Table 1: Substitution box). The corresponding input is matched with the inputs in the S-box to obtain the output consisting of 4 bytes.

3.2   Transmission

Once the encryption and hashing are completed, the encrypted payload and MDC are ready for preparing the packet for transmission except the value of counter. All nodes maintain individual counter values for each of its neighbouring nodes. To start with, the counter values maintained by all the nodes are initialized to zero. When a node (sender) starts transmission with another node (receiver), the sender increases its counter (corresponding to the receiver node) value by one. Similar to MiniSec-U, it also uses the concept of LB (Last Bits) optimization where instead of sending the entire counter bits (the size of the counter is 4 bits) only the last 8 bits of the counter are sent with each packet. After completion of 8 rounds the hash result of all blocks, encryption result and the LB bit of the counter are appended together to form the 7-tuple packet containing destination address, type, length, source address, encrypted payload, counter and MDC which is to be sent to the receiver/ destination.

3.3   Reception

At the receiving end, the receiver checks the destination address (μSec-U packet: Figure 2) of the received packet for verifying whether the packet is destined for the receiver.

3.3.1 Replay Attack Detection

The receiver compares the counter value in the 7-tuple packet with the counter value stored (section 3.2) by it. If both the counter values match then it can be confirmed that no replay attack has taken place and the packet is accepted. Once the packet is accepted the receiver increments the counter value by one.

3.3.2 Confidentiality Check

If there is no replay attack, the payload is split into blocks each of 64 bits and on each block mTEA algorithm is run for decrypting the data in each block for 8 rounds. If it is successfully decrypted, confidentiality is ensured.

3.3.3 Integrity Check

Once the blocks are decrypted the hash function is employed on each of the 64 bit decrypted blocks. The hash results of all the blocks are concatenated and if this hash result matches with MDC of the received packet then integrity is preserved.

3.4   Algorithm for μSec-U

The μSec-U algorithm for unicast communication is presented in two parts- one is run in a sender node and the other in a receiver node.

3.4.1 Sender

The following algorithm is running at sender side.

Input: Message X to be transmitted from node s to a node r.
Output: 7-tuple packet ready for transmission

Begin
1. apply unambiguous padding on X
2. obtain X'   // formatted message- $X' = X \parallel 1 \parallel 0^j$, where j is the smallest positive integer such that $L + j \equiv -1 \pmod{64}$
3. split X' into t blocks each of 64 bits   // $X' = x_0 x_1 x_2 ... x_{t-1}$
4. initialize H, E(X') to ϕ // H and E(X') store the hash value and encrypted m sage respectively
5. **for** (i=0; i≤t-1; i++)
6.   **for** (j=0; j≤7; j++)   // 8-round encryption start
7.   run mTEA on each block $X_i'^j$ // for ensuring confidentiality
8.   **end for**
9.   obtain E(X'$_i$)   // obtain encrypted ith block of X'
10.   compute E(X')=E(X') $\parallel$ E(X'$_i$)   // form encrypted payload
11.   compute H$_i$=(Extract LSB E(X'$_i$)) mod 4

12.   compute $H=H \parallel H_i$
13. **end for**
14. search S-box to find out the matched value for H
15. obtain search_result
16. compute MDC=search_result
17. generate 7-tuple packet   // attributes of the packet are destination address, type, length,
                                   source address, E(X'), $counter_s^r$, MDC

18. increase value of $counter_s^r$ by one

19. send 7-tuple packet to receiver
End

___

3.4.2   Receiver

Input: 7-tuple packet from sender/transmitter node
Output: Detection of replay attack and checking of basic securities

Begin
1.   receive 7-tuple packet from sender
2.   check packet header i.e. destination address   // verify whether the packet is for the
                                                       intended receiver

3.   retrieve $counter_s^r$ value from the packet

4.   **if** ($counter_s^r$ value in the packet $=counter_s^r$ value stored in the receiver)   // check for
                                                                                              replay attack
5.   accept packet
6.   increase $counter_s^r$ value by one
7.   **else**
8.   reject packet
9.   **exit**
10. obtain encrypted payload $E(X')$ from the packet

11. split the payload $E(X')$ into t blocks each of 64 bits   // $X' = x_0x_1x_2...x_{t-1}$

12. initialize D(X') and H to ϕ // H and D(X') are to store the hash value and decrypted
                                             message respectively

13. **for** (i=0; i≤t-1; i++)
14.   **for** (j=0; j≤7; j++)
15.   run mTEA on each block $X_i'^j$ // for confidentiality check

16.   **end for**
17.   obtain D(X'$_i$)   // obtain decrypted ith block of X'
18.   compute H_i =(Extract LSB D(X'$_i$)) mod 4
19.   compute H=H || Hi
20. **end for**
21. search S-box to find out the matched value for H
22. obtain search_result
23. compute MDC = search_result
24. **if** (computed MDC = MDC in the packet) // integrity and authenticity check

25.   accept packet
26. **else**
27.   reject packet
28. **end if**
End

---

4   Performance Analysis

The effectiveness of the proposed scheme for securing unicast communication reported in the earlier section is evaluated both by qualitative and quantitative analyses.

4.1   Qualitative Analysis

In this section primarily justification of selecting mTEA over other existing algorithms for encryption/ decryption is provided through qualitative analysis based on their memory requirements, CPU cycle count and average throughput to code size ratio.

4.1.1   mTEA vs. Its Competitors

Memory requirements
The cryptographic algorithm mTEA used in μSec-U has been compared with other existing cryptographic algorithms such as modified DES (mDES) [10], Skipjack [8], XTEA [10]. The memory usages in Figure 3 clearly reflect that mTEA outperforms all the other cryptographic algorithms with respect to total memory requirements.

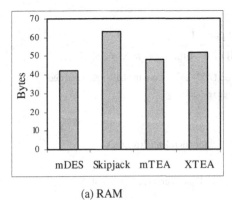
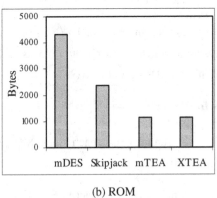

(a) RAM   (b) ROM

Fig. 3. Memory requirements for different ciphering schemes

CPU cycle count
The CPU cycle time requirement gives a measure of computational complexity and energy consumption. The amount of energy consumed is directly related to the CPU cycle time. Considering the amount of energy consumed per CPU cycle is fixed,

energy consumption is measured in terms of number of CPU cycles required for executing per data block of plaintext/ciphertext processed. The CPU cycle time required for encryption and decryption of various algorithms is shown in Figure 4. We observe from the figure that encryption and decryption cycle counts are minimum for mTEA thus ensuring that energy consumed is also least.

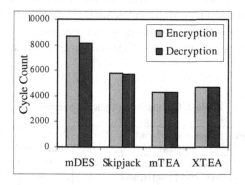

Fig. 4. Cycle Count for encryption and decryption

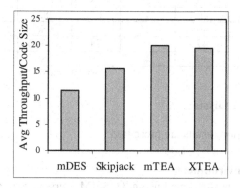

Fig. 5. Ratio of Average Throughput (bits/sec) to Code Size

Average throughput to code size ratio
We have also used the ratio of average throughput to the code size in logarithmic scale as a parameter for comparison. The ratio is calculated as-

$$10 \times \log_{10} \left(\frac{\text{Average Throughput}}{\text{Code Size}} \right).$$

As throughput is defined as the number of bits processed per second by an algorithm, it influences the performance of the algorithm. The ratio described above can be regarded as the figure of merit for the encryption/decryption algorithm. The value of this ratio for the different ciphering schemes is shown in Figure 5.

4.1.2 Overhead Comparison

Table 2 gives a comparison of μSec-U with TinyOS, TinySec and TinySec (AE). The comparison table illustrates that μSec-U outperforms all the other protocols in terms of security overhead. As all the schemes have evolved from the basic TinyOS scheme, the last two columns in the table are the illustration of how much increase in overhead over TinyOS has taken place in all the schemes with respect to packet size and bandwidth respectively. In packet overhead calculation we have used the term byte time, which is the time taken to transmit a single byte of data over the radio [4]. Also a 28-byte start symbol and a 4-byte synchronization message are also introduced as an extra overhead.

Table 2. Comparison of packet overhead

Scheme	Payload size (Bytes)	Packet overhead (Bytes)		Total Size (Bytes)	Transmission time (ms)	Size increasing over TinyOS (%)	BW overhead over TinyOS (%)
		Header overhead	Security overhead				
TinyOS	24	39	-	63	26.2	-	-
TinySec	24	38	2	64	26.7	1.58	1.7
TinySec(AE)	24	40	4	68	28.8	7.9	7.3
SenSec	24	40	4	68	28.8(e)	7.9	7.3
Minisec	24	47	3	74	31.3(e)	17.38	16.9
μSec-U	24	40	4	68	28.8(e)	7.9	7.3

4.2 Quantitative Analysis

In this section simulation results are presented.

4.2.1 Simulation Environment

Simulation of μSec-U is performed using TOSSIM (version 1.0), which is a discrete event simulator for WSN having nodes supporting TinyOS. In simulation the key has been randomly assigned, with every node having a unique key. We consider radio model as "simple" which is implemented in TOSSIM for testing single-hop algorithms. TOSSIM does not provide any power/energy consumption model. We assume the random model of ADC [17] where whenever sampling takes place it returns a 10-bit random value. Further, TOSSIM models EEPROM by means of a large, memory mapped file which is anonymous and is not available at the end of current session. However, we have used a name file which allows the EEPROM data to persist across multiple simulation invocations.

Table 3. Simulation Parameters and values

Parameters	Value
Number of nodes	5
Radio propagation speed	3×10^8 meters/s
Radio speed	19.2 Kbps
Payload size	24 bytes
CPU clock speed	8 MHz

We implemented μSec-U in nesC code [18], the programming language used for TinyOS. The relevant parameters used for simulation and their associated values are listed in Table 3.

4.2.2 Simulation Metric

As energy consumption by a node is greatly influenced by the time taken for cryptographic computations, we have analyzed the cryptographic computation time in a node. The cryptographic computation time considers the time required for encryption /decryption at the sender/receiver.

4.2.3 Simulation Results

We have simulated our proposed μSec-U scheme using TOSSIM for determining the efficiency of the ciphering algorithm employed in the scheme as well as for evaluating the authentication/integrity and replay attack protection mechanism used in the same. For these experiments, a network consisting of 5 sensor nodes are used for accurately determining the details of communication. The simulation is performed at a scale of 0.5 times the real speed in order to study the message exchange between the nodes. We have run the simulation 10 times and each time results are collected from one randomly chosen node. Finally, we have taken the average of the results and plotted.

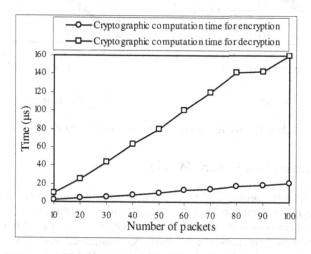

Fig. 6. Cryptographic computation time

Time required for cryptographic computations for encryption and decryption are plotted in Figure 6. Our primary observation is that as the number of packets increases the cryptographic computation time required for both encryption and decryption increases. To be more specific if number of packets is 10, cryptographic computation time required for encryption is 2.5 μs whereas for decryption it is 10 μs. Also if number of packet is 100, cryptographic computation time required for encryption is 21 μs and same for decryption is 160 μs. This is due to the fact that as the number of packets increases the time required for cryptographic computation also increases. Also it is observed that cryptographic computation time required for decryption is more than that for encryption. This is because during decryption more number of constraints are involved such as checking the packet header and retrieving the counter value from the received packet before doing the actual decryption process.

4.2.4 Comparative Study

Further, we compare μSec-U with TinySec based on the parameter cryptographic computation time for encryption and decryption.

Figure 7(a) shows that with number of packets up to 50, time required for encryption of the packet in μSec-U is nearly same as that of TinySec. But when the number of packets increases beyond 50, the time required in μSec-U is lesser than TinySec by about 18%. However, we observe that computation time required for decryption (Figure 7(b)) is about 11% more in case of μSec-U than TinySec. This is due to the constraints involved in counter value checking at the time of reception. This small overhead is affordable for getting replay attack protection which is not provided by TinySec.

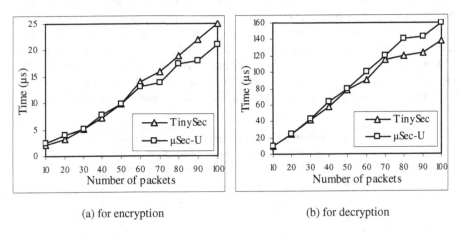

(a) for encryption   (b) for decryption

Fig. 7. Time required for cryptographic computations

5   Conclusion and Future Works

The proposed securing protocol μSec-U offers defense against replay attack in addition to provide fundamental security features for unicast communication. During the protocol design emphasis is given such that it meets both the desired requirements of keeping it lightweight in presence of resource-constrained nodes while achieving high-level security features. It uses lightweight cryptographic algorithm requiring less overhead in terms of computations and energy consumption. The µSec-U has been simulated in TOSSIM simulator, the simulator used for simulating protocols based on TinyOS. A detailed comparative analysis is performed where it is shown that our scheme requires significantly less overhead than its competitor scheme while both the schemes defend replay attack in addition to providing basic securities. To make our solution a complete one, as a future extension, the scheme may be extended for securing broadcast communication.

References

1. Hill, J., Szewczyk, R., Woo, A., Hollar, S., Culler, D.E., Pister, K.S.J.: System Architecture Directions for Networked Sensors. ACM SIGPLAN Notice 35(11), 93–104 (2000)
2. Perrig, A., Stankovic, J., Wagner, D.: Security in Wireless Sensor Setworks. Communications of the ACM, Special Issue on Wireless Sensor Networks 47(6), 53–57 (2004)
3. Ghosal, A., Halder, S., DasBit, S.: A Dynamic TDMA Based Scheme for Securing Query Processing in WSN. Wireless Networks 18(2), 165–184 (2012)
4. Karlof, C., Sastry, N., Wagner, D.: TinySec: A Link Layer Security Architecture for Wireless Sensor Networks. In: Proc. of 2nd Int'l Conf. SenSys, pp. 162–175 (2004)
5. Perrig, A., Szewczyk, R., Wen, V., Culler, D., Tygar, J.D.: SPINS: Security Protocols for Sensor Networks. In: Proc. of 7th Int'l Conf. MobiCom, pp. 189–199 (2001)
6. Li, T., Wu, H. Wang, X., Bao, F.: SenSec Design. I^2R Sensor Network Flagship Project (SNFP: Security part). Technical Report-TR v1.0 (February 2005)
7. Xue, Q., Ganz, A.: Runtime Security Composition for Sensor Networks (SecureSense). In: Proc. of IEEE VTC, vol. 5, pp. 2976–2980 (2003)
8. Luk, M., Mezzour, G., Perrig, A., Gligor, V.: MiniSec: A Secure Sensor Network Communication Architecture. In: Proc. of 6th Int'l Conf. IPSN, pp. 479–488 (2007)
9. Rogaway, P., Bellare, M., Black, J., Krovetz, T.: OCB: A Block-Cipher Mode of Operation for Efficient Authenticated Encryption. In: Proc. of ACM Int'l Conf. CCS, pp. 96–205 (2001)
10. Brands, S.A.: Rethinking Public Key Infrastructures and Digital Certificates Building in Privacy. MIT Press (2000)
11. Bellare, M., Desai, A., Jokipii, E., Rogaway, P.: A Concrete Security Treatment of Symmetric Encryption: Analysis of the DES Modes of Operation. In: Proc. of 38th Annual Symposium FOCS, pp. 394–403 (1997)
12. Housley, R., Whiting, D., Ferguson, N.: Counter with CBC-MAC (CCM), Submitted to N.I.S.T. (June 3, 2002), http://csrc.nist.gov/encryption/modes/proposedmodes/
13. Menezes, A., Oorschot, P.V., Vanstone, S.: Handbook of Applied Cryptography. CRC Press (1996)
14. David, R.R., Marchany, R.C., Midkiff, S.F.: Scalable, Cluster-based Anti-replay Protection for Wireless Sensor Networks. In: Proc. of IEEE Workshop on Information Assurance, pp. 127–134 (2007)
15. Wheeler, D., Needham, R.: TEA, A Tiny Encryption Algorithm. In: Preneel, B. (ed.) FSE 1994. LNCS, vol. 1008, pp. 363–366. Springer, Heidelberg (1995)
16. Murphy, S., Robshaw, M.: Essential Algebraic Structure within the AES. In: Yung, M. (ed.) CRYPTO 2002. LNCS, vol. 2442, pp. 1–16. Springer, Heidelberg (2002)
17. Levis, P., Lee, N.: TOSSIM: A Simulator for TinyOS Networks. User's manual, in TinyOS Documentation (March 23, 2007)
18. Gay, D., Levis, P., Behren, R.V., Welsh, M., Brewer, E., Culler, D.: The nesC Language: A Holistic Approach to Network Embedded Systems. In: Proc. of Programming Language Design and Implementation, pp. 1–11 (2003)

Security Monitoring for Content-Centric Networking

David Goergen, Thibault Cholez, Jérôme François, and Thomas Engel

SnT - University of Luxembourg, Luxembourg
`firstname.lastame@uni.lu`

Abstract. Content-Centric Networking (CCN) is one of the most promising research area for a future Internet. The goal is to obtain a more scalable, secure, collaborative Internet supporting context-aware services. However, as a new overlay infrastructure, CCN raises the need of a new monitoring architecture to assess security of CCN devices. In particular, the stateful nature of CCN routers introduces new attack threats that need to be addressed. We propose in this paper a monitoring approach for the instrumentation of CCN enabled network nodes. The rationale of our monitoring approach is demonstrated through real experimentations to detect and mitigate network level attacks against CCN.

1 Introduction

Content-Centric Networking (CCN) is a new routing paradigm developed at PARC by Van Jacobson et al [14] but also known as Named Data Networking at a larger scale [20]. Based on the observation that today's communications are more oriented toward content retrieval (Web, P2P, etc.) than point-to-point communications (VoIP, IM, etc.)[18], CCN proposes to deeply revise the Internet architecture to best match its current usage. In a nutshell, contents are addressable, routable and authenticated, while their locations do not matter anymore. They can be replicated and stored (especially popular contents) on any CCN node. People looking for a content can securely retrieve it from the best locations available.

On one side, the client-server architecture needs more and more investments in expensive content delivery networks and server farms to be scalable. Agreements between ISPs (Internet Service Providers) and content providers tend to benefit to big web-actors that centralize user-generated contents. On the other side, the P2P paradigm makes an inefficient use of resources being mostly unaware of the physical location of the peers. In this context, we think that CCN could be an answer to the challenges that Internet will face in the near future and deserves research efforts from the community to properly investigate the applicability of this paradigm.

From a management point of view, Content-Centric Networking introduces new challenges. Firstly, it is hard for a content provider to monitor and control the diffusion of its content over the network after the initial release which leads

R. Di Pietro et al. (Eds.): DPM 2012 and SETOP 2012, LNCS 7731, pp. 274–286, 2013.

to accountability issues because content can be distributed from any CCN node without requesting the original provider. While it is an important quest from a management point of view, we focus on the security aspects which present a more critical drawback of early deployment of CCN. Secondly, CCN routers are stateful as the route between a content and the requester has to be memorized. This stateful nature can lead to new possible DoS (Denial of Service) attacks which exploit the CCN routers limited memory size and these kind of attacks must be detected and mitigated. In this paper, we address this second issue because we think that security issues could highly decrease the appeal of the technology and reduce further research efforts. To that end, we (1) model a DoS attacks and (2) propose a Monitoring Architecture for Content-Centric Networking which is able to detect them.

Section 2 gives a brief overview of Content Centric Networking and its possible attacks. Section 3 describes our monitoring architecture adapted to CCN devices and our strategy to detect malicious traffic based on Support Vector Machines (SVM). Section 4 presents the experiments assessing the detection of real network attacks by the monitoring architecture. Finally, Section 5 presents the related work and Section 6 concludes the paper and outlines future work.

2 CCN Background

2.1 CCN Paradigm

The main idea behind CCN (also called Named Data Networking[3]) is a paradigm shift towards content oriented networking and routing. Today's Internet relies on the well established communication paradigm in which two end-points communicate over a network. However, regarding the behavior and habits of today's users, there is a strong shift towards content and not the location where this content is stored. Today, Internet is becoming more and more a content distribution network. Therefore some claim[11] that the best approach is to start from scratch building a new Internet architecture. However this involves long term investments for ISPs and CCN can thus be used over the already established architecture (for example CCN over IPv6).

2.2 CCN Node Model

CCN has two main types of packets, *Interest* and *Data* as seen in Figure 1. A user who wants to access a certain content sends out an *Interest* packet, specifying the name of the content (as defined by CCN nomenclature ContentName) to all its available faces. A Face can be anything which can serve as medium for transmitting and receiving data. A node which receives this packet and that can 'satisfy' the *Interest* sends out the corresponding *Data* packet onto the face from which it received the *Interest*. By definition, CCN nodes are stateful and only send *Data* if there was an *Interest* beforehand.

Data can only 'satisfy' a specific *Interest* if the ContentName of the *Interest* packet is a prefix of the *Data* packet. CCN names are defined in [14] as

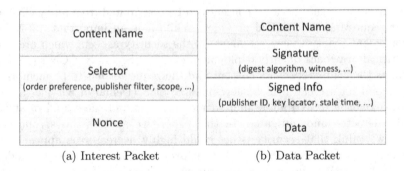

(a) Interest Packet   (b) Data Packet

Fig. 1. CCN packet structures

opaque, binary objects composed of an (explicitly specified) number of compo-nents. This structure allows a fast and efficient prefix-based lookup similar to the IP lookup currently used. It also allows names to be context dependent *i.e. /ThisRoom/Printer* references a printer in the current room. This context-naming could make possible efficient context-aware service discovery in the future Internet of Things.

CCN nodes are composed of three main table structures which handle the forwarding of packets. At the arrival of an *Interest* packet on any given face, the engine performs a longest-match lookup on its structures and action is taken depending on the lookup result. The first structure to be searched is the Content Store. It can be seen as a buffer memory of past *Data* packets on the current router. IP routers also have such a buffer but it is purged once the packet is forwarded. The Content Store however preserves the *Data* packet based on LRU (Least-Recently-Used) scheme and enables therefore a fast retrieval of currently popular demands. If there is a match, the router forwards its local copy of the content to the face on which it received the *Interest* and updates its Content Store accordingly.

If there is no match in the Content Store, the lookup is launched on the next structure which is the PIT. The PIT stands for Pending Interest Table and keeps record of *Interests* waiting to be resolved upstream by other content source(s). If a received *Interest* matches an entry in the PIT, the engine compares the faces recorded for that entry. If there is already one existing, no update is made. Otherwise, the face from which the *Interest* was emitted is simply added to the list of already waiting faces.

If no match-up is found in the PIT then the engine searches in its last struc-ture: the FIB. The Forward Information Base keeps record of potential content source(s) and works similarly to its IP counterpart except that it stores a list of possible providers for a given name rather than a single one only. If a match is found, the engine then creates a PIT entry for the given *Interest* and it is forwarded to all faces specified in the FIB entry. If no match could be made, it means that the current router has no information on the demanded content and discards the *Interest*.

CCN has also built-in strategy and security layers. The strategy layer is used to define policies to select which face is the best for given contents. In fact, due to its design, FIB entries contain multiple faces. CCN can send periodically *Interests* to all outgoing faces without fearing of loops and thereby testing which of the faces responds the fastest. This one will be used as preferred until another round of this experiment yields to a different result. Criteria for experimentation interval can be a threshold of packets sent, a time out, change of the SSID(Service Set Identifier), etc.

The security layer ensures that the content received by a previously announced *Interest* is authentic. As in CCN only the content matters but not the route it takes, the only thing which needs to be checked for authenticity, consistency and integrity is the content itself which reversely means that end-to-end encryption is not needed any more. Key management is another issue often discussed. In [14,13], several solutions are discussed which range from a PKI to PGP like web-of-trust.

2.3 Threats Description

Content Centric Networking improves the security of Internet communications in many ways. First of all, CCN messages can not be sent toward a node without any prior *Interest* request from that node which makes the classical denial of service scheme inefficient as the attacker would need his target to generate a lot of *Interests* to enable the DoS attack. Also, CCN strongly relies on cryptography to authenticate the contents so that users can clearly know who emitted the content and can discard those from untrustworthy sources to avoid malware. If CCN improves security in some points, it also raises the possibility of new kind of attack. Unlike a terminal host which is less exposed to attacks, CCN routers are more vulnerable than IP routers because of their stateful nature and the management of their inner tables from which result their performance and quality of service.

By focusing on CCN routers, new kinds of Denial of Service can be performed. We categorize these attacks regarding the tables they target.

PIT Attack. A first attack can be focused on the Pending Interest Table. This table is critical because of the stateful routing of CCN network. If an attacker can manage to fill the PIT with a lot of forged *Interests*, legitimate *Interests* might be dropped, resulting in the denial of service of the pending communications. The attack is easy to achieve from the technical aspects. The attacker only needs to generate a lot of *Interests* whatever is the requested content in order to create entries in its PIT. Such an attack would benefit from distributed attack sources that would make it more difficult to detect. Therefore, the monitoring of the PIT to avoid flooding is a critical point for a safe and efficient CCN infrastructure.

FIB Attack. Unlike the IP address space, the CCN address space is not clearly bounded as domains are defined through strings rather than a small IP prefix.

Therefore, a possible attack consists in generating and advertising a lot of contents belonging to different domains in order to fill the FIB on a face of the router. In that way, new legitimate domains can not be routed through the CCN device which interface is full. This DoS is critical because one of the major interest of CCN is to allow end-users to directly diffuse their content in a peer-to-peer way instead of relying on big Internet content providers. This attack could reduce the diversity of routable domains and consequently the interest of CCN.

Content Store Attack. DoS can also be launched against the Content Store in order to decrease the efficiency of the caching mechanism which is one of the main components that provides the incentive to deploy CCN infrastructures. According to the caching policy, an attacker could generate a lot of download requests for unpopular contents which would modify the distribution of the downloaded contents and update the cache in a inefficient way. From a technical point of view, this attack is hard to achieve for a single attacker as it would need a lot of bandwidth to have a significant impact on the distribution of contents passing through the router.

3   Monitoring Architecture

3.1   Requirements

The monitoring task consists of collecting information about the functioning and the current status of the CCN nodes. The objective is to correctly select and process the necessary information to highlight important facts. In this paper, we focus on the detection of anomalies resulting from attacks. As CCN works in a distributed manner with independent nodes, monitoring the network from a global perspective is thus hard. A solution could counter this problem by leveraging a central service interacting with a large set of CCN devices to collect and analyse information. However, this raises serious issues about reliability and scalability and does not fit to the CCN paradigm where each node has to be involved in the functioning of the network including the security related aspects.

Therefore, to stick to the CCN paradigm, our architecture is implemented at each CCN device which has to monitor itself for detecting anomalies. As presented in the previous section, a device has three main components: the FIB, the PIT and the Content Store. Each of them plays a crucial role in the well operation of CCN. For example, an abnormal Content Store can provide faulty contents or make the caching inefficient; a badly populated FIB may entail erroneous forwarding and so, some content may not be accessible any more similar to a bogus PIT which leads to disrupt the data content transmission over the back path of a request. Therefore, all of these three tables have to be monitored.

The objective of our monitoring architecture is to detect attack patterns by monitoring the recent past activity over the three tables. Since they may contain many information which are related to many actions (lookup, updates, etc.), monitoring and keeping track of all individual entry or action requires many resources that may delay the process or even affect the entire functioning of a node up to a denial of service in the worst case. To guarantee the scalability and the timeliness, our architecture is designed to represent the three monitored tables by condensed metrics which values can be easily tracked along time.

Finally, devices can also share knowledge for detecting the attacks, in particular for highly distributed ones like DDoS, as well as for preventing future ones or recovering efficiently from anomalies. This may be provided as a content where devices can express their interest through the underlying CCN itself. However, as the individual monitoring is already required prior, our paper focuses on it.

3.2   Instrumentation

As explained in the previous section, there are different components of a CCN node that can be monitored for detecting malicious activities. All of them are impacted and/or impacts the network activity. For example, a node may receive an *Interest* (ingoing network activity) which has to be forwarded (outgoing network activity), this will update its PIT. Therefore, monitoring the network activity will track the global functioning of a node and its internal components without having a particular monitoring function for each of them.

For detecting attacks, network statistics are retrieved periodically from the CCNx implementation [2], every τ seconds. So, for each time window t, the following metrics are considered for all active faces of the CCN devices:

- $recv\_byt_t$: number of received bytes per second
- $sent\_byt_t$: number of sent bytes per second
- $recv\_data_t$: number of received *Data* packets per second
- $sent\_data_t$: number of sent *Data* packets per second
- $recv\_intr_t$: number of received *Interests* per second
- $sent\_intr_t$: number of sent *Interests* per second

We also consider more synthetic values on the router status that are also provided by the CCNx implementation:

- on Content statistics: number of $accessioned_t$, $stored_t$, $staled_t$, $sparse_t$, $duplicated_t$ and $sent_t$ contents
- on recent *Interest* statistics: number of $named_t$, $pending_t$, $propagating_t$ and $noted_t$ Interests
- on total *Interest* statistics: number of $accepted_t$, $dropped_t$, $sent_t$ and $stuffed_t$ Interests

3.3   Classification Algorithm

The objective of the classification algorithm is to label each time window as anomalous or benign. A time window t_i is a tuple defined as:

$$< recv\_byt_{t_i}, sent\_byt_{t_i}, recv\_data_{t_i}, sent\_data_{t_i},$$
$$recv\_intr_{t_i}, sent\_intr_{t_i}, accessioned_{t_i}, stored_{t_i},$$
$$staled_{t_i}, sparse_{t_i}, duplicated_{t_i}, sent_{t_i}, named_{t_i},$$
$$pending_{t_i}, propagating_{t_i}, noted_{t_i}, accepted_{t_i},$$
$$dropped_{t_i}, sent_{t_i}, stuffed_{t_i} >$$

This paper leverages Support Vector Machines (SVM) [7] which are able to efficiently classify data, even if the data points are not separable linearly, while the complexity remains low [19] allowing our solution to detect in real time attacks affecting the monitored CCN nodes. For sake of clarity, we have considered a single attack at a certain time which is handled by 2-class SVM. However, multiple attacks could be detected by building a unique multi-class classifier [9].

2-class SVM is a supervised method and so requires M training samples: $Train = \{(t_1, l_1), \ldots, (t_M, l_M)\}$ with $l_i = 1$ if the time window t_i contains an attack, else -1. For enhancing the data separability, these samples are mapped into a higher dimensional space. Defining an efficient mapping function, ϕ, is a difficult task because it corresponds to add an additional dimensional space over data not given by any features. This however may be avoided by using the kernel function defined as:

$$K(t_i, t_j) = \langle \phi(t_i).\phi(t_j) \rangle \tag{1}$$

Because our data points are vectors representing the different metrics of a time window, the Radial Basis Function (RBF) is adapted:

$$K(t_i, t_j) = e^{-q||t_i - t_j||} \tag{2}$$

where q is tunable. Different values for q have been tested to choose an optimal which provides the best result.

Once in the space, the points may be linearly separable by a hyperplane which divides the samples of two classes with the maximum margins regarding the hyperplane. This leads to the following optimisation problem.

$$max \sum_{t_i \in Train} \alpha_{t_i} - \frac{1}{2} \sum_{\substack{t_i \in Train \\ t_j \in train}} \alpha_i \alpha_j l_i l_j K(t_i, t_j) \tag{3}$$

subject to where $C = 1.0$ determined through initial experiments:

$$\sum_{t_i \in Train} \alpha_i l_i = 0 \tag{4}$$

$$\forall \, t_i \in Train, 0 \le \alpha_i \le C$$

As highlighted by these equations, the problem solving leads also to determine α_i which is used afterwards for classifying a new time window. A major advantage of SVM is that it relies on a subset of initial samples for the decision function, i.e. the support vectors which represent the training points such that $\alpha_i \ne 0$.

Assuming, t_x, a time window which requires a prediction about the attack, it will be labelled by the following function:

$$f(t_x) = sgn(\sum_{(t_i,l_i) \in Train, \alpha_i \neq 0} \alpha_{t_i} l_i K(t_i, t_x) + b) \qquad (5)$$

4 Experiments

4.1 Attack Description and Test Environment

The most critical threat among the three described in Section 2.3 is clearly the attack on the PIT table. Attacks on Content Store can just reduce the efficiency of the cache and therefore do not present critical security issues. Also, attacks on the FIB will become critical when large deployments of CCN will occur, with many providers announcing contents, while PIT attacks is already a threat for local deployments involving few CCN nodes. Therefore the main threat we want to address when monitoring CCN nodes is the Pending Interest Table DoS attack as described in section 2.3. To realize the detection, we first implemented different attack strategies against the PIT in a single attack tool based on the source code of the *ccndsmoketest*[1] program provided in the CCNx implementation. The PIT stores *Interests* according to the faces they belong. To fill the PIT table we have to consider two dimensions, the number of faces created and the number of *Interests* requested.

- **Burst attack**: sending multiple *Interests* to multiple faces. Our first strategy sends a given number of *Interests* on a given number of faces. In extreme scenarios, we can send a lot of *Interests* to a single face or send a single *Interest* to several faces. Both dimensions can be combined leading to the following definition $Attack1(\#packets, \#faces)$ with the aforementioned remarkable values: $Attack1a(1, n)$, $Attack1b(n, 1)$, $Attack1c(n, 100)$, $Attack1d(100, n)$ where n defines the attack aggressiveness and may be tuned to study the impact of the attack.
- **Long duration attack**: keeping alive multiples faces with periodic *Interests*. Our second strategy consists into making the DoS more efficient by keeping alive a lot of faces with a small number of *Interests* that we send periodically. In this case, the attack aggressiveness, n, is the number of targeted faces. In this paper, keep alive *Interests* are sent every $t = 4$ seconds.

Our test-bed is composed of this attack tool and of two CCN devices running the routing daemon *ccnd* provided by CCNx. Both devices are on an restricted network used for this purpose. For each step in the experiment we transfer a 366MB video file from one device to the other.

We defined the impact factor of our attack as the time overhead introduced when transferring a content between our two CCN devices. Figure 2 shows the impact of the number of *Interest* packets we inject while targeting a constant number of faces. Firstly, we vary the *Interest* packet generation to inject them over one face (Attack 1b). The later we use the same principle but we inject them

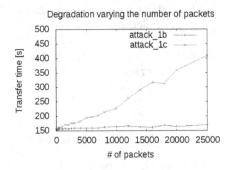

Fig. 2. Impact of varying # of packets (attack 1b, 1c)

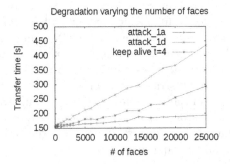

Fig. 3. Impact of varying # of faces (attack 1a, 1d, long duration)

on 100 faces (Attack 1c). Figure 3 is similar but we vary the number of faces while maintaining a constant number of injected *Interest* packets (Attack 1a and 1d). Logically, performances are more degraded when the number of faces or *Interest* packets increase in particular if both are combined (attack 1c and 1d). Moreover, multiplying the number of faces used has a similar effect than sending multiple *Interest* packets. The second attack strategy, keeping alive many interfaces, can also significantly degrade the performance.

4.2   Attack Detection

As previously described attack detection is based on SVM analysing metrics over time windows. In our evaluation, the size of a window is set to one second. To assess the detection, the following metrics are used:

- the True Positive Rate (TPR): proportion of correctly identified windows presenting an attack,
- the False Positive Rate (FPR): proportion of windows without attack classified as attacks.

In order to strengthen our evaluation, only one third of the data is used for the training while the remaining is considered for testing and computing the

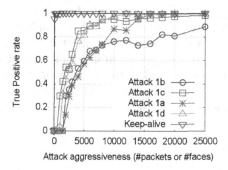

Fig. 4. True Positive Rate

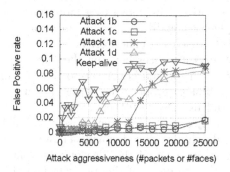

Fig. 5. False Positive Rate

previous metrics. Each experiment is run 10 times including a shuffle of windows for computing the average TPR and FPR. Initial experiments have been done to configure SVM for obtaining a good trade-off between TPR and FPR by using 5000 packets respectively faces as initial data.

In Figure 4 the true positive rate is plotted regarding the attack aggressiveness. This corresponds to the number of *Interest* packets for attacks 1b and 1c. The latter 1c is detected easier since the number of faces is multiplied meanwhile by 100 compared to 1b. Once the attack aggressiveness reaches 10,000 *Interest* packets, the TPR is higher than 95%. Similarly, the attack 1d is easier to monitor than 1a as the number of sent *Interest* packets is 100 times higher. Finally, the attack based on keep-alive *Interests* is well detected in any cases. In fact, such an attack last a longer time and is consequently much more visible.

Figure 5 shows that FPR remains low in most of cases. For the attacks 1b and 1c, generating a lot of *Interests*, they are never above 2%. The worst values are obtained for attacks involving a lot of faces (attack 1a, 1d and long duration attack) which seems contradictory as these attacks should be recognized easier when the number of solicited faces increases. In fact, this is due to two biases that we have investigated manually. First, the monitoring interface provided by CCNx gives metrics that are smoothed regarding the time. Hence, the impact of an attack is still visible on the monitoring interface in several time slots once it is finished (slow decrease of certain values over time) implying false positives. This all the more true with the keep alive which inject *Interest* packets periodically. This finding raises the need of a more accurate monitoring of inner values of CCN nodes for security purpose. Second, attacks involving many faces are longer to execute, which leads to have less windows without attacks. Thus, the training becomes less efficient for normal windows resulting in more false positives.

5   Related Work

5.1   Alternative Content Oriented Approaches

There are several architecture, like CCN, which aim to shift away of today Internet point-to-point primitives, move to a more data-oriented and content-centric paradigm, replace the end-to-end communication network model by pub-lish/subscribe model of a distribution network and to used cached copy of content for faster retrieval. Main differences between the different research approaches are the content naming scheme and how inter-domain routing is handled.

TRIAD [6] was the first to propose such an architecture. Names in TRIAD are based on URLs and use DNS for their resolution. Furthermore directories are used to map content to a replica server close-by. Shortly afterwards Brent Baccala in [4] expressed a similar idea of moving a more content-centric approach.

In 2007, *Koponen et al.* renewed the idea of a content-oriented network at Berkeley. DONA[15] was the name of this project. They followed another idea which consists into replacing DNS with flat and self-certifying names avoiding PKI for key verification.

The PSIRP[17] project introduces an architecture based on rendezvous points. Content is publish at the source. Each pieces has two labels, a public label used for the subscription to the content a private label used to verify the publisher.

Another research project focusing on content-centric networking is the 4WARD NetInf[8] project. Content is published using information units called Informa-tionObject (IO). As in general every IO needs a unique identifier by which it can be referenced, a multi-level DHT (Distributed Hash Table) handles the name res-olution and location lookup for a given IO.

5.2   Research Efforts on CCN

The most popular architecture for research purposes is the Content Centric Net-working proposed by Van Jacobson et al [12] from early 2007 and later introduced to the research community [14] in 2009. CCN current development is quite ad-vanced thanks to the CCNx open source framework [2]. PARC pursues research efforts of their architecture, describing and implementing advanced features and functionalities as the capacity of CCN to transport voice [13] with the adapted architecture. Many issues are described in [20] and still need to be addressed to make CCN (or Named Data Networking) a viable solution, for example: the scal-ability of routing on names, the efficiency of key management, the management of contents or the security of CCN nodes are critical questions deserving research efforts. Also, the design of a complete model to better understand the working and the benefit of a CCN architecture according to the network configuration, as proposed by Carofiglio et al [5], is an important step forward. Privacy on the Internet is more than ever a critical topic. DiBenedetto et al proposed in [10] a application over CCN that enables privacy preserving communications while introducing less relative overhead than TOR running over IP.

Among researches on CCN, a only few security issues have been investigated. In his master thesis, Tobias Lauinger [16] identified several attacks related to caches, in particular denial-of-service attacks against CCN routers, but he only investigated another attack "cache snooping" that enables attackers to efficiently monitor which content their neighbours are retrieving.

6 Conlusion

We presented in this paper a first monitoring architecture for CCN. While this new paradigm worth being investigated for the sake of future Internet, it also raises new management challenges we presented in this paper. Among those, we investigated one of the most important problem affecting CCN devices: the possible denial of service through the flooding of the PIT table. To address this issue, we used the monitoring features of the reference implementation coupled with a classification algorithm based on SVM and which can efficiently detect such attacks with a small computational cost. In fact, we implemented and experimented different attack strategies to perform DoS and all of them can be detected with very low error rates, which could be even lower with a more accurate report of operating values.

Our research opens directions for a lot of future works. First of all, our detection mechanism will be implemented within the CCNx libraries in order to enable real-time detection and the usage of associated countermeasure to mitigate attacks. We will then extend our monitoring architecture to monitor the other tables (FIB and Content Store tables) to detect other types of attacks. Finally, we want to extend our test-bed and generate more realistic traces including traffic from different applications. Attack detection was the focus point of our approach and future work will also focus on attack prevention.

References

1. CCNDSMOKETEST Manual Page, http://www.ccnx.org/releases/latest/doc/manpages/ccndsmoketest.1.html
2. Content Centric Networking, http://www.ccnx.org
3. Named Data Networking, http://named-data.net
4. Baccala, B.: Data-oriented networking. INTERNET-DRAFT (August 2002)
5. Carofiglio, G., Gallo, M., Muscariello, L., Perino, D.: Modeling data transfer in content-centric networking. In: Proceedings of the 23rd International Teletraffic Congress. pp. 111–118. ITC 2011, ITCP (2011), http://dl.acm.org/citation.cfm?id=2043468.2043487

6. Cheriton, D.R., Gritter, M.: Triad: A new next-generation internet architecture (July 2000)
7. Cristianini, N., Shawe-Taylor, J.: An introduction to support Vector Machines: and other kernel-based learning methods. Cambridge University Press, New York (2000)
8. Dannewitz, C., Herlich, M., Bauer, E., Becker, M., Beister, F., Dertmann, N., Hrestic, R., Kionka, M., Mohr, M., Mühe, M., Murali, D., Steffen, F., Stey, S., Unruh, E., Wang, Q., Weber, S.: Opennetinf documentation design and implementation (September 2011)
9. Debnath, R., Takahide, N., Takahashi, H.: A decision based one-against-one method for multi-class support vector machine. Pattern Anal. Appl. 7(2), 164–175 (2004)
10. DiBenedetto, S., Gasti, P., Tsudik, G., Uzun, E.: Andana: Anonymous named data networking application. CoRR abs/1112.2205 (2011), http://dblp.uni-trier.de/db/journals/corr/corr1112.html#abs-1112-2205
11. Ghodsi, A., Shenker, S., Koponen, T., Singla, A., Raghavan, B., Wilcox, J.: Information-centric networking: seeing the forest for the trees. In: Proceedings of the 10th ACM Workshop on Hot Topics in Networks, HotNets 2011, 1:1–1:6. ACM, New York (2011)
12. Jacobson, V., Mosko, M., Smetters, D., Garcia-Luna-Aceves, J.J.: Content-centric networking: Whitepaper describing future assurable global networks. Response to DARPA RFI SN07-12 (2007)
13. Jacobson, V., Smetters, D.K., Briggs, N.H., Plass, M.F., Stewart, P., Thornton, J.D., Braynard, R.L.: VoCCN: voice-over content-centric networks. In: Proceedings of the 2009 Workshop on Re-architecting the Internet, ReArch 2009, pp. 1–6. ACM, New York (2009)
14. Jacobson, V., Smetters, D.K., Thornton, J.D., Plass, M.F., Briggs, N.H., Braynard, R.L.: Networking named content. In: Proceedings of the 5th International Conference on Emerging Networking Experiments and Technologies, CoNEXT 2009, pp. 1–12. ACM, New York (2009)
15. Koponen, T., Chawla, M., Chun, B.G., Ermolinskiy, A., Kim, K.H., Shenker, S., Stoica, I.: A data-oriented (and beyond) network architecture. In: Proceedings of the 2007 Conference on Applications, Technologies, Architectures, and Protocols for Computer Communications, SIGCOMM 2007, pp. 181–192. ACM, New York (2007)
16. Lauinger, T.: Security & scalability of content-centric networking (September 2010), http://tubiblio.ulb.tu-darmstadt.de/46912/
17. Särelä, M., Rinta-aho, T., Tarkoma, S.: RTFM: Publish/Subscribe Internetworking Architecture. ICT-MobileSummit Conference (2008)
18. Schulze, H., Mochalski, K.: Internet study 2008/2009 (2009)
19. Wang, L. (ed.): Support Vector Machines: Theory and Applications. STUDFUZZ, vol. 177. Springer (2005)
20. Zhang, L., Estrin, D., Burke, J., Jacobson, V., Thornton, J.D., Smetters, D.K., Zhang, B., Tsudik, G., kc claffy, Krioukov, D., Massey, D., Papadopoulos, C., Abdelzaher, T., Wang, L., Crowley, P., Yeh, E.: Named Data Networking (NDN) Project (October 2010)

Towards Session-Aware RBAC Delegation: Function Switch

Meriam Ben Ghorbel-Talbi[1], Frédéric Cuppens[1], Nora Cuppens-Boulahia[1,2], and Stéphane Morucci[2]

[1] Institut TELECOM/Télécom Bretagne
2, rue de la Châtaigneraie, 35576 Cesson-Sévigné, France
[2] SWID, 5 Square du Chêne Germain, 35510 Cesson-Sévigné, France
{meriam.benghorbel,frederic.cuppens,nora.cuppens}@telecom-bretagne.eu,
stephane.morucci@swid.fr

Abstract. This paper shows how to extend RBAC sessions with dynamic aspects to deal with user switch. Users can authenticate using their functions which will create a dynamic session and automatically activate a set of privileges associated with this function. A dynamic session can be joined, left, restarted and reused by authorized users. Moreover, a user can switch the session to another user in order to continue the task by preserving the working context. We discuss in this paper how to manage users privileges in the dynamic session and how to deal with the switch mechanism.

1 Introduction

The delegation of privileges (permissions, roles) and duties (obligations, responsibilities) has been well studied in recent years and many RBAC extensions have been suggested to deal with these requirements [21,5,14,16]. In this paper we aim to introduce a new concept of dynamic session delegation which we call *switch*. Unlike traditional delegation models we consider that users may be able to "delegate" their whole activated session including their activated privileges and duties, but also their working context which contains running applications and files in use. Hence, the delegatee can continue to run the session exactly like the initial user without impacting the applications or services that are connected to this session, and without any additional authentication burden. This is very useful in many situations such as the continuity of work, where constant online user is required, or in the case of emergency management (e.g., in healthcare or public safety).

We first extend the notion of session suggested in RBAC [15] by dynamic session to enable (1) shareability: more than one user can use the same session (collaborative work), (2) reusability: a session can be reopened while keeping the same states and environments, (3) switchability: a user can transfer his session to another user which can be in a different time space or location. We focus in this paper on this last property and we consider that a session switch involves on itself an authentication, so that the user can directly access to the session

R. Di Pietro et al. (Eds.): DPM 2012 and SETOP 2012, LNCS 7731, pp. 287–302, 2013.
© Springer-Verlag Berlin Heidelberg 2013

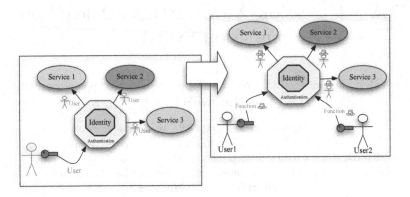

Fig. 1. Function authentication

without additional authentication and can have the whole privileges that are activated in this session. To deal with this aspect we introduce a new concept called *function*. A function can be seen as a job title, such as doctor on duty, that can be used as a virtual identity for the user (see figure 1). This means that, to be authenticated users can provide their function instead of their own identity. Once authenticated, they act as a function and a set of privileges (e.g., roles) that are associated with this function are automatically activated. Hence, if the user switches to another user, this later is authenticated through the same function and can reuse the session with the same environment. Moreover, in the case of collaborative work, many users can be authenticated through the same function and then can share the same session. During the session switch the user activity can be changed, it is what we call *activity switch*. This allows the user to reuse the working context in order to fulfill another task. Moreover, the working environment can be modified, in order to preserve the user privacy, for instance. It is what we call *context switch*.

These new concepts of switch have been introduced in [8] where authors have defined a new model called Smatch (Secure MAnagement of swiTCH) to deal with dynamic session. The Smatch model provides means to specify expressive contextual access control and authentication policies which apply to control functional behavior of dynamic sessions. We base our work on this model and we propose to extend the concept of switch in order to deal with the security administration. In fact, the notion of dynamic session and function authentication have been defined in this model, but the management of the security policy, which encompass users' actions on the dynamic session, has not yet been addressed. We show in this paper how the security administrator can define the security policy related to the function activation, the session joining/leaving, the user switching, the context switching or the function delegation.

This paper is organized as follows. In section 2, we present the basics of the smatch model that we need for our work. In section 3, we give a detailed description of dynamic sessions and how functions are managed in our model. In section 4, we focus on the notion of switch and how to manage the security policy in this context. Namely, how to manage users privileges in the dynamic session and how to control the switch mechanism (user and context switch). Finally, in section 5, we propose an implementation of our model using Eyeos, an open-source web based Operating System.

2   System Description

Our work is based on the Smatch model [8] which is defined as an extension of the Organization-Based Access Control model OrBAC [6]. This model is based on first order logic with action. First order logic is used to represent the system state at a given time. A system state is represented by a set of ground facts and a set of derivation rules having the form $P1 \wedge ... \wedge Pn \rightarrow P$. The derivation rules are syntactically compatible with Datalog [18]. Negative literals are allowed if it is possible to stratify the derivation rules. Stratifying a Datalog program consists in ordering derivation rules so that if a rule contains a negative literal then the rule that defines this literal is computed first. A stratified Datalog program with negation is computable in polynomial time through the computation of a fix point. Starting from the initial state, the system state can then change due to the execution of actions. Actions are specified through dynamic effect laws having the following form: $A(s, o)$ **causes** P **if** $Q1 \wedge ... \wedge Qn$ where $A(s, o)$ represents the execution of action A by subject s on object o and $P, Q1, ..., Qn$ are negated or unnegated application-dependent predicates.

In this model there are several concepts that are necessary to specify dynamic session and switch. Firstly, the concept of organization is central, which means that several organizations may specify their own security policy. More precisely, we will use the notion of dynamic organization [2] used in the smatch model to deal with dynamic session. Secondly, the administration model proposed by OrBAC [9] is very expressive and provides means to deal with different kinds of delegations [4,3], which is useful to manage the function switch. Moreover, the concept of context is explicitly introduced [6], this means that every security rule (permission, prohibition and obligation) can be associated with a context defined as constraints that a subject must satisfy to activate the rule. This allows us to define dynamic security policy. We give in the following the basics of the Smatch model that we need for our work.

The security policy is specified at the organization level that is independent of the implementation of this policy. Thus, instead of modeling the policy by using the concrete concepts of subject, action and object, it is specified using the roles that subjects, actions or objects play in the organization. The role of a subject is simply called a role, whereas the role of an action is called an activity and the role of an object is called a view. A view is an organizational concept used to structure the policy specification, i.e., a view groups objects to which the same security rules apply. We consider that there are nine basic sets of entities: Org (a set of organizations), F (a set of functions), S (a set of subjects), A (a set of actions), O (a set of objects), R (a set of roles), $\mathcal{A}$ (a set of activities), V (a set of views) and C (a set of contexts). And we consider the following built-in predicates:

- **Assign** is a predicate over domains $Org \times S \times R$. If org is an organization, s a subject and r a role, $Assign(org, s, r)$ means that s can activate role r in org.
- **Empower** is a predicate over domains $Org \times S \times R$. If org is an organization, s a subject and r a role, $Empower(org, s, r)$ means that role r is activated by subject s in org.
- **Use** is a predicate over domains $Org \times O \times V$. If org is an organization, o is an object and v is a view, then $Use(org, o, v)$ means that org uses o in v.
- **Consider** is a predicate over domains $Org \times A \times \mathcal{A}$. If org is an organization, α is an action and a is an activity, then $Consider(org, \alpha, a)$ means that org considers that action α implements activity a.
- **Hold** is a predicate over domains $Org \times S \times A \times O \times C$. If org is an organization, s a subject, α an action, o an object and c a context, $Hold(org, s, \alpha, o, c)$ means that within organization org, context c holds between s, α and o.

A security policy corresponds to a set of contextual organization privileges. Abstract permissions are defined using the following predicate:

- **Permission** is a predicate over domains $Org \times R \times A \times V \times C$. More precisely, if $auth$ is an organization, r is a role, v is a view, a is an activity and c is a context, then $Permission(auth, r, a, o, c)$ means that $auth$ grants permission to s to perform activity a on view v in context c.

Concrete permissions are derived from abstract permissions when the associated context holds (prohibitions and obligations are similarly defined). Five kinds of contexts have been defined [6]. The Temporal context that depends on the time at which the subject is requesting for an access to the system. The Spatial context that depends on the subject location. The User-declared context that depends on the subject objective (or purpose). The Prerequisite context that depends on characteristics that join the subject, the action and the object. Finally, the Provisional context that depends on previous actions the subject has performed in the system. We can also combine these elementary contexts to define new composed contexts by using conjunction, disjunction and negation operators: $\&$, $\oplus$ and $\bar{\ }$. This means that if c_1 and c_2 are two contexts, then $c_1 \& c_2$ is a conjunctive context, $c_1 \oplus c_2$ is a disjunctive context and $\bar{c_1}$ is a negative context.

Hierarchies [7] are defined over organizations, roles, activities, views and contexts using predicates $sub\_organization$, sub_role, $sub\_activity$, sub_view and $sub\_context$, respectively. Privileges are inherited through these hierarchies, for instance, permission inheritance is modeled by the following rule:

$$permission(org_2, r, a, v, c) \wedge sub\_organization(org_1, org_2)$$
$$\rightarrow permission(org_1, r, a, v, c).$$

The Smatch model proposes an authentication policy that activates user's privileges according to how users are authenticated: password authentication, strong authentication, one time password or also function authentication. In our work we focus on the function authentication that is defined as follows:

Action $function\_authentication(s, f, pass, org)$
Causes $function\_authenticated(org, s, f)$
If $password(org, f, pass)$

where ***function authentication(s, f, pass, org)*** is an authentication action and *pass* is the password associated with function f that subject s uses to authenticate in organization *org*. Obviously, other kinds of function authentication can be required, such as strong authentication using password and token.

3 Dynamic Session

Once authenticated through a function a set of privileges are automatically activated to the user in order to fulfill the task related to this function. And, according to the security policy, the user can switch to another user by preserving or not the activity and the working context. He/she can also allow another user to join the session to fulfill a collaborative task. How to deal with the security policy has not been addressed in the Smatch model, only the states of dynamic sessions and actions that users can perform on these sessions have been described. We give in the following sections our proposition to deal with administration aspects. For this purpose, we extend the function definition proposed in [8] and we give details on how to manage the switch in dynamic sessions.

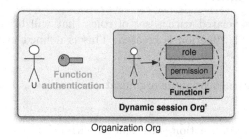

Fig. 2. Dynamic session

We consider that a dynamic session is created when a function is activated by a user, i.e., the user is authenticated through a function. This is different from the "traditional" RBAC session where users are authenticated using their own identity and activate or deactivate their privileges in the session according to their needs. A dynamic session is related to a given task (i.e., a function) so the set of privileges required to fulfill this function is automatically activated in the session. We use in our model the concept of dynamic organization introduced in [2] to define dynamic session. This means that, as described in figure 2, the creation of dynamic session is defined as the creation of a (dynamic) sub-organization (Org') of the organization in which the function was activated (Org). Privileges associated with the function (F) will be activated for the user (U) in this sub-organization.

As defined in [8] a dynamic session may have different states: active or idle, and users can ask to fulfill different actions in the session according to its state, such as create, join, share, asleep or awake (see figure 3). For the sake of simplicity we only consider in the following the active state and some actions that we need in our work.

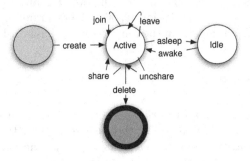

Fig. 3. Session states

We give in the following a description of how functions are defined in our model and the different steps required to create dynamic sessions.

3.1   Function Definition

Each function is associated with a set of roles that will be activated when a session related to this function is created. This is defined using the predicate *Assign* as follows:

- *Assign*(org, f, r) means that in organization *org* role r is assigned to function f.

We also consider that a function is associated with a context which holds when it is activated. We define for this purpose the predicate *function_context* as follows:

- *Function_context*(org, f, ctx_F) means that in organization *org* context ctx_F is associated with function f.

This context is used to activate permissions for the user in the dynamic organization, and more precisely permissions to administrate the session. Hence users can restrict the access to some of their data in order to preserve their privacy or to give fewer privileges to other users that join the session. More details about this context are given in the following section.

3.2   Function Activation

We give hereafter the different steps that are needed to activate a function.

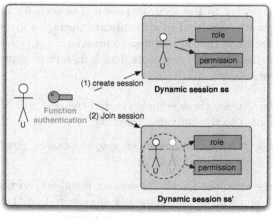

Fig. 4. Dynamic session

Session creation. After the authentication through function f, the user can choose to create a session as follows (see figure 4 part (1)):

Action $create\_session(subj, ss, org)$
Causes $use(org, ss, session) \land session\_initiator(ss, subj) \land$
$session\_function(ss, f)$
If $function\_authenticated(org, subj, f)$

where *session* is a special view and $use(org, ss, session)$ means that organization *org* uses object *ss* as a session. A session is associated with two attributes: *session_initiator*: the subject who creates the session and *session_function*: the function related to this session.

Then the created dynamic session becomes a sub-organization of the parent organization, so that it inherits all the privileges already defined [7]. The inheritance also applies to the assign, use, consider and hold predicates:

$$use(org, ss, session) \rightarrow sub\_organization(ss, org).$$

Session joining. Besides creating a new session, user *subj* can choose to join an existing session ss' related to function f that is already activated by another user $subj'$ in organization *org* (see figure 4 part (2)). We consider for this purpose a new attribute *session_member* as follows:

Action $join\_session(subj, ss, org)$
Causes $session\_member(ss, subj)$

The session initiator is also considered a session member:

$$session\_initiator(ss, subj) \rightarrow session\_member(ss, subj).$$

Obviously, the user can create or join the active session only if he/she is authorized to do so, according to the security policy. The security policy must also specify which users are permitted to authenticate through a given function, and the activation constraints that are related to functions, e.g., exclusive functions or function cardinality. We shall give more details on how to manage the security policy in the following section 4.

Privileges activation. Once the session is created the user will be empowered in roles that are assigned to the activated function:

$use(org, ss, session) \land session\_member(ss, subj) \land session\_function(ss, f) \land$
$assign(org, f, r) \rightarrow empower(ss, subj, r).$

Note that roles are activated for all the session members. So that when a user joins a session he/she will be automatically empowered on the function roles, and will lose these privileges when he/she leaves the session.

Moreover, the context related to the function is activated within the session. This is defined as follows:

$use(org, ss, session) \land session\_function(ss, f) \land function\_context(org, f, ctx_F)$
$\rightarrow hold(ss, s, a, o, ctx_F) \land session\_member(ss, s) \land consider(ss, a, \_) \land use(ss, o, \_).$

This context is used to activate a set of permissions related to the session administration. These permissions can be defined as follows:

$Permission(org, role, activity, view, ctx_F).$

where *activity* and *view* are administrative activities and views, respectively, and *role* can be defined as a default_role including the session members.

As we said previously, the dynamic session is a sub-organization of the parent organization then it will inherit these permissions. Moreover, the function context holds within the dynamic session so that these permissions will be activated only within the scope of this session. We give in the following more details about how we manage these administrative privileges.

4   Switch Management

We present in this section our proposition to manage the security policy. We specify how users can act on functions and dynamic sessions. These actions have been defined in the Smatch model, but how to control these actions has not been addressed. Namely, which users are allowed to authenticate through a function, which users are allowed to join an active session, to delegate their functions or also to switch to another user and under which conditions.

Activating a function. In our model, authenticated users are allowed to activate a given role only if they are assigned to this role:

$permission(org, authenticated\_user, activate, r, assigned\_role).$

where context *assigned_role* is defined as follows:

$$assign(org, u, r) \rightarrow hold(org, u, activate, r, assigned\_role).$$

Similarly, we consider that users are allowed to activate a dynamic session, i.e., a function, only if they are assigned to this function. This is defined as follows:

$$permission(org, default\_user, activate, f, assigned\_function).$$

where context *assigned_function* is defined as follows:

$$assign(org, u, f) \rightarrow hold(org, u, activate, f, assigned\_function).$$

Creating a session. Users are allowed to create a dynamic session only after function authentication:

$$permission(org, authenticated\_user, create, session, activated\_function).$$

where context *activated_function* is defined as follows:

$$function\_authenticated(org, subj, f) \wedge session\_initiator(ss, subj) \wedge$$
$$session\_function(ss, f)$$
$$\rightarrow hold(org, subj, create, ss, activated\_function).$$

Joining a session. This permission can be specified by the security administrator in order to allow users to join an existing session:

$$permission(org, r, join, session, existing\_session).$$

where context *existing_session* is defined as follows:

$$function\_authenticated(org, subj, f) \wedge use(org, ss, session) \wedge$$
$$session\_function(ss, f) \wedge session\_initiator(ss, subj')$$
$$\rightarrow hold(org, subj, join, ss, existing\_session).$$

This context means that session ss is already activated by another user $subj'$ and the user $subj$ is already authenticated through function f related to this session.

The security administrator can also specify other conditions using contexts (temporal, spatial, user-declared, prerequisite or provisional contexts [6]). For instance, we can specify that, in the case of an emergency, role *doctor* is allowed to join an existing session related to function *doctor_on_call*:

$$permission(org, doctor, join, session, activated\_session \ \& \ emergency\_doctor).$$

where context *emergency_doctor* holds in the case of an emergency and when the dynamic session is related to function *doctor_on_call*[1]:

$$hold(org, \_, \_, \_, emergency) \wedge session\_function(ss, doctor\_on\_call)$$
$$\rightarrow hold(org, \_, join, ss, emergency\_doctor).$$

We can also specify that a user is allowed to join a session only if the initiator is not available, or if a session member is leaving the session.

---

[1] The prolog symbol _ is interpreted as representing "do not care" condition.

Other actions on sessions. Similarly to create or to join a session, we can specify permissions to make other actions on sessions, namely to leave, to share, to unshare, to asleep or to awake a session. For instance, in the case of functions where continuity of work is required, a user is allowed to leave a session only if there is other members in this session:

$$permission(org, r, leave, session, other\_session\_member).$$

where context *other_session_member* is defined as follows:

$$session\_member(ss, u) \land session\_member(ss, u') \land \neg(u' = u)$$
$$\rightarrow hold(org, u, \_, ss, other\_session\_member).$$

User switch. This permission allows a user to assign new permissions to other users in order to join a given session, so that it is called administrative permission. To deal with this kind of permissions we use the administration model proposed by OrBAC [9,4]. This model is based on an object-oriented approach, thus we do not manipulate privileges directly (i.e., Permission and Prohibition), but we use objects having a specific semantic and belonging to specific views, called administrative views. Inserting an object in these views will enable to assign permissions, prohibitions or roles to users. Among these administrative views, we detail in the following the *License view* that is used to specify and manage the security policy. Objects belonging to this view have the following attributes: *Type*: the object type can be a license, a ban or a duty, *Auth*: organization in which the license applies, *Grantee*: subject to which the license is granted, *Privilege*: action permitted by the license, *Target*: object to which the license grants an access and *Context*: specific conditions that must be satisfied to use the license, the ban or the duty. The existence of an object in this view is interpreted as a permission, a prohibition or an obligation according to the object type. For instance, the existence of a valid license is interpreted as a permission by the following rule:

$$use(org, l, license) \land type(l, license) \land auth(l, auth) \land grantee(l, r) \land$$
$$privilege(l, act) \land target(l, v) \land context(l, context)$$
$$\rightarrow permission(auth, r, act, v, context).$$

We consider a sub-view of *license* view called *session_license* as follows:

$$use(org, l, license) \land target(l, ss) \land use(org, ss, session) \land privilege(l, a) \land$$
$$consider(org, a, session\_action) \rightarrow use(org, l, session\_license).$$

where *session_action* is an activity containing actions that users can perform on sessions (create, join, leave, etc.).

This means that the existence of an object in this sub-view is interpreted as the existence of an object in the license view having a session as a target and a session action as a privilege. Users that are allowed to add objects in this sub-view can create new permissions for other users related to sessions, such as a permission to join or to leave a given session.

As previously mentioned, a user switch creates a new permission to join the session, so we consider that a permission to switch in this view is a permission to add a new license with privilege *join*. Permissions to manage switch are defined as follows:

$$permission(org, r, switch, session\_license, authorized\_switch).$$

where context *authorized_switch* means that a switch is allowed only for the session members:

$$use(org, l, session\_license) \land target(l, ss) \land session\_member(ss, u)$$
$$\rightarrow hold(org, u, \_, l, authorized\_switch).$$

We can also add other contexts in order to specify more conditions on the switch. These conditions may concern, for instance, the user who switches the session (according to his/her roles, attributes, etc.), the function related to the session, the user to whom the switch is allowed, e.g., in the case of function *doctor on call* the session can only be switched to a doctor:

$$permission(org, r, switch, session\_license, session\_switch \ \& \ doctor\_switch).$$

$$auth(l, auth) \land target(l, ss) \land session\_function(ss, doctor\_on\_call) \land$$
$$grantee(l, u) \land assign(auth, u, doctor)$$
$$\rightarrow hold(org, u, \_, l, session\_license, doctor\_switch).$$

As a result of the user switch a new license is added to the view *session_license* and the user is no longer member of this session (see figure 5):

Action *user_switch(subj, usr, ss)*
Causes $use(org, l, session\_license) \land auth(l, org) \land grantee(l, usr) \land privilege(l,$
$join) \land target(l, ss) \land context(l, default\_context) \land \neg session\_member(ss, subj))$
If $sub\_organization(ss, org)$

Hence the grantee will be allowed to join the session, using his/her own identity, without the need to perform a function authentication as it is the case usually (see section 3.2). We can also activate an obligation for the grantee to join the session before a given deadline, for example before the other user leaves

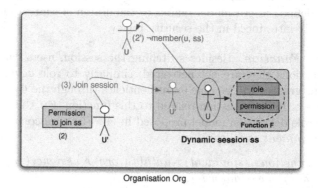

Organisation Org

Fig. 5. User switch

the session (in the case of continuity of work). Due to space limitation, we do not address the issue of how to deal with obligations in this paper (see [11] for more details about the management of obligations with deadlines).

The joining user has the same privileges (active roles, permissions, working environment, etc.) as the leaving one. Thus he/she can continue to run the session exactly as before. But, as previously mentioned, the user can modify the session context in order to limit the joining user privileges.

Context Switch. To deal with context switch, we consider that users have administrative privileges in the session, namely they are allowed to add prohibitions to other users in order to reduce their privileges. This is managed using the function context introduced previously in section 3.1. This context is used with administrative permissions to specify how users are allowed to administrate dynamic sessions. As defined in section 3.1, context ctx_f holds in the dynamic session after the activation of the function, thus permissions related to it are activated only in the scope of the session. For instance, we can specify that the session initiator of a given function f is allowed to add prohibitions for other users in this session:

$$permission(org, r, add, license\_view, ctx_f \ \& \ c\_prohibition).$$

where ctx_f is a context associated with function f, and $c\_prohibition$ is defined as follows:

$$session\_initiator(ss, u) \wedge type(l, ban) \rightarrow hold(ss, u, \_, l, c\_prohibition).$$

We can also use other contexts to specify more conditions related to the user to whom the session initiator can give prohibitions, and what kind of prohibition he/she can add. For instance, to preserve their privacy, users are allowed to prohibit the access to their personal data. Context switch can also be done automatically, according to the environment change. For instance, we can specify that sensitive information can only be accessed in secured context, e.g., when the user is in his/her office. If the user leaves the office then the access to this information will be automatically prohibited by the access control policy. This can be easily defined in our model thanks to the notion of contextual privileges that is explicitly introduced in the security policy.

Delegating a Function. Besides switching the session, users can also delegate their functions that are not activated, similarly to role delegation. This means that the grantee will be able to authenticate through the delegated function and create a dynamic session related to this function. For this purpose, we use the same role delegation model proposed in [4]. First, we consider the view *Function_assignment* as follows:

$$use(auth, fa, function\_assignment) \wedge auth(fa, org) \wedge assignee(fa, r) \wedge$$
$$assignment(fa, f) \rightarrow assign(org, f, r).$$

This means that the existence of a valid object fa in this view is interpreted as an assignment of function f to role (or subject) r in organization org. Then, to deal with function delegation, we consider a sub-view of $function\_ assignment$ called $function\_delegation$. Objects belonging to this view inherit the semantic and the attributes of view $function\_assignment$, but, also have an additional attribute called *Grantor*: the subject who is delegating the function. Thus inserting an object in this view will enable an authorized grantor to delegate a function to a grantee. The security administrator can specify which users/roles are allowed to delegate their functions and in which contexts as follows:

$$permission(org, r, delegate, function\_delegation, context).$$

The security administrator can also specify how much the function can be delegated and/or re-delegated (multiple and multi-step delegation, respectively), if the delegation is temporary or permanent, and if the grantor keeps the function or not after the delegation (transfer). More details about delegation are given in [4]. Hence to summarize this section, the security policy controls all the users actions on the session such as the activation, the joining, the switch and the delegation of functions. Authorized actions must also satisfy the global constraints specified by the security administrator, i.e., the separation of duty policies related to the activation/deactivation of functions, the joining/leaving of sessions, etc. For instance, we have to deal with dynamic separation of duties in the case of the user switch. Namely, when a user joins a session s_1, his/her roles that are activated in another session s_2 can conflict with roles activated in s_1. In this case, we can choose to refuse the switch or also to activate a pre-obligation to the user in order to leave the session s_2 before allowing him/her to join session s_1 (how to manage pre-obligations is presented in [10]). Many other constraints can be defined to deal with functions similarly to roles like cardinality, exclusive functions, etc. This is an important issue to consider and we aim to address it in our future work.

5   Switch Enforcement

For the implementation of our model we choose to use Eyeos [12], an efficient open-source web-based Operating System, following the cloud computing concept. It enables collaboration and communication among users. We have modified this OS to include a dedicated access control mechanism that overrides the Eyeos access control function to provide enhanced capabilities and demonstrate the switch concept. Access control policies are expressed using MotOrBAC [1] a tool developed at Telecom Bretagne that implements the OrBAC model. It provides a user-friendly interface to specify and manage the security policy.

As specified in figure 6, these policies are enforced using a specific Policy Enforcement Point (PEP) and two Policy Decision Points (PDP), only one PDP is active at a time. A PEP has been implemented in Eyeos as a replacement of current access control module. Two OrBAC-based PDPs, with two kinds of requesting methods: 1) A PDP which is queried using a standardized XACML protocol. OrBAC policies are translated into XACML and processed by the Swid XACML server. This PDP has the advantage of handling standard protocols.

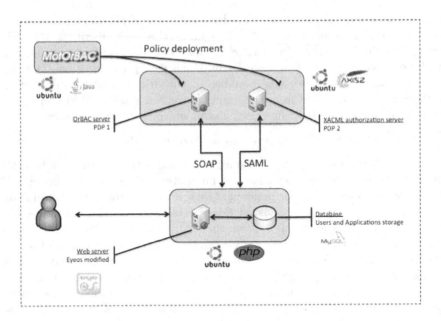

Fig. 6. Architecture

By contrast, XACML policies cannot express fine-grained access-control policies with complex context processing. 2) A PDP which is queried using dedicated Web-services. OrBAC policies are directly interpreted for each query. This PDP leverages the power of the OrBAC model, making it possible to have advanced security policies (through expressive context evaluation).

Swid software agents are integrated into Eyeos to handle communication (either SAML or Web-service) between Eyeos access control mechanism and PDPs. Using this application, users can be authenticated through a function, and get an access to a limited set of applications, depending on their rights (privileges that are assigned to the activated function). Several users can share the same session once authenticated through the same function. Users can close their sessions or perform a user switch. This second behavior is similar to the first one, but in addition it allows another user to join the session. In these two cases, the session can be resumed by authorized users, and all applications previously launched are displayed. Moreover, all data written by the previous user are kept, making it possible to append some additional information. The session context can change after the user switch, for instance, we may consider that if the user location is not in a secured area, then the security policy forbids the access to confidential information and applications. Note that the context can also be modified without the user switch, for instance, when the user moves from his/her office to another location, some applications will be prohibited or closed. Or also when an emergency occurs, the user will have an access to additional privileges in order to deal with urgent situations. As future work, we aim to extend this application with more administration features that we have discussed in this paper. For instance, in our model users are able to perform a context switch by forbidding the access to their personal data to the other session members. This will update the security policy by adding prohibition rules.

6 Discussion and Conclusion

To the best of our knowledge, we have addressed in this paper new issues that have not been previously considered by access control models. Our concept of dynamic session is different from traditional RBAC sessions [15] since, it supports new features namely, shareability, reusability and switchability. In our model, a user may create a dynamic session and starts the execution of a task, suspend the session, reopen it, and continue the execution of this task in another context. Also, using the switch operation, this task may be continued by another user. Moreover, we have introduced the concept of function that involves both authentication and access control mechanisms to ease the switch operation. When function authentication is used a set of privileges that are needed to perform the related task, are automatically activated for the user. This is different from the concept of task defined in task based RBAC models such as [20,17,19] since, in these models, the dynamic behavior of our approach is not addressed.

In [13] authors propose the concept of capability delegation, where a capability represents a self-authenticating permission to access a specified object in permitted operations. Our concept of function switch is different form delegation, since the working context of the initial session will not be lost when the joining user activates the dynamic session, which is not the case in "classical" delegation. During the switch, the context can change according to the security policy, to preserve user privacy or for security reasons. The user activity can also change to fulfill another task by preserving the working environment. Another switch issue that has not been addressed in this paper is the organization switch, when the user hands over to another user belonging to another organization. This is the most complex case to manage since the user, who is targeted by the switch, will not be probably assigned to the "same" role as the original user. We aim to further investigate this feature in future work. We also aim to study separation of duty policies related to the activation and deactivation of dynamic sessions especially in the case of user switch.

Acknowledgments. This research has been supported by the RoleID project. Role-ID is a european research project funded by Eureka, ITEA 2 programe. The project is coordinated by EADS Defense and Security Systems, France.

References

1. Autrel, F., Cuppens, F., Cuppens, N., Coma, C.: MotOrBAC 2: A Security Policy Tool. In: SARSSI (2008)
2. Autrel, F., Cuppens-Boulahia, N., Cuppens, F.: Reaction Policy Model Based on Dynamic Organizations and Threat Context. In: Gudes, E., Vaidya, J. (eds.) Data and Applications Security 2009. LNCS, vol. 5645, pp. 49–64. Springer, Heidelberg (2009)

3. Ben-Ghorbel-Talbi, M., Cuppens, F., Cuppens-Boulahia, N., Bouhoula, A.: An Extended Role-Based Access Control Model for Delegating Obligations. In: Fischer-Hübner, S., Lambrinoudakis, C., Pernul, G. (eds.) TrustBus 2009. LNCS, vol. 5695, pp. 127–137. Springer, Heidelberg (2009)
4. Ben-Ghorbel-Talbi, M., Cuppens, F., Cuppens-Boulahia, N., Bouhoula, A.: A Delegation Model for Extended RBAC. The International Journal of Information Security (IJIS) 9(3) (June 2010)
5. Crampton, J., Khambhammettu, H.: Delegation in Role-Based Access Control. International Journal of Information Security (September 2008)
6. Cuppens, F., Cuppens-Boulahia, N.: Modeling Contextual Security Policies. International Journal of Information Security 7(4) (2008)
7. Cuppens, F., Cuppens-Boulahia, N., Miège, A.: Inheritance hierarchies in the Or-BAC Model and application in a network environment. In: FCS (2004)
8. Cuppens, F., Cuppens-Boulahia, N., Nuadi, M.: Smatch Model: Extending RBAC Sessions in Virtualization Environment. In: ARES (2011)
9. Cuppens, F.C., Cuppens-Boulahia, N., Coma, C.: Multi-Granular Licences to Decentralize Security Administration. In: SSS/WRAS (2007)
10. El-Rakaiby, Y., Cuppens, F., Cuppens-Boulahia, N.: From Contextual Permission to Dynamic Pre-Obligation. In: ARES (2010)
11. Elrakaiby, Y., Cuppens, F., Cuppens-Boulahia, N.: Formal enforcement and management of obligation policies. Data & Knowledge Engineering (2011)
12. EYEOS, http://www.eyeos.org/
13. Hasebe, K., Mabuchi, M., Matsushita, A.: Capability-Based Delegation Model in RBAC. In: SACMAT (2010)
14. Ray, I., Toahchoodee, M.: A Spatio-temporal Access Control Model Supporting Delegation for Pervasive Computing Applications. In: Furnell, S.M., Katsikas, S.K., Lioy, A. (eds.) TrustBus 2008. LNCS, vol. 5185, pp. 48–58. Springer, Heidelberg (2008)
15. Sandhu, R., Coyne, E.J., Feinstein, H.L., Youman, C.E.: Role-Based Access Control Models. IEEE Computer 29(2), 38–47 (1996)
16. Schaad, A., Moffett, J.D.: Delegation of Obligations. In: POLICY (2002)
17. Oh, S., Park, S.: Task-Role-based Access Control Model. Information Systems 28 (2003)
18. Ullman, J.D.: Principles of Database and Knowledge-Base Systems: Volume II: The New Technologies. W. H. Freeman & Co., New York (1990)
19. Yao, L., Kong, X., Xu, Z.: A Task-Role Based Access Control Model With Multi-Constraints. In: NCM (2008)
20. Zhang, L., Luo, L., Zhang, L., Geng, T., Yue, Z.: Task-Role-Based Access Control in Application on MIS. In: APSCC (2006)
21. Zhang, X., Oh, S., Sandhu, R.: Pbdm: A Flexible Delegation Model in RBAC. In: SACMAT (2003)

Policy Chain for Securing Service Oriented Architectures

Wihem Arsac[1], Annett Laube[2], and Henrik Plate[1]

[1] SAP Research, 805 Avenue Dr M. Donat, 06250 Mougins, France
[2] Bern University of Applied Sciences, 2501 Biel/Bienne, Switzerland
{wihem.arsac,henrik.plate}@sap.com,
annett.laube@bfh.ch

Abstract. Service Providers using Service Oriented Architecture in order to deliver in-house services as well as on-demand and cloud services have to deal with two interdependent challenges: (1) to achieve, maintain and prove compliance with security requirements stemming from internal needs, 3rd party demands and international regulations and (2) to manage requirements, policies and security configuration in a cost-efficient manner. The deficiencies of current processes and tools force these service providers to trade off profitability against security and compliance. This paper summarizes a novel approach of a policy chain, which links high-level, abstract and declarative security policies on one side and low-level, imperative, and technical security configuration settings on the other side. The paper describes an architecture linking several applications and models via state-machines in order to provide a toolset supporting service providers to build such a holistic policy chain at design time, and to maintain and leverage it during system operation.

Keywords: Security of Service Oriented Architecture, Security Policy Management and Enforcement.

1   Introduction

Today, service providers offer services on different levels, providing a broad diversity of functions from low-level infrastructure services for data storage or bandwidth up to high-level IT services that support common business processes such as invoicing or enterprise resource planning. They have the freedom to integrate 3rd party services for their specific offering. As such, numerous combinations of in-house and on-demand services will be employed by future market participants, in its extremes ranging from service providers that operate entire service landscapes by themselves, to service providers that merely rebrand and resell services of suppliers. The technical composition of such services, typically based on service oriented architecture and using Web technologies, is accompanied by a multitude of contractual, binding agreements between service providers and consumers on security and compliance aspects. The PoSecCo[1] project takes the perspective of a service provider managing

---

[1] PoSecCo FP7 EU Project, http://posecco.eu/

R. Di Pietro et al. (Eds.): DPM 2012 and SETOP 2012, LNCS 7731, pp. 303–317, 2013.
© Springer-Verlag Berlin Heidelberg 2013

and operating such services, and possibly relying on one or multiple suppliers. The overall project goal is to increase and prove system compliance and security at reduced costs. It supports service providers in the design and enforcement of security policies, hereby involving a variety of company internal and external stakeholders. In order to ensure the applicability of project results in real-life environments, policy enforcement will not require the installation of a dedicated software infrastructure, but solely rely on standard security mechanisms present in a given landscape. The interface towards the system landscape is represented by IT service management solutions, e.g., Configuration Management Systems (CMS) and Databases (CMDB) that comprise system details and offer support for configuration provisioning.

2   Challenges

The challenges a typical service provider faces are related to:

(C1) The increasing number and complexity of regulatory requirements, multiplied by the number of countries a service provider and its customers are active in. For instance, a provider of an on-demand service for invoice management must consider country-specific requirements for digital signatures stemming from all countries its customers have business partners from. Typically, high-level policies are formulated and maintained in prose and manually translated into lower-level, service-specific configuration settings.

(C2) The number of stakeholders: A multitude of organization-internal and -external stakeholders are involved in security management and operation of a productive landscape. At a service provider, a wide range of stakeholders is involved in the process of defining the security requirements down to their enforcements: for instance, customer and vendor managers, both responsible to communicate with customers resp. suppliers, as well as operation, compliance and security managers, auditors and controllers also involved in the security enforcement process. In addition, the historic development of the IT and security domain as well as vendor or product specific languages and terminology often hinder the communication of stakeholders that work on different architectural layers. The process of breaking high-level requirements down to low-level settings spans across organizational boundaries and gains additional complexity in scenarios, where larger shares of a service infrastructure are outsourced or 3rd party business services are integrated by a provider into its own service offerings.

(C3) The steady evolution of a service provider's environment, business and IT landscape during operations time: [1, 2, 3] confirm the inefficiency of current processes that lead to outdated security policies not being aligned with current business requirements, and argues that companies have difficulties to prove the enforcement of their security policy at reasonable costs.

(C4) Potential conflicts at different levels: Both the high-level policies as well as enforcing security configuration settings of the various application and infrastructure services may overlap or conflict. For instance, invoice retention time requirements stemming from different countries may conflict with each other, or the virus scanning of PDF documents configured at a border firewall can fail due to the use of SSL/TLS when consumers of an invoice service exchange documents with business partners.

To summarize, today's shortcomings with regard to policy and security configuration management – i.e. the creation and maintenance of consistent security policies and their correct and traceable enforcement through security configurations of all infrastructure elements – impacts the trustworthiness, compliance and profitability of service providers. The impact on the Total Cost of Operations (TCO) and as such the profitability of service offerings is apparent from recent studies [2, 3], which state that system management costs – which include the cost of maintaining security configuration – have been growing out of control. At the same time, though being cost-intensive, the processes are error-prone and rarely documented [4], which impacts the trustworthiness of IT infrastructures, widely confirmed by studies, like [5, 6, 7]. The improvement and – where possible – automation of activities related to policy and configuration management can therefore be understood as one critical success factor of market actors. As such, we target the automation of activities where possible, and the assistance of responsible personnel with decision support systems where human intervention is required.

3   Related Work

Using policies to drive security management has been mentioned in [8]. The capturing and modeling of security requirements is an important concern. An extension of policy-based management and policy hierarchies is proposed in [9] to automatically derive configuration files for large-scale networks. As in our approach (cf. Section 5.2), their tool Mobasec supports the modeling phase of high-level security requirements and provides an automated derivation of the configuration. Their approach focuses on the design phase of policies and configuration, but does not investigate the usage of these artifacts during operations time, in order to cope with ongoing change (cf. challenge C3). The Power prototype [10] addresses the configuration management from a business point of view, supporting the creation of policy hierarchies by means of a tool-assisted policy refinement, but the syntax used is a Prolog-like language, far from both business and administrators' views. The framework developed in the scope of the Positif project [11] partially satisfies C2 and C3 by the policy-driven configuration of security services of networked systems within a single domain of administration. The Deserec project [12] defined a tiered architecture as a policy based framework to assure the dependability of critical systems. Both Positif and Deserec propose an abstraction of the policies close to the network layer, whereas PoSecCo considers all architectural layers, from network to application and services, as well as their related security capabilities (see Section 4). Moreover, Positif and Deserec aim at the full automation of configuration and change management processes, while we believe that human interaction is hardly evitable and sometimes even necessary, in particular with regard to authorization and responsibility related to decision-making, particularly regarding the harmonization and approval of high-level policies and the selection of to-be-implemented enforcement mechanisms among a set of alternatives.

Among the security enforcement tools, the authors of [13] present a policy-based dynamic adaptation and reconfiguration mechanisms of the deployed levels of security measures, hereby addressing C3 and C4, but their approach does not cover the design phase of the security requirements. Neither do the authors of MIRAGE [14], when they propose a management tool for the analysis, refinement and automatic deployment of configuration settings related to network layers (such as firewalls or VPN routers). MIRAGE does not currently address C3, but it is planned, as future work, to manage the update of components' configurations, comparing the discrepancies between the desired and actual configurations, a feature that we do support. Teo and Ahn [15] propose Chameleos-x, a policy framework designed to enforce security policies across security-aware systems on different kinds of equipment. However, they do not offer support for explicit modeling of the network architecture, making it difficult to understand the coverage of the model and the reuse of the policies in different environments. SmartFrog [16] is a framework for creating configuration-driven systems. However, only parts of the entire landscape are covered, as it provides configuration and change management for low-level system components like servers and network devices. Burns et al. [17] also address C3 with a tool that, given a security policy, automatically enables network elements to be reconfigured without human intervention.

With the aim to achieve, maintain and prove evidence of compliance with security requirements stemming from internal and external stakeholders, Ponder2 [18] tries to address all the challenges with a set of tools for the specification, deployment and management of policies, enriched with the implementation and conflict analysis of Ponder policies [19]. Despite the expressiveness of authorization and obligation policies, Ponder2 requires to install a policy-enforcement infrastructure whereas we rely on off-the-shelf security capabilities present in a given landscape, e.g., access control and channel protection as provided by J2EE containers. Hassan [20] proposed an interesting approach (addressing C1-C4) to refine network security policies to low-level security mechanisms. Their framework uses a policy-based approach to automate the implementation of security mechanisms, assessing the equivalence of the high-level security policy and the related low-level one. They focus on a fully automated approach, but they do not provide guidance in checking ambiguities and resolving conflicts.

4   Policy Chain

To meet these challenges, PoSecCo defines the so-called **policy chain**, a reliable, sustainable and traceable link between security artifacts of three different abstraction levels [21]: business policies, IT security policies, and security configurations. This link is crucial to ensure that a system is compliant to its security requirements, but difficult to establish and maintain in todays' practice.

Business policies represent high-level security requirements imposed on service providers, both from external and internal stakeholders. They are declarative and address the business domain, e.g., the requirement to "*ensure the confidentiality of invoice information*". They largely ignore details of the actual system used for service delivery, but focus on business concepts. Though structured and linkable to various business concepts, a business policy as such is described in natural language and does not support automated reasoning, e.g., conflict analysis.

IT security policies describe how to meet the requirements, hereby reflecting the service providers' organization and system. They are still declarative as they do not prescribe a given enforcement mechanism, e.g., to "*encrypt invoice data sent from the invoicing software to the archive*". A conflict-free set of such policies triggers a refinement process that selects the most efficient enforcement mechanisms existing in the current landscape, based on security capabilities offered by system components and associated metrics for performance and costs. Alternatives and their assessment will be presented to decision makers supposed to select one of the proposed alternatives for implementation. Continuing above example, WS-Security, SSL/TLS or VPN can be considered as alternative enforcement mechanisms.

Security configurations are imperative and implement IT security policies for previously selected mechanisms, e.g., SSL/TLS settings of a Web server that runs the archiving component. For PoSecCo, they are specific to a class of enforcement mechanisms, e.g., firewalls, but abstract from vendor specific formats. While the so-called abstract configuration is automatically created by PoSecCo tools, the translation of such an abstract configuration into a concrete, deployable configuration required by a given product is left to the CMS.

The policy chain is related to the lifecycle of an organization's security concept in that it is built during the design phase and leveraged at runtime to deal with on-going changes.

4.1 Building the Policy Chain

The construction of the policy chain relies on the presence of a **functional system model**, i.e., a comprehensive description of functional aspects characterizing a service provider's business and IT system. Similarly structured as the policy chain, the functional system model distinguishes three layers (see Fig. 1), one after the other considered during the top-down development of the policy chain.

The **business model** describes the service offering, the organizational structure of a service provider and relevant external institutions such as suppliers or customers. These concepts represent the starting point for the elicitation of above-described business policies in a collaborative process involving multiple security stakeholders. Thereby, stakeholders do not only contribute to requirement specification, but also declare ownership and responsibility for requirements, which in turn will be used to report and tackle security issues at operations time.

The **IT service interaction model** describes the choreography of logical software components jointly providing a given business service, hereby outlining their interfaces as well as the exchange and processing of data. The IT service model together with the business policies represent the basis for the specification of IT policies. A policy designer is supposed to specify IT security policies that satisfy the business policies in the given interaction model (resp. architecture). As IT security policies are formally specified, they allow reasoning about dependencies and conflicts prior to continuing with the refinement process.

The **infrastructure model** represents the implementation of the IT service interaction model, hereby describing the system in much detail, e.g., its network topology, installed software components, physical machines, or concrete service endpoints. This information is mainly retrieved from a CMDB, a central concept of ITIL[2] and commonly used for system and application management. Moreover, the infrastructure model comprises a description of security capabilities offered by the existing system elements, e.g., the capability of a given Web server to perform certificate-based user authentication. These capabilities will be searched and assessed during the policy refinement steps, in order to present human decision makers a set of alternative policy enforcement mechanisms. The assessment of alternatives is supported by mathematical optimization functions that consider cost and performance. Once a decision is taken, a capability-specific and abstract security configuration will be generated in an automated fashion. This represents the last element of the policy chain, and will be used as input for the generation and deployment of concrete configuration settings.

4.2   Leveraging the Policy Chain

After its construction during the design phase, the policy chain can be leveraged to deal with changes to high-level security requirements as well as to low-level system configuration.

On the level of security requirements, it facilitates the manual analysis of new security requirements imposed by, for instance, new customer contracts. Looking at comparable requirements and related IT security policies, the latter already being enforced in the landscape, one can more easily determine to what extent the current security concept already covers the new requirements and what is missing respectively.

On the level of the operational system landscape, it facilitates the impact analysis of configuration changes, an activity central to ITIL change management processes. By traversing the chain, change approvers can more easily determine the policies and requirements affected by a given change request. This application of the policy chain addresses a typical source of compliance and security issues, i.e., the ad-hoc change of low-level configuration settings in ignorance of security and compliance consequences.

Besides generating the configuration of selected policy enforcement mechanisms, the policy chain can also generate structured configuration checklists to validate the correctness of configuration settings and to assess misconfigurations. This use case acknowledges that real-life system configuration will be achieved in various ways, possibly bypassing ITIL processes.

The policy chain and the functional system model also serve as a comprehensive documentation of an organization's security concept, useful for company internal and external stakeholders: Selected parts may be of interest for security-aware prospects, herewith acknowledging the importance of security for purchase decisions in certain industries.

---

[2] IT Infrastructure Library, http://www.itil-officialsite.com/

Last, the policy chain provides a jump-start for internal and external auditors in scoping an audit to the relevant system and security elements. As such, it is expected that the policy chain decreases the time needed to draft and to execute an audit program (the latter due to automated validation of configuration settings).

4.3   Example

Fig.1 exemplifies the functional system model as well as the security model, i.e., the policy chain, looking at a simplified example of a service provider (*SP*) that offers an *eInvoice Business Service* allowing customers (*Cust*) to store *Invoices* in a long term archive according to legal requirements, and to make them available to their business partners over the Internet. Fig. 1 sketches all abstraction layers, hereby focusing on functional elements and security policies related only to the submission of invoices to the archive.

The eInvoice business service is implemented by an *eInvoice Business Process* comprising several activities, one of which is the invoice archiving (*InvoiceArch*), realized by the interaction of two logical software components on IT-level (*ERP, ArchWS*), and a corresponding communication link (*InvoiceComm*) with associated *eInvoice Data*. The logical software components are implemented in the service provider's system by an ERP system for invoice management and a Web service for invoice storage, the former arranged in a cluster, the latter running in a service platform of a public cloud.

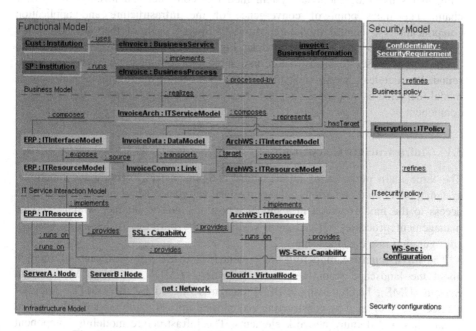

Fig. 1. Functional System and Security models of an eInvoice service

A high-level *Security Requirement* stemming from the service contract is to ensure the *Confidentiality* of invoice information (more requirements are omitted for simplification). Corresponding security policies were specified by policy designers on IT-level, one of which asks for the *Encryption* of invoice data sent over the communication link between the two logical software components. Based on security capabilities found in the service provider's system, *SSL/TLS* and *WS-Security* were considered as alternatives to enforce this IT security policy. The service provider's security manager decided for WS-Security, due to its increased, end-to-end security level and despite performance metrics in favor of SSL/TLS. Accordingly, the policy refinement process concluded with the generation of abstract configuration settings (based on CIM Policy) for WS-Security, to be translated and deployed to all software components in an ITIL change management process.

5   Architecture

This section sketches the PoSecCo architecture, that embraces a number of infrastructure and application components. All those components, implemented in the course of the project by the different PoSecCo partners, will be deployed in the premises of the service provider. The infrastructure components mainly create and provide access to the functional system model outlined in Section 4.1, achieved by interfacing various IT service management tools (CMS, CMDB). Application components use the functional system model to construct and leverage the policy chain. The main point of convergence of the infrastructure and application components is a central model repository, allowing each of them to access the functional system and security models. Fig. 2 provides an overview about the interaction of PoSecCo infrastructure and application components (both depicted as rounded rectangles), hereby indicating which elements of the functional and security model (depicted as straight rectangles) are consumed and produced by the respective component.

5.1   Infrastructure Components

The three main purposes of infrastructure components are to build the functional system model based on various data sources and automated where possible, to provide access to the models stored in a model repository, and to interact with IT service management processes offered by a CMS, for the purpose of deploying abstract configuration into the landscape.

The **infrastructure modeling** component [22] extracts the relevant information about the landscape from the service providers' CMDB and User Management System (UMS), hereby using WBEM standards offered by the DMTF[3]. Supplier services are integrated by constructing a simplified infrastructure model with attached capabilities and dummy network elements. The infrastructure modeling component

---

[3] http://dmtf.org/standards

has to ensure that the PoSecCo infrastructure model is always up-to-date, landscape changes have to be analyzed and reflected immediately in order to address challenge C3. Information about customers, business services and processes, linked to the roles of stakeholders in the involved organizations are extracted from Business Process Models (BPM) and Enterprise Architecture Management (EAM) tools. Last, UML components diagrams have been chosen as input to the construct the IT service interaction model.

The infrastructure and application components of PoSecCo interact by means of model artifacts stored in a central **model repository**. This container for all functional system and security models provides a WS-based API for accessing and modifying entire models as well as single model elements by means of CRUD operations, and offers versioning, change propagation on the basis of defined state-machines, access control, as well as an Object Constraint Language (OCL) and Hibernate SQL (hSQL)-based query interface. This repository is the central component assuring the link between the tools of the policy chain and providing a common access to the different models. The models are accompanied by an ontology used for formal reasoning.

The **configuration provisioning** component represents the link to the service providers' CMS. The deployment of abstract configurations at the end of the policy refinement process is signaled to the CMS by means of Requests For Change (RFC).

5.2   Application Components

The PoSecCo applications are used by the different stakeholders involved in security policy and configuration management. The policy chain ensures that work performed by any of these can be related to dependent artifacts on other levels, herewith guaranteeing a consistent model on all architecture layers and a holistic view of all security and compliance issues. One subset of applications focus on the policy chain construction, another set of applications leverages the chain, as described in Sections 4.1, 4.2.

Requirement engineering starts the construction of the policy chain with the capturing of security and compliance requirements stemming from internal needs, 3rd party demands and international regulations. This activity is embedded into a governance framework [23] defining organizational processes, roles as well as responsibilities with regard to requirements management, and which can be adapted to the particular needs of a given organization. Defined stakeholders use a graphical frontend to create and refine requirements as well as to maintain and monitor their fulfillment status. The security requirements, still high-level, relate to concepts embodied in the business layer. The business model is the result of BPM and EAM modeling, (cf. Fig. 2). This tool addresses the challenges C1, C2 and C4 from Section 2, as it allows to concentrate all (business) requirements in one place and to link them to involved stakeholders. This is a precondition to consolidate and prioritize security requirements and to manage them during operations time.

The process resulting in a conflict-free set of landscape-aware IT policies can be divided into **IT policy specification** and **policy harmonization** [24]. The semi-formal model of the business policies, result of the requirement engineering, is manually transformed to a formal, ontology-based representation of the security policy at the IT level taking the service interaction into account. The manual specification of IT policies requires the policy designer to establish an explicit link to the business requirement(s) addressed by a given policy. The documented link supports the analysis of requirement updates or of changes in the service landscape.

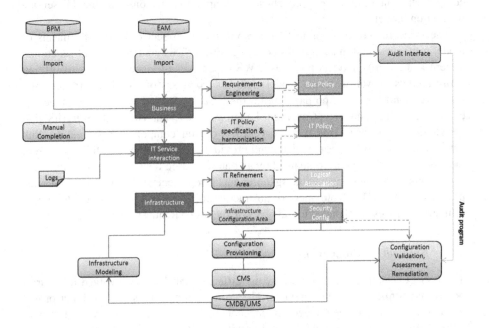

Fig. 2. PoSecCo Tool Chain

The policy harmonization then checks the consistency of the IT security policy and identifies conflicts, e.g., authorization conflicts related to subject and resource hierarchies. Conflict analysis is realized by using the Ontology Web Language OWL-DL, SPARQL Protocol and RDF Query Language (SPARQL) and Semantic Web Rule Language (SWRL). The defined challenged C4 (conflict detection) will be mainly provided by this tool.

The goal of the **IT refinement area** [25] is the transformation of the formal, declarative, and landscape-aware IT policies into the golden configuration, i.e., an ideal configuration complying with all security requirements and enforcing the policies in a cost-efficient way. In the first phase of the Policy Refinement, the Service Composition, Logical Associations (LAs) are used to bind concepts from the infrastructure layer of the system model to security properties from the IT layer. During this phase, behavioral and topological information about the landscape, including virtual environments are needed. Logical associations enable the specification of a policy from a behavioral point of view at the infrastructure layer without considering the full topology. For instance, a communication link defined in the IT service interaction model and a related policy for communication protection can result in a set of LAs, each LA specifying the desired security property together with two concrete communication endpoints, i.e., infrastructure implementations of the abstract components on IT level.

In a last step, referred to as **infrastructure configuration area** [26], suitable security capabilities are identified and assessed for single LAs (local optimization according to cost and performance functions), and finally for sets of LAs (global optimization). The results of the optimization process are presented to a human decision maker, who choses among the presented alternatives, which then triggers the automated generation of abstract configuration settings for the selected devices. The user is also guided to resolve conflicts that may arise when refining the IT policies in a deployed landscape.

During operations time, the **configuration validation** [27] component compares the actual system configuration retrieved from the CMDB or from the device itself, possibly changed outside of the PoSecCo scope, with the generated configuration resulting from the top-down refinement process. Discrepancies between the golden and actual configuration are identified and their relevance analyzed and reported. Tools for assessment and remediation support the evaluation of such discrepancies and can result in different remediation, e.g., the redeployment of golden configuration through CMS, or the acceptance of a configuration discrepancy since actual and golden configuration are assessed as being equivalent. Applications belonging to this category build on top of SCAP standards[4], well-known for their support of security automation. As such, the Configuration Validation is means to detect and react on discrepancies that may result from ongoing system changes (addressing C3).

PoSecCo applications integrate into well-defined ITIL processes for IT service management, centrally interfaced by the infrastructure components. For instance, the triggering of a change management process is used to provision the system with the generated, golden configuration resulting from the policy refinement. If, during runtime, a misconfiguration is detected, incident management processes are triggered.

5.3   Component Interaction and Communication

As shown in Fig. 3, the PoSecCo architecture consists of three layers [28]. The central model repository (see Section 5.1) provides persistency for the functional system and security models. The middle layer is composed of the different PoSecCo infrastructure and application components storing their results in the model repository. The upper layer is the presentation layer that provides a harmonized User Interface (UI) to the different applications.

---

[4] http://scap.nist.gov

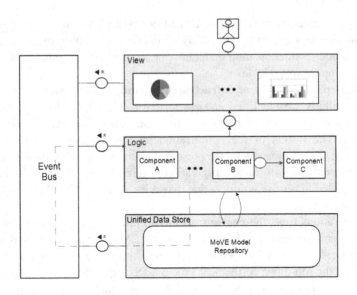

Fig. 3. PoSecCo Architecture FMC Diagram

We foresee two different types of communication in our architecture:

- **Direct communication** (solid arrows in Fig. 3) between two components according to an API, e.g., an application component using the CRUD interface of the model repository.
- **Indirect communication** (dotted arrows in Fig. 3) via the **event bus**.

Following the principles of an event-driven architecture, the components can register and consume events related to model changes and updates in order to react and to ensure the consistency of the policy chain. Thus, the model repository does not only store the various models, but also facilitates component interaction by the support of state machines and the creation of events in case of state transitions.

In fact, the interaction of the infrastructure and application components relies on a system of state-machines defined for the functional system model and the security model. State transitions of single model elements (or entire models) result in events that can be consumed by interested components to take appropriate action, e.g., to start or continue the refinement process (cf. Section 5.2).

The state-machines of the functional system model describe separately for each layer the completeness of the landscape description. When all layers are completed, manually confirmed by a human, the top-down policy refinement process can be started. While the state machines of the functional model are rather coarse-granular, those of the security models relate to single model elements, e.g., a single security requirement. This finer granularity allows tracing the **definition state** of single elements during design time, and the **operation state** during operations time.

Definition states link the application components in a top-down manner, in order to start the next phase of the policy refinement when the current phase has been completed. The fulfillment states indicate the deployment state of a configuration, the enforcement state of related policy element(s), as well as the fulfillment state of motivating requirement(s). Here, the state machines are used in a bottom-up manner to evaluate and signal the impact of not correctly implemented security policies, resulting from, for instance, the discrepancy between the golden, mandated configuration and the actual configuration in place.

5.4   Information Models and Languages

The different layers describing functional and security aspects of the service provider are modeled with help of the Unified Modeling Language (UML), classes belonging to the infrastructure model hereby correspond to a large extend with the DMTF Common Information Model (CIM).

Model instances are stored by the central model repository in a relational database. The Web service of the model repository, however, exchange model instances on the basis of XML Metadata Interchange (XMI), which can be processed with help of various Open Source tools. The use of XMI is also motivated by the fact that various tools support the editing and representation of XMI information.

In order to support automated reasoning, model instances represented as XMI are furthermore transformed into an ontology representation on the basis of the Web Ontology Language (OWL). IT Policies, in particular, can also be transformed into eXtensible Access Control Markup Language (XACML). Software components that do not need to reason about or exchange information with PoSecCo external tools work solely on the basis of XMI, e.g., the application component responsible for requirements engineering. The translation of abstract configuration represented as XMI and OWL happens outside of the scope of the project, and is left to technology and tool specific adapters provided by configuration management systems.

6   Conclusion

In this paper, we describe the PoSecCo concept of a policy chain to bridge the gap between high level business policies and low level security mechanisms and to address the challenges service providers must face. The architecture connects a set of linked tools allowing a service provider to create, maintain and leverage this policy chain during the security concept's design and operations time. Single prototypes, produced in the course of the PoSecCo project, implement the different components of that architecture. As a proof of concept, we build a demonstration platform, allowing to experience single services or to run pre-established scenarios to test PoSecCo infrastructure and application components. Although at the time of the publication, the assembly of the different components into a final prototype is yet not complete, the first results sound promising and will be subject to a follow-up paper.

Since it is hardly possible to cover requirements, policies and configurations for a domain as broad as IT security, the policy and tool chain only cover selected domains in its first version: These domains comprise (1) access control (including authentication, authorization and accountability) and (2) communication protection as a means to ensure the confidentiality and integrity of data. Additionally, we expect that our models allow statements about the degree of resource sharing among selected service consumers, herewith acknowledging that isolation is one important property in shared system landscapes.

Crucial to the success of the PoSecCo approach is the automation of model population; we hereby strongly depend on CMDBs for bigger parts of our functional system model. As such, the solution's applicability in real-life systems depends on the level of detail of landscape information maintained in CMDBs. This strong dependency was accepted due the increased adoption of IT service management methodologies and tools in the past decades, including, e.g., the possibility to federate single CMDBs. It is noteworthy that the policy refinement process identifies and configures standard security mechanisms being present in a system. In other words, the refinement process will not be able to suggest or even perform significant structural changes in order to enforce certain policies, e.g., the change of a service provider's network topology or software stack. However, the approach has the potential to assess simulated landscape changes, e.g., to determine if security policies are still enforceable anticipating a given change.

Acknowledgements. This work was partially funded by the European Commission under the Seventh Framework Project "PoSecCo" (IST 257129). The concepts described stem from joint efforts of all project partners.

References

1. Forrester Research: How To Manage Your Information Security Policy Framework (2006)
2. Forrester Research: The Change And Configuration Management Software Market (2007)
3. Gartner Research: Security Software and Services Spending Will Outpace Other IT Spending Areas in 2010 (2009)
4. Chen, H., Al-Nashif, Y.B., Qu, G., Hariri, S.: Self-Configuration of Network Security. In: 11th IEEE International Enterprise Distributed Object Computing Conference, p. 97 (2007)
5. Center for Strategic and International Studies: Securing Cyberspace for the 44th Presidency (2008)
6. Oppenheimer, D.: The importance of understanding distributed system configuration. In: Conference on Human Factors in Computer Systems Workshop (2003)
7. Patterson, D.A.: A simple way to estimate the cost of downtime. In: 16th Systems Administration Conference, LISA 2002, pp. 185–188 (2002)
8. Boutaba, R., Aib, I.: Policy-based Management: A Historical Perspective. Journal of Network and System Management 15(4), 447–480 (2007)

9. de Albuquerque, J.P., Krumm, H., de Geus, P.L., Jeruschkat, R.: Scalable model-based configuration management of security services in complex enterprise networks. Journal Software: Practice and Experience 41(3), 307–338 (2011)
10. Mont, M., Baldwin, A., Goh, C.: POWER prototype: Towards integrated policy-based management. In: IEEE/IFIP Network Operations and Management Symposium, pp. 789–802 (2000)
11. Basile, C., Lioy, A., Perez, G.M., Clemente, F.J.G., Skarmeta, A.F.G.: POSITIF: A Policy-Based Security Management System. In: 8th IEEE Workshop on Policies for Distributed Systems and Networks (2007)
12. Perez, M.G., Bernabe, J.B., Marin Perez, J.M., Martinez Manzano, D.J., Gomez Skarmeta, A.F.: A Policy-based Dependability Management Framework for Critical Services. International Journal on Advances in Internet Technology 2(4) (2009)
13. Alsubhi, K., Aib, I., François, J., Boutaba, R.: Policy-Based Security Configuration Management, Application to Intrusion Detection and Prevention. In: ICC, pp. 1–6 (2009)
14. Garcia-Alfaro, J., Cuppens, F., Cuppens-Boulahia, N., Preda, S.: MIRAGE: A Management Tool for the Analysis and Deployment of Network Security Policies. In: Garcia-Alfaro, J., Navarro-Arribas, G., Cavalli, A., Leneutre, J. (eds.) DPM 2010 and SETOP 2010. LNCS, vol. 6514, pp. 203–215. Springer, Heidelberg (2011)
15. Teo, L., Ahn, G.-J.: Managing heterogeneous network environments using an extensible policy framework. In: 2nd ACM symposium on Information, Computer and Communications Security, ASIACCS 2007, pp. 362–364 (2007)
16. Goldsack, P., Guijarro, J., Loughran, S., Coles, A., Farrell, A., Lain, A., Murray, P., Toft, P.: The SmartFrog configuration management framework. SIGOPS Oper. Syst. Rev. 43(1), 16–25 (2009)
17. Burns, J., Cheng, A., Gurung, P., Rajagopalan, S., et al.: Automatic management of network security policy. In: DARPA Information Survivability Conference and Exposition (DISCEX II 2001), vol. 2 (2001)
18. Twidle, K., Lupu, E., Dulay, N., Sloman, M.: Ponder2—A policy environment for autonomous pervasive systems. In: IEEE International Workshop on Policies for Distributed Systems and Networks, pp. 245–246 (2008)
19. Charalambides, M., Flegkas, P., Pavlou, G., et al.: Policy conflict analysis for diffserv quality of service management. IEEE Transactions on Network and Service Management 6(1), 15–30 (2009)
20. Hassan, A.A., Bahgat, W.M.: A Framework for Translating a High Level Security Policy into Low Level Security Mechanisms. Journal of Electrical Engineering 61(1), 20–28 (2010)
21. PoSecCo. Deliverable 4.2 – Structural Service Landscape Meta-Model (2011)
22. PoSecCo. Deliverable 4.4 – Concept and architecture for automated model creation, population, maintenance and audit (2012)
23. PoSecCo. Deliverable 2.1 – Framework for Business Level Policies (2011)
24. PoSecCo. Deliverable 2.2 – IT policy meta-model and language (2011)
25. PoSecCo. Deliverable 3.1 – Initial SDSS architecture and workflow (2011)
26. PoSecCo. Deliverable 3.3 – Configuration Meta-Model (2011)
27. Casalino, M.M., Mangili, M., Plate, H., Ponta, S.E.: Detection of configuration vulnerabilities in distributed (web) environments. In: Security and Privacy in Communication Networks - 8th Iternational ICST Conference, SecureComm (to appear, 2012)
28. PoSecCo. Deliverable 1.3 – Concept and Architecture of the overall Solution (2012)

Towards a Temporal Response Taxonomy

Wael Kanoun[1], Layal Samarji[1,2], Nora Cuppens-Boulahia[2], Samuel Dubus[1], and Frédéric Cuppens[2]

[1] Bell Labs, Alcatel-Lucent
[2] Telecom Bretagne

Abstract. Response systems play a growing role in modern security architectures. In order to select the most effective countermeasure, they adopt a dynamic and situation-aware approach. However, today's response systems are limited to the selection procedure. In other words, the follow-up and the deactivation phases are still performed manually. Consequently, existing response taxonomies failed to provide an appropriate set of requirements that covers the deactivation feature. In this paper, we tackle this issue by proposing a formal temporal taxonomy for response measures. Furthermore, we present an application of our work in the context of simultaneous attacks. This work provides a first step towards the deactivation and the transactional management of response measures.

Keywords: taxonomy, response, lifetime, defeasibility, deactivation, countermeasure, simultaneous attacks.

1 Introduction

The growth of critical information systems in size and complexity has driven the research community to find and propose intelligent and automated response systems. Furthermore, these response models and systems must cope with the steady progress of attacks' number, sophistication and effectiveness. For example [1] presents an adaptive intrusion response model that considers the intrusion's spread, using intrusion graphs. Moreover, [2,3,4,5,6] consider the cost (or the impact) of detected attacks and candidate countermeasures. Similarly, [7] and [8] consider service dependencies to calculate more accurately the impact of both ongoing attacks and candidate countermeasure(s). Furthermore, [9,10] calculates and considers the risk of the ongoing attack: the impact and the success likelihood of ongoing attacks are combined to assess dynamically the risk(s) and prioritize response measures.

Progressive advances in response models have driven the evolution of response taxonomies. The first response taxonomies were very limited, and presented as a part of intrusion detection taxonomies [11,12,13]. However, these taxonomies cannot cope with modern response systems. Later, Stakhanova *et al.* identified the gap between advanced response systems and the aforementioned taxonomies [14]. Consequently, they proposed the most complete response taxonomy in the literature to classify the most recent (and even future) response systems.

R. Di Pietro et al. (Eds.): DPM 2012 and SETOP 2012, LNCS 7731, pp. 318–331, 2013.

Response measure (i.e. countermeasures) are often temporary measures that are activated and deployed to counter a detected attack. Particularly, they can have an intrinsic cost, or affect the function of the system. Therefore, an activated response should be at certain time deactivated when it is no more necessary. We believe that the deactivation phase of the response process must be considered as importantly as the activation phase during the specification and operation. [15] raised this issue and proposed a risk-aware framework to activate and deactivate response policies. However, existing taxonomies do not take into account the deactivation phase. Thus, response measures (or systems) cannot be classified with respect to their effectiveness, lifetime, defeasibility, etc., which are relevant properties for the deactivation phase.

In this paper, we propose a novel temporal response taxonomy. In Section 2, we formally define this taxonomy using the *set theory*. It addresses the lifetime and the deactivation aspects of response measures. This taxonomy first distinguishes two major classes of countermeasures with respect to their lifetime: *one-shot* and *sustainable*. Afterwards, we show in Section 3 how *one-shot* countermeasures can be transformed, at the specification level, into a *sustainable* countermeasures. In Section 4, we present an application which demonstrates the relevance of this transformation, in the context of simultaneous attacks. Consequently, our work can be relevant to advanced and automated response systems with deactivation and transactional management feature of their countermeasures. We provide a discussion of related work in Section 5. Finally, Section 6 concludes our work.

2   Temporal Response Taxonomy

In this section, we propose a formal definition of our temporal taxonomy. While previous papers presented reaction and response taxonomies, none of them mentioned the lifetime of the countermeasures, or whether they can be deactivated. Our taxonomy considers the temporal dimension of response measures. We may refer to this taxonomy to classify any countermeasure. Thus, it may be also used to classify any security rule expressed in a response policy [15], with respect to their lifetime and the controllability of their lifetime.

We consider the set of the occurrences of all the attacks that target the monitored system χ. Deemed that not all attacks are detected, the set of detected attack occurrences χ^d constitutes a subset of the previous set ($\chi^d \subseteq \chi$). This set can be decomposed into several subsets (i.e. χ_X^d, χ_Y^d, etc.), with respect to the type of the attacks (X, Y, etc.). Thus, we can say that for an attack's type X, $\chi_X^d \subseteq \chi^d$. Finally, the set A_X is the set of terminated attack occurrences of the same type. On the other hand, the set of all the occurrences of all types of countermeasures, can be decomposed into several subsets. Each subset contains all the countermeasure occurrences of the same type. CM_X is the subset of successful countermeasure occurrences, which terminate successfully the associated attacks. Moreover, we will formally define a relation f_X between CM_X and A_X (see Figure 1): the properties of this relation will determine the classification of a countermeasure in the proposed taxonomy. In the remainder of this section we

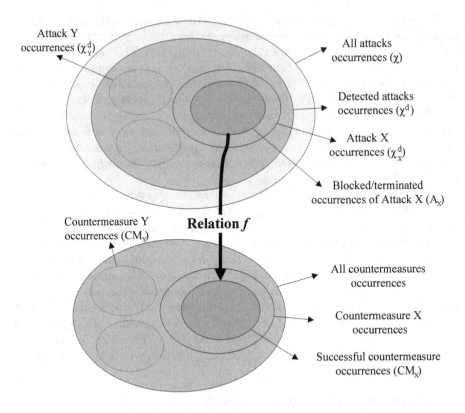

Fig. 1. Attack's and countermeasure's occurrences sets

will consider a single attack type. Thus, we can simply denote A_X and CM_X by A and CM respectively. However, the formal definition can be generalized for multiple attack types (X, Y, etc.) by defining for each one its associated sets and mapping function (f_X, f_Y, etc.) as presented in the remainder of this section.

First, considering their lifetime, countermeasures may be divided initially into two major classes: *one-shot* countermeasures and *sustainable* countermeasures. The latter class will be decomposed into two subclasses: *defeasible* and *indefeasible* countermeasures. Figure 2 depicts the proposed taxonomy.

2.1   One-Shot Countermeasures

A countermeasure has a one-shot lifetime when its effectiveness is limited to a single attack occurrence. Once a *one-shot* countermeasure is launched, it is automatically deactivated. The effective lifetime of this class of countermeasures is null (or negligible). Consequently, future attacks may occur, considering that this countermeasure was not re-launched. Therefore, a *one-shot* countermeasure must be launched for every attack occurrence. Examples of this class include: closing a malicious connection, restarting a server, notifying the administrator, etc.

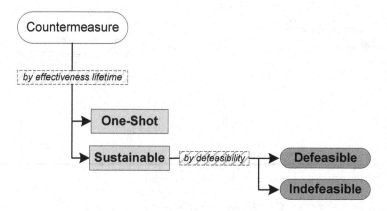

Fig. 2. Temporal response taxonomy

Let us consider an ideal response system which is capable of handling and blocking each detected attack occurrence with the associated and appropriate countermeasure. In such system, we consider A is a set of the attack occurrences, and CM the associated set of countermeasure occurrences. We define a relation $f : A \to CM$. This relation can be read as *"an element from A is ended by an element from CM"*. For an ideal system, each attack must be ended, and thus f is an application:

Hypothesis 1 $\forall a \in A, \exists! \; cm \in CM \mid cm = f(a)$

For each occurrence a of the attack A, a cm is required to end the attack. Therefore a cm_i that ended the attack occurrence a_i, has no effect on future attack a_j $(j > i)$. Thus, f is injective, and *one-shot* countermeasure can be defined as follows:

Definition 1. $\forall \; a_i, a_j \in A; \quad cm_i = f(a_i) \; and \; cm_i = f(a_j) \Rightarrow a_i = a_j$

Moreover, f is surjective, because each countermeasure cm in CM is launched to end at least one attack occurrence:

Proposition 1. $\forall \; cm \in CM; \; \exists \; a \in A \mid cm = f(a)$

Figure 3 depicts the effectiveness of a *one-shot* countermeasure over time. When the system detects the attack at $t_{attack\_detected}$, the response system decides to launch the associated countermeasure at t_{launch}. At $t_{activate}$, the *one-shot* countermeasure is deployed and active in the system, and consequently terminates the detected attack occurrence. Thus, in the case of *one-shot* countermeasure, $t_{activate} \approx t_{deactivate}$. After $t_{deactivate}$, the same attack can occur without being blocked, given that the *one-shot* countermeasure's effective lifetime expired.

2.2 Sustainable Countermeasures

A countermeasure has a sustainable lifetime when its effectiveness is not limited to a single attack occurrence. Once a *sustainable* countermeasure is activated, it

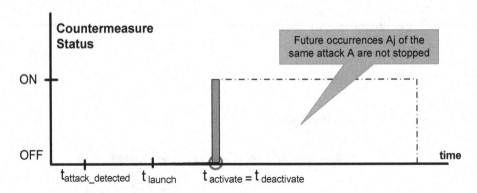

Fig. 3. One-shot countermeasure

remains active against at least one future attack occurrence. In other words, its lifetime sustains for a period of time (which may tend to infinite). Therefore, the activation of a *sustainable* countermeasure can be effective against future attack occurrences, until this countermeasure is deactivated. Examples of this class include: patching software, blocking a machine, deleting an account, suspending an account, etc.

Let us define the same function $f : A \to CM$. f is not injective because a *sustainable* countermeasure cm_i can block a sequence of attack occurrences $\{a_i, a_{i+1}, ...\}$ that may occur during the lifetime of cm_i. In other words, we can have several attack occurrences that are ended by the same countermeasure's occurrence. Thus, *sustainable* countermeasure can be defined as follows:

Definition 2. $\exists\, a_i, a_j \in A \mid (cm_i = f(a_i))$ *and* $(cm_i = f(a_j))$ *and* $(a_i \neq a_j)$

However, Proposition 1 ($\forall\, cm \in CM;\ \exists\, a \in A \mid cm = f(a)$) holds and f remains surjective, because each countermeasure cm in CM is launched to end at least one attack occurrence:

Figure 4 depicts the effectiveness of a *sustainable* countermeasure over time. When the system detects the first attack occurrence at $t_{attack\_detected}$, the response system launches the associated countermeasure at t_{launch}. At $t_{activate}$, the countermeasure is deployed and active in the system. In this case, all attacks that occur during $[t_{activate}; t_{deactivate}]$ will be blocked. Finally, it is obvious that after $t_{deactivate}$, the attack can occur without being blocked.

Moreover, *sustainable* class may be divided into two subclasses:

Defeasible. A *defeasible* countermeasure can be deactivated, and therefore its lifetime may be controlled by the administrator or the system. Examples of this class include: blocking a machine, suspending an account, dropping traffic, etc.

Indefeasible. An *indefeasible* countermeasure cannot be deactivated, or the deactivation of such countermeasure requires exceptional effort or policy modification(s). Examples of this class include: deleting an account, patching an OS, patching a software, etc. Thus, we can say that for *indefeasible* countermeasure we have $t_{deactivate} \to \infty$.

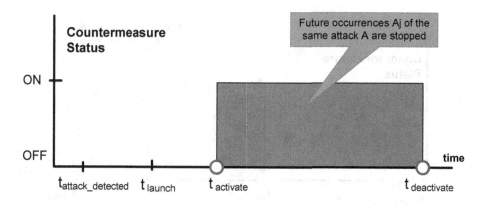

Fig. 4. Sustainable countermeasure

3 Transforming One-Shot Countermeasures into Sustainable Countermeasures

We can unify the *one-shot* and *sustainable* classes, or more precisely transform *one-shot* countermeasure into a *sustainable* countermeasure at the specification level. The advantages of this transformation are threefold:

- First, as we aim at addressing the deactivation issue of countermeasures, we will handle only one 'generic' type of countermeasures instead of two. This would make the deactivation models far more simple and effective.
- Second, when detecting bursts of the same attack, one *sustainable* countermeasure launch would be required to block the whole set of attack occurrences, instead of launching several *one-shot* countermeasures. In the former case, the response system will have a global understanding of the attacks and launched countermeasures. In the latter case, the response system will consider each attack occurrence (with the associated countermeasure) individually, which is by far less efficient for the response system. Therefore, this transformation allows the response model to have a better awareness, and a more accurate 'follow-up' of the system state.
- Third, this unification will have no impact on the monitored system, because it is only performed at the specification level. Launching this 'new' *sustainable* countermeasure, for instance *restarting service*, does not necessarily mean that the service will restart even an attack is not detected. In fact, we propose two methods to transform *one-shot* countermeasures to *sustainable* countermeasures: *synchronous* and *asynchronous*.

3.1 Synchronous Transformation: Check-to-Cease

The response system activates the 'new' *sustainable* countermeasure (e.g. kill process, close connection) by launching periodically the *one-shot* countermeasure

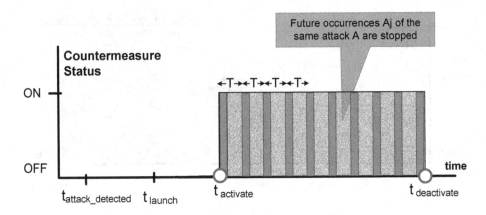

Fig. 5. Synchronous approach: Check-to-Cease

(see Figure 5). The response system is responsible of stopping this countermeasure when it is no more required. Concretely, the *one-shot* countermeasure's sequence will be launched, and potentially hold even if no other attack occurrence is detected.

3.2 Asynchronous Transformation: Check-to-Relaunch

Considering that the new *sustainable* countermeasure is a 'state', the monitored system will only launch (or re-launch) the corresponding countermeasure when the attack is re-detected (see Figure 6). Concretely, there will be no change in comparison with what is present prior to this work, but at the abstract level the monitored system is aware of the new state. The main advantage of the

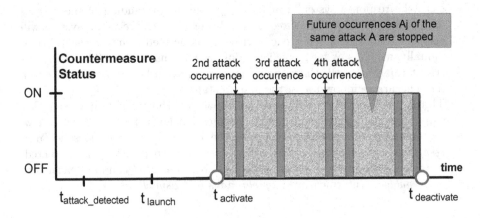

Fig. 6. Asynchronous approach: Check-to-relaunch

new *sustainable* countermeasure is that it would be re-launched only if the attack is re-detected. No countermeasure selection procedure will be re-done, and therefore:

Proposition 2. $t^i_{launch} = t^i_{detected\_attack}$ $(i > 1)$

4 Application for the One-Shot into Sustainable Transformation in a Simultaneous Attacks Context

When attackers gain access to corporate or university networks by compromising authorized users, computers or applications, the network and its resources can be used to perform distributed, coordinated and simultaneous attacks. Attackers may have a single or several attack objective(s). This section provides one advantage of transforming one-shot countermeasures into sustainable countermeasures in a multi-attacks response system. Indeed, it demonstrates the relevance of our taxonomy, by providing a scenario of simultaneous attacks and describing the corresponding response decisions in two cases: first, a one-shot countermeasure is considered; second, we consider that this countermeasure is transformed into a sustainable one. Finally, a concrete example is presented to illustrate our proposal.

4.1 Application Description

We consider a system where multiple attacks, are executed simultaneously. The response management system must launch different countermeasures at the same time to block the ongoing attacks. We will consider the following:

- A_1 and A_2 are two types of attacks; we will use $(i; j)$ to describe the jth occurrence of the attack type i.
- CM_1 and CM_2 are respectively the appropriate countermeasures against A_1 and A_2.
- CM_1 is a one-shot countermeasure, and CM_2 is a sustainable one.
- CM_1 and CM_2 can not be launched at the same time because either (1) they want to exclusively use the same asset (e.g. configuration file, server), or (2) they induce an execution conflict (e.g. a connection must be kept open for a countermeasure, and closed for another one). We also consider CM_1 has a higher priority over CM_2. For example, the total impact (or cost) of an attack on the system [3,7] while activating CM_1, is lower than the total impact while activating CM_2. Finally, we consider that CM_2, once launched, cannot be stopped or interrupted by another countermeasure.

4.2 One-Shot Countermeasure Case

Consider that $(1; 1)$ (i.e. a first occurrence of A_1) is detected at $t_{(1;1)}$, and the one-shot countermeasure CM_1 is activated then deactivated after blocking this attack (see Figure 7). At $t_{(2;1)}$, A_2 is detected, and the sustainable countermeasure CM_2 is activated. At $t_{(1;2)}$, the CM_2 is not deactivated yet, and a

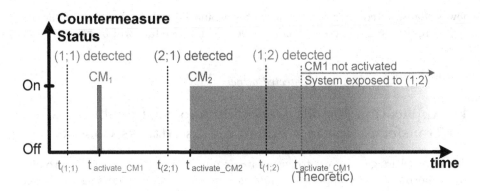

Fig. 7. Side effect of non-transformed one-shot countermeasure

second occurrence $(1; 2)$ of A_1 is detected. As we considered, CM_1 is prioritized over CM_2, but unfortunately, we are unable to interrupt the execution of CM_2 and launch CM_1 instead. Hence, the system will be exposed to $(1; 2)$, which is not desired considering its large impact on the system. This scenario reveals the main constraint of one-shot countermeasures. The limited lifetime aspect of the one-shot CM_1 allows other countermeasures to be launched before the next occurrence of A_1. In consequence, relaunching CM_1 will not be possible to respond to future occurrences of A_1, despite that A_1 has a higher impact. In the next section, we show how the transformation of a one-shot into a sustainable countermeasure can offer an interesting solution to this problem.

4.3   Transformed (Sustainable) Countermeasure Case

We consider now that we transformed the one-shot countermeasure CM_1 into a sustainable one. Similarly, the first occurrence of the A_1 is detected at $t_{(1;1)}$, and CM_1 is consequently launched. Since CM_1 is now sustainable, it remains activated until the system decides to deactivate it explicitly. After $t_{(1;2)}$, we will have a simultaneous attacks context $(A_1$ and $A_2)$ where the prioritized countermeasure CM_1 is activated instead of CM_2. The system will remain exposed to A_2 which is less critical, because it has a lower impact.

In this simultaneous attacks scenario, we showed how transforming a one-shot countermeasure to a sustainable one can help response systems to manage their responses, and consequently reduce the impact on the system. We also note that the activation lifetime of the sustainable countermeasure should be chosen with respect to its impact on the system.

4.4   Concrete Example

We consider a server 'S' that handles high confidential information and intellectual property of a company. Any attack that leads to confidentiality compromise (e.g. cracking an employee's password) is not tolerated. Moreover, the employees of this company do not have all the same privileges. For that, roles are affected to the employees depending on the function hierarchical level. For example, we have the *super user* role affected to administrators and managers, and the *normal user* role affected to the other employees. Furthermore, we consider the following attacks and associated countermeasures:

Attack A_1 consists in guessing/cracking the password of a legitimate identity discovered in the company's network.

Attack A_2 consists in flooding the server, by a group of internal machines infected with a Bot. This attack leads to a partial denial of service (DoS) on 'S'.

Countermeasure CM_1 consists in obligating the server 'S' to send a change-password request to the victim user. Consequently, the user must send a new password to the server 'S'. Using OrBAC language [16], an obligation rule corresponding to this response can be written as follows:

$$Obligation(server,\ change\_password\_request,\ user,\ password\_cracking)$$

Countermeasure CM_2 consists in obligating the server 'S', which suffers from a partial DoS, to drop the traffic coming from normal users. In consequence, the server can still handle the requests of super users (i.e. administrators and high-level managers). The obligation rule corresponding to this response can be written as follows:

$$Obligation(server,\ drop\_traffic,\ normal\_user,\ server\_dos)$$

A conflict, or more precisely an inability [17], occurs between *obligation (s, a_u, o)* and *obligation(s, a_v, o)*, if it is impossible to simultaneously execute both actions a_u and a_v. Hence, when both attack A_1 and A_2 are simultaneously detected together (see Figure 8), the system is unable to execute both CM_1 and CM_2. Server 'S', while dropping normal users traffic, blocks the proper execution of CM_1 because the victim user is unable to send his new password to 'S'.

Let us consider back the scenarios depicted in Sections 4.2 and 4.3.

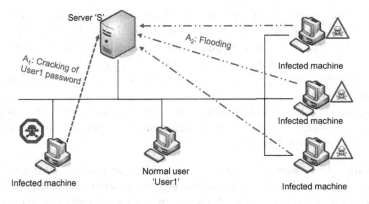

Fig. 8. Simultaneous attacks: (1) server flooding and (2) user's password cracking

- If CM_1 is specified as a one-shot countermeasure: When a second occurrence of A1 appears, the system will be unable to relaunch the CM1, due to the conflict with the already activated CM_2. This situation is unacceptable because the response system must handle in priority A_1 which compromise the confidentiality of the server.
- If CM_1 is transformed into a sustainable countermeasure: when A2 is detected after the detection of A_1, the CM_2 will not be launched immediately in order to avoid the potential conflict (and due the higher priority of A_1). When the second occurrence of A_1 is detected, CM_1 will block this attack.

We note that at the enforcement/system level, the one-shot into sustainable transformation is transparent. Such countermeasure will not be enforced all the long of the chosen lifetime. However, it will remain active (idle mode) during its lifetime: once a new attack occurrence appears, the countermeasure will be executed again (i.e. asynchronous transformation). On the other hand, this transformation provides a decisive advantage at the response management level of the response system. The transformation allows the administrator to prioritize a one-shot countermeasure.

In this section, we demonstrated the relevance of our proposal. We analyzed two classes of countermeasures: one-shot and transformed-sustainable (in the second scenario). Such scenarios (or challenges) cannot be handled using previous taxonomies, because none of them considered the deactivation phase of a countermeasure.

5   Related Work

Several taxonomies of response systems were proposed during the last decade [11,12,13,14]. All of these taxonomies have similar objectives, which consists in providing a comprehensive insight on existing response systems. Such taxonomies classify response measures and mechanisms according to the most relevant and exhaustive criterion. The main objectives of such taxonomies are:

- presenting a comprehensive overview of the major response systems' issues and giving the researchers a better understanding of theses systems.
- motivating the research community to investigate unexplored areas in the field. Response taxonomies can provide useful insight into the requirements of better and more effective response measures, and open new horizons of future research.
- providing a common foundation to organize research efforts of intrusion response. A complete and systematic taxonomy can offer a unified terminology, criteria and properties.

Particularly, [14] reviewed previous taxonomies. The authors established afterwards a unique vocabulary for intrusion response systems, by using the existing and already used terms, and by finding new terms for newly described classifications. Subsequently, they propose a complete taxonomy, adapted to current

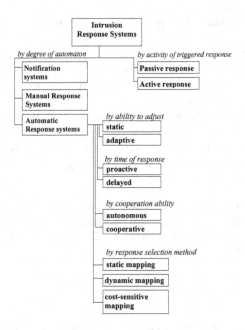

Fig. 9. Stakhanova *et al.*'s taxonomy

and advanced response systems. They classify response systems by *degree of automation*: (i) notification, (ii) manual, and (iii) automatic. The latter class is considered as the most sophisticated and advanced. Stakhanova *et al.* further develop this class in their taxonomy, by classifying advanced response systems by four following dimensions: ability to adjust, response time (proactive or delayed), ability to cooperate, response selection (see Figure 9).

Existing taxonomies were interested by the selection procedure of a countermeasure, and did not consider the deactivation phase. Stakhanova *et al.*'s taxonomy is the most comprehensive taxonomy in literature; and we believe that our work is complementary to their taxonomy. Thus, it offers a relevant extension for advanced response systems that handle both the activation and the deactivation of countermeasures. Ultimately, such extension is crucial for transactional response management, when several responses must be activated (and deactivated) simultaneously to counter several attacks.

6   Conclusion

In this paper, we presented a temporal response taxonomy that considers the lifetime and the defeasibility of response measures and mechanisms. The proposed taxonomy was formally specified using the set theory. We classify response measures with respect to their : (i) effective lifetime and (ii) defeasibility. In particular, we showed how *one-shot* countermeasures can be implemented as *sustainable* countermeasures at the specification level.

Advanced and automated response systems capable of managing several simultaneous responses must include the deactivation feature. Our work provides a first insight towards a better understanding of temporal aspects of response measures, by defining a set of appropriate temporal properties. Our taxonomy can foster research in response deactivation, and more generally, in transactional management of responses measures.

Future work include modeling the activation/deactivation of several countermeasures against simultaneous ongoing attacks using formal languages. As introduced briefly in Section 4, we need to describe concurrent actions, which is crucial for modeling simultaneous attacks actions.

Acknowledgements. This work was partially funded by the Association Nationale de Recherche et de Technologie (ANRT), and partially supported by the European Commission in the framework of the ITEA2 Predykot project (Grant agreement no. 10035).

References

1. Foo, B., Wu, Y.S., Mao, Y.C., Bagchi, S., Spafford, E.: Adepts: Adaptive intrusion response using attack graphs in an e-commerce environment. In: International Conference on Dependable Systems and Networks, pp. 508–517 (2005)
2. Wei, H., Frinke, D., Carter, O., Ritter, C.: Cost-benefit analysis for network intrusion detection systems. In: 28th Annual Computer Security Conference (CSI 2001) (October 2001)
3. Toth, T., Kruegel, C.: Evaluating the impact of automated intrusion response mechanisms. In: Proceedings of the 18th Annual Computer Security Applications Conference, ACSAC 2002, p. 301. IEEE Computer Society, Las Vegas (2002)
4. Lee, W., Fan, W., Miller, M., Stolfo, S.J., Zadok, E.: Toward cost-sensitive modeling for intrusion detection and response. Journal of Computer Security 10(1/2), 5–22 (2002)
5. Balepin, I., Maltsev, S., Rowe, J., Levitt, K.N.: Using Specification-Based Intrusion Detection for Automated Response. In: Vigna, G., Kruegel, C., Jonsson, E. (eds.) RAID 2003. LNCS, vol. 2820, pp. 136–154. Springer, Heidelberg (2003)
6. Stakhanova, N., Basu, S., Wong, J.: A cost-sensitive model for preemptive intrusion response systems. In: Proceedings of the 21st International Conference on Advanced Networking and Applications, AINA 2007, pp. 428–435. IEEE Computer Society, Washington, DC (2007)
7. Jahnke, M., Thul, C., Martini, P.: Graph based metrics for intrusion response measures in computer networks. In: Proceedings of the 32nd IEEE Conference on Local Computer Networks, LCN 2007, pp. 1035–1042. IEEE Computer Society, Washington, DC (2007)
8. Kheir, N.: Response Policies and Countermeasures: Management of Service Dependencies and Intrusion and Reaction Impacts. PhD thesis, Telecom Bretagne (2010)
9. Kanoun, W., Cuppens-Boulahia, N., Cuppens, F.: Advanced Reaction Using Risk Assessment in Intrusion Detection Systems. In: Lopez, J., Hämmerli, B.M. (eds.) CRITIS 2007. LNCS, vol. 5141, pp. 58–70. Springer, Heidelberg (2008)

10. Kanoun, W.: Intelligent Risk-Aware System for Activating and Deactivating Policy-Based Response. PhD thesis, Telecom Bretagne (2011)
11. Irvine, C., Levin, T.: Toward a taxonomy and costing method for security services. In: Proceedings of the 15th Annual Computer Security Applications Conference (ACSAC 1999), pp. 183–188 (1999)
12. Carver, C., Pooch, U.: An intrusion response taxonomy and its role in automatic intrusion response. In: The 2000 IEEE Workshop on Information Assurance and Security (June 2000)
13. Wang, H., Wang, G., Lan, Y., Wang, K., Liu, D.: A New Automatic Intrusion Response Taxonomy and Its Application. In: Shen, H.T., Li, J., Li, M., Ni, J., Wang, W. (eds.) APWeb 2006 Workshops. LNCS, vol. 3842, pp. 999–1003. Springer, Heidelberg (2006)
14. Stakhanova, N., Basu, S., Wong, J.: A taxonomy of intrusion response systems. International Journal of Information and Computer Security 1(1/2), 169–184 (2007)
15. Kanoun, W., Cuppens-Boulahia, N., Cuppens, F., Dubus, S.: Risk-aware framework for activating and deactivating policy-based response. In: The fourth International Conference on Network and System Security (NSS 2010), Melbourne, Australia (September 2010)
16. Abou El Kalam, A., Baida, R.E., Balbiani, P., Benferhat, S., Cuppens, F., Deswarte, Y., Miège, A., Saurel, C., Trouessin, G.: Organization Based Access Control. In: 4th IEEE Policy (June 2003)
17. Cuppens, F., Cuppens-Boulahia, N., Kanoun, W., Croissant, A.: A Formal Framework to Specify and Deploy Reaction Policies. In: Web-Based Information Technologies and Distributed Systems, pp. 159–188. Atlantis Press, Paris (2010)

Author Index